T0130725

Get the eBook FREE!

(PDF, ePub, Kindle, and liveBook all included)

We believe that once you buy a book from us, you should be able to read it in any format we have available. To get electronic versions of this book at no additional cost to you, purchase and then register this book at the Manning website.

Go to https://www.manning.com/freebook and follow the instructions to complete your pBook registration.

That's it!
Thanks from Manning!

Machine Learning
Bookcamp

BUILD A PORTFOLIO OF REAL-LIFE PROJECTS

ALEXEY GRIGOREV

MANNING

SHELTER ISLAND

For online information and ordering of this and other Manning books, please visit
www.manning.com. The publisher offers discounts on this book when ordered in quantity.
For more information, please contact

    Special Sales Department
    Manning Publications Co.
    20 Baldwin Road
    PO Box 761
    Shelter Island, NY 11964
    Email: orders@manning.com

Manning Publications Co.
20 Baldwin Road
PO Box 761
Shelter Island, NY 11964

Development editor:	Susan Ethridge
Technical development editor:	Michael Lund
Review editor:	Adriana Sabo
Production editor:	Deirdre S. Hiam
Copy editor:	Pamela Hunt
Proofreader:	Melody Dolab
Technical proofreader:	Al Krinker
Typesetter:	Dennis Dalinnik
Cover designer:	Marija Tudor

ISBN: 9781617296819
Printed in the United States of America

brief contents

1 ■ Introduction to machine learning   1

2 ■ Machine learning for regression   18

3 ■ Machine learning for classification   65

4 ■ Evaluation metrics for classification   113

5 ■ Deploying machine learning models   154

6 ■ Decision trees and ensemble learning   180

7 ■ Neural networks and deep learning   224

8 ■ Serverless deep learning   271

9 ■ Serving models with Kubernetes and Kubeflow   292

contents

foreword xi
preface xiii
acknowledgments xv
about this book xvii
about the author xxi
about the cover illustration xxii

1 Introduction to machine learning 1

1.1 Machine learning 2

*Machine learning vs. rule-based systems 4 ▪ When machine
learning isn't helpful 7 ▪ Supervised machine learning 7*

1.2 Machine learning process 9

*Business understanding 10 ▪ Data understanding 11
Data preparation 11 ▪ Modeling 11 ▪ Evaluation 12
Deployment 12 ▪ Iterate 12*

1.3 Modeling and model validation 12

2 Machine learning for regression 18

2.1 Car-price prediction project 19

Downloading the dataset 19

2.2 Exploratory data analysis   20

Exploratory data analysis toolbox   21 ▪ Reading and preparing data   22 ▪ Target variable analysis   25 ▪ Checking for missing values   28 ▪ Validation framework   29

2.3 Machine learning for regression   32

Linear regression   32 ▪ Training linear regression model   41

2.4 Predicting the price   43

Baseline solution   43 ▪ RMSE: Evaluating model quality   46 Validating the model   50 ▪ Simple feature engineering   51 Handling categorical variables   53 ▪ Regularization   57 Using the model   61

2.5 Next steps   62

Exercises   62 ▪ Other projects   63

3 **Machine learning for classification   65**

3.1 Churn prediction project   66

Telco churn dataset   67 ▪ Initial data preparation   67 Exploratory data analysis   75 ▪ Feature importance   78

3.2 Feature engineering   88

One-hot encoding for categorical variables   88

3.3 Machine learning for classification   92

Logistic regression   92 ▪ Training logistic regression   95 Model interpretation   100 ▪ Using the model   108

3.4 Next steps   110

Exercises   110 ▪ Other projects   110

4 **Evaluation metrics for classification   113**

4.1 Evaluation metrics   114

Classification accuracy   114 ▪ Dummy baseline   117

4.2 Confusion table   119

Introduction to the confusion table   119 ▪ Calculating the confusion table with NumPy   122 ▪ Precision and recall   126

4.3 ROC curve and AUC score   129

True positive rate and false positive rate   130 ▪ Evaluating a model at multiple thresholds   131 ▪ Random baseline model   134 The ideal model   136 ▪ ROC Curve   140 ▪ Area under the ROC curve (AUC)   144

4.4 Parameter tuning 147

K-fold cross-validation 147 ▪ Finding best parameters 149

4.5 Next steps 151

Exercises 151 ▪ Other projects 152

5 ***Deploying machine learning models 154***

5.1 Churn-prediction model 155

*Using the model 155 ▪ Using Pickle to save and load
the model 156*

5.2 Model serving 159

*Web services 160 ▪ Flask 161 ▪ Serving churn model
with Flask 163*

5.3 Managing dependencies 166

Pipenv 166 ▪ Docker 170

5.4 Deployment 174

AWS Elastic Beanstalk 175

5.5 Next steps 178

Exercises 179 ▪ Other projects 179

6 ***Decision trees and ensemble learning 180***

6.1 Credit risk scoring project 181

*Credit scoring dataset 181 ▪ Data cleaning 182
Dataset preparation 187*

6.2 Decision trees 190

*Decision tree classifier 191 ▪ Decision tree learning
algorithm 194 ▪ Parameter tuning for decision tree 201*

6.3 Random forest 203

*Training a random forest 206 ▪ Parameter tuning for
random forest 207*

6.4 Gradient boosting 210

*XGBoost: Extreme gradient boosting 211 ▪ Model performance
monitoring 213 ▪ Parameter tuning for XGBoost 214
Testing the final model 220*

6.5 Next steps 222

Exercises 222 ▪ Other projects 223

7 Neural networks and deep learning   224

7.1 Fashion classification   225

*GPU vs. CPU   225 ▪ Downloading the clothing dataset   226
TensorFlow and Keras   228 ▪ Loading images   228*

7.2 Convolutional neural networks   230

Using a pretrained model   230 ▪ Getting predictions   233

7.3 Internals of the model   234

Convolutional layers   234 ▪ Dense layers   237

7.4 Training the model   240

*Transfer learning   240 ▪ Loading the data   241 ▪ Creating
the model   242 ▪ Training the model   245 ▪ Adjusting the
learning rate   249 ▪ Saving the model and checkpointing   251
Adding more layers   252 ▪ Regularization and dropout   254
Data augmentation   259 ▪ Training a larger model   264*

7.5 Using the model   265

*Loading the model   265 ▪ Evaluating the model   266
Getting the predictions   267*

7.6 Next steps   269

Exercises   269 ▪ Other projects   269

8 Serverless deep learning   271

8.1 Serverless: AWS Lambda   272

*TensorFlow Lite   273 ▪ Converting the model to TF Lite
format   274 ▪ Preparing the images   274 ▪ Using the
TensorFlow Lite model   276 ▪ Code for the lambda
function   277 ▪ Preparing the Docker image   279
Pushing the image to AWS ECR   281 ▪ Creating the
lambda function   281 ▪ Creating the API Gateway   285*

8.2 Next steps   290

Exercises   290 ▪ Other projects   290

9 Serving models with Kubernetes and Kubeflow   292

9.1 Kubernetes and Kubeflow   293

9.2 Serving models with TensorFlow Serving   293

*Overview of the serving architecture   294 ▪ The saved_model
format   295 ▪ Running TensorFlow Serving locally   296
Invoking the TF Serving model from Jupyter   297 ▪ Creating
the Gateway service   301*

9.3 Model deployment with Kubernetes 304

Introduction to Kubernetes 304 ▪ Creating a Kubernetes cluster on AWS 305 ▪ Preparing the Docker images 307 ▪ Deploying to Kubernetes 310 ▪ Testing the service 316

9.4 Model deployment with Kubeflow 317

Preparing the model: Uploading it to S3 317 ▪ Deploying TensorFlow models with KFServing 318 ▪ Accessing the model 319 ▪ KFServing transformers 321 ▪ Testing the transformer 323 ▪ Deleting the EKS cluster 324

9.5 Next steps 324

Exercises 324 ▪ Other projects 325

appendix A Preparing the environment 326
appendix B Introduction to Python 357
appendix C Introduction to NumPy 374
appendix D Introduction to Pandas 404
appendix E AWS SageMaker 427

index 439

foreword

I've known Alexey for more than six years. We almost worked together at the same data science team in a tech company in Berlin: Alexey started a few months after I left. Despite that, we still managed to get to know each other through Kaggle, the data science competition platform, and a common friend. We participated on the same team in a Kaggle competition on natural language processing, an interesting project that required carefully using pretrained word embeddings and cleverly mixing them. At the same time, Alexey was writing a book, and he asked me to be a technical reviewer. The book was about Java and data science, and, while reading it, I was particularly impressed by how carefully Alexey planned and orchestrated interesting examples. This led soon to a new collaboration: we coauthored a project-based book about TensorFlow, working on different projects from reinforcement learning to recommender systems that aimed to be an inspiration and example for the readers.

When working with Alexey, I noticed that he prefers to learn things by doing and by coding, like many others who transitioned to data science from software engineering.

Therefore, I wasn't very surprised when I heard that he had started another project-based book. Invited to provide feedback on Alexey's work, I read the book from its early stages and found the reading fascinating. This book is a practical introduction to machine learning with a focus on hands-on experience. It's written for people with the same background that Alexey has — for developers interested in data science and needing to quickly build up useful and reusable experience with data and data problems.

As an author of more than a dozen books on data science and AI, I know there are already a lot of books and courses on this topic. However, this book is quite different.

In *Machine Learning Bookcamp*, you won't find the same déjà vu data problems that other books offer. It doesn't have the same pedantic, repetitive flow of topics, like a route already traced on maps that always leads to places that you already know and have seen.

Everything in the book revolves around practical and nearly real-world examples. You will learn how to predict the price of a car, determine whether or not a customer is going to churn, and assess the risk of not repaying a loan. After that, you will classify clothing photos into T-shirts, dresses, pants, and other categories. This project is especially curious and interesting because Alexey personally curated this dataset, and you can enrich it with the clothes from your own wardrobe.

By reading this book, of course, you are expected to apply machine learning to solve common problems, and you will use the simplest and most efficient solutions to achieve the best results. The first chapters begin by examining basic algorithms such as linear regression and logistic regression. The reader then gradually moves to gradient boosting and neural networks. Nevertheless, the strong point of the book is that, while teaching machine learning through practice, it also prepares you for the real world. You will deal with unbalanced classes and long-tail distributions, and discover how to handle dirty data. You will evaluate your models and deploy them with AWS Lambda and Kubernetes. And these are just a few of the new techniques you learn by working through the pages.

Thinking with the mind-set of an engineer, you can say that this book is arranged so that you'll get the core 20% knowledge that covers 80% of being a great data scientist. More importantly, I'll add that you'll be also reading and practicing under Alexey's guidance, which is distilled by his work and Kaggle experience. Given such premises, I wish you a great journey through the pages and the projects of this book. I am sure that it will help you find the best way to approach data science and its problems, tools, and solutions.

— Luca Massaron

preface

I started my career working as a Java developer. Around 2012–2013, I became interested in data science and machine learning. First, I watched online courses, and then I enrolled in a master's program and spent two years studying different aspects of business intelligence and data science. Eventually, I graduated in 2015, and started working as a data scientist.

At work, my colleague showed me Kaggle — a platform for data science competitions. I thought, "With all the skills I got from courses and my master's degree, I'll be able to win any competition easily." But when I tried competing, I failed miserably. All the theoretical knowledge I had was useless on Kaggle. My models were awful, and I ended up on the bottom of the leaderboard.

I spent the next nine months taking part in data science competitions. I didn't do exceptionally well, but this was when I actually learned machine learning.

I realized that for me, the best way to learn is to do projects. When I focus on the problem, when I implement something, when I experiment, then I really learn. But if I focus on courses and theory, I invest too much time in learning things that aren't important and useful in practice.

And I'm not alone. When telling this story, I've heard "Me, too!" many times. That's why the focus of *Machine Learning Bookcamp* is on learning by doing projects. I believe that software engineers — people with the same background as me — learn best by doing.

We start this book with a car-price prediction project and learn linear regression. Then, we determine if customers want to stop using the services of our company. For this, we learn logistic regression. To learn decision trees, we score the clients of a bank to determine if they can pay back a loan. Finally, we use deep learning to classify pictures of clothes into different classes like T-shirts, pants, shoes, outerwear, and so on.

Each project in the book starts with the problem description. We then solve this problem using different tools and frameworks. By focusing on the problem, we cover only the parts that are important for solving this problem. There is theory as well, but I keep it to a minimum and focus on the practical part.

Sometimes, however, I had to include formulas in some chapters. It's not possible to avoid formulas in a book about machine learning. I know that formulas are terrifying for some of us. I've been there, too. That's why I explain all the formulas with code as well. When you see a formula, don't let it scare you. Try to understand the code first and then get back to the formula to see how the code translates to the formula. Then the formula won't be intimidating anymore!

You won't find all possible topics in this book. I focused on the most fundamental things — things you will use with 100% certainty when you start working with machine learning. There are other important topics that I didn't cover: time series analysis, clustering, natural language processing. After reading this book, you will have enough background knowledge to learn these topics yourself.

Three chapters in this book focus on model deployment. These are very important chapters — maybe the most important ones. Being able to deploy a model makes the difference between a successful project and a failed one. Even the best model is useless if others can't use it. That's why it's worth investing your time in learning how to make it accessible for others. And that's the reason I cover it quite early in the book, right after we learn about logistic regression.

The last chapter is about deploying models with Kubernetes. It's not a simple chapter, but nowadays Kubernetes is the most commonly used container management system. It's likely that you'll need to work with it, and that's why it's included in the book.

Finally, each chapter of the book includes exercises. It might be tempting to skip them, but I don't recommend doing so. If you only follow the book, you will learn many new things. But if you don't apply this knowledge in practice, you will forget most of it quite soon. The exercises help you apply these new skills in practice — and you'll remember what you learned much better.

Enjoy your journey through the book, and feel free to get in touch with me at any time!

— Alexey Grigorev

acknowledgments

Working on this book took a lot of my free time. I spent countless evenings and sleepless nights working on it. That's why, first and foremost, I would like to thank my wife for her patience and support.

Next, I would like to thank my editor, Susan Ethridge, for her patience as well. The book's first early access version was released in January 2020. Shortly after that, the world around us went crazy, and everyone was locked down at home. Working on the book was extremely challenging for me. I don't know how many deadlines I missed (a lot!), but Susan wasn't pushing me and let me work at my own pace.

The first person who had to read all the chapters (after Susan) was Michael Lund. I would like to thank Michael for the invaluable feedback he provided and for all the comments he left on my drafts. One of the reviewers wrote that "the attention to detail across the book is marvelous," and the main reason for that is Michael's input.

Finding the motivation to work on the book during the lockdown was difficult. At times, I didn't feel any energy at all. But the feedback from the reviewers and the MEAP readers was very encouraging. It helped me to finish the book despite all the difficulties. So, I would like to thank you all for reviewing the drafts, for giving me the feedback and — most importantly — for your kind words, as well as your support!

I especially want to thank a few readers who shared their feedback with me: Martin Tschendel, Agnieszka Kamińska, and Alexey Shvets. Also, I'd like to thank everyone who left feedback in the LiveBook comments section or in the #ml-bookcamp channel of the DataTalks.Club Slack group.

In chapter 7, I use a dataset with clothes for the image classification project. This dataset was created and curated specifically for this book. I would like to thank everyone who contributed the images of their clothes, especially Kenes Shangerey and Tagias, who contributed 60% of the entire dataset.

In the last chapter, I covered model deployment with Kubernetes and Kubeflow. Kubeflow is a relatively new technology, and some things are not documented well enough yet. That's why I would like to thank my colleagues, Theofilos Papapanagiotou and Antonio Bernardino, for their help with Kubeflow.

Machine Learning Bookcamp would not have reached most of the readers without the help of Manning's marketing department. I specifically would like to thank Lana Klasic and Radmila Ercegovac for their help with arranging events for promoting the book and for running social media campaigns to attract more readers. I would also like to thank my project editor, Deirdre Hiam; my reviewing editor, Adriana Sabo; my copyeditor, Pamela Hunt; and my proofreader, Melody Dolab.

To all the reviewers: Adam Gladstone, Amaresh Rajasekharan, Andrew Courter, Ben McNamara, Billy O'Callaghan, Chad Davis, Christopher Kottmyer, Clark Dorman, Dan Sheikh, George Thomas, Gustavo Filipe Ramos Gomes, Joseph Perenia, Krishna Chaitanya Anipindi, Ksenia Legostay, Lurdu Matha Reddy Kunireddy, Mike Cuddy, Monica Guimaraes, Naga Pavan Kumar T, Nathan Delboux, Nour Taweel, Oliver Korten, Paul Silisteanu, Rami Madian, Sebastian Mohan, Shawn Lam, Vishwesh Ravi Shrimali, William Pompei, your suggestions help to make this a better book.

Last but not least, I would like to thank Luca Massaron for inspiring me to write books. I will never be such a prolific book writer like you, Luca, but thank you for being a great motivation for me!

about this book

Who should read this book

This book is written for people who can program and can grasp the basics of Python quickly. You don't need to have any prior experience with machine learning.

The ideal reader is a software engineer who would like to start working with machine learning. However, a motivated college student who needs to code for studies and side projects will succeed as well.

Additionally, people who already work with machine learning but want to learn more will also find the book useful. Many people who already work as data scientists and data analysts said that it was helpful for them, especially the chapters about deployment.

How this book is organized: a roadmap

This book contains nine chapters, and we work on four different projects throughout the book.

- In chapter 1, we introduce the topic — we discuss the difference between traditional software engineering and machine learning. We cover the process of organizing machine learning projects, from the initial step of understanding the business requirements to the last step of deploying the model. We cover the modeling step in the process in more detail and talk about how we should evaluate our models and select the best one. To illustrate the concepts in this chapter, we use the spam-detection problem.

- In chapter 2, we start with our first project — we predict the price of a car. We learn how to use linear regression for that. We first prepare a dataset and do a bit of data cleaning. Next, we perform exploratory data analysis to understand the data better. Then we implement a linear regression model ourselves with NumPy to understand how machine learning models work under the hood. Finally, we discuss topics like regularization and evaluating the quality of the model.

- In chapter 3, we tackle the churn-detection problem. We work in a telecom company and want to determine which customer might stop using our services soon. It's a classification problem that we solve with logistic regression. We start by performing feature importance analysis to understand which factors are the most important ones for this problem. Then we discuss one-hot encoding as a way to handle categorical variables (factors like gender, type of contract, and so on). Finally, we train a logistic regression model with Scikit-learn to understand which customers are going to churn soon.

- In chapter 4, we take the model we developed in chapter 3 and evaluate its performance. We cover the most important classification evaluation metrics: accuracy, precision, and recall. We discuss the confusion table and then go into the details of ROC analysis and calculate AUC. We wrap up this chapter with discussing K-fold cross-validation.

- In chapter 5, we take the churn-prediction model and deploy it as a web service. This is an important step in the process, because if we don't make our model available, it's not useful for anyone. We start with Flask, a Python framework for creating web services. Then we cover Pipenv and Docker for dependency management and finish with deploying our service on AWS.

- In chapter 6, we start a project on risk scoring. We want to understand if a customer of a bank will have problems paying back a loan. For that, we learn how decision trees work and train a simple model with Scikit-learn. Then we move to more complex tree-based models like random forest and gradient boosting.

- In chapter 7, we build an image classification project. We will train a model for classifying images of clothes into 10 categories like T-shirts, dresses, pants, and so on. We use TensorFlow and Keras for training our model, and we cover things like transfer learning for being able to train a model with a relatively small dataset.

- In chapter 8, we take the clothes classification model we trained in chapter 7 and deploy it with TensorFlow Lite and AWS Lambda.

- In chapter 9, we deploy the clothes classification model, but we use Kubernetes and TensorFlow Serving in the first part, and Kubeflow and Kubeflow Serving in the second.

To help you get started with the book as well as Python and libraries around it, we prepared five appendix chapters:

- Appendix A explains how to set up the environment for the book. We show how to install Python with Anaconda, how to run Jupyter Notebook, how to install Docker, and how to create an AWS account
- Appendix B covers the basics of Python.
- Appendix C covers the basics of NumPy and gives a short introduction to the most important linear algebra concepts that we need for machine learning: matrix multiplication and matrix inversion.
- Appendix D covers Pandas.
- Appendix E explains how to get a Jupyter Notebook with a GPU on AWS Sage-Maker.

These appendices are optional, but they are helpful, especially if you haven't used Python or AWS before.

You don't have to read the book from cover to cover. To help you navigate, you can use this map:

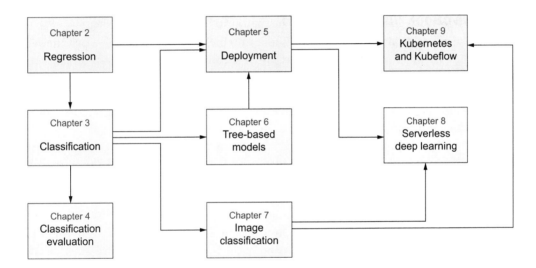

Chapters 2 and 3 are the most important ones. All the other chapters depend on them. After reading them, you jump to chapter 5 to deploy the model, chapter 6 to learn about tree-based models, or chapter 7 to learn about image classifications. Chapter 4, about evaluation metrics, depends on chapter 3: we evaluate the quality of the churn-prediction model from chapter 3. In chapters 8 and 9, we deploy the image classification model, so it's helpful to read chapter 7 before moving on to chapter 8 or 9.

Each chapter contains exercises. It's important to do these exercises — they will help you remember the material a lot better.

About the code

This book contains many examples of source code, both in numbered listings and in line with normal text. In both cases, source code is formatted in a `fixed-width font like this` to separate it from ordinary text. Sometimes code is also **in bold** to highlight code that has changed from previous steps in the chapter, such as when a new feature adds to an existing line of code.

In many cases, the original source code has been reformatted; we've added line breaks and reworked indentation to accommodate the available page space in the book. In rare cases, even this was not enough, and listings include line-continuation markers (➥). Additionally, comments in the source code have often been removed from the listings when the code is described in the text. Code annotations accompany many of the listings, highlighting important concepts.

The code for this book is available on GitHub at https://github.com/alexeygrigorev/mlbookcamp-code. This repository also contains a lot of useful links that will be helpful for you in your machine learning journey.

liveBook discussion forum

Purchase of Machine Learning Bookcamp includes free access to a private web forum run by Manning Publications where you can make comments about the book, ask technical questions, and receive help from the author and from other users. To access the forum, go to https://livebook.manning.com/book/machine-learning-bookcamp/welcome/v-11. You can also learn more about Manning's forums and the rules of conduct at https://livebook.manning.com/#!/discussion.

Manning's commitment to our readers is to provide a venue where a meaningful dialogue between individual readers and between readers and the author can take place. It is not a commitment to any specific amount of participation on the part of the author, whose contribution to the forum remains voluntary (and unpaid). We suggest you try asking the author some challenging questions lest his interest stray! The forum and the archives of previous discussions will be accessible from the publisher's website as long as the book is in print.

Other online resources

- The book's website: https://mlbookcamp.com/. It contains useful articles and courses based on the book.
- Community of data enthusiasts: https://datatalks.club. You can ask any question about data or machine learning there.
- There's also a channel for discussing book-related questions: #ml-bookcamp.

about the author

ALEXEY GRIGOREV lives in Berlin with his wife and son. He's an experienced software engineer who focuses on machine learning. He works at OLX Group as a principal data scientist, where he helps his colleagues bring machine learning to production.

After work, Alexey runs DataTalks.Club, a community of people who like data science and machine learning. He's the author of two other books: *Mastering Java for Data Science* and *TensorFlow Deep Learning Projects*.

about the cover illustration

The figure on the cover of Machine Learning Bookcamp is captioned "Femme de Brabant," or a woman from Brabant. The illustration is taken from a collection of dress costumes from various countries by Jacques Grasset de Saint-Sauveur (1757–1810), titled Costumes de Différents Pays, published in France in 1797. Each illustration is finely drawn and colored by hand. The rich variety of Grasset de Saint-Sauveur's collection reminds us vividly of how culturally apart the world's towns and regions were just 200 years ago. Isolated from each other, people spoke different dialects and languages. In the streets or in the countryside, it was easy to identify where they lived and what their trade or station in life was just by their dress.

The way we dress has changed since then and the diversity by region, so rich at the time, has faded away. It is now hard to tell apart the inhabitants of different continents, let alone different towns, regions, or countries. Perhaps we have traded cultural diversity for a more varied personal life — certainly for a more varied and fast-paced technological life.

At a time when it is hard to tell one computer book from another, Manning celebrates the inventiveness and initiative of the computer business with book covers based on the rich diversity of regional life of two centuries ago, brought back to life by Grasset de Saint-Sauveur's pictures.

Introduction to machine learning

This chapter covers

- Understanding machine learning and the problems it can solve
- Organizing a successful machine learning project
- Training and selecting machine learning models
- Performing model validation

In this chapter, we introduce machine learning and describe the cases in which it's most helpful. We show how machine learning projects are different from traditional software engineering (rule-based solutions) and illustrate the differences by using a spam-detection system as an example.

To use machine learning to solve real-life problems, we need a way to organize machine learning projects. In this chapter, we talk about CRISP-DM: a step-by-step methodology for implementing successful machine learning projects.

Finally, we take a closer look at one of the steps of CRISP-DM — the modeling step. In this step, we train different models and select the one that solves our problem best.

1.1   *Machine learning*

Machine learning is part of applied mathematics and computer science. It uses tools from mathematical disciplines such as probability, statistics, and optimization theory to extract patterns from data.

The main idea behind machine learning is learning from examples: we prepare a dataset with examples, and a machine learning system "learns" from this dataset. In other words, we give the system the input and the desired output, and the system tries to figure out how to do the conversion automatically, without asking a human.

We can collect a dataset with descriptions of cars and their prices, for example. Then we provide a machine learning model with this dataset and "teach" it by showing it cars and their prices. This process is called *training* or sometimes *fitting* (figure 1.1).

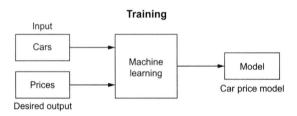

Figure 1.1   A machine learning algorithm takes in input data (descriptions of cars) and desired output (the cars' prices). Based on that data, it produces a model.

When training is done, we can use the model by asking it to predict car prices that we don't know yet (figure 1.2).

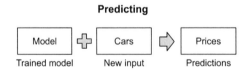

Figure 1.2   When training is done, we have a model that can be applied to new input data (cars without prices) to produce the output (predictions of prices).

All we need for machine learning is a dataset in which for each input item (a car) we have the desired output (the price).

This process is quite different from traditional software engineering. Without machine learning, analysts and developers look at the data they have and try to find patterns manually. After that, they come up with some logic: a set of rules for converting the input data to the desired output. Then they explicitly encode these rules using a programming language such as Java or Python, and the result is called software. So, in contrast with machine learning, a human does all the difficult work (figure 1.3).

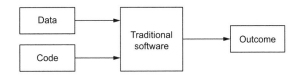

Figure 1.3　In traditional software, patterns are discovered manually and then encoded with a programming language. A human does all the work.

In summary, the difference between a traditional software system and a system based on machine learning is shown in figure 1.4. In machine learning, we give the system the input and output data, and the result is a model (code) that can transform the input into the output. The difficult work is done by the machine; we need only supervise the training process to make sure that the model is good (figure 1.4B). In contrast, in traditional systems, we first find the patterns in the data ourselves and then write code that converts the data to the desired outcome, using the manually discovered patterns (figure 1.4A).

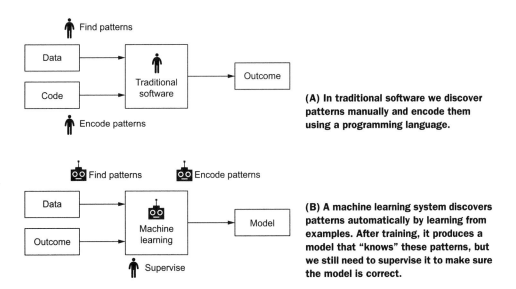

(A) In traditional software we discover patterns manually and encode them using a programming language.

(B) A machine learning system discovers patterns automatically by learning from examples. After training, it produces a model that "knows" these patterns, but we still need to supervise it to make sure the model is correct.

Figure 1.4　The difference between a traditional software system and a machine learning system. In traditional software engineering, we do all the work, whereas in machine learning, we delegate pattern discovery to a machine.

1.1.1 Machine learning vs. rule-based systems

To illustrate the difference between these two approaches and to show why machine learning is helpful, let's consider a concrete case. In this section, we talk about a spam-detection system to show this difference.

Suppose we are running an email service, and the users start complaining about unsolicited emails with advertisements. To solve this problem, we want to create a system that marks the unwanted messages as spam and forwards them to the spam folder.

The obvious way to solve the problem is to look at these emails ourselves to see whether they have any pattern. For example, we can check the sender and the content.

If we find that there's indeed a pattern in the spam messages, we write down the discovered patterns and come up with following two simple rules to catch these messages:

- If sender = promotions@online.com, then "spam"
- If title contains "buy now 50% off" and sender domain is "online.com," then "spam"
- Otherwise, "good email"

We write these rules in Python and create a spam-detection service, which we successfully deploy. At the beginning, the system works well and catches all the spam, but after a while, new spam messages start to slip through. The rules we have are no longer successful at marking these messages as spam.

To solve the problem, we analyze the content of the new messages and find that most of them contain the word *deposit*. So we add a new rule:

- If sender = "promotions@online.com" then "spam"
- If title contains "buy now 50% off" and sender domain is "online.com," then "spam"
- If body contains a word "deposit," then "spam"
- Otherwise, "good email"

After discovering this rule, we deploy the fix to our Python service and start catching more spam, making the users of our mail system happy.

Some time later, however, users start complaining again: some people use the word *deposit* with good intentions, but our system fails to recognize that fact and marks the messages as spam. To solve the problem, we look at the good messages and try to understand how they are different from spam messages. After a while, we discover a few patterns and modify the rules again:

- If sender = "promotions@online.com," then "spam"
- If title contains "buy now 50% off" and sender domain is "online.com," then "spam"

- If body contains "deposit," then
  - If the sender's domain is "test.com," then spam
  - If description length is >= 100 words, then spam
- Otherwise, "good email"

In this example, we looked at the input data manually and analyzed it in an attempt to extract patterns from it. As a result of the analysis, we got a set of rules that transforms the input data (emails) to one of the two possible outcomes: spam or not spam.

Now imagine that we repeat this process a few hundred times. As a result, we end up with code that is quite difficult to maintain and understand. At some point, it becomes impossible to include new patterns in the code without breaking the existing logic. So, in the long run, it's quite difficult to maintain and adjust existing rules such that the spam-detection system still performs well and minimizes spam complaints.

This is exactly the kind of situation in which machine learning can help. In machine learning, we typically don't attempt to extract these patterns manually. Instead, we delegate this task to statistical methods, by giving the system a dataset with emails marked as spam or not spam and describing each object (email) with a set of its characteristics (features). Based on this information, the system tries to find patterns in the data with no human help. In the end, it learns how to combine the features in such a way that spam messages are marked as spam and good messages aren't.

With machine learning, the problem of maintaining a hand-crafted set of rules goes away. When a new pattern emerges — for example, there's a new type of spam — we, instead of manually adjusting the existing set of rules, simply provide a machine learning algorithm with the new data. As a result, the algorithm picks up the new important patterns from the new data without damaging the old existing patterns — provided that these old patterns are still important and present in the new data.

Let's see how we can use machine learning to solve the spam-classification problem. For that, we first need to represent each email with a set of features. At the beginning we may choose to start with the following features:

- Length of title > 10? true/false
- Length of body > 10? true/false
- Sender "promotions@online.com"? true/false
- Sender "hpYOSKmL@test.com"? true/false
- Sender domain "test.com"? true/false
- Description contains "deposit"? true/false

In this particular case, we describe all emails with a set of six features. Coincidentally, these features are derived from the preceding rules.

With this set of features, we can encode any email as a feature vector: a sequence of numbers that contains all the feature values for a particular email.

Subject: Waiting for your reply
From: prince1@test.com

We are delighted to inform you that you won 1.000.000 (one million) US Dollars. To claim the prize, you need to pay a small processing fee. Please transfer $10 to our PayPal account at prince@test.com. Once we receive the money, we will start the transfer.

Congratulations again!

Spam: True

Figure 1.5   An email that a user marked as spam

Now imagine that we have an email that users marked as spam (figure 1.5). We can express this email as a vector [1, 1, 0, 0, 1, 1], and for each of the six features, we encode the value as 1 for true or 0 for false (figure 1.6). Because our users marked the message as spam, the target variable is 1 (true).

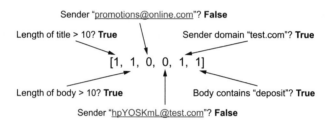

Figure 1.6   The six-dimensional feature vector for a spam email. Each of the six features is represented by a number. In this case, we use 1 if the feature is true and 0 if the feature is false.

This way, we can create feature vectors for all the emails in our database and attach a label to each one. These vectors will be the input to a model. Then the model takes all these numbers and combines the features in such a way that the prediction for spam messages is close to 1 (spam) and is 0 (not spam) for normal messages (figure 1.7).

```
      Features        Target
       (data)     (desired output)

[1, 1, 0, 0, 1, 1]      1
[0, 0, 0, 1, 0, 1]      0
[1, 1, 1, 0, 1, 0]      1
[1, 0, 0, 0, 0, 1]      1
[0, 0, 0, 1, 1, 0]      0
[1, 0, 1, 0, 1, 1]      0
```

Machine learning → Model

Figure 1.7   The input to a machine learning algorithm consists of multiple feature vectors and the target variable for each vector.

As a result, we have a tool that is more flexible than a set of hardcoded rules. If something changes in the future, we don't have to revisit all the rules manually and try to reorganize them. Instead, we use only the most recent data and replace the old model with the fresh one.

This example is just one way that machine learning can make our lives easier. Other applications of machine learning include

- Suggesting the price of a car.
- Predicting whether a customer will stop using the services of a company.
- Ordering documents by relevance with respect to a query.
- Showing users the ads they are more likely to click instead of irrelevant content.
- Classifying harmful and incorrect edits on Wikipedia. A system like this one can help Wikipedia's moderators prioritize their efforts when validating the suggested edits.
- Recommending items that customers may buy.
- Classifying images in different categories.

Applications of machine learning aren't limited to these examples, of course. We can use literally anything that we can express as (input data, desired output) to train a machine learning model.

1.1.2 When machine learning isn't helpful

Although machine learning is helpful and can solve many problems, it's not really needed in some cases.

For some simple tasks, rules and heuristics often work well, so it's better to start with them and then consider using machine learning. In our spam example, we started by creating a set of rules, but after maintaining this set became difficult, we switched to machine learning. We used some of the rules as features, however, and simply fed them to a model.

In some cases, it's simply not possible to use machine learning. To use machine learning, we need to have data. If no data is available, machine learning is not possible.

1.1.3 Supervised machine learning

The email-classification problem we just looked at is an example of supervised learning: we provide the model with features and the target variable, and it figures out how to use these features to arrive at the target. This type of learning is called *supervised* because we supervise or teach the model by showing it examples, exactly as we would teach children by showing them pictures of different objects and then telling them the names of those objects.

A bit more formally, we can express a supervised machine learning model mathematically as

$$y \approx g(X)$$

where

- *g* is the function that we want to learn with machine learning.
- *X* is the feature matrix in which rows are feature vectors.
- *y* is the target variable: a vector.

The goal of machine learning is to learn this function *g* in such a way that when it gets the matrix *X*, the output is close to the vector *y*. In other words, the function *g* must be able to take in *X* and produce *y*. The process of learning *g* is usually called *training* or *fitting*. We "fit" *g* to dataset *X* in such a way that it produces *y* (figure 1.8).

Figure 1.8   **When we train a model, an algorithm takes in a matrix *X* in which feature vectors are rows and the desired output is the vector *y*, with all the values we want to predict. The result of training is *g*, the model. After training, *g* should produce *y* when applied to *X* — or, in short, *g(X)* ≈ *y*.**

There are different types of supervised learning problems, and the type depends on the target variable *y*. The main types are

- Regression: the target variable *y* is numeric, such as a car price or the temperature tomorrow. We cover regression models in chapter 2.
- Classification: the target variable *y* is categorical, such as spam, not spam, or car make. We can further split classification into two subcategories: (1) *binary classification*, which has only two possible outcomes, such as spam or not spam, and (2) *multiclass classification*, which has more than two possible outcomes, such as a car make (Toyota, Ford, Volkswagen, and so on). Classification, especially binary classification, is the most common application of machine learning. We cover it in multiple chapters throughout the book, starting with chapter 3. In that chapter, we'll build a model for predicting whether a customer is going to churn — stop using the services of our company.
- Ranking: the target variable *y* is an ordering of elements within a group, such as the order of pages in a search-result page. The problem of ranking often happens in areas like search and recommendations, but it's out of the scope of this book and we won't cover it in detail.

Each supervised learning problem can be solved with different algorithms. Many types of models are available. These models define how exactly function *g* learns to predict *y* from *X*. These models include

- Linear regression for solving the regression problem, covered in chapter 2
- Logistic regression for solving the classification problem, covered in chapter 3
- Tree-based models for solving both regression and classification, covered in chapter 6
- Neural networks for solving both regression and classification, covered in chapter 7

Deep learning and neural networks have received a lot of attention recently, mostly because of breakthroughs in computer vision methods. These networks solve tasks such as image classification a lot better than earlier methods did. *Deep learning* is a subfield of machine learning in which the function g is a neural network with many layers. We will learn more about neural networks and deep learning starting in chapter 7, where we train a deep learning model for image classification.

1.2 Machine learning process

Creating a machine learning system involves more than just selecting a model, training it, and applying it to new data. The model-training part of the process is only a small step in the process.

Many other steps are involved, such as identifying the problem that machine learning can solve and using the predictions of the model to affect the end users. What is more, this process is iterative. When we train a model and apply it to a new dataset, we often identify cases in which the model doesn't perform well. We use these cases to retrain the model in such a way that the new version handles such situations better.

Certain techniques and frameworks help us organize a machine learning project in such a way that it doesn't get out of control. One such framework is CRISP-DM, which stands for *Cross-Industry Standard Process for Data Mining*. It was invented quite long ago, in 1996, but in spite of its age, it's still applicable to today's problems.

According to CRISP-DM (figure 1.9), the machine learning process has six steps:

1 Business understanding
2 Data understanding
3 Data preparation
4 Modeling
5 Evaluation
6 Deployment

Each phase covers typical tasks:

- In the business understanding step, we try to identify the problem, to understand how we can solve it, and to decide whether machine learning will be a useful tool for solving it.
- In the data understanding step, we analyze available datasets and decide whether we need to collect more data.

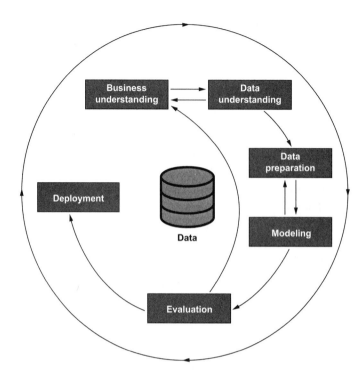

Figure 1.9 The CRISP-DM process. A machine learning project starts with understanding the problem and then moves into data preparation, training the model, and evaluating the results. Finally, the model goes to deployment. This process is iterative, and at each step, it's possible to go back to the previous one.

- In the data preparation step, we transform the data into a tabular form that we can use as input for a machine learning model.
- When the data is prepared, we move to the modeling step, in which we train a model.
- After the best model is identified, there's the evaluation step, where we evaluate the model to see if it solves the original business problem and measure its success at doing that.
- Finally, in the deployment step, we deploy the model to the production environment.

1.2.1 Business understanding

Let's consider the spam-detection example for an email service provider. We see more spam messages than ever before, and our current system cannot deal with it easily. This problem is addressed in the business understanding step: we analyze the problem and the existing solution and try to determine if adding machine learning to that system will help us stop spam messages. We also define the goal and how to measure it.

The goal could be "Reduce the amount of reported spam messages" or "Reduce the amount of complaints about spam that customer support receives per day," for example. In this step, we may also decide that machine learning is not going to help and propose a simpler way to solve the problem.

1.2.2 Data understanding

The next step is data understanding. Here, we try to identify the data sources we can use to solve the problem. If our site has a Report Spam button, for example, we can get data generated by users who marked their incoming emails as spam. Then we look at the data and analyze it to decide whether it's good enough to solve our problem.

This data may not be good enough, however, for a wide range of reasons. One reason could be that the dataset is too small for us to learn any useful patterns. Another reason could be that the data is too noisy. The users may not use the button correctly, so it will be useless for training a machine learning model, or the data-collection process could be broken, gathering only a small fraction of the data we want.

If we conclude that the data we currently have is not sufficient, we need to find a way to get better data, whether we acquire it from external sources or improve the way we collect it internally. It's also possible that discoveries we make in this step will influence the goal we set in the business understanding step, so we may need to go back to that step and adjust the goal according to our findings.

When we have reliable data sources, we go to the data preparation step.

1.2.3 Data preparation

In this step, we clean the data, transforming it in such a way that it can be used as input for a machine learning model. For the spam example, we transform the dataset into a set of features that we feed into a model later.

After the data is prepared, we go to the modeling step.

1.2.4 Modeling

In this step, we decide which machine learning model to use and how to make sure that we get the best out of it. For example, we may decide to try logistic regression and a deep neural network to solve the spam problem.

We need to know how we will measure the performance of the models to select the best one. For the spam model, we can look at how well the model predicts spam messages and choose the one that does it best. For this purpose, setting a proper validation framework is important, which is why we cover it in more detail in the next section.

It's very likely that in this step, we need to go back and adjust the way we prepare the data. Perhaps we came up with a great feature, so we go back to the data preparation step to write some code to compute that feature. When the code is done, we train the model again to check whether this feature is good. We might add a feature "length of the subject," retrain the model, and check whether this change improves the model's performance, for example.

After we select the best possible model, we go to the evaluation step.

1.2.5   *Evaluation*

In this step, we check whether the model lives up to expectations. When we set the goal in the business understanding step, we also define the way of establishing whether the goal is achieved. Typically, we do this by looking at an important business metric and making sure that the model moves the metric in the right direction. In the case of spam detection, the metric could be the number of people who click the Report Spam button or the number of complaints about the issue we're solving that customer support receives. In both cases, we hope that using the model reduces the number.

Nowadays, this step is tightly connected to the next step: deployment.

1.2.6   *Deployment*

The best way to evaluate a model is to battle-test it: roll it out to a fraction of users and then check whether our business metric changes for these users. If we want our model to reduce the number of reported spam messages, for example, we expect to see fewer reports from this group compared with the rest of the users.

After the model is deployed, we use everything we learned in all the steps and go back to the first step to reflect on what we achieved (or didn't achieve). We may realize that our initial goal was wrong and that what we actually want to do is *not* reduce the number of reports but increase customer engagement by decreasing the amount of spam. So we go all the way back to the business understanding step to redefine our goal. Then, when we evaluate the model again, we use a different business metric to measure its success.

1.2.7   *Iterate*

As we can see, CRISP-DM emphasizes the iterative nature of machine learning processes: after the last step, we are always expected to go back to the first step, refine the original problem, and change it based on the learned information. We never stop at the last step; instead, we rethink the problem and see what we can do better in the next iteration.

It's a common misconception that machine learning engineers and data scientists spend their entire day training machine learning models. In reality, this idea is incorrect, as we can see in the CRISP-DM diagram (figure 1.9). A lot of steps come before and after the modeling step, and all these steps are important for a successful machine learning project.

1.3   *Modeling and model validation*

As we saw previously, training models (the modeling step) is only one step in the whole process. But it's an important step because it's where we actually use machine learning to train models.

After we collect all the required data and determine that it's good, we find a way to process the data and then proceed to training a machine learning model. In our spam example, this happens after we get all the spam reports, process the emails, and have a matrix ready to be put to a model.

At this point, we may ask ourselves what to use: logistic regression or a neural network. If we decide to go with a neural network because we've heard it's the best model, how can we make sure that it's indeed better than any other model?

The goal at this step is to produce a model in such a way that it achieves the best predictive performance. To do this, we need to have a way to reliably measure the performance of each possible model candidate and then choose the best one.

One possible approach is to train a model, let it run on a live system, and observe what happens. In the spam example, we decide to use a neural network for detecting spam, so we train it and deploy it to our production system. Then we observe how the model behaves on new messages and record the cases in which the system is incorrect.

This approach, however, is not ideal for our case: we cannot possibly do it for every model candidate we have. What's worse, we can accidentally deploy a really bad model and see that it's bad only after it has been run on live users of our system.

> **NOTE** Testing a model on a live system is called online testing, and it's important for evaluating the quality of a model on real data. This approach, however, belongs to the evaluation and deployment steps of the process, not to the modeling step.

A better approach for selecting the best model before deploying it is emulating the scenario of going live. We get our complete dataset, take a part out of it, and train the model on the remaining part of the data. When the training is done, we pretend that the held-out dataset is the new, unseen data, and we use it to measure the performance of our models. This part of data is often called the *validation set*, and the process of keeping part of a dataset away and using it to evaluate performance is called *validation* (see figure 1.10).

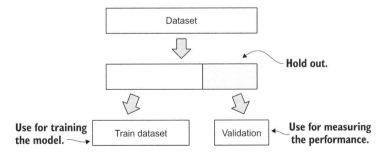

Figure 1.10   To evaluate the performance of a model, we set some data aside and use it only for validation purposes.

In the spam dataset, we can take out every tenth message. This way, we hold out 10% of the data, which we use only for validating the models, and use the remaining 90%

for training. Next, we train both logistic regression and a neural network on the training data. When the models are trained, we apply them to the validation dataset and check which one is more accurate at predicting spam.

If, after applying the models to validation, we see that logistic regression is correct in predicting the spam in only 90% of cases, whereas a neural network is correct in 93% of cases, we conclude that the neural network model is a better choice than logistic regression (figure 1.11).

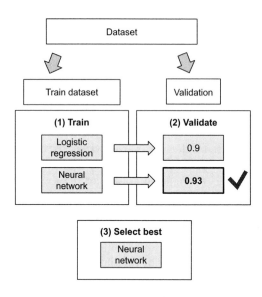

Figure 1.11   The validation process. We split the dataset into two parts, train the models on the training part, and evaluate the performance on the validation part. Using the evaluation results, we can choose the best model.

Often, we don't have just two models to try but a lot more. Logistic regression, for example, has a parameter, C, and depending on the value we set, the results can vary dramatically. Likewise, a neural network has many parameters, and each may have a great effect on the predictive performance of the final model. On top of that, we have other models, each with its own set of parameters. How do we select the best model with the best parameters?

To do so, we use the same evaluation scheme. We train the models with different parameters on the training data, apply them to the validation data, and then select the model and its parameters based on the best validation results (figure 1.12).

This approach has a subtle problem, however. If we repeat the process of model evaluation over and over again and use the same validation dataset for that purpose, the good numbers we observe in the validation dataset may appear just by chance. In other words, the "best" model may simply get lucky in predicting the outcomes for this particular dataset.

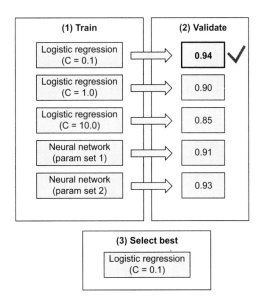

**Figure 1.12   Using the validation dataset to select the best model
with the best parameters**

NOTE   In statistics and other fields, this problem is known as the multiple-comparisons problem or multiple-tests problem. The more times we make predictions on the same dataset, the more likely we are to see good performance by chance.

To guard against this problem, we use the same idea: we hold out part of the data again. We call this part of data the *test* dataset. We use it rarely, only for testing the model that we selected as the best (figure 1.13).

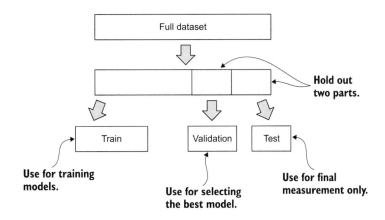

Figure 1.13   Splitting the data into training, testing, and validation parts

To apply this to the spam example, we first hold out 10% of the data as the test dataset and then hold out 10% of the data as the validation. We try multiple models on the validation dataset, select the best one, and apply it to the test dataset. If we see that the difference in performance between validation and test is not big, we confirm that this model is indeed the best one (figure 1.14).

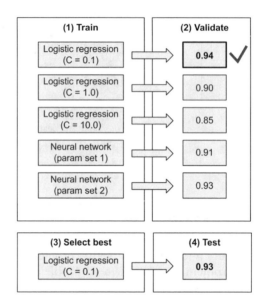

Figure 1.14   We use the test dataset to confirm that the performance of the best model on the validation set is good.

IMPORTANT   Setting the validation process is the most important step in machine learning. Without it, there's no reliable way to know whether the model we've just trained is good, useless, or even harmful.

The process of selecting the best model and the best parameters for the model is called *model selection*. We can summarize model selection as follows (figure 1.15):

1 We split the data into training, validation, and testing parts.
2 We train each model first on the training part and then evaluate it on validation.
3 Each time we train a different model, we record the evaluation results using the validation part.
4 At the end, we determine which model is the best and test it on the test dataset.

It's important to use the model selection process and to validate and test the models in offline settings first to make sure that the models we train are good. If the model behaves well offline, we can decide to move to the next step and deploy the model to evaluate its performance with real users.

Model selection process

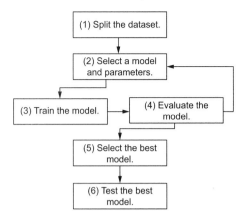

Figure 1.15 The model selection process. First, we split the dataset, select a model, and train it only on the training part of the data. Then we evaluate the model on the validation part. We repeat the process many times until we find the best model.

Summary

- Unlike traditional rule-based software engineering systems, in which rules are extracted and coded manually, machine learning systems can be taught to extract meaningful patterns from data automatically. This gives us a lot more flexibility and makes it easier to adapt to changes.

- Successfully implementing a machine learning project requires a structure and a set of guidelines. CRISP-DM is a framework for organizing a machine learning project that breaks down the process into six steps, from business understanding to deployment. The framework highlights the iterative nature of machine learning and helps us stay organized.

- Modeling is an important step in a machine learning project: the part where we actually use machine learning to train a model. During this step, we create models that achieve the best predictive performance.

- Model selection is the process of choosing the best model to solve a problem. We split all the available data into three parts: training, validation, and testing. We train models on the training set and select the best model by using the validation set. When the best model is selected, we use the test step as a final check to ensure that the best model behaves well. This process helps us create useful models that work well with no surprises.

Machine learning for regression

2

This chapter covers

- Creating a car-price prediction project with a linear regression model
- Doing an initial exploratory data analysis with Jupyter notebooks
- Setting up a validation framework
- Implementing the linear regression model from scratch
- Performing simple feature engineering for the model
- Keeping the model under control with regularization
- Using the model to predict car prices

In chapter 1, we talked about supervised machine learning, in which we teach machine learning models how to identify patterns in data by giving them examples.

Suppose that we have a dataset with descriptions of cars, like make, model, and age, and we would like to use machine learning to predict their prices. These characteristics of cars are called *features*, and the price is the *target variable* — something we want to predict. Then the model gets the features and combines them to output the price.

This is an example of supervised learning: we have some information about the price of some cars, and we can use it to predict the price of others. In chapter 1, we also talked about different types of supervised learning: regression and classification. When the target variable is numerical, we have a regression problem, and when the target variable is categorical, we have a classification problem.

In this chapter, we create a regression model, starting with the simplest one: linear regression. We implement the algorithms ourselves, which is simple enough to do in a few lines of code. At the same time, it's very illustrative, and it will teach you how to deal with NumPy arrays and perform basic matrix operations such as matrix multiplication and matrix inversion. We also come across problems of numerical instability when inverting a matrix and see how regularization helps solve them.

2.1 Car-price prediction project

The problem we solve in this chapter is predicting the price of a car. Suppose that we have a website where people can sell and buy used cars. When posting an ad on our website, sellers often struggle to come up with a meaningful price. We want to help our users with automatic price recommendations. We ask the sellers to specify the model, make, year, mileage, and other important characteristics of a car, and based on that information, we want to suggest the best price.

One of the product managers in the company accidentally came across an open dataset with car prices and asked us to have a look at it. We checked the data and saw that it contained all the important features as well as the recommended price — exactly what we needed for our use case. Thus, we decided to use this dataset for building the price-recommendation algorithm.

The plan for the project is the following:

1 First, we download the dataset.
2 Next, we do some preliminary analysis of the data.
3 After that, we set up a validation strategy to make sure our model produces correct predictions.
4 Then we implement a linear regression model in Python and NumPy.
5 Next, we cover feature engineering to extract important features from the data to improve the model.
6 Finally, we see how to make our model stable with regularization and use it to predict car prices.

2.1.1 Downloading the dataset

The first thing we do for this project is install all the required libraries: Python, NumPy, Pandas, and Jupyter Notebook. The easiest way to do it is to use a Python distribution called Anaconda (https://www.anaconda.com). Please refer to appendix A for installation guidelines.

After the libraries are installed, we need to download the dataset. We have multiple options for doing this. You can download it manually through the Kaggle web interface, available at https://www.kaggle.com/CooperUnion/cardataset. (You can read more about the dataset and the way it was collected at https://www.kaggle.com/jshih7/car-price-prediction.) Go there, open it, and click the download link. The other option is using the Kaggle command-line interface (CLI), which is a tool for programmatic access to all datasets available via Kaggle. For this chapter, we will use the second option. We describe how to configure the Kaggle CLI in appendix A.

> **NOTE** Kaggle is an online community for people who are interested in machine learning. It is mostly known for hosting machine learning competitions, but it is also a data-sharing platform where anyone can share a dataset. More than 16,000 datasets are available for anyone to use. It is a great source of project ideas and very useful for machine learning projects.

In this chapter, as well as throughout the book, we will actively use NumPy. We cover all necessary NumPy operations as we go along, but please refer to appendix C for a more in-depth introduction.

The source code for this project is available in the book's repository in GitHub at https://github.com/alexeygrigorev/mlbookcamp-code in chapter-02-car-price.

As the first step, we will create a folder for this project. We can give it any name, such as chapter-02-car-price:

```
mkdir chapter-02-car-price
cd chapter-02-car-price
```

Then we download the dataset:

```
kaggle datasets download -d CooperUnion/cardataset
```

This command downloads the cardataset.zip file, which is a zip archive. Let's unpack it:

```
unzip cardataset.zip
```

Inside, there's one file: data.csv.

When we have the dataset, let's move on to the next step: understanding it.

2.2 *Exploratory data analysis*

Understanding data is an important step in the machine learning process. Before we can train any model, we need to know what kind of data we have and whether it is useful. We do this with exploratory data analysis (EDA).

We look at the dataset to learn

- The distribution of the target variable
- The features in this dataset
- The distribution of values in these features

- The quality of the data
- The number of missing values

2.2.1 Exploratory data analysis toolbox

The main tools for this analysis are Jupyter Notebook, Matplotlib, and Pandas:

- Jupyter Notebook is a tool for interactive execution of Python code. It allows us to execute a piece of code and immediately see the outcome. In addition, we can display charts and add notes with comments in free text. It also supports other languages such as R or Julia (hence the name: Jupyter stands for Julia, Python, R), but we will use it only for Python.
- Matplotlib is a library for plotting. It is very powerful and allows you to create different types of visualizations, such as line charts, bar charts, and histograms.
- Pandas is a library for working with tabular data. It can read data from any source, be it a CSV file, a JSON file, or a database.

We will also use Seaborn, another tool for plotting that is built on top of Matplotlib and makes it easier to draw charts.

Let's start a Jupyter Notebook by executing the following command:

```
jupyter notebook
```

This command starts a Jupyter Notebook server in the current directory and opens it in the default web browser (figure 2.1).

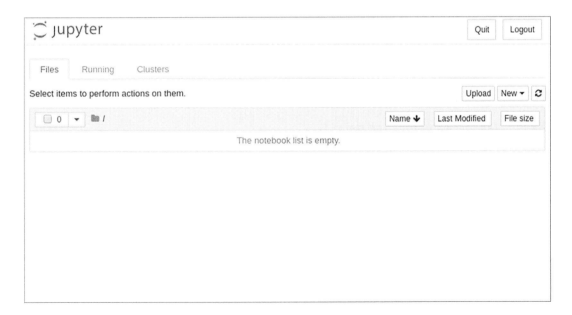

Figure 2.1 The starting screen of the Jupyter Notebook service

If Jupyter is running on a remote server, it requires additional configuration. Please refer to appendix A for details on the setup.

Now let's create a notebook for this project. Click New, then select Python 3 in the Notebooks section. We can call it chapter-02-car-price-project — click the current title (Untitled), and replace it with the new one.

First, we need to import all the libraries required for this project. Write the following in the first cell:

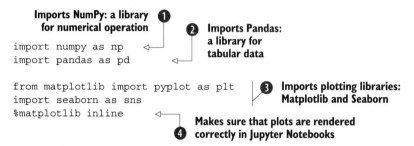

The first two lines, ❶ and ❷, are imports for required libraries: NumPy for numeric operations and Pandas for tabular data. The convention is to import these libraries using shorter aliases (such as pd in import pandas as pd). This convention is common in the Python machine learning community, and everybody follows it.

The next two lines, ❸, are imports for plotting libraries. The first one, Matplotlib, is a library for creating good-quality visualizations. It's not always easy to use this library as is. Some libraries make using Matplotlib simpler, and Seaborn is one of them.

Finally, %matplotlib inline in line ❹ tells Jupyter to expect plots in the notebook, so it will be able to render them when we need them.

Press Shift+Enter or click Run to execute the content of the selected cell.

We will not get into more detail about Jupyter Notebooks. Check the official website (https://jupyter.org) to learn more about it. The site has plenty of documentation and examples that will help you master it.

2.2.2   *Reading and preparing data*

Now let's read our dataset. We can use the read_csv function from Pandas for that purpose. Put the following code in the next cell and again press Shift+Enter:

```
df = pd.read_csv('data.csv')
```

This line of code reads the CSV file and writes the results to a variable named df, which is short for *DataFrame*. Now we can check how many rows there are. Let's use the len function:

```
len(df)
```

The function prints 11914, which means that there are almost 12,000 cars in this dataset (figure 2.2).

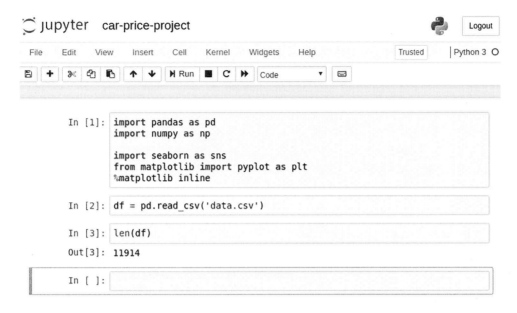

Figure 2.2 Jupyter Notebooks are interactive. We can type some code in a cell, execute it, and see the results immediately, which is ideal for exploratory data analysis.

Now let's use df.head() to look at the first five rows of our DataFrame (figure 2.3).

In [4]: `df.head()`

Out[4]:

	Make	Model	Year	Engine Fuel Type	Engine HP	Engine Cylinders	Transmission Type	Driven_Wheels	Number of Doors	
0	BMW	1 Series M	2011	premium unleaded (required)	335.0	6.0	MANUAL	rear wheel drive	2.0	T
1	BMW	1 Series	2011	premium unleaded (required)	300.0	6.0	MANUAL	rear wheel drive	2.0	Lux
2	BMW	1 Series	2011	premium unleaded (required)	300.0	6.0	MANUAL	rear wheel drive	2.0	
3	BMW	1 Series	2011	premium unleaded (required)	230.0	6.0	MANUAL	rear wheel drive	2.0	Lu
4	BMW	1 Series	2011	premium unleaded (required)	230.0	6.0	MANUAL	rear wheel drive	2.0	

Figure 2.3 The output of the head() function of a Pandas DataFrame: it shows the first five rows of the dataset. This output allows us to understand what the data looks like.

This gives us an idea of what the data looks like. We can already see that there are some inconsistencies in this dataset: the column names sometimes have spaces, and sometimes have underscores (_). The same is true for feature values: sometimes they're capitalized, and sometimes they are short strings with spaces. This is inconvenient and confusing, but we can solve this by normalizing them — replacing all spaces with underscores and lowercase all letters:

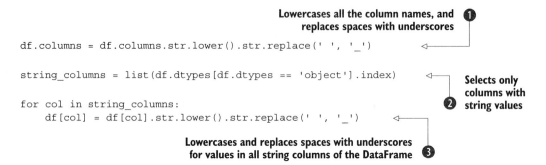

In ❶ and ❸, we use the special `str` attribute. Using it, we can apply string operations to the entire column at that same time without writing any `for` loops. We use it to lowercase the column names and the content of these columns as well as to replace spaces with underscores.

We can use this attribute only for columns with string values inside. This is exactly why we first select such columns in ❷.

> **NOTE** In this chapter and subsequent chapters, we cover relevant Pandas operations as we go along, but at a fairly high level. Please refer to appendix D for a more consistent and in-depth introduction to Pandas.

After this initial preprocessing, the DataFrame looks more uniform (figure 2.4).

```
In [6]: df.head()
```

Out[6]:

	make	model	year	engine_fuel_type	engine_hp	engine_cylinders	transmission_type	driven_wheels	n
0	bmw	1_series_m	2011	premium_unleaded_(required)	335.0	6.0	manual	rear_wheel_drive	
1	bmw	1_series	2011	premium_unleaded_(required)	300.0	6.0	manual	rear_wheel_drive	
2	bmw	1_series	2011	premium_unleaded_(required)	300.0	6.0	manual	rear_wheel_drive	
3	bmw	1_series	2011	premium_unleaded_(required)	230.0	6.0	manual	rear_wheel_drive	
4	bmw	1_series	2011	premium_unleaded_(required)	230.0	6.0	manual	rear_wheel_drive	

Figure 2.4   The result of preprocessing the data. The column names and values are normalized: they are lowercase, and the spaces are converted to underscores.

As we see, this dataset contains multiple columns:

- make: make of a car (BMW, Toyota, and so on)
- model: model of a car
- year: year when the car was manufactured
- engine_fuel_type: type of fuel the engine needs (diesel, electric, and so on)
- engine_hp: horsepower of the engine
- engine_cylinders: number of cylinders in the engine
- transmission_type: type of transmission (automatic or manual)
- driven_wheels: front, rear, all
- number_of_doors: number of doors a car has
- market_category: luxury, crossover, and so on
- vehicle_size: compact, midsize, or large
- vehicle_style: sedan or convertible
- highway_mpg: miles per gallon (mpg) on the highway
- city_mpg: miles per gallon in the city
- popularity: number of times the car was mentioned in a Twitter stream
- msrp: manufacturer's suggested retail price

For us, the most interesting column here is the last one: MSRP (manufacturer's suggested retail price, or simply the price of a car). We will use this column for predicting the prices of a car.

2.2.3 Target variable analysis

The MSRP column contains the important information — it's our target variable, the y, which is the value that we want to learn to predict.

One of the first steps of exploratory data analysis should always be to look at what the values of y look like. We typically do this by checking the distribution of y: a visual description of what the possible values of y can be and how often they occur. This type of visualization is called a *histogram*.

We will use Seaborn to plot the histogram, so type the following in the Jupyter Notebook:

```
sns.histplot(df.msrp, bins=40)
```

After plotting this graph, we immediately notice that the distribution of prices has a very long tail. There are many cars with low prices on the left side, but the number quickly drops, and there's a long tail of very few cars with high prices (see figure 2.5).

We can have a closer look by zooming in a bit and looking at values below $100,000 (figure 2.6):

```
sns.histplot(df.msrp[df.msrp < 100000])
```

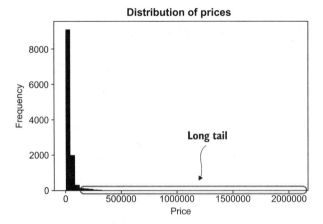

Figure 2.5   The distribution of the prices in the dataset. We see many values at the low end of the price axis and almost nothing at the high end. This is a long tail distribution, which is a typical situation for many items with low prices and very few expensive ones.

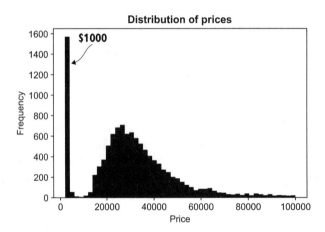

Figure 2.6   The distribution of the prices for cars below $100,000. Looking only at car prices below $100,000 allows us to see the head of the distribution better. We also notice a lot of cars that cost $1,000.

The long tail makes it quite difficult for us to see the distribution, but it has an even stronger effect on a model: such distribution can greatly confuse the model, so it won't learn well enough. One way to solve this problem is log transformation. If we apply the log function to the prices, it removes the undesired effect (figure 2.7).

$$y_{\text{new}} = \log(y + 1)$$

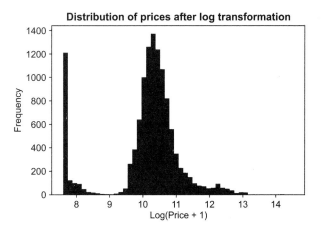

Figure 2.7   The logarithm of the price. The effect of the long tail is removed, and we can see the entire distribution in one plot.

The +1 part is important in cases that have zeros. The logarithm of zero is minus infinity, but the logarithm of one is zero. If our values are all non-negative, by adding 1, we make sure that the transformed values do not go below zero.

For our specific case, zero values are not an issue — all the prices we have start at $1,000 — but it's still a convention that we follow. NumPy has a function that performs this transformation:

```
log_price = np.log1p(df.msrp)
```

To look at the distribution of the prices after the transformation, we can use the same `histplot` function (figure 2.7):

```
sns.histplot(log_price)
```

As we see, this transformation removes the long tail, and now the distribution resembles a bell-shaped curve. This distribution is not normal, of course, because of the large peak in lower prices, but the model can deal with it more easily.

NOTE   Generally, it's good when the target distribution looks like the normal distribution (figure 2.8). Under this condition, models such as linear regression perform well.

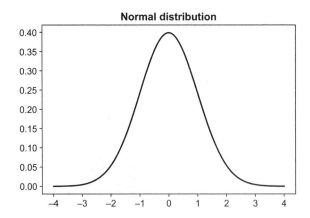

Figure 2.8   The normal distribution, also known as Gaussian, follows the bell-shaped curve, which is symmetrical and has a peak in the center.

Exercise 2.1

The head of a distribution is a range where there are many values. What is a long tail of a distribution?

  a A big peak around 1,000 USD
  b A case when many values are spread very far from the head — and these values visually appear as a "tail" on the histogram
  c A lot of very similar values packed together within a short range

---

2.2.4   *Checking for missing values*

We will look more closely at other features a bit later, but one thing we should do now is check for missing values in the data. This step is important because, typically, machine learning models cannot deal with missing values automatically. We need to know whether we need to do anything special to handle those values.

Pandas has a convenient function that checks for missing values:

```
df.isnull().sum()
```

This function shows

```
make                    0
model                   0
year                    0
engine_fuel_type        3
engine_hp              69
engine_cylinders       30
transmission_type       0
driven_wheels           0
number_of_doors         6
```

```
market_category       3742
vehicle_size             0
vehicle_style            0
highway_mpg              0
city_mpg                 0
popularity               0
msrp                     0
```

The first thing we see is that MSRP — our target variable — doesn't have any missing values. This result is good, because otherwise, such records won't be useful to us: we always need to know the target value of an observation to use it for training the model. Also, a few columns have missing values, especially market_category, in which we have almost 4,000 rows with missing values.

We need to deal with missing values later when we train the model, so we should keep this problem in mind. For now, we don't do anything else with these features and proceed to the next step: setting up the validation framework so that we can train and test machine learning models.

2.2.5 Validation framework

As we learned previously, it's important to set up the validation framework as early as possible to make sure that the models we train are good and can generalize — that is, that the model can be applied to new, unseen data. To do that, we put aside some data and train the model only on one part. Then we use the held-out dataset — the one we didn't use for training — to make sure that the predictions of the model make sense.

This step is important because we train the model by using optimization methods that fit the function $g(X)$ to the data X. Sometimes these optimization methods pick up spurious patterns — patterns that appear to be real patterns to the model but in reality are random fluctuations. If we have a small training dataset in which all BMW cars cost only $10,000, for example, the model will think that this is true for all BMW cars in the world.

To ensure that this doesn't happen, we use validation. Because the validation dataset is not used for training the model, the optimization method did not see this data. When we apply the model to this data, it emulates the case of applying the model to new data that we've never seen. If the validation dataset has BMW cars with prices higher than $10,000, but our model will predict $10,000 on them, we will notice that the model doesn't perform well on these examples.

As we already know, we need to split the dataset into three parts: train, validation, and test (figure 2.9).

Let's split the DataFrame such that

- 20% of data goes to validation.
- 20% goes to test.
- The remaining 60% goes to train.

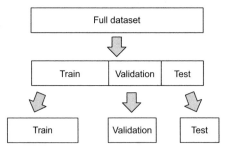

Figure 2.9   The entire dataset is split into three parts: train, validation and test.

Listing 2.1   Splitting Data into validation, test, and training sets

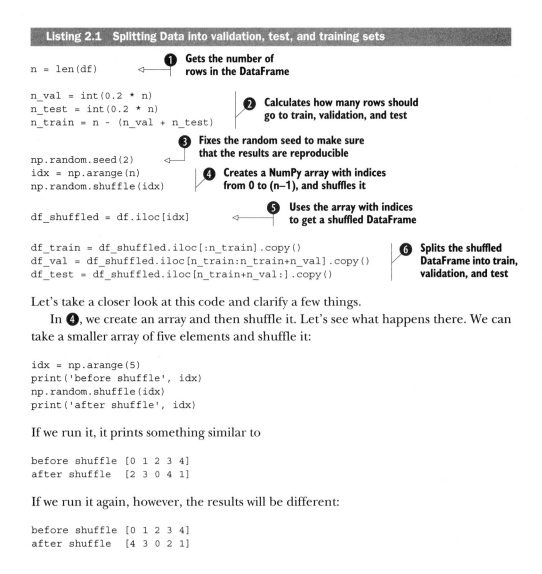

```
n = len(df)
```
❶ Gets the number of rows in the DataFrame

```
n_val = int(0.2 * n)
n_test = int(0.2 * n)
n_train = n - (n_val + n_test)
```
❷ Calculates how many rows should go to train, validation, and test

```
np.random.seed(2)
```
❸ Fixes the random seed to make sure that the results are reproducible

```
idx = np.arange(n)
np.random.shuffle(idx)
```
❹ Creates a NumPy array with indices from 0 to (n–1), and shuffles it

```
df_shuffled = df.iloc[idx]
```
❺ Uses the array with indices to get a shuffled DataFrame

```
df_train = df_shuffled.iloc[:n_train].copy()
df_val = df_shuffled.iloc[n_train:n_train+n_val].copy()
df_test = df_shuffled.iloc[n_train+n_val:].copy()
```
❻ Splits the shuffled DataFrame into train, validation, and test

Let's take a closer look at this code and clarify a few things.

In ❹, we create an array and then shuffle it. Let's see what happens there. We can take a smaller array of five elements and shuffle it:

```
idx = np.arange(5)
print('before shuffle', idx)
np.random.shuffle(idx)
print('after shuffle', idx)
```

If we run it, it prints something similar to

```
before shuffle [0 1 2 3 4]
after shuffle  [2 3 0 4 1]
```

If we run it again, however, the results will be different:

```
before shuffle [0 1 2 3 4]
after shuffle  [4 3 0 2 1]
```

To make sure that every time we run it, the results are the same, in ❸ we fix the random seed:

```
np.random.seed(2)
idx = np.arange(5)
print('before shuffle', idx)
np.random.shuffle(idx)
print('after shuffle', idx)
```

The function `np.random.seed` takes in any number and uses this number as the starting seed for all the generated data inside NumPy's random package.

When we execute this code, it prints

```
before shuffle [0 1 2 3 4]
after shuffle  [2 4 1 3 0]
```

In this case the results are still random, but when we re-execute it, the result turns out to be the same as the previous run:

```
before shuffle [0 1 2 3 4]
after shuffle  [2 4 1 3 0]
```

This is good for reproducibility. If we want somebody else to run this code and get the same results, we need to make sure that everything is fixed, even the "random" component of our code.

NOTE This makes the results reproducible on the same computer. With a different operating system and a different version of NumPy, the result may be different.

After we create an array with indices `idx`, we can use it to get a shuffled version of our initial DataFrame. For that purpose in ❺, we use `iloc`, which is a way to access the rows of the DataFrame by their numbers:

```
df_shuffled = df.iloc[idx]
```

If `idx` contains shuffled consequent numbers, this code will produce a shuffled DataFrame (figure 2.10).

	make	model	year	msrp
0	lotus	evora_400	2017	91900
1	aston_martin	v8_vantage	2014	136900
2	hyundai	genesis	2015	38000
3	suzuki	samurai	1993	2000
4	mitsubishi	outlander	2015	26195

`df.iloc[idx]`

⟹

	make	model	year	msrp
2	hyundai	genesis	2015	38000
4	mitsubishi	outlander	2015	26195
1	aston_martin	v8_vantage	2014	136900
3	suzuki	samurai	1993	2000
0	lotus	evora_400	2017	91900

idx = [2, 4, 1, 3, 0]

Figure 2.10 Using `iloc` to shuffle a DataFrame. When used with a shuffled array of indices, it creates a shuffled DataFrame.

In this example, we used `iloc` with a list of indices. We can also use ranges with the colon operator (:), and this is exactly what we do in ❻ for splitting the shuffled Data-Frame into train, validation, and test:

```
df_train = df_shuffled.iloc[:n_train].copy()
df_val = df_shuffled.iloc[n_train:n_train+n_val].copy()
df_test = df_shuffled.iloc[n_train+n_val:].copy()
```

Now the DataFrame is split into three parts, and we can continue. Our initial analysis showed a long tail in the distribution of prices, and to remove its effect, we need to apply the log transformation. We can do that for each DataFrame separately:

```
y_train = np.log1p(df_train.msrp.values)
y_val = np.log1p(df_val.msrp.values)
y_test = np.log1p(df_test.msrp.values)
```

To avoid accidentally using the target variable later, let's remove it from the dataframes:

```
del df_train['msrp']
del df_val['msrp']
del df_test['msrp']
```

> **NOTE** Removing the target variable is an optional step. But it's helpful to make sure that we don't use it when training a model: if that happens, we'd use price for predicting the price, and our model would have perfect accuracy.

When the validation split is done, we can go to the next step: training a model.

2.3 *Machine learning for regression*

After performing the initial data analysis, we are ready to train a model. The problem we are solving is a regression problem: the goal is to predict a number — the price of a car. For this project we will use the simplest regression model: linear regression.

2.3.1 *Linear regression*

To predict the price of a car, we need to use a machine learning model. To do this, we will use linear regression, which we will implement ourselves. Typically, we don't do this by hand; instead, we let a framework do this for us. In this chapter, however, we want to show that there is no magic inside these frameworks: it's just code. Linear regression is a perfect model because it's relatively simple and can be implemented with just a few lines of NumPy code.

First, let's understand how linear regression works. As we know from chapter 1, a supervised machine learning model has the form

$$y \approx g(X)$$

This is a matrix form. *X* is a matrix where the features of observations are rows of the matrix, and *y* is a vector with the values we want to predict.

These matrices and vectors may sound confusing, so let's take a step back and consider what happens with a single observation x_i and the value y_i that we want to predict. The index *i* here means that this is an observation number *i*, one of *m* observations that we have in our training dataset.

Then, for this single observation, the previous formula looks like

$$y_i \approx g(x_i)$$

If we have *n* features, our vector x_i is *n*-dimensional, so it has *n* components:

$$x_i = (x_{i1}, x_{i2}, ..., x_{in})$$

Because it has *n* components, we can write the function *g* as a function with *n* parameters, which is the same as the previous formula:

$$y_i = g(x_i) = g(x_{i1}, x_{i2}, ..., x_{in})$$

For our case, we have 7,150 cars in the training dataset. This means that *m* = 7,150, and *i* can be any number between 0 and 7,149. For *i* = 10, for example, we have the following car:

```
make                          rolls-royce
model                phantom_drophead_coupe
year                                   2015
engine_fuel_type    premium_unleaded_(required)
engine_hp                               453
engine_cylinders                         12
transmission_type                 automatic
driven_wheels              rear_wheel_drive
number_of_doors                           2
market_category      exotic,luxury,performance
vehicle_size                          large
vehicle_style                   convertible
highway_mpg                              19
city_mpg                                 11
popularity                               86
msrp                                 479775
```

Let's pick a few numerical features and ignore the rest for now. We can start with horsepower, MPG in the city, and popularity:

```
engine_hp          453
city_mpg            11
popularity          86
```

Then let's assign these features to x_{i1}, x_{i2}, and x_{i3}, respectively. This way, we get the feature vector x_i with three components:

$$x_i = (x_{i1}, x_{i2}, x_{i3}) = (453, 11, 86)$$

To make it easier to understand, we can translate this mathematical notation to Python. In our case, the function g has the following signature:

```
def g(xi):
    # xi is a list with n elements
    # do something with xi
    # return the result
    pass
```

In this code, the variable xi is our vector x_i. Depending on implementation, xi could be a list with n elements or a NumPy array of size n.

For the car described previously, xi is a list with three elements:

```
xi = [453, 11, 86]
```

When we apply the function g to a vector xi, it produces y_pred as the output, which is the g's prediction for xi:

```
y_pred = g(xi)
```

We expect this prediction to be as close as possible to y_i, which is the real price of the car.

> **NOTE** In this section, we will use Python to illustrate the ideas behind mathematical formulas. We don't need to use these code snippets for doing the project. On the other hand, taking this code, putting it into Jupyter, and trying to run it could be helpful for understanding the concepts.

There are many ways the function g could look, and the choice of a machine learning algorithm defines the way it works.

If g is the linear regression model, it has the following form:

$$g(x_i) = g(x_{i1}, x_{i2}, ..., x_{in}) = w_0 + x_{i1}w_1 + x_{i2}w_2 + \cdots + x_{in}w_n$$

The variables w_0, w_1, w_2, ..., w_n are the parameters of the model:

- w_0 is the *bias* term.
- w_1, w_2, ..., w_n are the *weights* for each feature x_{i1}, x_{i2}, ..., x_{in}.

These parameters define exactly how the model should combine the features so that the predictions at the end are as good as possible. It's okay if the meaning behind these parameters is not clear yet, because we will cover them later in this section.

To keep the formula shorter, let's use sum notation:

$$g(x_i) = g(x_{i1}, x_{i2}, ..., x_{in}) = w_0 + \sum_{j=1}^{n} x_{ij} w_j$$

Exercise 2.2

For supervised learning, we use a machine learning model for a single observation $y_i \approx g(x_i)$. What are x_i and y_i for this project?

    a x_i is a feature vector — a vector that contains a few numbers that describe the object (a car) — and y_i is the logarithm of the price of this car.

    b y_i is a feature vector — a vector that contains a few numbers that describe the object (a car) — and x_i is the logarithm of the price of this car.

These weights are what the model learns when we train it. To better understand how the model uses these weights, let's consider the following values (table 2.1).

Table 2.1   An example of weights that a linear regression model learned

w_0	w_1	w_2	w_3
7.17	0.01	0.04	0.002

So if we want to translate this model to Python, it will look like this:

```
w0 = 7.17
#    [w1    w2    w3   ]
w = [0.01, 0.04, 0.002]
n = 3

def linear_regression(xi):
    result = w0
    for j in range(n):
        result = result + xi[j] * w[j]
    return result
```

We put all the feature weights inside a single list w — just like we did with xi previously. All we need to do now is loop over these weights and multiply them by the corresponding feature values. This is nothing else but the direct translation of the previous formula to Python.

This is easy to see. Have another look at the formula:

$$w_0 + \sum_{j=1}^{n} x_{ij} w_j$$

Our example has three features, so $n = 3$, and we have

$$g(x_i) = g(x_{i1}, x_{i2}, x_{i3}) = w_0 + \sum_{j=1}^{3} x_{ij}w_j = w_0 + x_{i1}w_1 + x_{i2}w_2 + x_{i3}w_3$$

This is exactly what we have in the code

```
result = w0 + xi[0] * w[0] + xi[1] * w[1] + xi[2] * w[2]
```

with the simple exception that indexing in Python starts with 0, x_{i1} becomes `xi[0]` and w_1 is `w[0]`.

Now let's see what happens when we apply the model to our observation x_i and replace the weights with their values:

$$g(x_i) = 7.17 + 453 \cdot 0.01 + 11 \cdot 0.04 + 86 \cdot 0.002 = 12.31$$

The prediction we get for this observation is 12.31. Remember that during preprocessing, we applied the logarithmic transformation to our target variable y. This is why the model we trained on this data also predicts the logarithm of the price. To undo the transformation, we need to take the exponent of the logarithm. In our case, when we do it, the prediction becomes $603,000:

$$\exp(12.31 + 1) = 603,000$$

The bias term (7.17) is the value we would predict if we didn't know anything about the car; it serves as a baseline.

We do know something about the car, however: horsepower, MPG in the city, and popularity. These features are the x_{i1}, x_{i2}, and x_{i3} features, each of which tells us something about the car. We use this information to adjust the baseline.

Let's consider the first feature: horsepower. The weight for this feature is 0.01, which means that for each extra unit of horsepower, we adjust the baseline by adding 0.01. Because we have 453 horses in the engine, we add 4.53 to the baseline: 453 horses · 0.01 = 4.53.

The same happens with MPG. Each additional mile per gallon increases the price by 0.04, so we add 0.44: 11 MPG · 0.04 = 0.44.

Finally, we take popularity into account. In our example, each mention in the Twitter stream results in a 0.002 increase. In total, popularity contributes 0.172 to the final prediction.

This is exactly why we get 12.31 when we combine everything (figure 2.11).

$$g(x_i) = 7.17 + 453 \cdot 0.01 + 11 \cdot 0.04 + 86 \cdot 0.002 = 12.31$$

Bias	Horsepower	MPG	Popularity
	4.53	0.44	0.172

Figure 2.11   The prediction of linear regression is the baseline of 7.17 (the bias term) adjusted by information we have from the features. Horsepower contributes 4.53 to the final prediction; MPG, 0.44; and popularity, 0.172.

Now, let's remember that we are actually dealing with vectors, not individual numbers. We know that x_i is a vector with n components:

$$x_i = (x_{i1}, x_{i2}, ..., x_{in})$$

We can also put all the weights together in a single vector w:

$$w = (w_0, w_1, w_2, ..., w_n)$$

In fact, we already did that in the Python example when we put all the weights in a list, which was a vector of dimensionality 3 with weights for each individual feature. This is how the vectors look for our example:

$$x_i = (x_{i1}, x_{i2}, x_{i3}) = (453, 11, 86)$$

$$w = (0.01, 0.04, 0.002)$$

Because we now think of both features and weights as vectors x_i and w, respectively, we can replace the sum of the elements of these vectors with a dot product between them:

$$x_i^T w = \sum_{j=1}^{n} x_{ij} w_j = x_{i1} w_1 + x_{i2} w_2 + ... + x_{in} w_n$$

The dot product is a way of multiplying two vectors: we multiply corresponding elements of the vectors and then sum the results. Refer to appendix C for more details about vector-vector multiplication.

The translation of the formula for dot product to the code is straightforward:

```
def dot(xi, w):
    n = len(w)
    result = 0.0
    for j in range(n):
```

```
        result = result + xi[j] * w[j]
    return result
```

Using the new notation, we can rewrite the entire equation for linear regression as

$$g(x_i) = w_0 + x_i^T w$$

where

- w_0 is the bias term.
- w is the n-dimensional vector of weights.

Now we can use the new dot function, so the linear regression function in Python becomes very short:

```
def linear_regression(xi):
    return w0 + dot(xi, w)
```

Alternatively, if xi and w are NumPy arrays, we can use the built-in dot method for multiplication:

```
def linear_regression(xi):
    return w0 + xi.dot(w)
```

To make it even shorter, we can combine w_0 and w into one $(n+1)$-dimensional vector by prepending w_0 to w right in front of w_1:

$$w = (w_0, w_1, w_2, ..., w_n)$$

Here, we have a new weights vector w that consists of the bias term w_0 followed by the weights w_1, w_2, ... from the original weights vector w.

In Python, this is very easy to do. If we already have the old weights in a list w, all we need to do is the following:

```
w = [w0] + w
```

Remember that the plus operator in Python concatenates lists, so [1] + [2, 3, 4] will create a new list with four elements: [1, 2, 3, 4]. In our case, w is already a list, so we create a new w with one extra element at the beginning: w0.

Because now w becomes a $(n+1)$-dimensional vector, we also need to adjust the feature vector x_i so that the dot product between them still works. We can do this easily by adding a dummy feature x_{i0}, which always takes the value 1. Then we prepend this new dummy feature to x_i right before x_{i1}:

$$x_i = (x_{i0}, x_{i1}, x_{i2}, ..., x_{in}) = (1, x_{i1}, x_{i2}, ..., x_{in})$$

Or, in code:

```
xi = [1] + xi
```

We create a new list `xi` with 1 as the first element followed by all the elements from the old list `xi`.

With these modifications, we can express the model as the dot product between the new x_i and the new w:

$$g(x_i) = x_i^T w$$

The translation to the code is simple:

```
w0 = 7.17
w = [0.01, 0.04, 0.002]
w = [w0] + w

def linear_regression(xi):
    xi = [1] + xi
    return dot(xi, w)
```

These formulas for linear regressions are equivalent because the first feature of the new x_i is 1, so when we multiply the first component of x_i by the first component of w, we get the bias term, because $w_0 \cdot 1 = w_0$.

We are ready to consider the bigger picture again and talk about the matrix form. There are many observations and x_i is one of them. Thus, we have m feature vectors x_1, $x_2, ..., x_i, ..., x_m$, and each of these vectors consists of $n+1$ features:

$$x_1 = (1, x_{11}, x_{12}, ..., x_{1n})$$
$$x_2 = (1, x_{21}, x_{22}, ..., x_{2n})$$
$$...$$
$$x_i = (1, x_{i1}, x_{i2}, ..., x_{in})$$
$$...$$
$$x_m = (1, x_{m1}, x_{m2}, ..., x_{mn})$$

We can put these vectors together as rows of a matrix. Let's call this matrix X (figure 2.12).

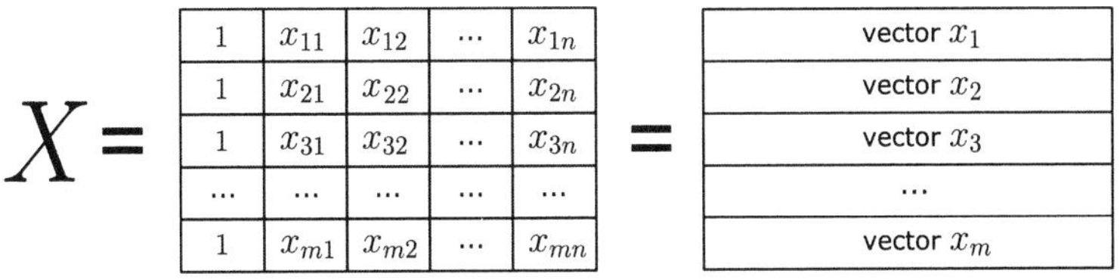

Figure 2.12   Matrix X, in which observations x_1, x_2, ..., x_m are rows

Let's see how it looks in code. We can take a few rows from the training dataset, such as the first, second, and tenth:

```
x1  = [1, 148, 24, 1385]
x2  = [1, 132, 25, 2031]
x10 = [1, 453, 11, 86]
```

Now let's put the rows together in another list:

```
X = [x1, x2, x10]
```

List X now contains three lists. We can think of it as a 3x4 matrix — a matrix with three rows and four columns:

```
X = [[1, 148, 24, 1385],
     [1, 132, 25, 2031],
     [1, 453, 11, 86]]
```

Each column of this matrix is a feature:

1 The first column is a dummy feature with "1."
2 The second column is the engine horsepower.
3 The third — MPG in the city.
4 And the last one — popularity, or the number of mentions in a Twitter stream.

We already learned that to make a prediction for a single feature vector, we need to calculate the dot product between this feature vector and the weights vector. Now we have a matrix X, which in Python is a list of feature vectors. To make predictions for all the rows of the matrix, we can simply iterate over all rows of X and compute the dot product:

```
predictions = []

for xi in X:
    pred = dot(xi, w)
    predictions.append(pred)
```

In linear algebra, this is the matrix-vector multiplication: we multiply the matrix X by the vector w. The formula for linear regression becomes

$$g(X) = w_0 + Xw$$

The result is an array with predictions for each row of X. Refer to appendix C for more details about matrix-vector multiplication.

With this matrix formulation, the code for applying linear regression to make predictions becomes very simple. The translation to NumPy becomes straightforward:

```
predictions = X.dot(w)
```

Exercise 2.3

When we multiply the matrix X by the weights vector w, we get

    a A vector y with the actual price
    b A vector y with price predictions
    c A single number y with price predictions

2.3.2 *Training linear regression model*

So far, we've only covered making predictions. To be able to do that, we need to know the weights w. How do we get them?

We learn the weights from data: we use the target variable y to find such w that combines the features of X in the best possible way. "Best possible" in the case of linear regression means that it minimizes the error between the predictions $g(X)$ and the actual target y.

We have multiple ways to do that. We will use normal equation, which is the simplest method to implement. The weight vector w can be computed with the following formula:

$$w = (X^T X)^{-1} X^T y$$

NOTE Covering the derivation of the normal equation is out of scope for this book. We give a bit of intuition of how it works in appendix C, but you should consult a machine learning textbook for a more in-depth introduction. *The Elements of Statistical Learning*, 2nd edition by Hastie, Tibshirani, and Friedman is a good start.

This piece of math may appear scary or confusing, but it's quite easy to translate to NumPy:

- X^T is the transpose of X. In NumPy, it's `X.T`.
- $X^T X$ is a matrix–matrix multiplication, which we can do with the `dot` method from NumPy: `X.T.dot(X)`.
- X^{-1} is the inverse of X. We can use `np.linalg.inv` function to calculate the inverse.

So the formula above translates directly to

```
inv(X.T.dot(X)).dot(X.T).dot(y)
```

Please refer to appendix C for more details about this equation.

To implement the normal equation, we need to do the following:

    1 Create a function that takes in a matrix X with features and a vector y with the target.

  2 Add a dummy column (the feature that is always set to 1) to the matrix *X*.

  3 Train the model: compute the weights *w* by using the normal equation.

  4 Split this *w* into the bias w_0 and the rest of the weights, and return them.

The last step — splitting *w* into the bias term and the rest — is optional and mostly for convenience; otherwise, we need to add the dummy column every time we want to make predictions instead of doing it once during training.

  Let's implement it.

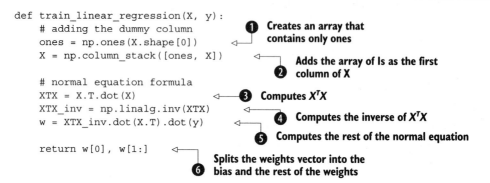

Listing 2.2 Linear regression implemented with NumPy

```
def train_linear_regression(X, y):
    # adding the dummy column                    ❶ Creates an array that
    ones = np.ones(X.shape[0])                      contains only ones
    X = np.column_stack([ones, X])
                                                  ❷ Adds the array of 1s as the first
                                                    column of X
    # normal equation formula
    XTX = X.T.dot(X)                              ❸ Computes X^T X
    XTX_inv = np.linalg.inv(XTX)
    w = XTX_inv.dot(X.T).dot(y)                   ❹ Computes the inverse of X^T X
                                                  ❺ Computes the rest of the normal equation
    return w[0], w[1:]
                                                  ❻ Splits the weights vector into the
                                                    bias and the rest of the weights
```

With six lines of code, we have implemented our first machine learning algorithm. In ❶, we create a vector containing only ones, which we append to the matrix *X* as the first column; this is the dummy feature in ❷. Next, we compute $X^T X$ in ❸ and its inverse in ❹, and we put them together to calculate *w* in ❺. Finally, we split the weights into the bias w_0 and the remaining weights *w* in ❻.

  The `column_stack` function from NumPy that we used for adding a column of ones might be confusing at first, so let's have a closer look at it:

```
np.column_stack([ones, X])
```

It takes in a list of NumPy arrays, which in our case contains `ones` and `X` and stacks them (figure 2.13).

  If weights are split into the bias term and the rest, the linear regression formula for making predictions changes slightly:

$$g(X) = w_0 + Xw$$

This is still very easy to translate to NumPy:

```
y_pred = w0 + X.dot(w)
```

Let's use it for our project!

```
ones = np.array([1, 1])
ones
```

```
array([1, 1])
```

```
X = np.array([[2, 3], [4, 5]])
X
```

```
array([[2, 3],
       [4, 5]])
```

```
np.column_stack([ones, X])
```

```
array([[ 1  2, 3 ],
       [ 1  4, 5 ]])
         Ones    X
```

Figure 2.13 The function `column_stack` takes a list of NumPy arrays and stacks them in columns. In our case, the function appends the array with ones as the first column of the matrix.

2.4 *Predicting the price*

We've covered a great deal of theory, so let's come back to our project: predicting the price of a car. We now have a function for training a linear regression model at our disposal, so let's use it to build a simple baseline solution.

2.4.1 *Baseline solution*

To be able to use it, however, we need to have some data: a matrix X and a vector with the target variable y. We have already prepared the y, but we still don't have the X: what we have right now is a data frame, not a matrix. So we need to extract some features from our dataset to create this matrix X.

We will start with a very naive way of creating features: select a few numerical features, and form the matrix X from them. In the previous example, we used only three features. This time, we include a couple more features and use the following columns:

- engine_hp
- engine_cylinders
- highway_mpg
- city_mpg
- popularity

Let's select the features from the data frame and write them to a new variable, df_num:

```
base = ['engine_hp', 'engine_cylinders', 'highway_mpg', 'city_mpg',
        'popularity']
df_num = df_train[base]
```

As discussed in the section on exploratory data analysis, the dataset has missing values. We need to do something because the linear regression model cannot deal with missing values automatically.

One option is to drop all the rows that contain at least one missing value. This approach, however, has some disadvantages. Most important, we will lose the information that we have in the other columns. Even though we may not know the number of doors of a car, we still know other things about the car, such as make, model, age, and other things that we don't want to throw away.

The other option is filling the missing values with some other value. This way, we don't lose the information in other columns and still can make predictions, even if the row has missing values. The simplest possible approach is to fill the missing values with zeros. We can use the `fillna` method from Pandas:

```
df_num = df_num.fillna(0)
```

This method may not be the best way to deal with missing values, but often, it's good enough. If we set the missing feature value to zero, the respective feature is simply ignored.

> **NOTE** An alternative option is to replace the missing values with the average values. For some variables, for example, the number of cylinders, the value of zero doesn't make much sense: a car cannot have zero cylinders. However, this will make our code more complex and won't have a significant impact on the results. That's why we follow a simpler approach and replace the missing values with zeros.

It's not difficult to see why setting a feature to zero is the same as ignoring it. Let's recall the formula for linear regression. In our case, we have five features, so the formula is

$$g(x_i) = w_0 + x_{i1}w_1 + x_{i2}w_2 + x_{i3}w_3 + x_{i4}w_4 + x_{i5}w_5$$

If feature three is missing, and we fill it with zero, x_{i3} becomes zero:

$$g(x_i) = w_0 + x_{i1}w_1 + x_{i2}w_2 + 0\ w_3 + x_{i4}w_4 + x_{i5}w_5$$

In this case, regardless of the weight w_3 for this feature, the product $x_{i3}w_3$ will always be zero. In other words, this feature will have no contribution to the final prediction, and we will base our prediction only on features that aren't missing:

$$g(x_i) = w_0 + x_{i1}w_1 + x_{i2}w_2 + x_{i4}w_4 + x_{i5}w_5$$

Now we need to convert this DataFrame to a NumPy array. The easiest way to do it is to use its `values` property:

```
X_train = df_num.values
```

X_train is a matrix — a two-dimensional NumPy array. It's something we can use as input to our `linear_regresson` function. Let's call it

```
w_0, w = train_linear_regression(X_train, y_train)
```

We have just trained the first model! Now we can apply it to the training data to see how well it predicts:

```
y_pred = w_0 + X_train.dot(w)
```

To see how good the predictions are, we can use `histplot` — a function from Seaborn for plotting histograms that we used previously — to plot the predicted values and compare them with the actual prices:

```
sns.histplot(y_pred, label='prediction')
sns.histplot(y_train, label='target')
plt.legend()
```

We can see from the plot (figure 2.14) that the distribution of values we predicted looks quite different from the actual values. This result may indicate that the model is not powerful enough to capture the distribution of the target variable. This shouldn't be a surprise to us: the model we used is quite basic and includes only five very simple features.

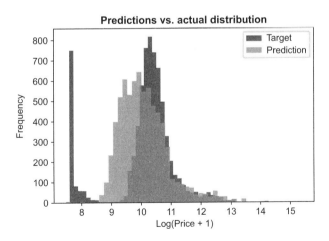

Figure 2.14 **The distribution of the predicted values (light gray) and the actual values (dark gray). We see that our predictions aren't very good; they are very different from the actual distribution.**

2.4.2   *RMSE: Evaluating model quality*

Looking at plots and comparing the distributions of the actual target variable with the predictions is a good way to evaluate quality, but we cannot do this every time we change something in the model. Instead, we need to use a metric that quantifies the quality of the model. We can use many metrics to evaluate how well a regression model behaves. The most commonly used one is *root mean squared error* — RMSE for short.

RMSE tells us how large the errors are that our model makes. It's computed with the following formula:

$$\text{RMSE} = \sqrt{\frac{1}{m} \sum_{i=1}^{m} \left(g(x_i) - y_i \right)^2}$$

Let's try to understand what's going on here. First, let's look inside the sum. We have

$$\left(g(x_i) - y_i \right)^2$$

This is the difference between the prediction we make for the observation and the actual target value for that observation (figure 2.15).

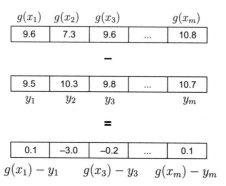

Figure 2.15   The difference between the predictions g(x₁) and the actual values y₁

Then we use the square of the difference, which gives a lot more weight to larger differences. If we predict 9.5, for example, and the actual value is 9.6, the difference is 0.1, so its square is 0.01, which is quite small. But if we predict 7.3, and the actual value is 10.3, the difference is 3, and the square of the difference is 9 (figure 2.16).

This is the SE part (*squared error*) of RMSE.

$$\left(\begin{array}{|c|c|c|c|c|} \hline 0.1 & -3.0 & -0.2 & \ldots & 0.1 \\ \hline \end{array}\right)^2 = \begin{array}{|c|c|c|c|c|} \hline 0.01 & 9.0 & 0.04 & \ldots & 0.01 \\ \hline \end{array}$$

Figure 2.16 The square of the difference between the predictions and the actual values. For large differences, the square is quite big.

Next, we have a sum:

$$\sum_{i=1}^{m} \left(g(x_i) - y_i \right)^2$$

This summation goes over all m observations and puts all the squared errors together (figure 2.17) into a single number.

$$\sum_{i=1}^{m} \left(\begin{array}{|c|c|c|c|c|} \hline 0.01 & 9.0 & 0.04 & \ldots & 0.01 \\ \hline \end{array} \right) = \begin{array}{|c|} \hline 9.06 \\ \hline \end{array}$$

Figure 2.17 The result of the summation of all the square differences is a single number.

If we divide this sum by m, we get the mean squared error:

$$\frac{1}{m} \sum_{i=1}^{m} \left(g(x_i) - y_i \right)^2$$

This is the squared error that our model makes on average — the M part (*mean*) of RMSE, or *mean squared error* (MSE). MSE is also a good metric on its own (figure 2.18).

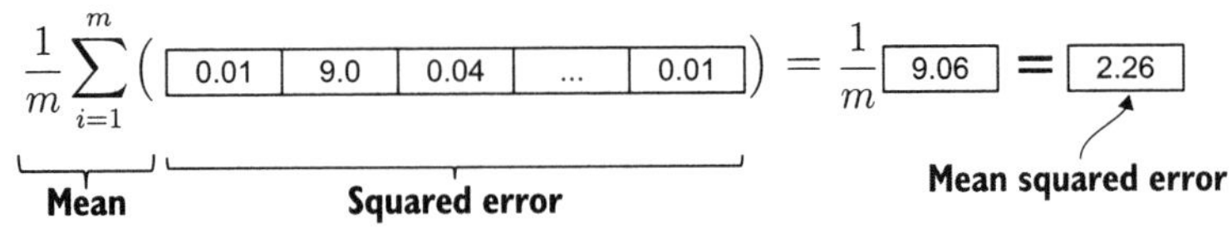

$$\frac{1}{m} \sum_{i=1}^{m} \left(\begin{array}{|c|c|c|c|c|} \hline 0.01 & 9.0 & 0.04 & \ldots & 0.01 \\ \hline \end{array} \right) = \frac{1}{m} \begin{array}{|c|} \hline 9.06 \\ \hline \end{array} = \begin{array}{|c|} \hline 2.26 \\ \hline \end{array}$$

Mean   Squared error   Mean squared error

Figure 2.18 MSE is computed by calculating the mean of the squared errors.

Finally, we take the square root of that:

$$\text{RMSE} = \sqrt{\frac{1}{m} \sum_{i=1}^{m} \left(g(x_i) - y_i \right)^2}$$

This is the R part (*root*) of RMSE (figure 2.19).

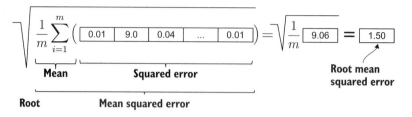

Figure 2.19   RMSE: we first compute MSE and then calculate its square root.

When using NumPy to implement RMSE, we can take advantage of *vectorization*: the process of applying the same operation to all elements of one or more NumPy arrays. We get multiple benefits from using vectorization. First, the code is more concise: we don't have to write any loops to apply the same operation to each element of the array. Second, vectorized operations are a lot faster than simple Python for loops.

Consider the following implementation.

Listing 2.3   The implementation of root mean squared error

```
def rmse(y, y_pred):
    error = y_pred - y          ❶ Computes the difference
    mse = (error ** 2).mean()      between the prediction and the
    return np.sqrt(mse)
```

❶ Computes the difference between the prediction and the

❷ Computes MSE: first computes the squared error, and then calculates its mean

❸ Takes the square root to get RMSE

In ❶, we compute element-wise difference between the vector with predictions and the vector with the target variable. The result is a new NumPy array `error` that contains the differences. In ❷, we do two operations in one line: compute the square of each element of the `error` array and then get the mean value of the result, which gives us MSE. In ❸, we compute the square root to get RMSE.

Element-wise operations in NumPy and Pandas are quite convenient. We can apply an operation to an entire NumPy array (or a Pandas series) without writing loops.

In the first line of our `rmse` function, for example, we compute the difference between the predictions and the actual prices:

```
error = y_pred - y
```

What happens here is that for each element of `y_pred`, we subtract the corresponding element of `y` and then put the result to the new array `error` (figure 2.20).

Next, we compute the square of each element of the `error` array and then calculate its mean to get the mean squared error of our model (figure 2.21).

To see exactly what happens, we need to know that the power operator (**) is also applied element-wise, so the result is another array in which all elements of the

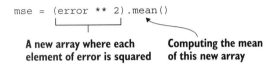

Figure 2.20 The element-wise difference between `y_pred` and `y`. The result is written to the `error` array.

```
mse = (error ** 2).mean()
```

A new array where each   Computing the mean
element of error is squared   of this new array

Figure 2.21 To calculate MSE, we first compute the square of each element in the error array and then compute the mean value of the result.

original array are squared. When we have this new array with squared elements, we simply compute its mean by using the `mean()` method (figure 2.22).

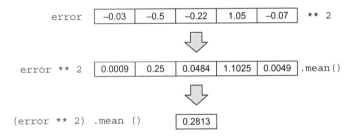

Figure 2.22 The power operator (`**`) applied element-wise to the error array. The result is another array in which each element is squared. Then we compute the mean of the array with the squared error to compute MSE.

Finally, we compute the square root of the mean value to get RMSE:

```
np.sqrt(mse)
```

Now we can use RMSE to evaluate the quality of the model:

```
rmse(y_train, y_pred)
```

The code prints 0.75. This number tells us that on average, the model's predictions are off by 0.75. This result alone may not be very useful, but we can use it to compare this model with other models. If one model has a better (lower) RMSE than the other, it indicates that model is better.

2.4.3 *Validating the model*

In the example from the previous section we computed RMSE on the training set. The result is useful to know but doesn't reflect the way the model will be used later. The model will be used to predict the price of cars that it didn't see before. For that purpose, we set aside a validation dataset. We intentionally don't use it for training and keep it for validating the model.

We have already split our data into multiple parts: df_train, df_val, and df_test. We have also created a matrix X_train from df_train and used X_train and y_train to train the model. Now we need to do the same steps to get X_val — a matrix with features computed from the validation dataset. Then we can apply the model to X_val to get predictions and compare them with y_val.

First, we create the X_val matrix, following the same steps as for X_train:

```
df_num = df_val[base]
df_num = df_num.fillna(0)
X_val = df_num.values
```

We're ready to apply the model to X_val to get predictions:

```
y_pred = w_0 + X_val.dot(w)
```

The y_pred array contains the predictions for the validation dataset. Now we use y_pred and compare it with the actual prices from y_val, using the RMSE function that we implemented previously:

```
rmse(y_val, y_pred)
```

The value this code prints is 0.76, which is the number we should use for comparing models.

In the previous code we already see some duplication: training and validation tests require the same preprocessing, and we wrote the same code twice. Thus, it makes sense to move this logic to a separate function and avoid duplicating the code.

We can call this function prepare_X because it creates a matrix X from a Data-Frame.

Listing 2.4 The `prepare_X` function for converting a DataFrame into a matrix

```
def prepare_X(df):
    df_num = df[base]
    df_num = df_num.fillna(0)
    X = df_num.values
    return X
```

Now the whole training and evaluation becomes simpler and looks like this:

```
X_train = prepare_X(df_train)
w_0, w = train_linear_regression(X_train, y_train)
```
Trains the model

```
X_val = prepare_X(df_val)
y_pred = w_0 + X_val.dot(w)
print('validation:', rmse(y_val, y_pred))
```
Applies the model to
the validation dataset

Computes RMSE on
the validation data

This gives us a way to check whether any model adjustments lead to improvements in the predictive quality of the model. As the next step, let's add more features and check whether it gets lower RMSE scores.

2.4.4 Simple feature engineering

We already have a simple baseline model with simple features. To improve our model further, we can add more features to the model: we create others and add them to the existing features. As we already know, this process is called *feature engineering*.

Because we have already set up the validation framework, we can easily verify whether adding new features improves the quality of the model. Our aim is to improve the RMSE calculated on the validation data.

First, we create a new feature, "age," from the feature "year." The age of a car should be very helpful when predicting its price: intuitively, the newer the car, the more expensive it should be.

Because the dataset was created in 2017 (which we can verify by checking `df_train.year.max()`), we can calculate the age by subtracting the year when the car was made from 2017:

```
df_train['age'] = 2017 - df_train.year
```

This operation is an element-wise operation. We calculate the difference between 2017 and each element of the year series. The result is a new Pandas series containing the differences, which we write back to the dataframe as the age column.

We already know that we will need to apply the same preprocessing twice: to the training and validation sets. Because we don't want to repeat the feature extraction code multiple times, let's put this logic into the `prepare_X` function.

Listing 2.5   Creating the age feature in the `prepare_X` function

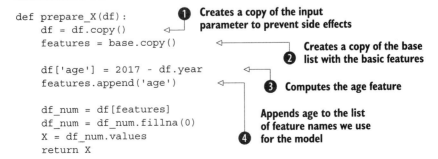

```
def prepare_X(df):
    df = df.copy()
    features = base.copy()

    df['age'] = 2017 - df.year
    features.append('age')

    df_num = df[features]
    df_num = df_num.fillna(0)
    X = df_num.values
    return X
```

❶ Creates a copy of the input
parameter to prevent side effects

❷ Creates a copy of the base
list with the basic features

❸ Computes the age feature

❹ Appends age to the list
of feature names we use
for the model

The way we implement the function this time is slightly different from the previous version. Let's look at these differences. First, in ❶, we create a copy of the DataFrame `df` that we pass in the function. Later in the code, we modify `df` by adding extra rows in ❸. This kind of behavior is known as a *side effect*: the caller of the function may not expect the function to change the DataFrame. To prevent the unpleasant surprise, we instead modify the copy of the original DataFrame. In ❷, we create a copy for the list with the base features for the same reason. Later, we extend this list with new features ❹, but we don't want to change the original list. The rest of the code is the same as previously.

Let's test if adding the feature "age" leads to any improvements:

```
X_train = prepare_X(df_train)
w_0, w = train_linear_regression(X_train, y_train)

X_val = prepare_X(df_val)
y_pred = w_0 + X_val.dot(w)
print('validation:', rmse(y_val, y_pred))
```

The code prints

```
validation: 0.517
```

The validation error is 0.517, which is a good improvement from 0.76 — the value we had in the baseline solution. Thus, we conclude that adding "age" is indeed helpful when making predictions.

We can also look at the distribution of the predicted values:

```
sns.histplot(y_pred, label='prediction')
sns.histplot(y_val, label='target')
plt.legend()
```

We see (figure 2.23) that the distribution of the predictions follows the target distribution a lot more closely than previously. Indeed, the validation RMSE score confirms it.

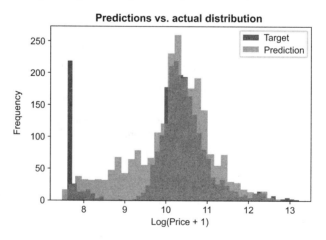

Figure 2.23   The distribution of predicted (light gray) versus actual (dark gray). With the new features, the model follows the original distribution closer than previously.

2.4.5 *Handling categorical variables*

We see that adding "age" is quite helpful for the model. Let's continue adding more features. One of the columns we can use next is the number of doors. This variable appears to be numeric and can take three values: 2, 3, and 4 doors. Even though it's tempting to put the variable to the model as is, it's not really a numeric variable: we cannot say that by adding one more door, the price of a car grows (or drops) by a certain amount of money. Rather, the variable is categorical.

Categorical variables describe characteristics of objects and can take one of a few possible values. The make of a car is a categorical variable; for example, it can be Toyota, BWM, Ford, or any other make. It's easy to recognize a categorical variable by its values, which typically are strings and not numbers. That's not always the case, however. The number of doors, for example, is categorical: it can take only one of the three possible values (2, 3, and 4).

We can use categorical variables in a machine learning model in multiple ways. One of the simplest ways is to encode such variables by a set of binary features, with a separate feature for each distinct value.

In our case, we will create three binary features: num_doors_2, num_doors_3, and num_doors_4. If the car has two doors, num_doors_2 will be set to 1, and the rest will be 0. If the car has three doors, num_doors_3 will get the value 1, and the same goes for num_doors_4.

This method of encoding categorical variables is called *one-hot encoding*. We will learn more about this way of encoding categorical variables in chapter 3. For now, let's choose the simplest way to do this encoding: looping over the possible values (2, 3, and 4) and, for each value, checking whether the value of the observation matches it.

Let's add these lines to the prepare_X function:

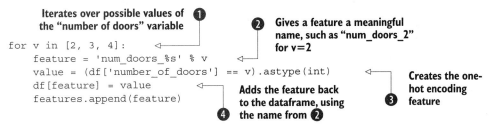

This code may be difficult to understand, so let's take a closer look at what's going on here. The most difficult line is ❸:

```
(df['number_of_doors'] == v).astype(int)
```

Two things happen here. The first one is the expression inside the parentheses, where we use the equals (==) operator. This operation is also an element-wise operation, like the ones we used previously when computing RMSE. In this case, the operation creates a new Pandas series. If elements of the original series equal v, the corresponding elements in the result is True; otherwise, the elements are False. The operation creates a series of True/False values. Because v has three values (2, 3, and 4), and we apply this operation to every value of v, we create three series (figure 2.24).

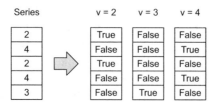

Figure 2.24   We use the == operator to create the new series from the original one: one for two doors, one for three doors, and one for four doors.

Next, we convert the Boolean series to integers in such a way that True becomes 1 and False becomes 0, which is easy to do with the `astype(int)` method (figure 2.25). Now we can use the results as features and put them into linear regression.

Figure 2.25   Using `astype(int)` to convert series with Boolean values to integers

The number of doors, as we discussed, is a categorical variable that appears to be numerical because the values are integers (2, 3 and 4). All the remaining categorical variables we have in the dataset are strings.

   We can use the same approach to encode other categorical variables. Let's start with `make`. For our purposes, it should be enough to get and use only the most frequently occurring values. Let's find out what the five most frequent values are:

```
df['make'].value_counts().head(5)
```

The code prints

```
chevrolet     1123
ford           881
volkswagen     809
toyota         746
dodge          626
```

We take these values and use them to encode `make` in the same way that we encoded the number of doors.

Next, we create five new variables called is_make_chevrolet, is_make_ford, is_make_volkswagen, is_make_toyota, and is_make_dodge:

```
for v in ['chevrolet', 'ford', 'volkswagen', 'toyota', 'dodge']:
    feature = 'is_make_%s' % v
    df[feature] = (df['make'] == v).astype(int)
    features.append(feature)
```

Now the whole prepare_X should look like the following.

Listing 2.6   Handling categorical variables number of doors and make

```
def prepare_X(df):
    df = df.copy()
    features = base.copy()

    df['age'] = 2017 - df.year
    features.append('age')                        ┐ Encodes the number
                                                  │ of doors variable
    for v in [2, 3, 4]:                      ◄────┘
        feature = 'num_doors_%s' % v
        df[feature] = (df['number_of_doors'] == v).astype(int)    Encodes
        features.append(feature)                                  the make
                                                                  variable
    for v in ['chevrolet', 'ford', 'volkswagen', 'toyota', 'dodge']:   ◄──┘
        feature = 'is_make_%s' % v
        df[feature] = (df['make'] == v).astype(int)
        features.append(feature)

    df_num = df[features]
    df_num = df_num.fillna(0)
    X = df_num.values
    return X
```

Let's check whether this code improves the RMSE of the model:

```
X_train = prepare_X(df_train)
w_0, w = train_linear_regression(X_train, y_train)

X_val = prepare_X(df_val)
y_pred = w_0 + X_val.dot(w)
print('validation:', rmse(y_val, y_pred))
```

The code prints

```
validation: 0.507
```

The previous value was 0.517, so we managed to improve the RMSE score further.

We can use a few more variables: engine_fuel_type, transmission_type, driven_wheels, market_category, vehicle_size, and vehicle_style. Let's do the same thing for them. After the modifications, the prepare_X starts looking a bit more complex.

Listing 2.7 Handling more categorical variables in the `prepare_X` function

```
def prepare_X(df):
    df = df.copy()
    features = base.copy()

    df['age'] = 2017 - df.year
    features.append('age')

    for v in [2, 3, 4]:
        feature = 'num_doors_%s' % v
        df[feature] = (df['number_of_doors'] == v).astype(int)
        features.append(feature)

    for v in ['chevrolet', 'ford', 'volkswagen', 'toyota', 'dodge']:
        feature = 'is_make_%s' % v
        df[feature] = (df['make'] == v).astype(int)
        features.append(feature)

    for v in ['regular_unleaded', 'premium_unleaded_(required)',
              'premium_unleaded_(recommended)',
              'flex-fuel_(unleaded/e85)']:              ⟵  Encodes the
        feature = 'is_type_%s' % v                          type variable
        df[feature] = (df['engine_fuel_type'] == v).astype(int)
        features.append(feature)
                                                                 Encodes the
                                                                 transmission
                                                                 variable
    for v in ['automatic', 'manual', 'automated_manual']:   ⟵
        feature = 'is_transmission_%s' % v
        df[feature] = (df['transmission_type'] == v).astype(int)
        features.append(feature)

    for v in ['front_wheel_drive', 'rear_wheel_drive',
              'all_wheel_drive', 'four_wheel_drive']:    ⟵  Encodes the number
        feature = 'is_driven_wheels_%s' % v                  of driven wheels
        df[feature] = (df['driven_wheels'] == v).astype(int)
        features.append(feature)
                                                              Encodes
                                                              the market
                                                              category
    for v in ['crossover', 'flex_fuel', 'luxury',
              'luxury,performance', 'hatchback']:        ⟵
        feature = 'is_mc_%s' % v
        df[feature] = (df['market_category'] == v).astype(int)
        features.append(feature)

    for v in ['compact', 'midsize', 'large']:    ⟵  Encodes the size
        feature = 'is_size_%s' % v
        df[feature] = (df['vehicle_size'] == v).astype(int)
        features.append(feature)

    for v in ['sedan', '4dr_suv', 'coupe', 'convertible',
              '4dr_hatchback']:
        feature = 'is_style_%s' % v
        df[feature] = (df['vehicle_style'] == v).astype(int)
        features.append(feature)
```

Encodes
the style ⟶

```
    df_num = df[features]
    df_num = df_num.fillna(0)
    X = df_num.values
    return X
```

Let's test it:

```
X_train = prepare_X(df_train)
w_0, w = train_linear_regression(X_train, y_train)

X_val = prepare_X(df_val)
y_pred = w_0 + X_val.dot(w)
print('validation:', rmse(y_val, y_pred))
```

The number we see is significantly worse than before. We get 34.2, which is a lot more than the 0.5 we had before.

> **NOTE** The number you get may be different, depending on the Python version, the NumPy version, the versions of NumPy dependencies, the OS, and other factors. But the jump in the validation metric from 0.5 to something significantly bigger should always alert us.

Instead of helping, the new features made the score a lot worse. Luckily, we have validation to help us spot this problem. In the next section, we will see why it happens and how to deal with it.

2.4.6 *Regularization*

We saw that adding new features does not always help, and in our case, it made things a lot worse. The reason for this behavior is numerical instability. Recall the formula of the normal equation:

$$w = (X^T X)^{-1} X^T y$$

One of the terms in the equation is the inverse of the $X^T X$ matrix:

$$(X^T X)^{-1}$$

The inversion is the issue in our case. Sometimes, when adding new columns to X, we can accidentally add a column that is a combination of other columns. For example, if we already have the MPG in the city feature and decide to add kilometers per liter in the city, the second feature is the same as the first one but multiplied by a constant.

When this happens, $X^T X$ becomes *undetermined* or *singular*, which means that it's not possible to find an inverse for this matrix. If we try to invert a singular matrix, NumPy will tell us about that by raising a LinAlgError:

```
LinAlgError: Singular matrix
```

Our code didn't raise any exceptions, however. It happened because we don't typically have columns that are perfect linear combinations of other columns. The real data is often noisy, with measurement errors (such as recording 1.3 instead of 13 for MPG), rounding errors (such as storing 0.0999999 instead of 0.1), and many other errors. Technically, such matrices are not singular, so NumPy doesn't complain.

For this reason, however, some of the values in the weights become extremely large — a lot larger than they are supposed to be.

If we look at the values of our w_0 and w, we see that this is indeed the case. The bias term w_0 has the value 5788519290303866.0, for example (the value may vary depending on the machine, OS, and version of NumPy), and a few components of w have extremely large negative values as well.

In numerical linear algebra, such issues are called *numerical instability issues,* and they are typically solved with regularization techniques. The aim of *regularization* is to make sure that the inverse exists by forcing the matrix to be invertible. Regularization is an important concept in machine learning: it means "controlling" — controlling the weights of the model so that they behave correctly and don't grow too large, as in our case.

One way to do regularization is to add a small number to each diagonal element of the matrix. Then we get the following formula for linear regression:

$$w = (X^T X + \alpha I)^{-1} X^T y$$

> **NOTE**   Regularized linear regression is often called *ridge regression.* Many libraries, including Scikit-learn, use *ridge* to refer to regularized linear regression and *linear regression* to refer to the unregularized model.

Let's look at the part that changed: the matrix that we need to invert. This is how it looks:

$$X^T X + \alpha I$$

This formula says that we need I — an *identity matrix,* which is a matrix with ones on the main diagonal and zeros everywhere else. We multiply this identity matrix by a number α. This way, all the ones on the diagonal of I become α. Then we sum αI and $X^T X$, which adds α to all the diagonal elements of $X^T X$.

This formula can directly translate to NumPy code:

```
XTX = X_train.T.dot(X_train)
XTX = XTX + 0.01 * np.eye(XTX.shape[0])
```

The np.eye function creates a two-dimensional NumPy array that is also an identity matrix. When we multiply by 0.01, the ones on the diagonal become 0.01, so when we add this matrix to XTX, we add only 0.01 to its main diagonal (figure 2.26).

```
np.eye(4)
```
```
array([[1., 0., 0., 0.],
       [0., 1., 0., 0.],
       [0., 0., 1., 0.],
       [0., 0., 0., 1.]])
```

(A) The eye function from NumPy creates an identity matrix.

```
np.eye(4) * 0.01
```
```
array([[0.01, 0.  , 0.  , 0.  ],
       [0.  , 0.01, 0.  , 0.  ],
       [0.  , 0.  , 0.01, 0.  ],
       [0.  , 0.  , 0.  , 0.01]])
```

(B) When we multiply the identity matrix by a number, this number goes to the main diagonal of the result.

```
XTX = np.array([
    [0, 1, 2, 3],
    [0, 1, 2, 3],
    [0, 1, 2, 3],
    [0, 1, 2, 3],
])
```
```
XTX + 0.01 * np.eye(4)
```
```
array([[0.01, 1.  , 2.  , 3.  ],
       [0.  , 1.01, 2.  , 3.  ],
       [0.  , 1.  , 2.01, 3.  ],
       [0.  , 1.  , 2.  , 3.01]])
```

(C) The effect of adding an identity matrix multiplied by 0.01 to another matrix is the same as adding 0.01 to the main diagonal of that matrix.

Figure 2.26 Using an identity matrix to add 0.01 to the main diagonal of a square matrix

Let's create a new function that uses this idea and implements linear regression with regularization.

Listing 2.8 Linear regression with regularization

```
def train_linear_regression_reg(X, y, r=0.0):       ◁──┐  Controls the amount of
    ones = np.ones(X.shape[0])                          │  regularization by using
    X = np.column_stack([ones, X])                      │  the parameter r

    XTX = X.T.dot(X)
    reg = r * np.eye(XTX.shape[0])      Adds r to the main
    XTX = XTX + reg                     diagonal of XTX

    XTX_inv = np.linalg.inv(XTX)
    w = XTX_inv.dot(X.T).dot(y)

    return w[0], w[1:]
```

The function is very similar to linear regression, but a few lines are different. First, there's an extra parameter r that controls the amount of regularization — this corresponds to the number α in the formula that we add to the main diagonal of X^TX.

Regularization affects the final solution by making the components of w smaller. We can see that the more regularization we add, the smaller the weights become.

Let's check what happens with our weights for different values of r:

```
for r in [0, 0.001, 0.01, 0.1, 1, 10]:
    w_0, w = train_linear_regression_reg(X_train, y_train, r=r)
    print('%5s, %.2f, %.2f, %.2f' % (r, w_0, w[13], w[21]))
```

The code prints

```
    0, 5788519290303866.00, -9.26, -5788519290303548.00
0.001, 7.20, -0.10, 1.81
 0.01, 7.18, -0.10, 1.81
  0.1, 7.05, -0.10, 1.78
    1, 6.22, -0.10, 1.56
   10, 4.39, -0.09, 1.08
```

We start with 0, which is an unregularized solution, and get very large numbers. Then we try 0.001 and increase it 10 times on each step: 0.01, 0.1, 1, and 10. We see that the values that we selected become smaller as r grows.

Now let's check whether regularization helps with our problem and what RMSE we get after that. Let's run it with r=0.001:

```
X_train = prepare_X(df_train)
w_0, w = train_linear_regression_reg(X_train, y_train, r=0.001)

X_val = prepare_X(df_val)
y_pred = w_0 + X_val.dot(w)
print('validation:', rmse(y_val, y_pred))
```

The code prints

```
Validation: 0.460
```

This result is an improvement over the previous score: 0.507.

> **NOTE** Sometimes, when adding a new feature causes performance degradation, simply removing this feature may be enough to solve the problem. Having a validation dataset is important to decide whether to add regularization, remove the feature, or do both: we use the score on the validation data to choose the best option. In our particular case, we see that adding regularization helps: it improves the score we had previously.

We tried using r=0.001, but we should try other values as well. Let's try a couple of different ones to select the best parameter r:

```
X_train = prepare_X(df_train)
X_val = prepare_X(df_val)

for r in [0.000001, 0.0001, 0.001, 0.01, 0.1, 1, 5, 10]:
    w_0, w = train_linear_regression_reg(X_train, y_train, r=r)
    y_pred = w_0 + X_val.dot(w)
    print('%6s' %r, rmse(y_val, y_pred))
```

We see that the best performance is achieved with a smaller r:

```
1e-06 0.460225
0.0001 0.460225
0.001 0.460226
0.01 0.460239
0.1 0.460370
1 0.461829
5 0.468407
10 0.475724
```

We also notice that the performance for values below 0.1 don't change much except in the sixth digit, which we shouldn't consider to be significant.

Let's take the model with r=0.01 as the final model. Now we can check it against the test dataset to verify if the model works:

```
X_train = prepare_X(df_train)
w_0, w = train_linear_regression_reg(X_train, y_train, r=0.01)

X_val = prepare_X(df_val)
y_pred = w_0 + X_val.dot(w)
print('validation:', rmse(y_val, y_pred))

X_test = prepare_X(df_test)
y_pred = w_0 + X_test.dot(w)
print('test:', rmse(y_test, y_pred))
```

The code prints

```
validation: 0.460
test: 0.457
```

Because these two numbers are pretty close, we conclude that the model can generalize well to the new unseen data.

Exercise 2.4

Regularization is needed because

a It can control the weights of the model and not let them grow too large.

b Real-world data is noisy.

c We often have numerical instability problems.

Multiple answers are possible.

2.4.7 Using the model

Because we now have a model, we can start using it for predicting the price of a car.

Suppose that a user posts the following ad on our website:

```
ad = {
    'city_mpg': 18,
```

```
'driven_wheels': 'all_wheel_drive',
'engine_cylinders': 6.0,
'engine_fuel_type': 'regular_unleaded',
'engine_hp': 268.0,
'highway_mpg': 25,
'make': 'toyota',
'market_category': 'crossover,performance',
'model': 'venza',
'number_of_doors': 4.0,
'popularity': 2031,
'transmission_type': 'automatic',
'vehicle_size': 'midsize',
'vehicle_style': 'wagon',
'year': 2013
}
```

We'd like to suggest the price for this car. For that, we use our model:

```
df_test = pd.DataFrame([ad])
X_test = prepare_X(df_test)
```

First, we create a small DataFrame with one row. This row contains all the values of the ad dictionary we created earlier. Next, we convert this DataFrame to a matrix.

Now we can apply our model to the matrix to predict the price of this car:

```
y_pred = w_0 + X_test.dot(w)
```

This prediction is not the final price, however; it's the logarithm of the price. To get the actual price, we need to undo the logarithm and apply the exponent function:

```
suggestion = np.expm1(y_pred)
suggestion
```

The output is 28,294.13. The real price of this car is $31,120, so our model is not far from the actual price.

2.5   Next steps

2.5.1   Exercises

You can try the following things to make the model better:

- *Write a function for binary encoding.* In this chapter we implemented the category encoding manually: we looked at the top five values, wrote them in a list, and then looped over the list to create binary features. Doing it this way is cumbersome, which is why it's a good idea to write a function that will do this automatically. It should have multiple arguments: the dataframe, the name of the categorical variable, and the number of most frequent values it should consider. This function should also help us do the previous exercise.

- *Try more feature engineering.* When implementing category encoding, we included only the top five values for each categorical variable. Including more values during the encoding process might improve the model. Try doing that, and reevaluate the quality of the model in terms of RMSE.

2.5.2 Other projects

There are other projects you can do now:

- Predict the price of a house. You can take the New York City Airbnb Open Data dataset from https://www.kaggle.com/dgomonov/new-york-city-airbnb-open-data or the California housing dataset from https://scikit-learn.org/stable/modules/generated/sklearn.datasets.fetch_california_housing.html.
- Check other datasets, such as https://archive.ics.uci.edu/ml/datasets.php?task=reg, that have numerical target values. For example, we can use the data from the student performance dataset (http://archive.ics.uci.edu/ml/datasets/Student+Performance) to train a model for determining the performance of students.

Summary

- Doing simple initial exploratory analysis is important. Among other things, it helps us find out whether the data has missing values. It's not possible to train a linear regression model when there are missing values, so it's important to check our data and fill in the missing values if necessary.
- As a part of exploratory data analysis, we need to check the distribution of the target variable. If the target distribution has a long tail, we need to apply the log transformation. Without it, we may get inaccurate and misleading predictions from the linear regression model.
- The train/validation/test split is the best way to check our models. It gives us a way to measure the performance of the model reliably, and things like numerical instability issues won't go unnoticed.
- The linear regression model is based on a simple mathematical formula, and understanding this formula is the key to successful application of the model. Knowing these details helps us learn how the model works before coding it.
- It's not difficult to implement linear regression from scratch using Python and NumPy. Doing so helps us understand that there's no magic behind machine learning: it's simple math translated to code.
- RMSE gives us a way to measure the predictive performance of our model on the validation set. It lets us confirm that the model is good and helps us compare multiple models to find the best one.
- Feature engineering is the process of creating new features. Adding new features is important for improving the performance of a model. While adding new features, we always need to use the validation set to make sure that our

model indeed improves. Without constant monitoring, we risk getting medio-cre or very bad performance.

- Sometimes, we face numerical instability issues that we can solve with regularization. Having a good way to validate models is crucial for spotting a problem before it's too late.

- After the model is trained and validated, we can use it to make predictions, such as applying it to cars with unknown prices to estimate how much they may cost.

In chapter 3, we will learn how to do classification with machine learning, using logistic regression to predict customer churn.

Answers to exercises

- Exercise 2.1 B) Values spread far from the head.
- Exercise 2.2 A) x_i is a feature vector and y_i is the logarithm of the price.
- Exercise 2.3 B) A vector y with price predictions.
- Exercise 2.4 A), B), and C) All three answers are correct.

Machine learning for classification

This chapter covers

- Performing exploratory data analysis for identifying important features
- Encoding categorical variables to use them in machine learning models
- Using logistic regression for classification

In this chapter, we are going to use machine learning to predict churn.

Churn is when customers stop using the services of a company. Thus, churn prediction is about identifying customers who are likely to cancel their contracts soon. If the company can do that, it can offer discounts on these services in an effort to keep the users.

Naturally, we can use machine learning for that: we can use past data about customers who churned and, based on that, create a model for identifying present customers who are about to leave. This is a binary classification problem. The target variable that we want to predict is categorical and has only two possible outcomes: churn or not churn.

In chapter 1, we learned that many supervised machine learning models exist, and we specifically mentioned ones that can be used for binary classification, including logistic regression, decision trees, and neural networks. In this chapter, we start with the simplest one: logistic regression. Even though it's indeed the simplest, it's still powerful and has many advantages over other models: it's fast and easy to understand, and its results are easy to interpret. It's a workhorse of machine learning and the most widely used model in the industry.

3.1 *Churn prediction project*

The project we prepared for this chapter is churn prediction for a telecom company. We will use logistic regression and Scikit-learn for that.

Imagine that we are working at a telecom company that offers phone and internet services, and we have a problem: some of our customers are churning. They no longer are using our services and are going to a different provider. We would like to prevent that from happening, so we develop a system for identifying these customers and offer them an incentive to stay. We want to target them with promotional messages and give them a discount. We also would like to understand why the model thinks our customers churn, and for that, we need to be able to interpret the model's predictions.

We have collected a dataset where we've recorded some information about our customers: what type of services they used, how much they paid, and how long they stayed with us. We also know who canceled their contracts and stopped using our services (churned). We will use this information as the target variable in the machine learning model and predict it using all other available information.

The plan for the project follows:

1 First, we download the dataset and do some initial preparation: rename columns and change values inside columns to be consistent throughout the entire dataset.

2 Then we split the data into train, validation, and test so we can validate our models.

3 As part of the initial data analysis, we look at feature importance to identify which features are important in our data.

4 We transform categorical variables into numeric variables so we can use them in the model.

5 Finally, we train a logistic regression model.

In the previous chapter, we implemented everything ourselves, using Python and NumPy. In this project, however, we will start using Scikit-learn, a Python library for machine learning. Namely, we will use it for

- Splitting the dataset into train and test
- Encoding categorical variables
- Training logistic regression

3.1.1 *Telco churn dataset*

As in the previous chapter, we will use Kaggle datasets for data. This time we will use data from https://www.kaggle.com/blastchar/telco-customer-churn.

According to the description, this dataset has the following information:

- Services of the customers: phone; multiple lines; internet; tech support and extra services such as online security, backup, device protection, and TV streaming
- Account information: how long they have been clients, type of contract, type of payment method
- Charges: how much the client was charged in the past month and in total
- Demographic information: gender, age, and whether they have dependents or a partner
- Churn: yes/no, whether the customer left the company within the past month

First, we download the dataset. To keep things organized, we first create a folder, chapter-03-churn-prediction. Then we go to that directory and use Kaggle CLI for downloading the data:

```
kaggle datasets download -d blastchar/telco-customer-churn
```

After downloading it, we unzip the archive to get the CSV file from there:

```
unzip telco-customer-churn.zip
```

We are ready to start now.

3.1.2 *Initial data preparation*

The first step is creating a new notebook in Jupyter. If it's not running, start it:

```
jupyter notebook
```

We name the notebook chapter-03-churn-project (or any other name that we like).

As previously, we begin with adding the usual imports:

```
import pandas as pd
import numpy as np

import seaborn as sns
from matplotlib import pyplot as plt
%matplotlib inline
```

And now we can read the dataset:

```
df = pd.read_csv('WA_Fn-UseC_-Telco-Customer-Churn.csv')
```

We use the `read_csv` function to read the data and then write the results to a dataframe named df. To see how many rows it contains, let's use the `len` function:

```
len(df)
```

It prints 7043, so there are 7,043 rows in this dataset. The dataset is not large but should be enough to train a decent model.

Next, let's look at the first couple of rows using `df.head()` (figure 3.1). By default, it shows the first five rows of the dataframe.

```
df.head()
```

	customerID	gender	SeniorCitizen	Partner	Dependents	tenure	PhoneService	MultipleLines	InternetService	OnlineSecurity	...	DeviceProtection	Tech
0	7590-VHVEG	Female	0	Yes	No	1	No	No phone service	DSL	No	...	No	
1	5575-GNVDE	Male	0	No	No	34	Yes	No	DSL	Yes	...	Yes	
2	3668-QPYBK	Male	0	No	No	2	Yes	No	DSL	Yes	...	No	
3	7795-CFOCW	Male	0	No	No	45	No	No phone service	DSL	Yes	...	Yes	
4	9237-HQITU	Female	0	No	No	2	Yes	No	Fiber optic	No	...	No	

Figure 3.1   The output of the `df.head()` command showing the first five rows of the telco churn dataset

This dataframe has quite a few columns, so they all don't fit on the screen. Instead, we can transpose the dataframe using the `T` function, switching columns and rows so the columns (customerID, gender, and so on) become rows. This way we can see a lot more data (figure 3.2):

```
df.head().T
```

We see that the dataset has a few columns:

- CustomerID: the ID of the customer
- Gender: male/female
- SeniorCitizen: whether the customer is a senior citizen (0/1)
- Partner: whether they live with a partner (yes/no)
- Dependents: whether they have dependents (yes/no)
- Tenure: number of months since the start of the contract
- PhoneService: whether they have phone service (yes/no)
- MultipleLines: whether they have multiple phone lines (yes/no/no phone service)
- InternetService: the type of internet service (no/fiber/optic)
- OnlineSecurity: if online security is enabled (yes/no/no internet)
- OnlineBackup: if online backup service is enabled (yes/no/no internet)
- DeviceProtection: if the device protection service is enabled (yes/no/no internet)
- TechSupport: if the customer has tech support (yes/no/no internet)
- StreamingTV: if the TV streaming service is enabled (yes/no/no internet)

```
df.head().T
```

	0	1	2
customerID	7590-VHVEG	5575-GNVDE	3668-QPYBK
gender	Female	Male	Male
SeniorCitizen	0	0	0
Partner	Yes	No	No
Dependents	No	No	No
tenure	1	34	2
PhoneService	No	Yes	Yes
MultipleLines	No phone service	No	No
InternetService	DSL	DSL	DSL
OnlineSecurity	No	Yes	Yes
OnlineBackup	Yes	No	Yes
DeviceProtection	No	Yes	No
TechSupport	No	No	No
StreamingTV	No	No	No
StreamingMovies	No	No	No
Contract	Month-to-month	One year	Month-to-month
PaperlessBilling	Yes	No	Yes
PaymentMethod	Electronic check	Mailed check	Mailed check
MonthlyCharges	29.85	56.95	53.85
TotalCharges	29.85	1889.5	108.15
Churn	No	No	Yes

Figure 3.2 The output of the `df.head().T` command showing the first three rows of the telco churn dataset. The original rows are shown as columns: this way, it's possible to see more data without having to use the slider.

- StreamingMovies: if the movie streaming service is enabled (yes/no/no internet)
- Contract: the type of contract (monthly/yearly/two years)
- PaperlessBilling: if the billing is paperless (yes/no)
- PaymentMethod: payment method (electronic check, mailed check, bank transfer, credit card)
- MonthlyCharges: the amount charged monthly (numeric)
- TotalCharges: the total amount charged (numeric)
- Churn: if the client has canceled the contract (yes/no)

The most interesting one for us is Churn. As the target variable for our model, this is what we want to learn to predict. It takes two values: yes if the customer churned and no if the customer didn't.

When reading a CSV file, Pandas tries to automatically determine the proper type of each column. However, sometimes it's difficult to do it correctly, and the inferred types aren't what we expect them to be. This is why it's important to check whether the actual types are correct. Let's have a look at them by using `df.dtypes`:

```
df.dtypes
```

We see (figure 3.3) that most of the types are inferred correctly. Recall that object means a string value, which is what we expect for most of the columns. However, we may notice two things. First, SeniorCitizen is detected as int64, so it has a type of integer, not object. The reason for this is that instead of the values yes and no, as we have in other columns, there are 1 and 0 values, so Pandas interprets this as a column with integers. It's not really a problem for us, so we don't need to do any additional preprocessing for this column.

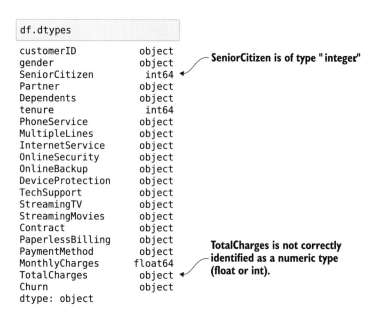

Figure 3.3 **Automatically inferred types for all the columns of the dataframe. Object means a string. TotalCharges is incorrectly identified as "object," but it should be "float."**

The other thing to note is the type for TotalCharges. We would expect this column to be numeric: it contains the total amount of money the client was charged, so it should be a number, not a string. Yet Pandas infers the type as "object." The reason is that in some cases this column contains a space (" ") to represent a missing value. When coming across nonnumeric characters, Pandas has no other option but to declare the column "object."

IMPORTANT Watch out for cases when you expect a column to be numeric, but Pandas says it's not: most likely the column contains special encoding for missing values that require additional preprocessing.

We can force this column to be numeric by converting it to numbers using a special function in Pandas: `to_numeric`. By default, this function raises an exception when it sees nonnumeric data (such as spaces), but we can make it skip these cases by specifying the `errors='coerce'` option. This way Pandas will replace all nonnumeric values with a `NaN` (not a number):

```
total_charges = pd.to_numeric(df.TotalCharges, errors='coerce')
```

To confirm that data indeed contains nonnumeric characters, we can now use the `isnull()` function of `total_charges` to refer to all the rows where Pandas couldn't parse the original string:

```
df[total_charges.isnull()][['customerID', 'TotalCharges']]
```

We see that indeed there are spaces in the TotalCharges column (figure 3.4).

```
total_charges = pd.to_numeric(df.TotalCharges, errors='coerce')
df[total_charges.isnull()][['customerID', 'TotalCharges']]
```

	customerID	TotalCharges
488	4472-LVYGI	
753	3115-CZMZD	
936	5709-LVOEQ	
1082	4367-NUYAO	
1340	1371-DWPAZ	
3331	7644-OMVMY	
3826	3213-VVOLG	
4380	2520-SGTTA	
5218	2923-ARZLG	
6670	4075-WKNIU	
6754	2775-SEFEE	

Figure 3.4 We can spot nonnumeric data in a column by parsing the content as numeric and see at which rows the parsing fails.

Now it's up to us to decide what to do with these missing values. Although we could do many things with them, we are going to do the same thing we did in the previous chapter — set the missing values to zero:

```
df.TotalCharges = pd.to_numeric(df.TotalCharges, errors='coerce')
df.TotalCharges = df.TotalCharges.fillna(0)
```

In addition, we notice that the column names don't follow the same naming convention. Some of them start with a lower letter, whereas others start with a capital letter, and there are also spaces in the values.

Let's make it uniform by lowercasing everything and replacing spaces with underscores. This way we remove all the inconsistencies in the data. We use the exact same code we used in the previous chapter:

```
df.columns = df.columns.str.lower().str.replace(' ', '_')

string_columns = list(df.dtypes[df.dtypes == 'object'].index)

for col in string_columns:
    df[col] = df[col].str.lower().str.replace(' ', '_')
```

Next, let's look at our target variable: churn. Currently, it's categorical, with two values, "yes" and "no" (figure 3.5A). For binary classification, all models typically expect a number: 0 for "no" and 1 for "yes." Let's convert it to numbers:

```
df.churn = (df.churn == 'yes').astype(int)
```

When we use `df.churn == 'yes'`, we create a Pandas series of type boolean. A position in the series is equal to `True` if it's "yes" in the original series and `False` otherwise. Because the only other value it can take is "no," this converts "yes" to `True` and "no" to `False` (figure 3.5B). When we perform casting by using the `astype(int)` function, we

```
df.churn.head()

0    no
1    no
2    yes
3    no
4    yes
Name: churn, dtype: object
```

(A) The original Churn column: it's a Pandas series that contains only "yes" and "no" values.

```
(df.churn == 'yes').head()

0    False
1    False
2     True
3    False
4     True
Name: churn, dtype: bool
```

(B) The result of the == operator: it's a Boolean series with `True` when the elements of the original series are "yes" and `False` otherwise.

```
(df.churn == 'yes').astype(int).head()

0    0
1    0
2    1
3    0
4    1
Name: churn, dtype: int64
```

(C) The result of converting the Boolean series to integer: `True` is converted to 1 and `False` is converted to 0.

Figure 3.5   The expression `(df.churn == 'yes').astype(int)` broken down by individual steps

convert `True` to 1 and `False` to 0 (figure. 3.5C). This is exactly the same idea that we used in the previous chapter when we implemented category encoding.

We've done a bit of preprocessing already, so let's put aside some data for testing. In the previous chapter, we implemented the code for doing it ourselves. This is great for understanding how it works, but typically we don't write such things from scratch every time we need them. Instead, we use existing implementations from libraries. In this chapter we use Scikit-learn, and it has a module called `model_selection` that can handle data splitting. Let's use it.

The function we need to import from `model_selection` is called `train_test_split`:

```
from sklearn.model_selection import train_test_split
```

After importing, it's ready to be used:

```
df_train_full, df_test = train_test_split(df, test_size=0.2, random_state=1)
```

The function `train_test_split` takes a dataframe `df` and creates two new dataframes: `df_train_full` and `df_test`. It does this by shuffling the original dataset and then splitting it in such a way that the test set contains 20% of the data and the train set contains the remaining 80% (figure 3.6). Internally, it's implemented similarly to what we did ourselves in the previous chapter.

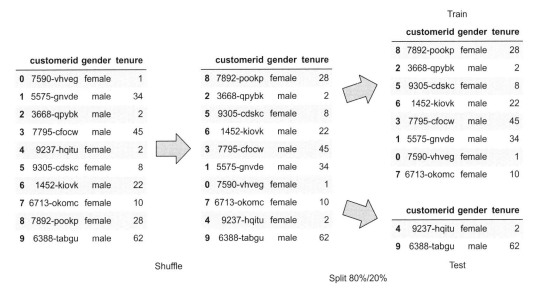

Figure 3.6 When using `train_test_split`, the original dataset is shuffled and then split such that 80% of the data goes to the train set and the remaining 20% goes to the test set.

This function contains a few parameters:

1 The first parameter that we pass is the dataframe that we want to split: df.
2 The second parameter is test_size, which specifies the size of the dataset we want to set aside for testing — 20% for our case.
3 The third parameter we pass is random_state. It's needed for ensuring that every time we run this code, the dataframe is split in the exact same way.

Shuffling of data is done using a random-number generator; it's important to fix the random seed to ensure that every time we shuffle the data, the final arrangement of rows will be the same.

```
df_train_full.head()
```

	customerid	gender	seniorcitizen	partner	dependents	tenure	phoneservice
1814	5442-pptjy	male	0	yes	yes	12	yes
5946	6261-rcvns	female	0	no	no	42	yes
3881	2176-osjuv	male	0	yes	no	71	yes
2389	6161-erdgd	male	0	yes	yes	71	yes
3676	2364-ufrom	male	0	no	no	30	yes

Figure 3.7   The side effect of train_test_split: the indices (the first column) are shuffled in the new dataframes, so instead of consecutive numbers like 0, 1, 2, ..., they look random.

We do see a side effect from shuffling: if we look at the dataframes after splitting by using the head() method, for example, we notice that the indices appear to be randomly ordered (figure 3.7).

In the previous chapter, we split the data into three parts: train, validation, and test. However, the train_test_split function splits the data into only two parts: train and test. In spite of that, we can still split the original dataset into three parts; we just take one part and split it again (figure 3.8).

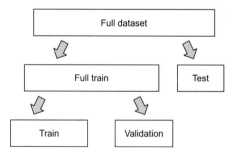

Figure 3.8   Because train_test_split splits a dataset into only two parts, we perform the split two times because we need three parts. First, we split the entire dataset into full train and test, and then we split full train into train and validation.

Let's take the `df_train_full` dataframe and split it one more time into train and validation:

```
df_train, df_val = train_test_split(df_train_full, test_size=0.33,
      random_state=11)
```

Sets the random seed when doing the split to make sure that every time we run the code, the result is the same

```
y_train = df_train.churn.values
y_val = df_val.churn.values
```

Takes the column with the target variable, churn, and saves it outside the dataframe

```
del df_train['churn']
del df_val['churn']
```

Deletes the churn columns from both dataframes to make sure we don't accidentally use the churn variable as a feature during training

Now the dataframes are prepared, and we are ready to use the training dataset for performing initial exploratory data analysis.

3.1.3 *Exploratory data analysis*

Looking at the data before training a model is important. The more we know about the data and the problems inside, the better the model we can build afterward.

We should always check for any missing values in the dataset because many machine learning models cannot easily deal with missing data. We have already found a problem with the TotalCharges column and replaced the missing values with zeros. Now let's see if we need to perform any additional null handling:

```
df_train_full.isnull().sum()
```

It prints all zeros (figure 3.9), so we have no missing values in the dataset and don't need to do anything extra.

```
df_train_full.isnull().sum()
customerid          0
gender              0
seniorcitizen       0
partner             0
dependents          0
tenure              0
phoneservice        0
multiplelines       0
internetservice     0
onlinesecurity      0
onlinebackup        0
deviceprotection    0
techsupport         0
streamingtv         0
streamingmovies     0
contract            0
paperlessbilling    0
paymentmethod       0
monthlycharges      0
totalcharges        0
churn               0
dtype: int64
```

Figure 3.9 We don't have to handle missing values in the dataset: all the values in all the columns are present.

Another thing we should do is check the distribution of values in the target variable. Let's take a look at it using the `value_counts()` method:

```
df_train_full.churn.value_counts()
```

It prints

```
0    4113
1    1521
```

The first column is the value of the target variable, and the second is the count. As we see, the majority of the customers didn't churn.

We know the absolute numbers, but let's also check the proportion of churned users among all customers. For that, we need to divide the number of customers who churned by the total number of customers. We know that 1,521 of 5,634 churned, so the proportion is

$$1521 \; / \; 5634 = 0.27$$

This gives us the proportion of churned users, or the probability that a customer will churn. As we see in the training dataset, approximately 27% of the customers stopped using our services, and the rest remained as customers.

The proportion of churned users, or the probability of churning, has a special name: churn rate.

There's another way to calculate the churn rate: the `mean()` method. It's more convenient to use than manually calculating the rate:

```
global_mean = df_train_full.churn.mean()
```

Using this method, we also get 0.27 (figure 3.10).

```
global_mean = df_train_full.churn.mean()
round(global_mean, 3)
```
```
0.27
```

Figure 3.10   Calculating the global churn rate in the training dataset

The reason it produces the same result is the way we calculate the mean value. If you don't remember, the formula for that is

$$\frac{1}{n} \sum_{i=1}^{n} y_i$$

where n is the number of items in the dataset.

Because y_i can take only zeros and ones, when we sum all of them, we get the number of ones, or the number of people who churned. Then we divide it by the total number of customers, which is exactly the same as the formula we used for calculating the churn rate previously.

Our churn dataset is an example of a so-called *imbalanced* dataset. There were three times as many people who didn't churn in our dataset as those who did churn, and we say that the nonchurn class dominates the churn class. We can clearly see that: the churn rate in our data is 0.27, which is a strong indicator of class imbalance. The opposite of *imbalanced* is the *balanced* case, when positive and negative classes are equally distributed among all observations.

Exercise 3.1

The mean of a Boolean array is

   a The percentage of `False` elements in the array: the number of `False` elements divided by the length of the array

   b The percentage of `True` elements in the array: the number of `True` elements divided by the length of the array

   c The length of an array

Both the categorical and numerical variables in our dataset are important, but they are also different and need different treatment. For that, we want to look at them separately.

We will create two lists:

- `categorical`, which will contain the names of categorical variables
- `numerical`, which, likewise, will have the names of numerical variables

Let's create them:

```
categorical = ['gender', 'seniorcitizen', 'partner', 'dependents',
               'phoneservice', 'multiplelines', 'internetservice',
               'onlinesecurity', 'onlinebackup', 'deviceprotection',
               'techsupport', 'streamingtv', 'streamingmovies',
               'contract', 'paperlessbilling', 'paymentmethod']
numerical = ['tenure', 'monthlycharges', 'totalcharges']
```

First, we can see how many unique values each variable has. We already know we should have just a few for each column, but let's verify it:

```
df_train_full[categorical].nunique()
```

Indeed, we see that most of the columns have two or three values and one (paymentmethod) has four (figure 3.11). This is good. We don't need to spend extra time preparing and cleaning the data; everything is already good to go.

Now we come to another important part of exploratory data analysis: understanding which features may be important for our model.

```
df_train_full[categorical].nunique()
```

```
gender              2
seniorcitizen       2
partner             2
dependents          2
phoneservice        2
multiplelines       3
internetservice     3
onlinesecurity      3
onlinebackup        3
deviceprotection    3
techsupport         3
streamingtv         3
streamingmovies     3
contract            3
paperlessbilling    2
paymentmethod       4
dtype: int64
```

Figure 3.11   **The number of distinct values for each categorical variable. We see that all the variables have very few unique values.**

3.1.4   *Feature importance*

Knowing how other variables affect the target variable, churn, is the key to understanding the data and building a good model. This process is called *feature importance analysis*, and it's often done as a part of exploratory data analysis to figure out which variables will be useful for the model. It also gives us additional insights about the dataset and helps answer questions like "What makes customers churn?" and "What are the characteristics of people who churn?"

We have two different kinds of features: categorical and numerical. Each kind has different ways of measuring feature importance, so we will look at each separately.

CHURN RATE

Let's start by looking at categorical variables. The first thing we can do is look at the churn rate for each variable. We know that a categorical variable has a set of values it can take, and each value defines a group inside the dataset.

We can look at all the distinct values of a variable. Then, for each variable, there's a group of customers: all the customers who have this value. For each such group, we can compute the churn rate, which is the group churn rate. When we have it, we can compare it with the global churn rate — the churn rate calculated for all the observations at once.

If the difference between the rates is small, the value is not important when predicting churn because this group of customers is not really different from the rest of the customers. On the other hand, if the difference is not small, something inside that group sets it apart from the rest. A machine learning algorithm should be able to pick this up and use it when making predictions.

Let's check first for the gender variable. This gender variable can take two values, female and male. There are two groups of customers: ones that have gender == 'female' and ones that have gender == 'male' (figure 3.12). To compute the churn rate for all

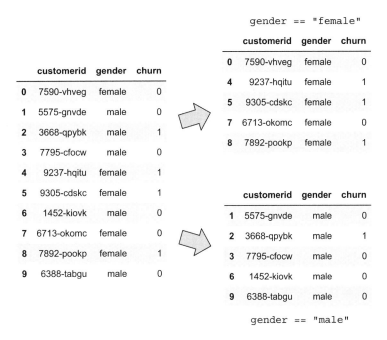

	customerid	gender	churn
0	7590-vhveg	female	0
1	5575-gnvde	male	0
2	3668-qpybk	male	1
3	7795-cfocw	male	0
4	9237-hqitu	female	1
5	9305-cdskc	female	1
6	1452-kiovk	male	0
7	6713-okomc	female	0
8	7892-pookp	female	1
9	6388-tabgu	male	0

gender == "female"

	customerid	gender	churn
0	7590-vhveg	female	0
4	9237-hqitu	female	1
5	9305-cdskc	female	1
7	6713-okomc	female	0
8	7892-pookp	female	1

	customerid	gender	churn
1	5575-gnvde	male	0
2	3668-qpybk	male	1
3	7795-cfocw	male	0
6	1452-kiovk	male	0
9	6388-tabgu	male	0

gender == "male"

Figure 3.12 **The dataframe is split by the values of the** `gender` **variable into two groups: a group with** `gender == "female"` **and a group with** `gender == "male"`.

female customers, we first select only rows that correspond to gender == 'female' and then compute the churn rate for them:

```
female_mean = df_train_full[df_train_full.gender == 'female'].churn.mean()
```

We then do the same for all male customers:

```
male_mean = df_train_full[df_train_full.gender == 'male'].churn.mean()
```

When we execute this code and check the results, we see that the churn rate of female customers is 27.7% and that of male customers is 26.3%, whereas the global churn rate is 27% (figure 3.13). The difference between the group rates for both females and males is quite small, which indicates that knowing the gender of the customer doesn't help us identify whether they will churn.

Now let's take a look at another variable: partner. It takes values of yes and no, so there are two groups of customers: the ones for which partner == 'yes' and the ones for which partner == 'no'.

We can check the group churn rates using the same code as we used previously. All we need to change is the filter conditions:

```
partner_yes = df_train_full[df_train_full.partner == 'yes'].churn.mean()
partner_no = df_train_full[df_train_full.partner == 'no'].churn.mean()
```

```
global_mean = df_train_full.churn.mean()
round(global_mean, 3)
```

```
0.27
```

```
female_mean = df_train_full[df_train_full.gender == 'female'].churn.mean()
print('gender == female:', round(female_mean, 3))

male_mean = df_train_full[df_train_full.gender == 'male'].churn.mean()
print('gender == male:  ', round(male_mean, 3))
```

```
gender == female: 0.277
gender == male:   0.263
```

Figure 3.13   The global churn rate compared with churn rates among males and females. The numbers are quite close, which means that `gender` is not a useful variable when predicting churn.

As we see, the rates for those who have a partner are quite different from rates for those who don't: 20% and 33%, respectively. It means that clients with no partner are more likely to churn than the ones with a partner (figure 3.14).

```
partner_yes = df_train_full[df_train_full.partner == 'yes'].churn.mean()
print('partner == yes:', round(partner_yes, 3))

partner_no = df_train_full[df_train_full.partner == 'no'].churn.mean()
print('partner == no :', round(partner_no, 3))
```

```
partner == yes: 0.205
partner == no : 0.33
```

Figure 3.14   The churn rate for people with a partner is significantly less than the rate for the ones without a partner — 20.5% versus 33% — which indicates that the `partner` variable is useful for predicting churn.

RISK RATIO

In addition to looking at the difference between the group rate and the global rate, it's interesting to look at the ratio between them. In statistics, the ratio between probabilities in different groups is called the *risk ratio*, where *risk* refers to the risk of having the effect. In our case, the effect is churn, so it's the risk of churning:

$$risk = group\ rate\ /\ global\ rate$$

For `gender == female`, for example, the risk of churning is 1.02:

$$risk = 27.7\%\ /\ 27\% = 1.02$$

Risk is a number between zero and infinity. It has a nice interpretation that tells you how likely the elements of the group are to have the effect (churn) compared with the entire population.

If the difference between the group rate and the global rate is small, the risk is close to 1: this group has the same level of risk as the rest of the population. Customers in the group are as likely to churn as anyone else. In other words, a group with a risk close to 1 is not risky at all (figure 3.15, group A).

If the risk is lower than 1, the group has lower risks: the churn rate in this group is smaller than the global churn. For example, the value 0.5 means that the clients in this group are two times less likely to churn than clients in general (figure 3.15, group B).

On the other hand, if the value is higher than 1, the group is risky: there's more churn in the group than in the population. So a risk of 2 means that customers from the group are two times more likely to churn (figure 3.15, group C).

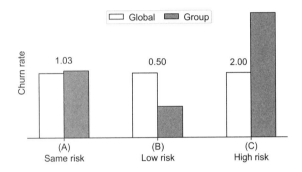

Figure 3.15 Churn rate of different groups compared with the global churn rate. In group (A), the rates are approximately the same, so the risk of churn is around 1. In group (B), the group churn rate is smaller than the global rate, so the risk is around 0.5. Finally, in group (C), the group churn rate is higher than the global rate, so the risk is close to 2.

The term *risk* originally comes from controlled trials, in which one group of patients is given a treatment (a medicine) and the other group isn't (only a placebo). Then we compare how effective the medicine is by calculating the rate of negative outcomes in each group and then calculating the ratio between the rates:

risk = negative outcome rate in group 1 / negative outcome rate in group 2

If medicine turns out to be effective, it's said to reduce the risk of having the negative outcome, and the value of the risk is less than 1.

Let's calculate the risks for gender and partner. For the gender variable, the risks for both males and females is around 1 because the rates in both groups aren't significantly different from the global rate. Not surprisingly, it's different for the partner variable; having no partner is more risky (table 3.1).

We did this from only two variables. Let's now do this for all the categorical variables. To do that, we need a piece of code that checks all the values a variable has and computes churn rate for each of these values.

Table 3.1 Churn rates and risks for the `gender` and `partner` variables. The churn rates for females and males are not significantly different from the global churn rates, so the risks for them to churn are low: both have risks values around 1. On the other hand, the churn rate for people with no partner is significantly higher than average, making them risky, with the risk value of 1.22. People with partners tend to churn less, so for them, the risk is only 0.75.

Variable	Value	Churn rate	Risk
gender	Female	27.7%	1.02
	Male	26.3%	0.97
partner	Yes	20.5%	0.75
	No	33%	1.22

If we used SQL, that would be straightforward to do. For gender, we'd need to do something like this:

```
SELECT
    gender, AVG(churn),
    AVG(churn) - global_churn,
    AVG(churn) / global_churn
FROM
    data
GROUP BY
    gender
```

This is a rough translation to Pandas:

```
global_mean = df_train_full.churn.mean()                                    Computes the ❶
                                                                            AVG(churn)

df_group = df_train_full.groupby(by='gender').churn.agg(['mean'])  ⟵
df_group['diff'] = df_group['mean'] - global_mean      ⟵
df_group['risk'] = df_group['mean'] / global_mean      ⟵                Calculates the difference
                                                                        between group churn
df_group                          Calculates the risk of churning ❸  ❷  rate and global rate
```

In ❶ we calculate the `AVG(churn)` part. For that, we use the agg function to indicate that we need to aggregate data into one value per group: the mean value. In ❷ we create another column, diff, where we will keep the difference between the group mean and the global mean. Likewise, in ❸ we create the column risk, where we calculate the fraction between the group mean and the global mean.

We can see the results in figure 3.16.

	mean	diff	risk
gender			
female	0.276824	0.006856	1.025396
male	0.263214	-0.006755	0.974980

Figure 3.16 The churn rate for the `gender` variable. We see that for both values, the difference between the group churn rate and the global churn rate is not very large.

Let's now do that for all categorical variables. We can iterate through them and apply the same code for each:

```
from IPython.display import display

for col in categorical:
    df_group = df_train_full.groupby(by=col).churn.agg(['mean'])
    df_group['diff'] = df_group['mean'] - global_mean
    df_group['rate'] = df_group['mean'] / global_mean
    display(df_group)
```

Loops over all categorical variables

Performs groupby for each categorical variable

Displays the resulting dataframe

Two things are different in this code. First, instead of manually specifying the column name, we iterate over all categorical variables.

The second difference is more subtle: we need to call the `display` function to render a dataframe inside the loop. The way we typically display a dataframe is to leave it as the last line in a Jupyter Notebook cell and then execute the cell. If we do it that way, the dataframe is displayed as the cell output. This is exactly how we managed to see the content of the dataframe at the beginning of the chapter (figure 3.1). However, we cannot do this inside a loop. To still be able to see the content of the dataframe, we call the `display` function explicitly.

From the results (figure 3.17) we learn that

- For gender, there is not much difference between females and males. Both means are approximately the same, and for both groups the risks are close to 1.
- Senior citizens tend to churn more than nonseniors: the risk of churning is 1.53 for seniors and 0.89 for nonseniors.
- People with a partner churn less than people with no partner. The risks are 0.75 and 1.22, respectively.
- People who use phone service are not at risk of churning: the risk is close to 1, and there's almost no difference with the global churn rate. People who don't use phone service are even less likely to churn: the risk is below 1, and the difference with the global churn rate is negative.

	mean	diff	risk
gender			
female	0.276824	0.006856	1.025396
male	0.263214	-0.006755	0.974980

(A) Churn ratio and risk: `gender`

	mean	diff	risk
seniorcitizen			
0	0.242270	-0.027698	0.897403
1	0.413377	0.143409	1.531208

(B) Churn ratio and risk: `seniorcitizen`

	mean	diff	risk
partner			
no	0.329809	0.059841	1.221659
yes	0.205033	-0.064935	0.759472

(C) Churn ratio and risk: `partner`

	mean	diff	risk
phoneservice			
no	0.241316	-0.028652	0.893870
yes	0.273049	0.003081	1.011412

(D) Churn ratio and risk: `phoneservice`

Figure 3.17   Churn rate difference and risk for four categorical variables: `gender`, `seniorcitizen`, `partner`, **and** `phoneservice`

Some of the variables have quite significant differences (figure 3.18):

- Clients with no tech support tend to churn more than those who do.
- People with monthly contracts cancel the contract a lot more often than others, and people with two-year contacts churn very rarely.

	mean	diff	risk
techsupport			
no	0.418914	0.148946	1.551717
no_internet_service	0.077805	-0.192163	0.288201
yes	0.159926	-0.110042	0.592390

(A) Churn ratio and risk: `techsupport`

	mean	diff	risk
contract			
month-to-month	0.431701	0.161733	1.599082
one_year	0.120573	-0.149395	0.446621
two_year	0.028274	-0.241694	0.104730

(B) Churn ratio and risk: `contract`

Figure 3.18   Difference between the group churn rate and the global churn rate for `techsupport` **and** `contract`. **People with no tech support and month-to-month contracts tend to churn a lot more than clients from other groups, whereas people with tech support and two-year contracts are very low-risk clients.**

This way, just by looking at the differences and the risks, we can identify the most discriminative features: the features that are helpful for detecting churn. Thus, we expect that these features will be useful for our future models.

MUTUAL INFORMATION

The kinds of differences we just explored are useful for our analysis and important for understanding the data, but it's hard to use them to say what the most important feature is and whether tech support is more useful than the type of contract.

Luckily, the metrics of importance can help us: we can measure the degree of dependency between a categorical variable and the target variable. If two variables are dependent, knowing the value of one variable gives us some information about another. On the other hand, if a variable is completely independent of the target variable, it's not useful and can be safely removed from the dataset.

In our case, knowing that the customer has a month-to-month contract may indicate that this customer is more likely to churn than not.

> **IMPORTANT** Customers with month-to-month contracts tend to churn a lot more than customers with other kinds of contracts. This is exactly the kind of relationship we want to find in our data. Without such relationships in data, machine learning models will not work — they will not be able to make predictions. The higher the degree of dependency, the more useful a feature is.

For categorical variables, one such metric is mutual information, which tells how much information we learn about one variable if we learn the value of the other variable. It's a concept from information theory, and in machine learning, we often use it to measure the mutual dependency between two variables.

Higher values of mutual information mean a higher degree of dependence: if the mutual information between a categorical variable and the target is high, this categorical variable will be quite useful for predicting the target. On the other hand, if the mutual information is low, the categorical variable and the target are independent, and thus the variable will not be useful for predicting the target.

Mutual information is already implemented in Scikit-learn in the `mutual_info_score` function from the `metrics` package, so we can just use it:

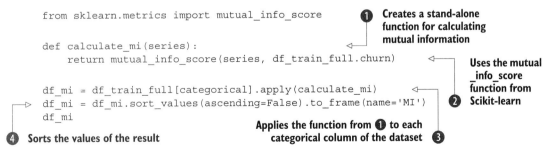

In ❸, we use the `apply` method to apply the `calculate_mi` function we defined in ❶ to each column of the `df_train_full` dataframe. Because we include an additional step of selecting only categorical variables, it's applied only to them. The function we define in ❶ takes only one parameter: `series`. This is a column from the dataframe on which we invoked the `apply()` method. In ❷, we compute the mutual information score between the series and the target variable churn. The output is a single number, so the output of the `apply()` method is a Pandas series. Finally, we sort the elements of the series by the mutual information score and convert the series to a dataframe. This way, the result is rendered nicely in Jupyter.

As we see, `contract`, `onlinesecurity`, and `techsupport` are among the most important features (figure 3.19). Indeed, we've already noted that `contract` and `techsupport` are quite informative. It's also not surprising that `gender` is among the least important features, so we shouldn't expect it to be useful for the model.

	MI
contract	0.098320
onlinesecurity	0.063085
techsupport	0.061032
internetservice	0.055868
onlinebackup	0.046923

(A) The most useful features according to the mutual information score.

	MI
partner	0.009968
seniorcitizen	0.009410
multiplelines	0.000857
phoneservice	0.000229
gender	0.000117

(B) The least useful features according to the mutual information score.

Figure 3.19   Mutual information between categorical variables and the target variable. Higher values are better. According to it, `contract` is the most useful variable, whereas `gender` is the least useful.

CORRELATION COEFFICIENT

Mutual information is a way to quantify the degree of dependency between two categorical variables, but it doesn't work when one of the features is numerical, so we cannot apply it to the three numerical variables that we have.

We can, however, measure the dependency between a binary target variable and a numerical variable. We can pretend that the binary variable is numerical (containing only the numbers zero and one) and then use the classical methods from statistics to check for any dependency between these variables.

One such method is the *correlation* coefficient (sometimes referred as *Pearson's correlation coefficient*). It is a value from −1 to 1:

- Positive correlation means that when one variable goes up, the other variable tends to go up as well. In the case of a binary target, when the values of the variable are high, we see ones more often than zeros. But when the values of the variable are low, zeros become more frequent than ones.
- Zero correlation means no relationship between two variables: they are completely independent.

- Negative correlation occurs when one variable goes up and the other goes down. In the binary case, if the values are high, we see more zeros than ones in the target variable. When the values are low, we see more ones.

It's very easy to calculate the correlation coefficient in Pandas:

```
df_train_full[numerical].corrwith(df_train_full.churn)
```

We see the results in figure 3.20:

- The correlation between `tenure` and churn is –0.35: it has a negative sign, so the longer customers stay, the less often they tend to churn. For customers staying with the company for two months or less, the churn rate is 60%; for customers with tenure between 3 and 12 months, the churn rate is 40%; and for customers staying longer than a year, the churn rate is 17%. So the higher the value of tenure, the smaller the churn rate (figure 3.21A).
- `monthlycharges` has a positive coefficient of 0.19, which means that customers who pay more tend to leave more often. Only 8% of those who pay less than $20 monthly churned; customers paying between $21 and $50 churn more frequently with a churn rate of 18%; and 32% of people paying more than $50 churned (figure 3.21B).
- `totalcharges` has a negative correlation, which makes sense: the longer people stay with the company, the more they have paid in total, so it's less likely that they will leave. In this case, we expect a pattern similar to `tenure`. For small values, the churn rate is high; for larger values, it's lower.

	correlation
tenure	-0.351885
monthlycharges	0.196805
totalcharges	-0.196353

Figure 3.20   Correlation between numerical variables and churn. `tenure` **has a high negative correlation: as tenure grows, churn rate goes down.** `monthlycharges` **has positive correlation: the more customers pay, the more likely they are to churn.**

After doing initial exploratory data analysis, identifying important features, and getting some insights into the problem, we are ready to do the next step: feature engineering and model training.

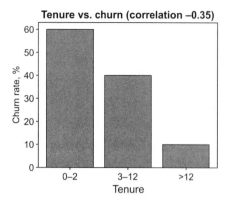

(A) Churn rate for different values of tenure.
The correlation coefficient is negative, so the
trend is downward: for higher values of
tenure, **the churn rate is smaller.**

(B) Churn rate for different values of monthlycharges.
The correlation coefficient is positive, so the trend is
upward: for higher values of monthlycharges, **the**
churn rate is higher.

Figure 3.21   Churn rate for tenure **(negative correlation of –0.35) and** monthlycharges
(positive correlation of 0.19)

3.2   Feature engineering

We had an initial look at the data and identified what could be useful for the model.
After doing that, we have a clear understanding how other variables affect churn —
our target.

Before we proceed to training, however, we need to perform the feature engineering step: transforming all categorical variables to numeric features. We'll do
that in the next section, and after that, we'll be ready to train the logistic regression
model.

3.2.1   One-hot encoding for categorical variables

As we already know from the first chapter, we cannot just take a categorical variable
and put it into a machine learning model. The models can deal only with numbers
in matrices. So, we need to convert our categorical data into a matrix form, or
encode.

One such encoding technique is *one-hot encoding*. We already saw this encoding
technique in the previous chapter, when creating features for the make of a car and
other categorical variables. There, we mentioned it only briefly and used it in a very
simple way. In this chapter, we will spend more time understanding and using it.

If a variable contract has possible values (monthly, yearly, and two-year), we can
represent a customer with the yearly contract as (0, 1, 0). In this case, the yearly value
is active, or *hot*, so it gets 1, whereas the remaining values are not active, or *cold*, so they
are 0.

To understand this better, let's consider a case with two categorical variables and see how we create a matrix from them. These variables are

- gender, with values female and male
- contract, with values monthly, yearly, and two-year

Because the gender variable has only two possible values, we create two columns in the resulting matrix. The contract variable has three columns, and in total, our new matrix will have five columns:

- gender=female
- gender=male
- contract=monthly
- contract=yearly
- contract=two-year

Let's consider two customers (figure 3.22):

- A female customer with a yearly contract
- A male customer with a monthly contract

For the first customer, the gender variable is encoded by putting 1 in the gender =female column and 0 in the gender=male column. Likewise, contract=yearly gets 1, whereas the remaining contract columns, contract=monthly and contract=two-year, get 0.

As for the second customer, gender=male and contract=monthly get ones, and the rest of the columns get zeros (figure 3.22).

gender	contract
male	monthly
female	yearly

gender		contract		
female	male	monthly	yearly	two-year
0	1	1	0	0
1	0	0	1	0

Figure 3.22 The original dataset with categorical variables is on the left and the one-hot encoded representation on the right. For the first customer, gender=male and contract=monthly are the hot columns, so they get 1. For the second customer, the hot columns are gender=female and contract=yearly.

The way we implemented it previously was simple but quite limited. We first looked at the top five values of the variable and then looped over each value and manually created a column in the dataframe. When the number of features grows, however, this process becomes tedious.

Luckily, we don't need to implement this by hand: we can use Scikit-learn. We can perform one-hot encoding in multiple ways in Scikit-learn, but we will use DictVectorizer.

As the name suggests, DictVectorizer takes in a dictionary and *vectorizes* it — that is, it creates vectors from it. Then the vectors are put together as rows of one matrix. This matrix is used as input to a machine learning algorithm (figure 3.23).

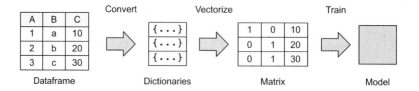

Figure 3.23   The process of creating a model. First, we convert a dataframe to a list of dictionaries, then we vectorize the list to a matrix, and finally, we use the matrix to train a model.

To use this method, we need to convert our dataframe to a list of dictionaries, which is simple to do in Pandas using the to_dict method with the orient="records" parameter:

```
train_dict = df_train[categorical + numerical].to_dict(orient='records')
```

If we take a look at the first element of this new list, we see

```
{'gender': 'male',
 'seniorcitizen': 0,
 'partner': 'yes',
 'dependents': 'yes',
 'phoneservice': 'yes',
 'multiplelines': 'no',
 'internetservice': 'no',
 'onlinesecurity': 'no_internet_service',
 'onlinebackup': 'no_internet_service',
 'deviceprotection': 'no_internet_service',
 'techsupport': 'no_internet_service',
 'streamingtv': 'no_internet_service',
 'streamingmovies': 'no_internet_service',
 'contract': 'two_year',
 'paperlessbilling': 'no',
 'paymentmethod': 'mailed_check',
 'tenure': 12,
 'monthlycharges': 19.7,
 'totalcharges': 258.35}
```

Each column from the dataframe is the key in this dictionary, with values coming from the actual dataframe row values.

Now we can use DictVectorizer. We create it and then fit it to the list of dictionaries we created previously:

```
from sklearn.feature_extraction import DictVectorizer

dv = DictVectorizer(sparse=False)
dv.fit(train_dict)
```

In this code we create a `DictVectorizer` instance, which we call `dv`, and "train" it by invoking the `fit` method. The `fit` method looks at the content of these dictionaries and figures out the possible values for each variable and how to map them to the columns in the output matrix. If a feature is categorical, it applies the one-hot encoding scheme, but if a feature is numerical, it's left intact.

The `DictVectorizer` class can take in a set of parameters. We specify one of them: `sparse=False`. This parameter means that the created matrix will not be sparse and instead will create a simple NumPy array. If you don't know about sparse matrices, don't worry: we don't need them in this chapter.

After we fit the vectorizer, we can use it for converting the dictionaries to a matrix by using the `transform` method:

```
X_train = dv.transform(train_dict)
```

This operation creates a matrix with 45 columns. Let's have a look at the first row, which corresponds to the customer we looked at previously:

```
X_train[0]
```

When we put this code into a Jupyter Notebook cell and execute it, we get the following output:

```
array([  0.  ,    0.  ,    1.  ,    1.  ,    0.  ,    0.  ,    0.  ,    1.  ,
         0.  ,    1.  ,    1.  ,    0.  ,    0.  ,   86.1,    1.  ,    0.  ,
         0.  ,    0.  ,    0.  ,    1.  ,    0.  ,    0.  ,    1.  ,    0.  ,
         1.  ,    0.  ,    1.  ,    1.  ,    0.  ,    0.  ,    0.  ,    0.  ,
         1.  ,    0.  ,    0.  ,    0.  ,    1.  ,    0.  ,    0.  ,    1.  ,
         0.  ,    0.  ,    1.  ,   71.  , 6045.9])
```

As we see, most of the elements are ones and zeros — they're one-hot encoded categorical variables. Not all of them are ones and zeros, however. We see that three of them are other numbers. These are our numeric variables: `monthlycharges`, `tenure`, and `totalcharges`.

We can learn the names of all these columns by using the `get_feature_names` method:

```
dv.get_feature_names()
```

It prints

```
['contract=month-to-month',
 'contract=one_year',
 'contract=two_year',
 'dependents=no',
```

```
'dependents=yes',
# some rows omitted
'tenure',
'totalcharges']
```

As we see, for each categorical feature it creates multiple columns for each of its distinct values. For contract, we have contract=month-to-month, contract=one_year, and contract=two_year, and for dependents, we have dependents=no and dependents =yes. Features such as tenure and totalcharges keep the original names because they are numerical; therefore, DictVectorizer doesn't change them.

Now our features are encoded as a matrix, so we can move to the next step: using a model to predict churn.

Exercise 3.2

How would DictVectorizer encode the following list of dictionaries?

```
records = [
    {'total_charges': 10, 'paperless_billing': 'yes'},
    {'total_charges': 30, 'paperless_billing': 'no'},
    {'total_charges': 20, 'paperless_billing': 'no'}
]
```

a   Columns: ['total_charges', 'paperless_billing=yes', 'paperless_
    billing=no']
    Values: [10, 1, 0], [30, 0, 1], [20, 0, 1]

b   Columns: ['total_charges=10', 'total_charges=20', 'total_charges=
    30', 'paperless_billing=yes', 'paperless_billing=no']
    Values: [1, 0, 0, 1, 0], [0, 0, 1, 0, 1], [0, 1, 0, 0, 1]

3.3   *Machine learning for classification*

We have learned how to use Scikit-learn to perform one-hot encoding for categorical variables, and now we can transform them into a set of numerical features and put everything together into a matrix.

When we have a matrix, we are ready to do the model training part. In this section we learn how to train the logistic regression model and interpret its results.

3.3.1   *Logistic regression*

In this chapter, we use logistic regression as a classification model, and now we train it to distinguish churned and not-churned users.

Logistic regression has a lot in common with linear regression, the model we learned in the previous chapter. If you remember, the linear regression model is a regression model that can predict a number. It has the form

$$g(x_i) = w_0 + x_i^T w$$

where

- x_i is the feature vector corresponding to the ith observation.
- w_0 is the bias term.
- w is a vector with the weights of the model.

We apply this model and get $g(x_i)$ — the prediction of what we think the value for x_i should be. Linear regression is trained to predict the target variable y_i — the actual value of the observation i. In the previous chapter, this was the price of a car.

Linear regression is a linear model. It's called *linear* because it combines the weights of the model with the feature vector *linearly*, using the dot product. Linear models are simple to implement, train, and use. Because of their simplicity, they are also fast.

Logistic regression is also a linear model, but unlike linear regression, it's a classification model, not regression, even though the name might suggest that. It's a binary classification model, so the target variable y_i is binary; the only values it can have are zero and one. Observations with $y_i = 1$ are typically called *positive examples*: examples in which the effect we want to predict is present. Likewise, examples with $y_i = 0$ are called *negative examples*: the effect we want to predict is absent. For our project, $y_i = 1$ means that the customer churned, and $y_i = 0$ means the opposite: the customer stayed with us.

The output of logistic regression is probability — the probability that the observation x_i is positive, or, in other words, the probability that $y_i = 1$. For our case, it's the probability that the customer i will churn.

To be able to treat the output as a probability, we need to make sure that the predictions of the model always stay between zero and one. We use a special mathematical function for this purpose called *sigmoid*, and the full formula for the logistic regression model is

$$g(x_i) = \text{sigmoid}(w_0 + x_i^T w)$$

If we compare it with the linear regression formula, the only difference is this sigmoid function: in case of linear regression, we have only $w_0 + x_i^T w$. This is why both of these models are linear; they are both based on the dot product operation.

The sigmoid function maps any value to a number between zero and one (figure 3.24). It's defined this way:

$$\text{sigmoid}(x) = \frac{1}{1 + \exp(-x)}$$

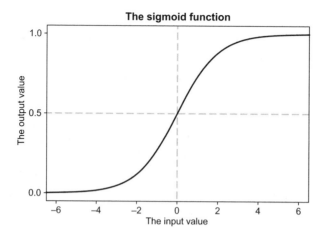

Figure 3.24 The sigmoid function outputs values that are always between 0 and 1. When the input is 0, the result of sigmoid is 0.5; for negative values, the results are below 0.5 and start approaching 0 for input values less than –6. When the input is positive, the result of sigmoid is above 0.5 and approaches 1 for input values starting from 6.

We know from chapter 2 that if the feature vector x_i is n-dimensional, the dot product $x_i^T w$ can be unwrapped as a sum, and we can write $g(x_i)$ as

$$g(x_i) = \text{sigmoid}(w_0 + x_{i1}w_1 + x_{i2}w_2 + \dots + x_{in}w_n)$$

Or, using sum notation, as

$$g(x_i) = \text{sigmoid}\left(w_0 + \sum_{j=1}^{n} x_{ij}w_j\right)$$

Previously, we translated the formulas to Python for illustration. Let's do the same here. The linear regression model has the following formula:

$$g(x_i) = w_0 + \sum_{j=1}^{n} x_{ij}w_j$$

If you remember from the previous chapter, this formula translates to the following Python code:

```
def linear_regression(xi):
    result = bias
```

```
    for j in range(n):
        result = result + xi[j] * w[j]
    return result
```

The translation of the logistic regression formula to Python is almost identical to the linear regression case, except that at the end, we apply the sigmoid function:

```
def logistic_regression(xi):
    score = bias
    for j in range(n):
        score = score + xi[j] * w[j]
    prob = sigmoid(score)
    return prob
```

Of course, we also need to define the sigmoid function:

```
import math

def sigmoid(score):
    return 1 / (1 + math.exp(-score))
```

We use *score* to mean the intermediate result before applying the sigmoid function. The score can take any real value. The *probability* is the result of applying the sigmoid function to the score; this is the final output, and it can take only the values between zero and one.

The parameters of the logistic regression model are the same as for linear regression:

- w_0 is the bias term.
- $w = (w_1, w_2, ..., w_n)$ is the weights vector.

To learn the weights, we need to train the model, which we will do now using Scikit-learn.

> **Exercise 3.3**
> Why do we need sigmoid for logistic regression?
>
> a Sigmoid converts the output to values between –6 and 6, which is easier to deal with.
> b Sigmoid makes sure the output is between zero and one, which can be interpreted as probability.

3.3.2 Training logistic regression

To get started, we first import the model:

```
from sklearn.linear_model import LogisticRegression
```

Then we train it by calling the `fit` method:

```
model = LogisticRegression(solver='liblinear', random_state=1)
model.fit(X_train, y_train)
```

The class `LogisticRegression` from Scikit-learn encapsulates the training logic behind this model. It's configurable, and we can change quite a few parameters. In fact, we already specify two of them: `solver` and `random_state`. Both are needed for reproducibility:

- `random_state`. The seed number for the random-number generator. It shuffles the data when training the model; to make sure the shuffle is the same every time, we fix the seed.
- `solver`. The underlying optimization library. In the current version (at the moment of writing, v0.20.3), the default value for this parameter is `liblinear`, but according to the documentation (https://scikit-learn.org/stable/modules/generated/sklearn.linear_model.LogisticRegression.html), it will change to a different one in version v0.22. To make sure our results are reproducible in the later versions, we also set this parameter.

Other useful parameters for the model include `C`, which controls the regularization level. We talk about it in the next chapter when we cover parameter tuning. Specifying `C` is optional; by default, it gets the value 1.0.

The training takes a few seconds, and when it's done, the model is ready to make predictions. Let's see how well the model performs. We can apply it to our validation data to obtain the probability of churn for each customer in the validation dataset.

To do that, we need to apply the one-hot encoding scheme to all the categorical variables. First, we convert the dataframe to a list of dictionaries and then feed it to the `DictVectorizer` we fit previously:

```
val_dict = df_val[categorical + numerical].to_dict(orient='records')
X_val = dv.transform(val_dict)
```

Instead of fit and then transform, we use transform, which we fit previously.

We perform one-hot encoding in exactly the same way as during training.

As a result, we get `X_val`, a matrix with features from the validation dataset. Now we are ready to put this matrix to the model. To get the probabilities, we use the `predict_proba` method of the model:

```
y_pred = model.predict_proba(X_val)
```

The result of `predict_proba` is a two-dimensional NumPy array, or a two-column matrix. The first column of the array contains the probability that the target is negative (no churn), and the second column contains the probability that the target is positive (churn) (figure 3.25).

These columns convey the same information. We know the probability of churn — it's p — and the probability of not churning is always $1 - p$, so we don't need both columns.

```
model.predict_proba(X_val)
```

Probability that the
observation belongs
to the negative class,
that is, customer will
not churn

```
array([[0.76508957, 0.23491043],
       [0.73113584, 0.26886416],
       [0.68054864, 0.31945136],
       ...,
       [0.94274779, 0.05725221],
       [0.38476995, 0.61523005],
       [0.9387273 , 0.0612727 ]])
```

Probability that the
observation belongs
to the positive class,
that is, customer will
churn

Figure 3.25   The predictions of the model: a two-column matrix. The first column contains
the probability that the target is zero (the client won't churn). The second column contains
the opposite probability (the target is one, and the client will churn).

Thus, it's enough to take only the second column of the prediction. To select only one column from a two-dimensional array in NumPy, we can use the slicing operation [:, 1]:

```
y_pred = model.predict_proba(X_val)[:, 1]
```

This syntax might be confusing, so let's break it down. Two positions are inside the brackets, the first one for rows and the second one for columns.

When we use [:, 1], NumPy interprets it this way:

- : means select all the rows.
- 1 means select only the column at index 1, and because the indexing starts at 0, it's the second column.

As a result, we get a one-dimensional NumPy array that contains the values from the second column only.

This output (probabilities) is often called *soft* predictions. These tell us the probability of churning as a number between zero and one. It's up to us to decide how to interpret this number and how to use it.

Remember how we wanted to use this model: we wanted to retain customers by identifying those who are about to cancel their contract with the company and send them promotional messages, offering discounts and other benefits. We do this in the hope that after receiving the benefit, they will stay with the company. On the other hand, we don't want to give promotions to all our customers, because it will hurt us financially: we will make less profit, if any.

To make the actual decision about whether to send a promotional letter to our customers, using the probability alone is not enough. We need *hard* predictions — binary values of True (churn, so send the mail) or False (not churn, so don't send the mail).

To get the binary predictions, we take the probabilities and cut them above a certain threshold. If the probability for a customer is higher than this threshold, we predict churn, otherwise, not churn. If we select 0.5 to be this threshold, making the binary predictions is easy. We just use the ">=" operator:

```
y_pred >= 0.5
```

The comparison operators in NumPy are applied element-wise, and the result is a new array that contains only Boolean values: True and False. Under the hood, it performs the comparison for each element of the y_pred array. If the element is greater than 0.5 or equal to 0.5, the corresponding element in the output array is True, and otherwise, it's False (figure 3.26).

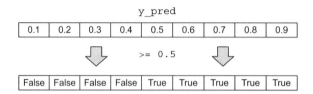

Figure 3.26   The >= operator is applied element-wise in NumPy. For every element, it performs the comparison, and the result is another array with True or False values, depending on the result of the comparison.

Let's write the results to the churn array:

```
churn = y_pred >= 0.5
```

When we have these hard predictions made by our model, we would like to understand how good they are, so we are ready to move to the next step: evaluating the quality of these predictions. In the next chapter, we will spend a lot more time learning about different evaluation techniques for binary classification, but for now, let's do a simple check to make sure our model learned something useful.

The simplest thing to check is to take each prediction and compare it with the actual value. If we predict churn and the actual value is churn, or we predict non-churn and the actual value is non-churn, our model made the correct prediction. If the predictions don't match, they aren't good. If we calculate the number of times our predictions match the actual value, we can use it for measuring the quality of our model.

This quality measure is called *accuracy*. It's very easy to calculate accuracy with NumPy:

```
(y_val == churn).mean()
```

Even though it's easy to calculate, it might be difficult to understand what this expression does when you see it for the first time. Let's try to break it down into individual steps.

First, we apply the == operator to compare two NumPy arrays: y_val and churn. If you remember, the first array, y_val, contains only numbers: zeros and ones. This is our target variable: one if the customer churned and zero otherwise. The second array contains Boolean predictions: True and False values. In this case True means we predict the customer will churn, and `False` means the customer will not churn (figure 3.27).

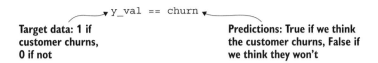

Figure 3.27   Applying the == operator to compare the target data with our predictions

Even though these two arrays have different types inside (integer and Boolean), it's still possible to compare them. The Boolean array is cast to integer such that `True` values are turned to "1" and `False` values are turned to "0." Then it's possible for NumPy to perform the actual comparison (figure 3.28).

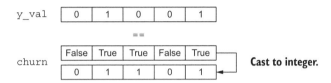

Figure 3.28   To compare the prediction with the target data, the array with predictions is cast to integer.

Like the `>=` operator, the `==` operator is applied element-wise. In this case, however, we have two arrays to compare, and here, we compare each element of one array with the respective element of the other array. The result is again a Boolean array with `True` or `False` values, depending on the outcome of the comparison (figure 3.29).

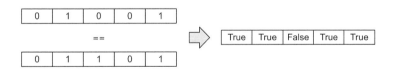

Figure 3.29   The == operator from NumPy is applied element-wise for two NumPy arrays.

In our case, if the true value in `y_pred` matches our prediction in `churn`, the label is `True`, and if it doesn't, the label is `False`. In other words, we have `True` if our prediction is correct and `False` if it's not.

Finally, we take the results of comparison — the Boolean array — and compute its mean using the `mean()` method. This method, however, is applied to numbers, not

Boolean values, so before calculating the mean, the values are cast to integers: `True` values to "1" and `False` values to "0" (figure 3.30).

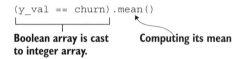

Figure 3.30   When computing the mean of a Boolean array, NumPy first casts it to integers and then computes the mean.

Finally, as we already know, if we compute the mean of an array that contains only ones and zeros, the result is the fraction of ones in that array, which we already used for calculating the churn rate. Because "1" (`True`) in this case is a correct prediction and "0" (`False`) is an incorrect prediction, the resulting number tells us the percentage of correct predictions.

After executing this line of code, we see 0.8 in output. This means that the model predictions matched the actual value 80% of the time, or the model makes correct predictions in 80% of cases. This is what we call the accuracy of the model.

Now we know how to train a model and evaluate its accuracy, but it's still useful to understand how it makes the predictions. In the next section, we try to look inside the models and see how we can interpret the coefficients it learned.

3.3.3   *Model interpretation*

We know that the logistic regression model has two parameters that it learns from data:

- w_0 is the bias term.
- $w = (w_1, w_2, ..., w_n)$ is the weights vector.

We can get the bias term from `model.intercept_[0]`. When we train our model on all features, the bias term is –0.12.

The rest of the weights are stored in `model.coef_[0]`. If we look inside, it's just an array of numbers, which is hard to understand on its own.

To see which feature is associated with each weight, let's use the `get_feature_names` method of the `DictVectorizer`. We can zip the feature names together with the coefficients before looking at them:

```
dict(zip(dv.get_feature_names(), model.coef_[0].round(3)))
```

This prints

```
{'contract=month-to-month': 0.563,
 'contract=one_year': -0.086,
 'contract=two_year': -0.599,
 'dependents=no': -0.03,
 'dependents=yes': -0.092,
```

```
... # the rest of the weights is omitted
'tenure': -0.069,
'totalcharges': 0.0}
```

To understand how the model works, let's consider what happens when we apply this model. To build the intuition, let's train a simpler and smaller model that uses only three variables: `contract`, `tenure`, and `totalcharges`.

The variables `tenure` and `totalcharges` are numeric so we don't need to do any additional preprocessing; we can take them as is. On the other hand, `contract` is a categorical variable, so to be able to use it, we need to apply one-hot encoding.

Let's redo the same steps we did for training, this time using a smaller set of features:

```
small_subset = ['contract', 'tenure', 'totalcharges']
train_dict_small = df_train[small_subset].to_dict(orient='records')
dv_small = DictVectorizer(sparse=False)
dv_small.fit(train_dict_small)

X_small_train = dv_small.transform(train_dict_small)
```

So as not to confuse it with the previous model, we add `small` to all the names. This way, it's clear that we use a smaller model, and it saves us from accidentally overwriting the results we already have. Additionally, we will use it to compare the quality of the small model with the full one.

Let's see which features the small model will use. For that, as previously, we use the `get_feature_names` method from `DictVectorizer`:

```
dv_small.get_feature_names()
```

It outputs the feature names:

```
['contract=month-to-month',
 'contract=one_year',
 'contract=two_year',
 'tenure',
 'totalcharges']
```

There are five features. As expected, we have `tenure` and `totalcharges`, and because they are numeric, their names are not changed.

As for the `contract` variable, it's categorical, so `DictVectorizer` applies the one-hot encoding scheme to convert it to numbers. `contract` has three distinct values: month-to-month, one year, and two years. Thus, one-hot encoding scheme creates three new features: `contract=month-to-month`, `contract=one_year`, and `contract=two_years`.

Let's train the small model on this set of features:

```
model_small = LogisticRegression(solver='liblinear', random_state=1)
model_small.fit(X_small_train, y_train)
```

The model is ready after a few seconds, and we can look inside the weights it learned. Let's first check the bias term:

```
model_small.intercept_[0]
```

It outputs –0.638. Then we can check the other weights, using the same code as previously:

```
dict(zip(dv_small.get_feature_names(), model_small.coef_[0].round(3)))
```

This line of code shows the weight for each feature:

```
{'contract=month-to-month': 0.91,
 'contract=one_year': -0.144,
 'contract=two_year': -1.404,
 'tenure': -0.097,
 'totalcharges': 0.000}
```

Let's put all these weights together in one table and call them w_1, w_2, w_3, w_4, and w_5 (table 3.2).

Table 3.2   The weights of a logistic regression model

	contract				
Bias	**month**	**year**	**2-year**	**tenure**	**charges**
w_0	w_1	w_2	w_3	w_4	w_5
—0.639	0.91	—0.144	—1.404	—0.097	0.0

Now let's take a look at these weights and try to understand what they mean and how we can interpret them.

First, let's think about the bias term and what it means. Recall that in the case of linear regression, it's the baseline prediction: the prediction we would make without knowing anything else about the observation. In the car price prediction project, it would be the price of a car on average. This is not the final prediction; later, this baseline is corrected with other weights.

In the case of logistic regression, it's similar: it's the baseline prediction — or the score we would make on average. Likewise, we later correct this score with the other weights. However, for logistic regression, interpretation is a bit trickier because we also need to apply the sigmoid function before we get the final output. Let's consider an example to help us understand that.

In our case, the bias term has the value of –0.639. This value is negative. If we look at the sigmoid function, we can see that for negative values, the output is lower than 0.5 (figure 3.31). For –0.639, the resulting probability of churning is 34%. This means that on average, a customer is more likely to stay with us than churn.

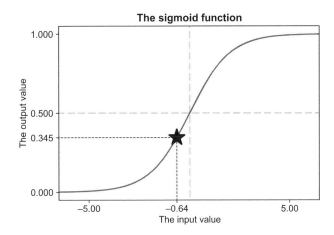

Figure 3.31 The bias term –0.639 on the sigmoid curve. The resulting probability is less than 0.5, so the average customer is more likely to not churn.

The reason why the sign before the bias term is negative is the class imbalance. There are a lot fewer churned users in the training data than non-churned ones, meaning the probability of churn on average is low, so this value for the bias term makes sense.

The next three weights are the weights for the contract variable. Because we use one-hot encoding, we have three `contract` features and three weights, one for each feature:

```
'contract=month-to-month': 0.91,
'contract=one_year': -0.144,
'contract=two_year': -1.404.
```

To build our intuition on how one-hot encoded weights can be understood and interpreted, let's think of a client with a month-to-month contract. The `contract` variable has the following one-hot encoding representation: the first position corresponds to the month-to-month value and is hot, so it's set to "1." The remaining positions correspond to one_year and two_years, so they are cold and set to "0" (figure 3.32).

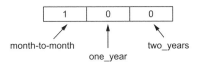

Figure 3.32 The one-hot encoding representation for a customer with a month-to-month contract

We also know the weights w_1, w_2, and w_3 that correspond to `contract=month-to-month`, `contract=one_year`, and `contract=two_years` (figure 3.33).

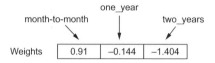

Figure 3.33   The weights of the contract=month-to-month, contract=one_year, and contract=two_years features

To make a prediction, we perform the dot product between the feature vector and the weights, which is multiplication of the values in each position and then summation. The result of the multiplication is 0.91, which turns out to be the same as the weight of the contract=month-to-month feature (figure 3.34).

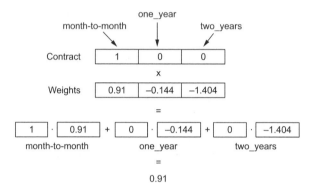

Figure 3.34   The dot product between the one-hot encoding representation of the contract variable and the corresponding weights. The result is 0.91, which is the weight of the hot feature.

Let's consider another example: a client with a two-year contract. In this case, the contract=two_year feature is hot and has a value of "1," and the rest are cold. When we multiply the vector with the one-hot encoding representation of the variable by the weight vector, we get –1.404 (figure 3.35).

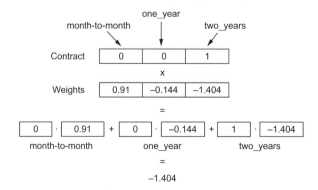

Figure 3.35   For a customer with a two-year contract, the result of the dot product is –1.404.

As we see, during the prediction, only the weight of the hot feature is taken into account, and the rest of the weights are not considered in calculating the score. This makes sense: the cold features have values of zero, and when we multiply by zero, we get zero again (figure 3.36).

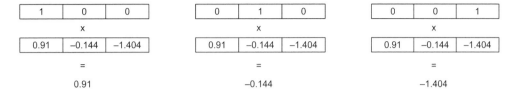

Figure 3.36 When we multiply the one-hot encoding representation of a variable by the weight vector from the model, the result is the weight corresponding to the hot feature.

The interpretation of the signs of the weights for one-hot encoded features follows the same intuition as the bias term. If a weight is positive, the respective feature is an indicator of churn, and vice versa. If it's negative, it's more likely to belong to a non-churning customer.

Let's look again at the weights of the `contract` variable. The first weight for `contract=month-to-month` is positive, so customers with this type of contract are more likely to churn than not. The other two features, `contract=one_year` and `contract=two_years`, have negative signs, so such clients are more likely to remain loyal to the company (figure 3.37).

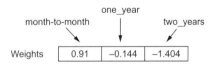

Figure 3.37 The sign of the weight matters. If it's positive, it's a good indicator of churn; if it's negative, it indicates a loyal customer.

The magnitude of the weights also matters. For `two_year`, the weight is –1.404, which is greater in magnitude than –0.144 — the weight for `one_year`. So, a two-year contract is a stronger indicator of not churning than a one-year one. It confirms the feature importance analysis we did previously. The risk ratios (the risk of churning) for this set of features are 1.55 for monthly, 0.44 for one-year, and 0.10 for two-year (figure 3.38).

Now let's have a look at the numerical features. We have two of them: `tenure` and `totalcharges`. The weight of the `tenure` feature is –0.097, which has a negative sign. This means the same thing: the feature is an indicator of no churn. We already know

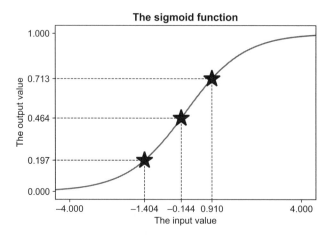

Figure 3.38 The weights for the contract features and their translation to probabilities. For `contract=two_year`, the weight is –1.404, which translates to very low probability of churn. For `contract=one_year`, the weight is –0.144, so the probability is moderate. And for `contract=month-to-month`, the weight is 0.910, and the probability is quite high.

from the feature importance analysis that the longer clients stay with us, the less likely they are to churn. The correlation between `tenure` and churn is –0.35, which is also a negative number. The weight of this feature confirms it: for every month that the client spends with us, the total score gets lower by 0.097.

The other numerical feature, `totalchanges`, has weight of zero. Because it's zero, no matter what the value of this feature is, the model will never consider it, so this feature is not really important for making the predictions.

To understand it better, let's consider a couple of examples. For the first example, let's imagine we have a user with a month-to-month contract, who spent a year with us and paid $1,000 (figure 3.39).

$$-0.639 + 0.91 - 12 \cdot 0.097 + 0 \cdot 1000 = -0.893$$

| **Bias** | **Monthly contract** | **12 months of tenure** | **Total charges don't matter.** | **Negative, so low likelihood of churn** |

Figure 3.39 The score the model calculates for a customer with a month-to-month contract and 12 months of tenure

This is the prediction we make for this customer:

- We start with the baseline score. It's the bias term with the value of –0.639.
- Because it's a month-to-month contract, we add 0.91 to this value and get 0.271. Now the score becomes positive, so it may mean that the client is going to churn. We know that a monthly contract is a strong indicator of churning.

- Next, we consider the `tenure` variable. For each month that the customer stayed with us, we subtract 0.097 from the score so far. Thus, we get $0.271 - 12 \cdot 0.097 = -0.893$. Now the score is negative again, so the likelihood of churn decreases.
- Now we add the amount of money the customer paid us (`totalcharges`) multiplied by the weight of this feature, but because it's zero, we don't do anything. The result stays –0.893.
- The final score is a negative number, so we believe that the customer is not very likely to churn soon.
- To see the actual probability of churn, we compute the sigmoid of the score, and it's approximately 0.29. We can treat this as the probability that this customer will churn.

If we have another client with a yearly contract who stayed 24 months with us and spent \$2,000, the score is –2.823 (figure 3.40).

$$-0.639 + 0.144 - 24 \cdot 0.097 + 0 \cdot 2000 = -2.823$$

| **Bias** | **Yearly contract** | **24 months of tenure** | **Total charges don't matter.** | **Negative, very low likelihood of churn** |

Figure 3.40 The score that the model calculates for a customer with a yearly contract and 24 months of tenure

After taking sigmoid, the score of –2.823 becomes 0.056, so the probability of churn for this customer is even lower (figure 3.41).

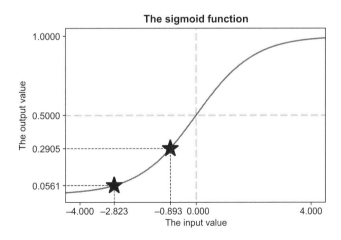

Figure 3.41 The scores of –2.823 and –0.893 translated to probability: 0.05 and 0.29, respectively

3.3.4   *Using the model*

Now we know a lot better how logistic regression, and we can also interpret what our model learned and understand how it makes the predictions.

Additionally, we applied the model to the validation set, computed the probabilities of churning for every customer there, and concluded that the model is 80% accurate. In the next chapter we will evaluate whether this number is satisfactory, but for now, let's try to use the model we trained. Now we can apply the model to customers for scoring them. It's quite easy.

First, we take a customer we want to score and put all the variable values in a dictionary:

```
customer = {
    'customerid': '8879-zkjof',
    'gender': 'female',
    'seniorcitizen': 0,
    'partner': 'no',
    'dependents': 'no',
    'tenure': 41,
    'phoneservice': 'yes',
    'multiplelines': 'no',
    'internetservice': 'dsl',
    'onlinesecurity': 'yes',
    'onlinebackup': 'no',
    'deviceprotection': 'yes',
    'techsupport': 'yes',
    'streamingtv': 'yes',
    'streamingmovies': 'yes',
    'contract': 'one_year',
    'paperlessbilling': 'yes',
    'paymentmethod': 'bank_transfer_(automatic)',
    'monthlycharges': 79.85,
    'totalcharges': 3320.75,
}
```

> **NOTE** When we prepare items for prediction, they should undergo the same preprocessing steps we did for training the model. If we don't do it in exactly the same way, the model might not get things it expects to see, and, in this case, the predictions could get really off. This is why in the previous example, in the customer dictionary, the field names and string values are lowercased and spaces are replaced with underscores.

Now we can use our model to see whether this customer is going to churn. Let's do it.

First, we convert this dictionary to a matrix by using the DictVectorizer:

```
X_test = dv.transform([customer])
```

The input to the vectorizer is a list with one item: we want to score only one customer. The output is a matrix with features, and this matrix contains only one row — the features for this one customer:

```
[[   0.  ,   1.  ,   0.  ,   1.  ,   0.  ,   0.  ,    0.  ,
     1.  ,   1.  ,   0.  ,   1.  ,   0.  ,   0.  ,   79.85,
     1.  ,   0.  ,   0.  ,   1.  ,   0.  ,   0.  ,    0.  ,
     0.  ,   1.  ,   0.  ,   1.  ,   1.  ,   0.  ,    1.  ,
     0.  ,   0.  ,   0.  ,   0.  ,   1.  ,   0.  ,    0.  ,
     0.  ,   1.  ,   0.  ,   0.  ,   1.  ,   0.  ,    0.  ,
     1.  ,  41.  , 3320.75]]
```

We see a bunch of one-hot encoding features (ones and zeros) as well as some numeric ones (`monthlycharges`, `tenure`, and `totalcharges`).

Now we take this matrix and put it into the trained model:

```
model.predict_proba(X_test)
```

The output is a matrix with predictions. For each customer, it outputs two numbers, which are the probability of staying with the company and the probability of churn. Because there's only one customer, we get a tiny NumPy array with one row and two columns:

```
[[0.93, 0.07]]
```

All we need from the matrix is the number at the first row and second column: the probability of churning for this customer. To select this number from the array, we use the brackets operator:

```
model.predict_proba(X_test)[0, 1]
```

We used this operator to select the second column from the array. However, this time there's only one row, so we can explicitly ask NumPy to return the value from that row. Because indexes start from 0 in NumPy, `[0, 1]` means first row, second column.

When we execute this line, we see that the output is 0.073, so that the probability that this customer will churn is only 7%. It's less than 50%, so we will not send this customer a promotional mail.

We can try to score another client:

```
customer = {
    'gender': 'female',
    'seniorcitizen': 1,
    'partner': 'no',
    'dependents': 'no',
    'phoneservice': 'yes',
    'multiplelines': 'yes',
    'internetservice': 'fiber_optic',
    'onlinesecurity': 'no',
    'onlinebackup': 'no',
    'deviceprotection': 'no',
    'techsupport': 'no',
    'streamingtv': 'yes',
    'streamingmovies': 'no',
    'contract': 'month-to-month',
```

```
        'paperlessbilling': 'yes',
        'paymentmethod': 'electronic_check',
        'tenure': 1,
        'monthlycharges': 85.7,
        'totalcharges': 85.7
}
```

Let's make a prediction:

```
X_test = dv.transform([customer])
model.predict_proba(X_test)[0, 1]
```

The output of the model is 83% likelihood of churn, so we should send this client a promotional mail in the hope of retaining them.

So far, we've built intuition on how logistic regression works, how to train it with Scikit-learn, and how to apply it to new data. We haven't covered the evaluation of the results yet; this is what we will do in the next chapter.

3.4 *Next steps*

3.4.1 *Exercises*

You can try a couple of things to learn the topic better:

- In the previous chapter, we implemented many things ourselves, including linear regression and dataset splitting. In this chapter we learned how to use Scikit-learn for that. Try to redo the project from the previous chapter using Scikit-learn. To use linear regression, you need `LinearRegression` from the `sklearn.linear_model` package. To use regularized regression, you need to import `Ridge` from the same package `sklearn.linear_model`.
- We looked at feature importance metrics to get some insights into the dataset but did not really use this information for other purposes. One way to use this information could be removing features that aren't useful from the dataset to make the model simpler, faster, and potentially better. Try to exclude the two least useful features (`gender` and `phoneservices`) from the training data matrix, and see what happens to validation accuracy. What if we remove the most useful feature (`contract`)?

3.4.2 *Other projects*

We can use classification in numerous ways to solve real-life problems, and now, after learning the materials of this chapter, you should have enough knowledge to apply logistic regression to solve similar problems. In particular, we suggest these:

- Classification models are often used for marketing purposes, and one of the problems it solves is *lead scoring*. A *lead* is a potential customer who may convert (become an actual customer) or not. In this case, the conversion is the target we want to predict. You can take a dataset from https://www.kaggle.com/ashydv/leads-dataset and build a model for that. You may notice that the lead-scoring problem is similar to churn prediction, but in one case, we want to get a new client to sign a contract with us, and in another case, we want a client not to cancel the contract.

- Another popular application of classification is default prediction, which is estimating the risk of a customer's not paying back a loan. In this case, the variable we want to predict is default, and it also has two outcomes: whether the customer managed to pay back the loan in time (good customer) or not (default). You can find many datasets online for training a model, such as https://archive.ics.uci.edu/ml/datasets/default+of+credit+card+clients (or the same one available via Kaggle: https://www.kaggle.com/pratjain/credit-card-default).

Summary

- The *risk* of a categorical feature tells us if a group that has the feature will have the condition we model. For churn, values lower than 1.0 indicate low risk of churning, whereas values higher than 1.0 indicate high risk of churning. It tells us which features are important for predicting the target variable and helps us better understand the problem we're solving.

- Mutual information measures the degree of (in)dependence between a categorical variable and the target. It's a good way of determining important features: the higher the mutual information is, the more important the feature.

- Correlation measures the dependence between two numerical variables, and it can be used for determining if a numerical feature is useful for predicting the target variable.

- One-hot encoding gives us a way to represent categorical variables as numbers. Without it, it wouldn't be possible to easily use these variables in a model. Machine learning models typically expect all input variables to be numeric, so having an encoding scheme is crucial if we want to use categorical features in modeling.

- We can implement one-hot encoding by using `DictVectorizer` from Scikit-learn. It automatically detects categorical variables and applies the one-hot encoding scheme to them while leaving numerical variables intact. It's very convenient to use and doesn't require a lot of coding on our side.

- Logistic regression is a linear model, just like linear regression. The difference is that logistic regression has an extra step at the end: it applies the sigmoid function to convert the scores to probabilities (a number between zero and one). That allows us to use it for classification. The output is the probability of belonging to a positive class (churn, in our case).

- When the data is prepared, training logistic regression is very simple: we use the `LogisticRegression` class from Scikit-learn and invoke the `fit` function.

- The model outputs probabilities, not hard predictions. To binarize the output, we cut the predictions at a certain threshold. If the probability is greater than or equal to 0.5, we predict `True` (churn), and `False` (no churn) otherwise. This allows us to use the model for solving our problem: predicting customers who churn.
- The weights of the logistic regression model are easy to interpret and explain, especially when it comes to the categorical variables encoded using the one-hot encoding scheme. It helps us understand the behavior of the model better and explain to others what it's doing and how it's working.

In the next chapter we will continue with this project on churn prediction. We will look at ways of evaluating binary classifiers and then use this information for tuning the model's performance.

Answers to exercises

- Exercise 3.1 B) The percentage of `True` elements
- Exercise 3.2 A) It will keep a numeric variable as is and encode only the categorical variable.
- Exercise 3.3 B) Sigmoid converts the output to a value between zero and one.

Evaluation metrics *for classification*

In this chapter, we continue with the project we started in the previous chapter: churn prediction. We have already downloaded the dataset, performed the initial preprocessing and exploratory data analysis, and trained the model that predicts whether customers will churn. We have also evaluated this model on the validation dataset and concluded that it has 80% accuracy.

The question we postponed until now was whether 80% accuracy is good and what it actually means in terms of the quality of our model. We answer this question in this chapter and discuss other ways of evaluating a binary classification model: the confusion table, precision and recall, the ROC curve, and AUC.

This chapter provides a lot of complex information, but the evaluation metrics we cover here are essential for doing practical machine learning. Don't worry if you don't immediately understand all the details of the different evaluation metrics: it requires time and practice. Feel free to come back to this chapter to revisit the finer points.

4.1   Evaluation metrics

We have already built a binary classification model for predicting churning customers. Now we need to be able to determine how good it is.

For this, we use a *metric* — a function that looks at the predictions the model makes and compares them with the actual values. Then, based on the comparison, it calculates how good the model is. This is quite useful: we can use it to compare different models and select the one with the best metric value.

There are different kinds of metrics. In chapter 2, we used RMSE (root mean squared error) to evaluate regression models. However, this metric can be used only for regression models and doesn't work for classification.

For evaluating classification models, we have other more suitable metrics. In this section, we cover the most common evaluation metrics for binary classification, starting with accuracy, which we already saw in chapter 3.

4.1.1   Classification accuracy

As you probably remember, the accuracy of a binary classification model is the percentage of correct predictions it makes (figure 4.1).

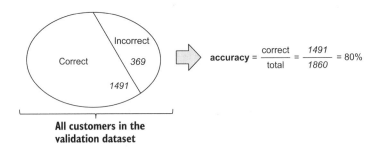

$$\text{accuracy} = \frac{\text{correct}}{\text{total}} = \frac{1491}{1860} = 80\%$$

Figure 4.1   The accuracy of a model is the fraction of predictions that turned out to be correct.

This accuracy is the simplest way to evaluate a classifier: by counting the number of cases in which our model turned out to be right, we can learn a lot about the model's behavior and quality.

Computing accuracy on the validation dataset is easy — we simply calculate the fraction of correct predictions:

```
y_pred = model.predict_proba(X_val)[:, 1]          ◁———┐   Gets the predictions
churn = y_pred >= 0.5              ◁———┐                ❶  from the model
(churn == y_val).mean()   ◁———┐        Makes "hard"
                              ❷        predictions
        Computes the accuracy  ❸
```

We first apply the model to the validation set to get the predictions in ❶. These predictions are probabilities, so we cut them at 0.5 in ❷. Finally, we calculate the fraction of predictions that matched reality in ❷.

The result is 0.8016, which means that our model is 80% accurate.

The first thing we should ask ourselves is why we chose 0.5 as the threshold and not any other number. That was an arbitrary choice, but it's actually not difficult to check other thresholds as well: we can just loop over all possible threshold candidates and compute the accuracy for each. Then we can choose the one with the best accuracy score.

Even though it's easy to implement accuracy ourselves, we can use existing implementations as well. The Scikit-learn library offers a variety of metrics, including accuracy and many others that we will use later. You can find these metrics in the metrics package.

We'll continue working on the same notebook that we started in chapter 3. Let's open it and add the `import` statement to import accuracy from Scikit-learn's metrics package:

```
from sklearn.metrics import accuracy_score
```

Now we can loop over different thresholds and check which one gives the best accuracy:

```
thresholds = np.linspace(0, 1, 11)       ◁———┐   Creates an array with
                                                 different thresholds:
                                                 0.0, 0.1, 0.2, and so on
┌─▷ for t in thresholds:
│       churn = y_pred >= t
│       acc = accuracy_score(y_val, churn)       ┐  Uses the accuracy_score
│       print('%0.2f %0.3f' % (t, acc))   ◁——┐      function from Scikit-learn
│                                                   for computing accuracy
│   Loops over each        Prints the thresholds and the
│   threshold value        accuracy values to standard output
```

In this code, we first create an array with thresholds. We use the `linspace` function from NumPy for that: it takes two numbers (0 and 1, in our case) and the number of elements the array should have (11). As a result, we get an array with the numbers 0.0,

0.1, 0.2, ..., 1.0. You can learn more about `linspace` and other NumPy functions in appendix C.

We use these numbers as thresholds: we loop over them, and for each one, we calculate the accuracy. Finally, we print the thresholds and the accuracy scores so we can decide which threshold is the best.

When we execute the code, it prints the following:

```
0.00 0.261
0.10 0.595
0.20 0.690
0.30 0.755
0.40 0.782
0.50 0.802
0.60 0.790
0.70 0.774
0.80 0.742
0.90 0.739
1.00 0.739
```

As we see, using the threshold of 0.5 gives us the best accuracy. Typically, 0.5 is a good threshold value to start with, but we should always try other threshold values to make sure 0.5 is the best choice.

To make it more visual, we can use Matplotlib to create a plot that shows how accuracy changes depending on the threshold. We repeat the same process as previously, but instead of just printing the accuracy scores, we first put the values to a list:

Creates different threshold values (this time 21 instead of 11)   **Creates an empty list to hold the accuracy values**

```
thresholds = np.linspace(0, 1, 21)
accuracies = []
for t in thresholds:
    acc = accuracy_score(y_val, y_pred >= t)
    accuracies.append(acc)
```

Calculates the accuracy for a given threshold

Records the accuracy for this threshold

And then we plot these values using Matplotlib:

```
plt.plot(thresholds, accuracies)
```

After executing this line, we should see a plot that shows the relationship between the threshold and the accuracy (figure 4.2). As we already know, the 0.5 threshold is the best in terms of accuracy.

So, the best threshold is 0.5, and the best accuracy for this model that we can achieve is 80%.

In the previous chapter, we trained a simpler model: we called it model_small. It was based on only three variables: `contract`, `tenure`, and `totalcharges`.

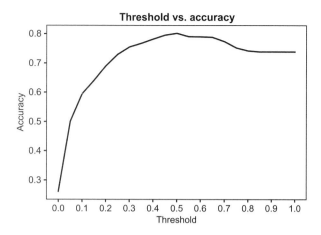

Figure 4.2 **Accuracy of our model evaluated at different thresholds. The best accuracy is achieved when cutting the predictions at the 0.5 threshold: if a prediction is higher than 0.5, we predict "churn," and otherwise, we predict "no churn."**

Let's also check its accuracy. For that, we first make predictions on the validation dataset and then compute the accuracy score:

```
val_dict_small = df_val[small_subset].to_dict(orient='records')

X_small_val = dv_small.transform(val_dict_small)
y_pred_small = model_small.predict_proba(X_small_val)[:, 1]

churn_small = y_pred_small >= 0.5
accuracy_score(y_val, churn_small)
```

Applies one-hot encoding to the validation data

Predicts churn using the small model

Calculates the accuracy of the predictions

When we run this code, we see that the accuracy of the small model is 76%. So, the large model is actually 4% more accurate than the small model.

However, this still doesn't tell us whether 80% (or 76%) is a good accuracy score.

4.1.2 *Dummy baseline*

Although it seems like a decent number, to understand whether 80% is actually good, we need to relate it to something — for example, a simple baseline that's easy to understand. One such baseline could be a dummy model that always predicts the same value.

In our example, the dataset is imbalanced, and we don't have many churned users. So, the dummy model can always predict the majority class — "no churn." In other words, this model will always output False, regardless of the features. This is not a super useful model, but we can use it as a baseline and compare it with the other two models.

Let's create this baseline prediction:

Gets the number of customers in the validation set

```
size_val = len(y_val)
baseline = np.repeat(False, size_val)
```

Creates an array with only False elements

To create an array with the baseline predictions, we first need to determine how many elements are in the validation set.

Next, we create an array of dummy predictions — all the elements of this array are False values. We do this using the `repeat` function from NumPy: it takes in an element and repeats it as many times as we ask. For more details about the `repeat` function and other NumPy functions, please refer to appendix C.

Now we can check the accuracy of this baseline prediction using the same code as we used previously:

```
accuracy_score(baseline, y_val)
```

When we run this code, it shows 0.738. This means that the accuracy of the baseline model is around 74% (figure 4.3).

```
size_val = len(y_val)
baseline = np.repeat(False, size_val)
baseline
```

```
array([False, False, False, ..., False, False, False])
```

```
accuracy_score(baseline, y_val)
```

```
0.7387096774193549
```

Figure 4.3   The baseline is a "model" that always predicts the same value for all the customers. The accuracy of this baseline is 74%.

As we see, the small model is only 2% better than the naive baseline, and the large one is 6% better. If we think about all the trouble we have gone through to train this large model, 6% doesn't seem like a significant improvement over the dummy baseline.

Churn prediction is a complex problem, and maybe this improvement is great. However, that's not evident from the accuracy score alone. According to accuracy, our model is only slightly better than a dummy model that treats all the customers as non-churning and doesn't attempt to keep any of them.

Thus, we need other metrics — other ways of measuring the quality of our model. These metrics are based on the confusion table, the concept that we cover in the next section.

4.2 Confusion table

Even though accuracy is easy to understand, it's not always the best metric. In fact, it sometimes can be misleading. We've already seen this occur: the accuracy of our model is 80%, and although that seems like a good number, it's just 6% better than the accuracy of a dummy model that always outputs the same prediction of "no churn."

This situation typically happens when we have a class imbalance (more instances of one class than another). We know that this is definitely the case for our problem: 74% of customers did not churn, and only 26% did churn.

For such cases, we need a different way of measuring the quality of our models. We have a few options, and most of them are based on the confusion table: a table that concisely represents every possible outcome for our model's predictions.

4.2.1 Introduction to the confusion table

We know that for a binary classification model, we can have only two possible predictions: True and False. In our case, we can predict that a customer is either going to churn (True) or not (False).

When we apply the model to the entire validation dataset with customers, we split it into two parts (figure 4.4):

- Customers for whom the model predicts "churn"
- Customers for whom the model predicts "no churn"

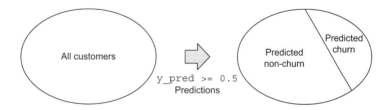

Figure 4.4   Our model splits all the customers in the validation dataset into two groups: customers who we think will churn and customers who will not.

Only two possible correct outcomes can occur: again, True or False. A customer has either actually churned (True) or not (False).

This means that by using the ground truth information — the information about the target variable — we can again split the dataset into two parts (figure 4.5):

- The customers who churned
- The customers who didn't churn

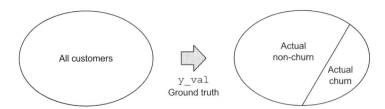

Figure 4.5   Using the ground truth data, we can split the validation dataset into two groups: customers who actually churned and customers who didn't.

When we make a prediction, it will either turn out to be correct or not:

- If we predict "churn," the customer may indeed churn, or they may not.
- If we predict "no churn," it's possible that the customer indeed doesn't churn, but it's also possible that they do churn.

This gives us four possible outcomes (figure 4.6):

- We predict False, and the answer is False.
- We predict False, and the answer is True.
- We predict True, and the answer is False.
- We predict True, and the answer is True.

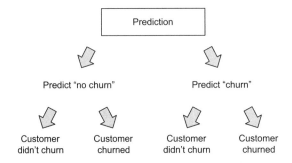

Figure 4.6   There are four possible outcomes: we predict "churn," and the customers either churn or do not, and we predict "no churn," and the customers again either churn or do not.

Two of these situations — the first and last ones — are good: the prediction matched the actual value. The two remaining ones are bad: we didn't make a correct prediction.

Each of these four situations has its own name (figure 4.7):

- True negative (TN): we predict False ("no churn"), and the actual label is also False ("no churn").
- True positive (TP): we predict True ("churn"), and the actual label is True ("churn").

- False negative (FN): we predict False ("no churn"), but it's actually True (the customer churned).
- False positive (FP): we predict True ("churn"), but it's actually False (the customer stayed with us).

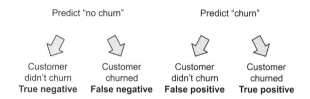

Predict "no churn"   Predict "churn"

Customer	Customer	Customer	Customer
didn't churn	churned	didn't churn	churned
True negative	**False negative**	**False positive**	**True positive**

Figure 4.7   Each of the four possible outcomes has its own name: true negative, false negative, false positive, and true positive.

It's visually helpful to arrange these outcomes in a table. We can put the predicted classes (False and True) in the columns and the actual classes (False and True) in the rows (figure 4.8).

Predictions

	False ("no churn")	True ("churn")
Actual False ("no churn")	TN	FP
Actual True ("churn")	FN	TP

Figure 4.8   We can organize the outcomes in a table — the predicted values as columns and the actual values as rows. This way, we break down all prediction scenarios into four distinct groups: TN (true negative), TP (true positive), FN (false negative), and FP (false positive).

When we substitute the number of times each outcome happens, we get the confusion table for our model (figure 4.9).

Predictions

	False ("no churn")	True ("churn")
Actual False ("no churn")	1202	172
Actual True ("churn")	197	289

Figure 4.9   In the confusion table, each cell contains the number of times each outcome happens.

Calculating the values in the cells of the confusion matrix is quite easy with NumPy. Next, we see how to do it.

4.2.2 *Calculating the confusion table with NumPy*

To help us understand our confusion table better, we can visually depict what it does to the validation dataset (figure 4.10).

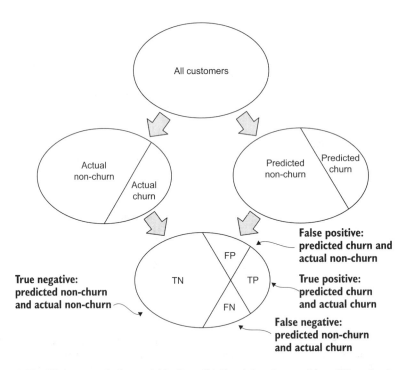

Figure 4.10 When we apply the model to the validation dataset, we get four different outcomes (TN, FP, TP, and FN).

To calculate the confusion table, we need to do these steps:

- First, the predictions split the dataset into two parts: the part for which we predict True ("churn") and the part for which we predict False ("no churn").
- At the same time, the target variable splits this dataset into two different parts: the customers who actually churned ("1" in y_val) and the customers who didn't ("0" in y_val).
- When we combine these splits, we get four groups of customers, which are exactly the four different outcomes from the confusion table.

Translating these steps to NumPy is straightforward:

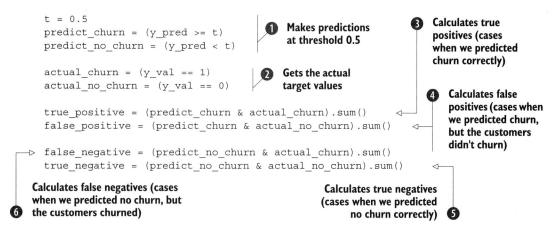

```
t = 0.5
predict_churn = (y_pred >= t)
predict_no_churn = (y_pred < t)

actual_churn = (y_val == 1)
actual_no_churn = (y_val == 0)

true_positive = (predict_churn & actual_churn).sum()
false_positive = (predict_churn & actual_no_churn).sum()

false_negative = (predict_no_churn & actual_churn).sum()
true_negative = (predict_no_churn & actual_no_churn).sum()
```

① Makes predictions at threshold 0.5

② Gets the actual target values

③ Calculates true positives (cases when we predicted churn correctly)

④ Calculates false positives (cases when we predicted churn, but the customers didn't churn)

⑥ Calculates false negatives (cases when we predicted no churn, but the customers churned)

⑤ Calculates true negatives (cases when we predicted no churn correctly)

We begin by making predictions at the threshold of 0.5.

The results are two NumPy arrays:

- In the first array (predict_churn), an element is True if the model thinks the respective customer is going to churn and False otherwise.
- Likewise, in the second array (predict_no_churn), True means that the model thinks the customer isn't going to churn.

The second array, predict_no_churn, is the exact opposite of predict_churn: if an element is True in predict_churn, it's False in predict_no_churn and vice versa (figure 4.11). This is the first split of the validation dataset into two parts — the one that's based on the predictions.

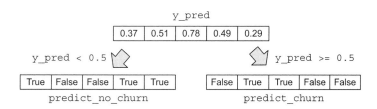

Figure 4.11 Splitting the predictions into two Boolean NumPy arrays: predict_churn if the probability is higher than 0.5, and predict_no_churn if it's lower

Next, we record the actual values of the target variable in **②**. The results are two NumPy arrays as well (figure 4.12):

- If the customer churned (value "1"), then the respective element of actual_churn is True, and it's False otherwise.
- For actual_no_churn it's exactly the opposite: it's True when the customer didn't churn.

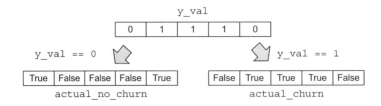

**Figure 4.12   Splitting the array with actual values into two Boolean NumPy arrays:
`actual_no_churn` if the customer didn't churn (`y_val == 0`) and `actual_churn`
if the customer churned (`y_val == 1`)**

That's the second split of the dataset — the one that's based on the target variable.

Now we combine these two splits — or, to be exact, these four NumPy arrays.

To calculate the number of true positive outcomes in ❸, we use the logical "and"
operator of NumPy (`&`) and the `sum` method:

```
true_positive = (predict_churn & actual_churn).sum()
```

The logical "and" operator evaluates to True only if both values are True. If at least
one is False or both are False, it's False. In case of `true_positive`, it will be True only
if we predict "churn" and the customer actually churned (figure 4.13).

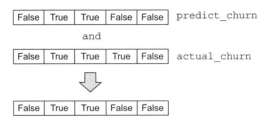

**Figure 4.13   Applying the element-wise and operator (`&`) to two NumPy arrays,
`predict_churn` and `actual_churn`; this creates another array with True in
any position where both arrays contained True and False in all others.**

Then we use the `sum` method from NumPy, which simply counts how many `True` values
are in the array. It does that by first casting the Boolean array to integers and then
summing it (figure 4.14). We already saw similar behavior in the previous chapter
when we used the `mean` method.

**Figure 4.14   Invoking the `sum` method on a Boolean array: we get the number
of elements in this array that are True.**

As a result, we have the number of true positive cases. The other values are computed similarly in lines ❹, ❺, and ❻.

Now we just need to put all these values together in a NumPy array:

```
confusion_table = np.array(
 [[true_negative, false_positive],
 [false_negative, true_positive]])
```

When we print it, we get the following numbers:

```
[[1202, 172],
 [ 197, 289]]
```

The absolute numbers may be difficult to understand, so we can turn them into fractions by dividing each value by the total number of items:

```
confusion_table / confusion_table.sum()
```

This prints the following numbers:

```
[[0.646, 0.092],
[0.105, 0.155]]
```

We can summarize the results in a table (table 4.1). We see that the model predicts negative values quite well: 65% of the predictions are true negatives. However, it makes quite a few mistakes of both types: the number of false positives and false negatives is roughly equal (9% and 11%, respectively).

Table 4.1 The confusion table for the churn classifier at the threshold of 0.5. We see that it's easy for the model to correctly predict non-churning users, but it's more difficult for it to identify churning users.

Full model with all features			
		Predicted	
		False	True
Actual	False	1202 (65%)	172 (9%)
	True	197 (11%)	289 (15%)

This table gives us a better understanding of the performance of the model — it's now possible to break down the performance into different components and understand where the model makes mistakes. We actually see that the performance of the model is not great: it makes quite a few errors when trying to identify users that will churn. This is something we couldn't see with the accuracy score alone.

We can repeat the same process for the small model using exactly the same code (table 4.2).

Table 4.2   The confusion table for the small model

		Predicted	
Small model with three features			
		False	**True**
Actual	**False**	1189 (63%)	185 (10%)
	True	248 (12%)	238 (13%)

When we compare the smaller model with the full model, we see that it's 2% worse at correctly identifying non-churning users (63% versus 65% for true negatives) and 2% worse at correctly identifying churning users (13% versus 15% for true positives), which together accounts for the 4% difference between the accuracies of these two models (76% versus 80%).

The values from the confusion table serve as the basis for many other evaluation metrics. For example, we can calculate accuracy by taking all the correct predictions — TN and TP together — and dividing that number by the total number of observations in all four cells of the table:

$$accuracy = (TN + TP) \ / \ (TN + TP + FN + FP)$$

Apart from accuracy, we can calculate other metrics based on the values from the confusion table. The most useful ones are precision and recall, which we will cover next.

Exercise 4.1
What is a false positive?

- a   A customer for whom we predicted "not churn," but they stopped using our services
- b   A customer for whom we predicted "churn," but they didn't churn
- c   A customer for whom we predicted "churn," and they churned

4.2.3   *Precision and recall*

As already mentioned, accuracy can be misleading when dealing with imbalanced datasets such as ours. Other metrics are helpful to use for such cases: precision and recall.

Both precision and recall are calculated from the values of the confusion table. They both help us understand the quality of the model in cases of class imbalance.

Let's start with precision. The precision of a model tells us how many of the positive predictions turned out to be correct. It's the fraction of correctly predicted positive examples. In our case, it's the number of customers who actually churned (TP) out of all the customers we thought would churn (TP + FP) (figure 4.15):

$$P = TP / (TP + FP)$$

For our model, the precision is 62%:

$$P = 289 / (289 + 172) = 172 / 461 = 0.62$$

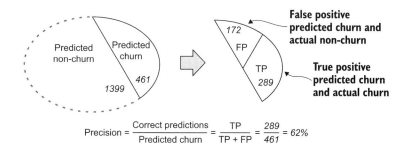

Figure 4.15   The precision of a model is the fraction of correct predictions (TP) among all positive predictions (TP + FP).

Recall is the fraction of correctly classified positive examples among all positive examples. In our case, to calculate recall we first look at all the customers who churned and see how many of them we managed to identify correctly.

The formula for calculating recall is

$$R = TP / (TP + FN)$$

Like in the formula for precision, the numerator is the number of true positives, but the denominator is different: it's the number of all positive examples (y_val == 1) in our validation dataset (figure 4.16).

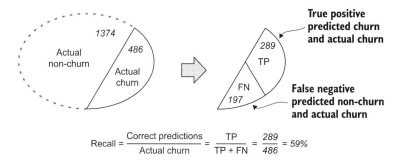

Figure 4.16   The recall of a model is the fraction of correctly predicted churning customers (TP) among all customers who churned (TP + FN).

For our model, the recall is 59%:

$$R = 286 \,/\, (289 + 197) = 289 \,/\, 486 = 0.59$$

The difference between precision and recall may seem subtle at first. In both cases, we look at the number of correct predictions, but the difference is in the denominators (figure 4.17):

- Precision: what's the percent of correct predictions (TP) among customers predicted as churning (TP + FP)?
- Recall: what's the percentage correctly predicted as churning (TP) among all churned customers (TP + FN)?

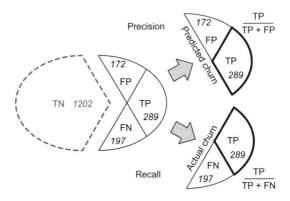

Figure 4.17 Both precision and recall look at the correct predictions (TP), but the denominators are different. For precision, it's the number of customers predicted as churning, whereas for recall, it's the number of customers who churned.

We can also see that both precision and recall don't take true negatives into account (figure 4.17). This is exactly why they are good evaluation metrics for imbalanced datasets. For situations with class imbalance, true negatives typically outnumber everything else — but at the same time, they are also often not really interesting for us. Let's see why.

The goal of our project is to identify customers who are likely to churn. Once we do, we can send them promotional messages in the hopes that they'll change their mind.

When doing this, we make two types of mistakes:

- We accidentally send messages to people who weren't going to churn — these people are the false positives of the model.
- We also sometimes fail to identify people who are actually going to churn. We don't send messages to these people — they are our false negatives.

Precision and recall help us quantify these errors.

Precision helps us understand how many people received a promotional message by mistake. The better the precision, the fewer false positives we have. The precision of 62% means that 62% of the reached customers indeed were going to churn (our true positives), whereas the remaining 38% were not (false positives).

Recall helps us understand how many of the churning customers we failed to find. The better the recall, the fewer false negatives we have. The recall of 59% means that we reach only 59% of all churning users (true positives) and fail to identify the remaining 41% (false negatives).

As we can see, in both cases, we don't really need to know the number of true negatives: even though we can correctly identify them as not churning, we aren't going to do anything with them.

Although the accuracy of 80% might suggest that the model is great, looking at its precision and recall tells us that it actually makes quite a few errors. This is typically not a deal-breaker: with machine learning it's inevitable that models make mistakes, and at least now we have a better and more realistic understanding of the performance of our churn-prediction model.

Precision and recall are useful metrics, but they describe the performance of a classifier only at a certain threshold. Often it's useful to have a metric that summarizes the performance of a classifier for all possible threshold choices. We look at such metrics in the next section.

Exercise 4.2

What is precision?

- a The percent of correctly identified churned customers in the validation dataset
- b The percent of customers who actually churned among the customers who we predicted as churning

---

Exercise 4.3

What is recall?

- a The percent of correctly identified churned customers among all churned customers
- b The percent of correctly classified customers among customers we predicted as churning

---

4.3   *ROC curve and AUC score*

The metrics we have covered so far work only with binary predictions — when we have only True and False values in the output. However, we do have ways to evaluate the performance of a model across all possible threshold choices. ROC curves is one of these options.

ROC stands for "receiver operating characteristic," and it was initially designed for evaluating the strength of radar detectors during World War II. It was used to assess how well a detector could separate two signals: whether an airplane was there or not. Nowadays it's used for a similar purpose: it shows how well a model can separate two classes, positive and negative. In our case, these classes are "churn" and "no churn."

We need two metrics for ROC curves: TPR and FPR, or true positive rate and false positive rate. Let's take a look at these metrics.

4.3.1   True positive rate and false positive rate

The ROC curve is based on two quantities, FPR and TPR:

- False positive rate (FPR): the fraction of false positives among all negative examples
- True positive rate (TPR): the fraction of true positives among all positive examples

Like precision and recall, these values are based on the confusion matrix. We can calculate them using the following formulas:

$$FPR = FP \ / \ (FP + TN)$$

$$TPR = TP \ / \ (TP + FN)$$

FPR and TPR involve two separate parts of the confusion table (figure 4.18):

- For FPR, we look at the first row of the table: the fraction of false positives among all negatives.
- For TPR, we look at the second row of the table: the fraction of true positives among all positives.

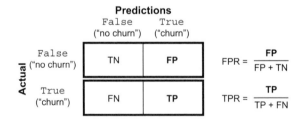

Figure 4.18   For calculating FPR, we look at the first row of the confusion table, and for calculating TPR, we look at the second row.

Let's calculate these values for our model (figure 4.19):

$$FPR = 172 \ / \ 1374 = 12.5\%$$

FPR is the fraction of users we predicted as churning among everybody who didn't churn. A small value for FPR tells us that a model is good — it has few false positives:

$$TPR = 289 \; / \; 486 = 59\%$$

TPR is the fraction of users who we predicted as churning among everybody who actually did churn. Note that TPR is the same as recall, so the higher the TPR is, the better.

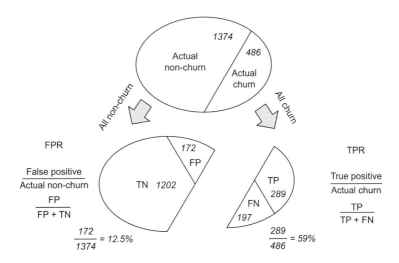

Figure 4.19   FPR is the fraction of false positives among all non-churning customers: the smaller the FPR, the better. TPR is the fraction of true positives among all churning customers: the larger the TPR, the better.

However, we still consider FPR and TPR metrics at only one threshold value — in our case, 0.5. To be able to use them for ROC curves, we need to calculate these metrics for many different threshold values.

4.3.2   *Evaluating a model at multiple thresholds*

Binary classification models, such as logistic regression, typically output a probability — a score between zero and one. To make actual predictions, we binarize the output by setting some threshold to get only True and False values.

Instead of evaluating the model at one particular threshold, we can do it for a range of them — in the same way we did it for accuracy earlier in this chapter.

For that, we first iterate over different threshold values and compute the values of the confusion table for each.

Listing 4.1   Computing the confusion table for different thresholds

```
scores = []          ◄──┤  Creates a list where
                            we'll keep the results

thresholds = np.linspace(0, 1, 101)          Creates an array with different
                                             threshold values, and loops over them
for t in thresholds:
    tp = ((y_pred >= t) & (y_val == 1)).sum()       Computes the confusion
    fp = ((y_pred >= t) & (y_val == 0)).sum()       table for predictions at
    fn = ((y_pred < t) & (y_val == 1)).sum()        each threshold
    tn = ((y_pred < t) & (y_val == 0)).sum()
    scores.append((t, tp, fp, fn, tn))    ◄──┐
                                              Appends the results to the scores list
```

The idea is similar to what we previously did with accuracy, but instead of recording just one value, we record all the four outcomes for the confusion table.

It's not easy to deal with a list of tuples, so let's convert it to a Pandas dataframe:

```
                                          Turns the list into a              Assigns names
                                          Pandas dataframe                   to the columns
df_scores = pd.DataFrame(scores)   ◄──┘                                      of the dataframe
df_scores.columns = ['threshold', 'tp', 'fp', 'fn', 'tn']   ◄──┘
```

This gives us a dataframe with five columns (figure 4.20).

```
df_scores[::10]
```

	threshold	tp	fp	fn	tn
0	0.0	486	1374	0	0
10	0.1	458	726	28	648
20	0.2	421	512	65	862
30	0.3	380	350	106	1024
40	0.4	337	257	149	1117
50	0.5	289	172	197	1202
60	0.6	200	105	286	1269
70	0.7	99	34	387	1340
80	0.8	7	1	479	1373
90	0.9	0	0	486	1374
100	1.0	0	0	486	1374

Figure 4.20   The dataframe with the elements of the confusion matrix evaluated at different threshold levels. The [::10] expression selects every 10th record of the dataframe.

Now we can compute the TPR and FPR scores. Because the data is now in a dataframe, we can do it for all the values at once:

```
df_scores['tpr'] = df_scores.tp / (df_scores.tp + df_scores.fn)
df_scores['fpr'] = df_scores.fp / (df_scores.fp + df_scores.tn)
```

After running this code, we have two new columns in the dataframe: tpr and fpr (figure 4.21).

```
df_scores[::10]
```

	threshold	tp	fp	fn	tn	tpr	fpr
0	0.0	486	1374	0	0	1.000000	1.000000
10	0.1	458	726	28	648	0.942387	0.528384
20	0.2	421	512	65	862	0.866255	0.372635
30	0.3	380	350	106	1024	0.781893	0.254731
40	0.4	337	257	149	1117	0.693416	0.187045
50	0.5	289	172	197	1202	0.594650	0.125182
60	0.6	200	105	286	1269	0.411523	0.076419
70	0.7	99	34	387	1340	0.203704	0.024745
80	0.8	7	1	479	1373	0.014403	0.000728
90	0.9	0	0	486	1374	0.000000	0.000000
100	1.0	0	0	486	1374	0.000000	0.000000

Figure 4.21 The dataframe with the values of the confusion matrix as well as TPR and FPR evaluated at different thresholds

Let's plot them (figure 4.22):

```
plt.plot(df_scores.threshold, df_scores.tpr, label='TPR')
plt.plot(df_scores.threshold, df_scores.fpr, label='FPR')
plt.legend()
```

Both TPR and FPR start at 100% — at the threshold of 0.0, we predict "churn" for everyone:

- FPR is 100% because we have only false positives in the prediction. There are no true negatives: nobody is predicted as non-churning.
- TPR is 100% because we have only true positives and no false negatives.

As the threshold grows, both metrics decline but at different rates.

Ideally, FPR should go down very quickly. A small FPR indicates that the model makes very few mistakes predicting negative examples (false positives).

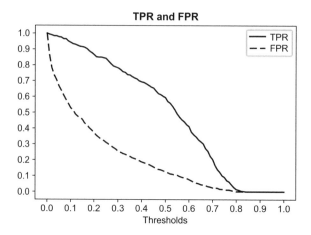

Figure 4.22   The TPR and FPR for our model, evaluated at different thresholds

On the other hand, TPR should go down slowly, ideally staying near 100% all the time: that will mean that the model predicts true positives well.

To better understand what these TPR and FPR mean, let's compare it with two baseline models: a random model and the ideal model. We will start with a random model.

4.3.3   *Random baseline model*

A random model outputs a random score between 0 and 1, regardless of the input. It's easy to implement — we simply generate an array with uniform random numbers:

```
np.random.seed(1)
y_rand = np.random.uniform(0, 1, size=len(y_val))
```

Fixes the random seed for reproducibility

Generates an array with random numbers between 0 and 1

Now we can simply pretend that y_rand contains the predictions of our "model."

Let's calculate FPR and TPR for our random model. To make it simpler, we'll reuse the code we wrote previously and put it into a function.

Listing 4.2   Function for calculating TPR and FPR at different thresholds

```
def tpr_fpr_dataframe(y_val, y_pred):
    scores = []

    thresholds = np.linspace(0, 1, 101)

    for t in thresholds:
        tp = ((y_pred >= t) & (y_val == 1)).sum()
        fp = ((y_pred >= t) & (y_val == 0)).sum()
        fn = ((y_pred < t) & (y_val == 1)).sum()
        tn = ((y_pred < t) & (y_val == 0)).sum()
        scores.append((t, tp, fp, fn, tn))
```

Defines a function that takes in actual and predicted values

Calculates the confusion table for different thresholds

Calculates TPR and FPR using the confusion table numbers

```
df_scores = pd.DataFrame(scores)
df_scores.columns = ['threshold', 'tp', 'fp', 'fn', 'tn']

df_scores['tpr'] = df_scores.tp / (df_scores.tp + df_scores.fn)
df_scores['fpr'] = df_scores.fp / (df_scores.fp + df_scores.tn)

    return df_scores
```

Converts the confusion table numbers to a dataframe

Returns the resulting dataframe

Now let's use this function to calculate the TPR and FPR for the random model:

```
df_rand = tpr_fpr_dataframe(y_val, y_rand)
```

This creates a dataframe with TPR and FPR values at different thresholds (figure 4.23).

```
np.random.seed(1)
y_rand = np.random.uniform(0, 1, size=len(y_val))
df_rand = tpr_fpr_dataframe(y_val, y_rand)
df_rand[::10]
```

	threshold	tp	fp	fn	tn	tpr	fpr
0	0.0	486	1374	0	0	1.000000	1.000000
10	0.1	440	1236	46	138	0.905350	0.899563
20	0.2	392	1101	94	273	0.806584	0.801310
30	0.3	339	972	147	402	0.697531	0.707424
40	0.4	288	849	198	525	0.592593	0.617904
50	0.5	239	723	247	651	0.491770	0.526201
60	0.6	193	579	293	795	0.397119	0.421397
70	0.7	152	422	334	952	0.312757	0.307132
80	0.8	98	302	388	1072	0.201646	0.219796
90	0.9	57	147	429	1227	0.117284	0.106987
100	1.0	0	0	486	1374	0.000000	0.000000

Figure 4.23   The TPR and FPR values of a random model

Let's plot them:

```
plt.plot(df_rand.threshold, df_rand.tpr, label='TPR')
plt.plot(df_rand.threshold, df_rand.fpr, label='FPR')
plt.legend()
```

We see that both TPR and FPR curves go from 100% to 0%, almost following the straight line (figure 4.24).

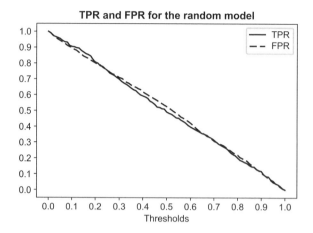

Figure 4.24   Both TPR and FPR of a random classifier decrease from 100% to 0% as a straight line.

At the threshold of 0.0, we treat everybody as churning. Both TPR and FPR are 100%:

- FPR is 100% because we have only false positives: all non-churning customers are identified as churning.
- TPR is 100% because we have only true positives: we can correctly classify all churning customers as churning.

As we increase the threshold, both TPR and FPR decrease.

At the threshold of 0.4, the model with a probability of 40% predicts "non-churn," and with a probability of 60% predicts "churn." Both TPR and FPR are 60%:

- FPR is 60% because we incorrectly classify 60% of non-churning customers as churning.
- TPR is 60% because we correctly classify 60% of churning customers as churning.

Finally, at 1.0, both TPR and FPR are 0%. At this threshold, we predict everybody as non-churning:

- FPR is 0% because we have no false positives: we can correctly classify all non-churning customers as non-churning.
- TPR is 0% because we have no true positives: all churning customers are identified as non-churning.

Let's now move on to the next baseline and see how TPR and FPR look for the ideal model.

4.3.4   *The ideal model*

The ideal model always makes correct decisions. We'll take it a step further and consider the ideal ranking model. This model outputs scores in such a way that churning customers always have higher scores than non-churning ones. In other words, the predicted probability for all churned ones should be higher than the predicted probability for non-churned ones.

So, if we apply the model to all the customers in our validation set and then sort them by the predicted probability, we first will have all the non-churning customers, followed by the churning ones (figure 4.25).

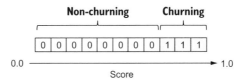

Figure 4.25 **The ideal model orders customers such that first we have non-churning customers and then churning ones.**

Of course, we cannot have such a model in real life. It's still useful, however: we can use it for comparing our TPR and FPR to the TPR and FPR of the ideal model.

Let's generate the ideal predictions. To make it easier, we generate an array with fake target variables that are already ordered: first it contains only 0s and then only 1s (figure 4.25). As for "predictions," we simply can create an array with numbers that grow from 0 in the first cell to 1 in the last cell using the np.linspace function.

Let's do it:

```
num_neg = (y_val == 0).sum()          | Calculates the number of negative and
num_pos = (y_val == 1).sum()          | positive examples in the dataset

y_ideal = np.repeat([0, 1], [num_neg, num_pos])
y_pred_ideal = np.linspace(0, 1, num_neg + num_pos)

df_ideal = tpr_fpr_dataframe(y_ideal, y_pred_ideal)
```

Generates an array that first repeats 0s num_neg number of times, followed by 1s repeated num_pos number of times

Generates the predictions of the "model": numbers that grow from 0 in the first cell to 1 in the last

Computes the TPR and FPR curves for the classifier

As a result, we get a dataframe with the TPR and FPR values of the ideal model (figure 4.26). You can read more about np.linspace and np.repeat functions in appendix C.

Now we can plot it (figure 4.27):

```
plt.plot(df_ideal.threshold, df_ideal.tpr, label='TPR')
plt.plot(df_ideal.threshold, df_ideal.fpr, label='FPR')
plt.legend()
```

	threshold	tp	fp	fn	tn	tpr	fpr
0	0.0	486	1374	0	0	1.000000	1.000000
10	0.1	486	1188	0	186	1.000000	0.864629
20	0.2	486	1002	0	372	1.000000	0.729258
30	0.3	486	816	0	558	1.000000	0.593886
40	0.4	486	630	0	744	1.000000	0.458515
50	0.5	486	444	0	930	1.000000	0.323144
60	0.6	486	258	0	1116	1.000000	0.187773
70	0.7	486	72	0	1302	1.000000	0.052402
80	0.8	372	0	114	1374	0.765432	0.000000
90	0.9	186	0	300	1374	0.382716	0.000000
100	1.0	1	0	485	1374	0.002058	0.000000

Figure 4.26   The TPR and FPR values for the ideal model

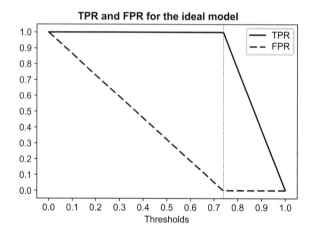

Figure 4.27   The TPR and FPR curves for the ideal model

From the plot, we can see that

- Both TPR and FPR start at 100% and end at 0%.
- For thresholds lower than 0.74, we always correctly classify all churning customers as churning; that's why TRP stays at 100%. On the other hand, we incorrectly classify some non-churning ones as churning — those are our false positives. As we increase the threshold, fewer and fewer non-churning customers are classified as churning, so FPR goes down. At 0.6, we misclassify 258 non-churning customers as churning (figure 4.28, A).

- The threshold of 0.74 is the ideal situation: all churning customers are classified as churning, and all non-churning are classified as non-churning; that's why TPR is 100% and FPR is 0% (figure 4.28, B).
- Between 0.74 and 1.0, we always correctly classify all non-churning customers, so FPR stays at 0%. However, as we increase the threshold, we start incorrectly classifying more and more churning customers as non-churning, so TPR goes down. At 0.8, 114 out of 446 churning customers are incorrectly classified as non-churning. Only 372 predictictions are correct, so TPR is 76% (figure 4.28, C).

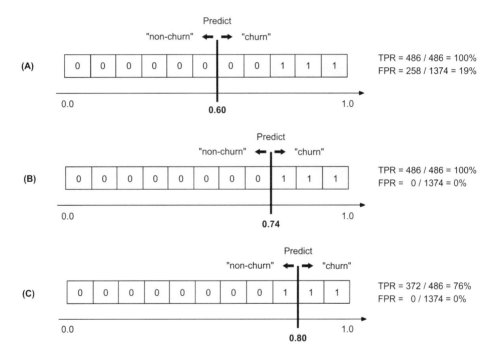

Figure 4.28   TPR and FPR of the ideal ranking model evaluated at different thresholds

Now we're ready to build the ROC curve.

Exercise 4.4
What does the ideal ranking model do?

a When applied to the validation data, it scores the customers such that for non-churning customers, the score is always lower than for churning ones.
b It scores non-churning customers higher than churning ones.

4.3.5 ROC Curve

To create an ROC curve, instead of plotting FPR and TPR against different threshold values, we plot them against each other. For comparison, we also add the ideal and random models to the plot:

```
plt.figure(figsize=(5, 5))        ◁───────  Makes the plot square

plt.plot(df_scores.fpr, df_scores.tpr, label='Model')      Plots the ROC curve
plt.plot(df_rand.fpr, df_rand.tpr, label='Random')         for the model and
plt.plot(df_ideal.fpr, df_ideal.tpr, label='Ideal')        baselines

plt.legend()
```

As a result, we get an ROC curve (figure 4.29). When we plot it, we can see that the ROC curve of the random classifier is an approximately straight line from bottom left to top right. For the ideal model, however, the curve first goes up until it reaches 100% TPR, and from there it goes right until it reaches 100% FPR.

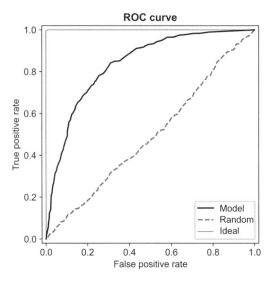

Figure 4.29   The ROC curve shows the relationship between the FPR and TPR of a model.

Our models should always be somewhere between these two curves. We want our model to be as close to the ideal curve as possible and as far as possible from the random curve.

The ROC curve of a random model serves as a good visual baseline — when we add it to the plot, it helps us to judge how far our model is from this baseline — so it's a good idea to always include this line in the plot.

However, we don't really need to generate a random model each time we want to have an ROC curve: we know what it looks like, so we can simply include a straight line from (0, 0) to (1, 1) in the plot.

As for the ideal model, we know that it always goes up to (0, 1) and then goes right to (1, 1). The top-left corner is called the "ideal spot": it's the point when the ideal model gets 100% TPR and 0% FPR. We want our models to get as close to the ideal spot as possible.

With this information, we can reduce the code for plotting the curve to the following:

```
plt.figure(figsize=(5, 5))
plt.plot(df_scores.fpr, df_scores.tpr)
plt.plot([0, 1], [0, 1])
```

This produces the result in figure 4.30.

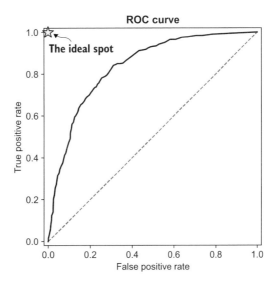

Figure 4.30 **The ROC curve. The baseline makes it easier to see how far the ROC curve of our model is from that of a random model. The top-left corner (0, 1) is the "ideal spot": the closer our models get to it, the better.**

Although computing all the FPR and TPR values across many thresholds is a good exercise, we don't need to do it ourselves every time we want to plot an ROC curve. We simply can use the roc_curve function from the metrics package of Scikit-learn:

```
from sklearn.metrics import roc_curve

fpr, tpr, thresholds = roc_curve(y_val, y_pred)

plt.figure(figsize=(5, 5))
plt.plot(fpr, tpr)
plt.plot([0, 1], [0, 1])
```

As a result, we get a plot identical to the previous one (figure 4.30).

Now let's try to make more sense of the curve and understand what it can actually tell us. To do this, we visually map the TPR and FPR values to their thresholds on the ROC curve (figure 4.31).

In the ROC plot, we start from the $(0, 0)$ point — this is the point at the bottom left. It corresponds to 0% FPR and 0% TPR, which happens at high thresholds like 1.0, when

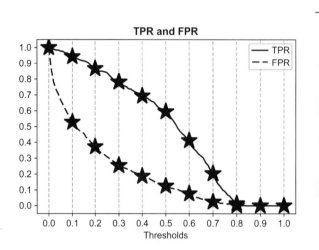

(A) TPR and FPR at different thresholds

threshold		fpr	tpr
100	1.0	0.000000	0.000000
90	0.9	0.000000	0.000000
80	0.8	0.000728	0.014403
70	0.7	0.024745	0.203704
60	0.6	0.076419	0.411523
50	0.5	0.125182	0.594650
40	0.4	0.187045	0.693416
30	0.3	0.254731	0.781893
20	0.2	0.372635	0.866255
10	0.1	0.528384	0.942387
0	0.0	1.000000	1.000000

(B) FPR and TPR values of the model for different thresholds

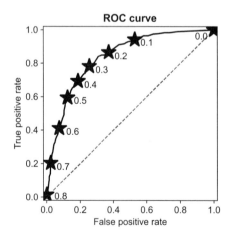

(C) FPR and TPR values for selected thresholds

Figure 4.31   Translation of the TPR and FPR plots against different threshold values (A and B) to the ROC curve (C). In the ROC plot, we start from the bottom left with high threshold values, where most of the customers are predicted as non-churning, and gradually go to the top right with low thresholds, where most of the customers are predicted as churning.

no customers are above that score. For these cases we simply end up predicting "no churn" for everyone. That's why our TPR is 0%: we are never correctly predicting churned customers. FPR, on the other hand, is 0% because this dummy model can correctly predict all non-churning customers as non-churning, so there are no false positives.

As we go up the curve, we consider FPR and TPR values evaluated at smaller thresholds. At 0.7, FPR changes only slightly, from 0% to 2%, but the TPR increases from 0% to 20% (figure 4.31, B and C).

As we follow the line, we keep decreasing the threshold and evaluating the model at smaller values, predicting more and more customers as churning. At some point, we cover most of the positives (churning customers). For example, at the threshold of 0.2, we predict most of the users as churning, which means that many of these predictions are false positives. FPR then starts to grow faster than TPR; at the threshold of 0.2, it's already at almost 40%.

Eventually, we reach the 0.0 threshold and predict that everyone is churning, thus reaching the top-right corner of the ROC plot.

When we start at high threshold values, all models are equal: any model at high threshold values degrades to the constant "model" that predicts False all the time. As we decrease the threshold, we start predicting some of the customers as churning. The better the model, the more customers are correctly classified as churning, resulting in a better TPR. Likewise, good models have a smaller FPR because they have fewer false positives.

Thus, the ROC curve of a good model first goes up as high as it can and only then starts turning right. Poor models, on the other hand, from the start have higher FPRs and lower TPRs, so their curves tend to go to the right earlier (figure 4.32).

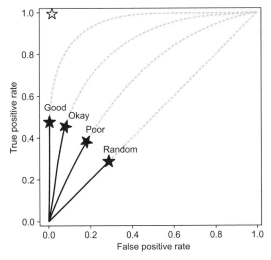

Figure 4.32 **ROC curves of good models go up as much as they can before turning right. Poor models, on the other hand, tend to have more false positives from the beginning, so they tend to go right earlier.**

We can use this for comparing multiple models: we can simply plot them on the same graph and see which of them is closer to the ideal point of (0, 1). For example, let's take a look at the ROC curves of the large and small models and plot them on the same graph:

```
fpr_large, tpr_large, _ = roc_curve(y_val, y_pred)
fpr_small, tpr_small, _ = roc_curve(y_val, y_pred_small)

plt.figure(figsize=(5, 5))

plt.plot(fpr_large, tpr_large, color='black', label='Large')
plt.plot(fpr_small, tpr_small, color='black', label='Small')
plt.plot([0, 1], [0, 1])
plt.legend()
```

This way we can get two ROC curves on the same plot (figure 4.33). We can see that the large model is better than the small model: it's closer to the ideal point for all the thresholds.

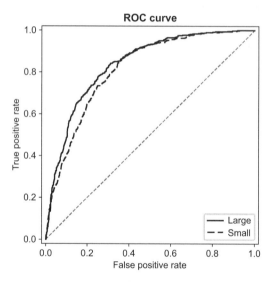

Figure 4.33   Plotting multiple ROC curves on the same graph helps us visually identify which model performs better.

ROC curves are quite useful on their own, but we also have another metric that's based on it: AUC, or the area under the ROC curve.

4.3.6   *Area under the ROC curve (AUC)*

When evaluating our models using the ROC curve, we want them to be as close to the ideal spot and as far from the random baseline as possible.

We can quantify this "closeness" by measuring the area under the ROC curve. We can use this metric — abbreviated as AU ROC, or often simply AUC — as a metric for evaluating the performance of a binary classification model.

The ideal model forms a 1x1 square, so the area under its ROC curve is 1, or 100%. The random model takes only half of that, so its AUC is 0.5, or 50%. The AUCs of our two models — the large one and the small one — will be somewhere between the random baseline of 50% and the ideal curve of 100%.

IMPORTANT   An AUC of 0.9 is indicative of a reasonably good model; 0.8 is okay, 0.7 is not very performant, and 0.6 indicates quite poor performance.

To calculate the AUC for our models we can use auc, a function from the metrics package of Scikit-learn:

```
from sklearn.metrics import auc
auc(df_scores.fpr, df_scores.tpr)
```

For the large model, the result is 0.84; for the small model, it's 0.81 (figure 4.34). Churn prediction is a complex problem, so an AUC of 80% is quite good.

```
from sklearn.metrics import auc
auc(df_scores.fpr, df_scores.tpr)
```
```
0.8359001084215382
```

```
auc(df_scores_small.fpr, df_scores_small.tpr)
```
```
0.8125475467380692
```

Figure 4.34 **The AUC for our models: 84% for the large model and 81% for the small model**

If all we need is the AUC, we don't need to compute the ROC curve first. We can take a shortcut and use the roc_auc_score function from Scikit-learn, which takes care of everything and simply returns the AUC of our model:

```
from sklearn.metrics import roc_auc_score
roc_auc_score(y_val, y_pred)
```

We get approximately the same results as previously (figure 4.35).

NOTE   The values from roc_auc_score may be slightly different from AUC computed from the dataframes where we calculated TPR and FPR ourselves: Scikit-learn internally uses a more precise method for creating ROC curves.

ROC curves and AUC scores tell us how well the model separates positive and negative examples. What is more, AUC has a nice probabilistic interpretation: it tells us what

```
from sklearn.metrics import roc_auc_score
roc_auc_score(y_val, y_pred)
```

0.8363366398907399

```
roc_auc_score(y_val, y_pred_small)
```

0.8129354083179088

Figure 4.35   Calculating AUC using Scikit-learn's `roc_auc_score` function.

the probability is that a randomly selected positive example will have a score higher than a randomly selected negative example.

Suppose we randomly pick a customer that we know churned and a customer who didn't and then apply the model to these customers and see what the score is for each. We want the model to score the churning customer higher than the non-churning one. AUC tells us the probability of that happening: it's the probability that the score of a randomly selected churning customer is higher than the score of a randomly selected non-churning one.

We can verify this. If we do this experiment 10,000 times and then count how many times the score of the positive example was higher than the score of the negative one, the percentage of cases when it's true should roughly correspond to the AUC:

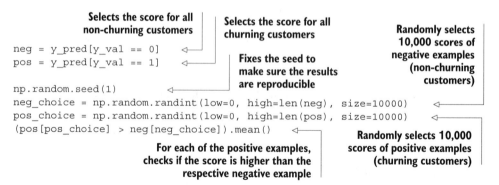

This prints 0.8356, which is indeed pretty close to the AUC value of our classifier.

This interpretation of AUC gives us additional insight into the quality of our models. The ideal model orders all the customers such that we first have non-churning customers and then churning customers. With this order, the AUC is always 1.0: the score of a randomly chosen churning customer is always higher than the score of a non-churning customer. On the other hand, the random model just shuffles the customers, so the score of a churning customer has only a 50% chance of being higher than the score of a non-churning one.

AUC thus not only gives us a way of evaluating the models at all possible thresholds but also describes how well the model separates two classes: in our case, churning and non-churning. If the separation is good, then we can order the customers such that most of the churning users come first. Such a model will have a good AUC score.

> **NOTE** You should keep this interpretation in mind: it provides an easy way to explain the meaning behind AUC to people without a machine learning background, such as managers and other decision makers.

This makes AUC the default classification metric in most situations, and it's often the metric we use when finding the best parameter set for our models.

The process of finding the best parameters is called "parameter tuning," and in the next section we will see how to do this.

4.4 Parameter tuning

In the previous chapter, we used a simple hold-out validation scheme for testing our models. In this scheme, we take part of the data out and keep it for validation purposes only. This practice is good but doesn't always give us the whole picture. It tells us how well the model will perform on these specific data points. However, it doesn't necessarily mean the model will perform equally well on other data points. So, how do we check if the model indeed works well in a consistent and predictable manner?

4.4.1 K-fold cross-validation

It's possible to use all the available data to assess the quality of models and get more reliable validation results. We can simply perform validation multiple times.

First, we split the entire dataset into a certain number of parts (say, three). Then we train a model on two parts and validate on the remaining one. We repeat this process three times and at the end get three different scores. This is exactly the idea behind K-fold cross-validation (figure 4.36).

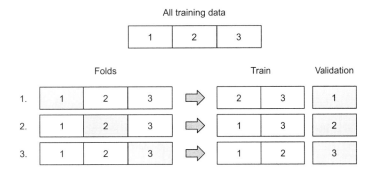

Figure 4.36 K-fold cross-validation (K=3). We split the entire dataset into three equal parts, or folds. Then, for each fold, we take it as the validation dataset and use the remaining K – 1 folds as the training data. After training the model, we evaluate it on the validation fold, and at the end we get k metric values.

Before we implement it, we need to make the training process simpler, so it's easy to run this process multiple times. For that, we'll put all the code for training into a `train` function, which first converts the data into a one-hot encoding representation and then trains the model.

Listing 4.3 Training the model

```
def train(df, y):
    cat = df[categorical + numerical].to_dict(orient='records')

    dv = DictVectorizer(sparse=False)          Applies one-
    dv.fit(cat)                                 hot encoding

    X = dv.transform(cat)

    model = LogisticRegression(solver='liblinear')    Trains the model
    model.fit(X, y)

    return dv, model
```

Likewise, we also put the prediction logic into a `predict` function. This function takes in a dataframe with customers, the vectorizer we "trained" previously — for doing one-hot encoding — and the model. Then we apply the vectorizer to the dataframe, get a matrix, and finally apply the model to the matrix to get predictions.

Listing 4.4 Applying the model to new data

```
def predict(df, dv, model):
    cat = df[categorical + numerical].to_dict(orient='records')    Applies the same
                                                                   one-hot encoding
    X = dv.transform(cat)                                          scheme as in training
    y_pred = model.predict_proba(X)[:, 1]      Uses the model to
                                               make predictions
    return y_pred
```

Now we can use these functions for implementing K-fold cross-validation.

We don't need to implement cross-validation ourselves: in Scikit-learn there's a class for doing that. It's called `KFold`, and it lives in the `model_selection` package.

Listing 4.5 K-fold cross-validation

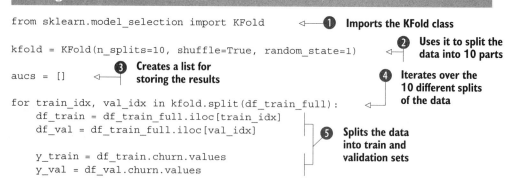

```
from sklearn.model_selection import KFold          ① Imports the KFold class

kfold = KFold(n_splits=10, shuffle=True, random_state=1)    ② Uses it to split the
                                                               data into 10 parts
aucs = []        ③ Creates a list for                       ④ Iterates over the
                    storing the results                        10 different splits
                                                               of the data
for train_idx, val_idx in kfold.split(df_train_full):
    df_train = df_train_full.iloc[train_idx]
    df_val = df_train_full.iloc[val_idx]          ⑤ Splits the data
                                                     into train and
    y_train = df_train.churn.values                  validation sets
    y_val = df_val.churn.values
```

```
dv, model = train(df_train, y_train)
y_pred = predict(df_val, dv, model)
```
❻ **Trains the model and makes predictions**

```
auc = roc_auc_score(y_val, y_pred)
aucs.append(auc)
```

Saves the AUC to the list with the results ❽

Evaluates the quality of the train model on the validation data using AUC ❼

Note that when defining the splitting in the KFold class in ❷, we set three parameters:

- n_splits = 10: That's K, which specifies the number of splits.
- shuffle = True: We ask it to shuffle the data before splitting it.
- random_state = 1: Because there's randomization in the process (shuffling data), we want the results to be reproducible, so we fix the seed for the random-number generator.

Here we used K-fold cross-validation with K =10. Thus, when we run it, at the end we get 10 different numbers — 10 AUC scores evaluated on 10 different validation folds:

```
0.849, 0.841, 0.859, 0.833, 0.824, 0.841, 0.844, 0.822, 0.845, 0.861
```

It's not a single number anymore, and we can think of it as a distribution of AUC scores for our model. We can get some statistics from this distribution, such as the mean and standard deviation:

```
print('auc = %0.3f ± %0.3f' % (np.mean(aucs), np.std(aucs)))
```

This prints "0.842 ± 0.012".

Now, not only do we know the average performance, but we also have an idea of how volatile that performance is, or how far it may deviate from the average.

A good model should be quite stable across different folds: this way, we make sure we don't get a lot of surprises when the model goes live. The standard deviation tells us about that: the smaller it is, the more stable the model is.

Now we can use K-fold cross-validation for parameter tuning: selecting the best parameters.

4.4.2 Finding best parameters

We learned how we can use K-fold cross-validation for evaluating the performance of our model. The model we trained previously was using the default value for the parameter C, which controls the amount of regularization.

Let's select our cross-validation procedure for selecting the best parameter C. For that, we first adjust the train function to take in an additional parameter.

Listing 4.6 Function for training the model with parameter C for controlling regularization

Adds an extra parameter to the train function

```
def train(df, y, C):
    cat = df[categorical + numerical].to_dict(orient='records')
```

```
dv = DictVectorizer(sparse=False)
dv.fit(cat)

X = dv.transform(cat)                                        Uses this
                                                             parameter
model = LogisticRegression(solver='liblinear', C=C)    ◁——  during training
model.fit(X, y)

return dv, model
```

Now let's find the best parameter C. The idea is simple:

- Loop over different values of C.
- For each C, run cross-validation and record the mean AUC across all folds as well as the standard deviation.

Listing 4.7   Tuning the model: selecting the best parameter C using cross-validation

```
nfolds = 5
kfold = KFold(n_splits=nfolds, shuffle=True, random_state=1)

for C in [0.001, 0.01, 0.1, 0.5, 1, 10]:
    aucs = []

    for train_idx, val_idx in kfold.split(df_train_full):
        df_train = df_train_full.iloc[train_idx]
        df_val = df_train_full.iloc[val_idx]

        y_train = df_train.churn.values
        y_val = df_val.churn.values

        dv, model = train(df_train, y_train, C=C)
        y_pred = predict(df_val, dv, model)

        auc = roc_auc_score(y_val, y_pred)
        aucs.append(auc)

    print('C=%s, auc = %0.3f ± %0.3f' % (C, np.mean(aucs), np.std(aucs)))
```

When we run it, it prints

```
C=0.001, auc = 0.825 ± 0.013
C=0.01, auc = 0.839 ± 0.009
C=0.1, auc = 0.841 ± 0.008
C=0.5, auc = 0.841 ± 0.007
C=1, auc = 0.841 ± 0.007
C=10, auc = 0.841 ± 0.007
```

What we see is that after C = 0.1, the average AUC is the same and doesn't grow anymore.

However, the standard deviation is smaller for C = 0.5 than for C = 0.1, so we should use that. The reason we prefer C = 0.5 to C = 1 and C = 10 is simple: when the

C parameter is small, the model is more regularized. The weights of this model are more restricted, so in general, they are smaller. Small weights in the model give us additional assurance that the model will behave well when we use it on real data. So we select C = 0.5.

Now we need to do the last step: train the model on the entire train and validation datasets and apply it to the test dataset to verify it indeed works well.

Let's use our `train` and `predict` functions for that:

```
y_train = df_train_full.churn.values
y_test = df_test.churn.values

dv, model = train(df_train_full, y_train, C=0.5)
y_pred = predict(df_test, dv, model)

auc = roc_auc_score(y_test, y_pred)
print('auc = %.3f' % auc)
```

Trains the model on the full training dataset

Applies it to the test dataset

Evaluates the predictions on the test data

When we execute the code, we see that the performance of the model (AUC) on the held-out test set is 0.858.

That's a little higher than what we had on the validation set, but that's not an issue; it could happen just by chance. What's important is that the score is not significantly different from the validation score.

Now we can use this model for scoring real customers and think about our marketing campaign for preventing churn. In the next chapter, we will see how to deploy this model in a production environment.

4.5 Next steps

4.5.1 Exercises

Try the following exercises to further explore the topics of model evaluation and model selection:

- In this chapter, we plotted TPR and FPR for different threshold values, and it helped us understand what these metrics mean and also how the performance of our model changes when we choose a different threshold. It's helpful to do a similar exercise for precision and recall, so try to repeat this experiment, this time using precision and recall instead of TPR and FPR.

- When plotting precision and recall for different threshold values, we can see that a conflict exists between precision and recall: when one goes up, the other goes down, and the other way around. This is called the "precision-recall trade-off": we cannot select a threshold that makes both precision and recall good. However, we do have strategies for selecting the threshold, even though precision and recall are conflicting. One of them is plotting precision and recall curves and seeing where they intersect, and using this threshold for binarizing the predictions. Try implementing this idea.

- Another idea for working around the precision-recall trade-off is the F1 score — a score that combines both precision and recall into one value. Then, to select the best threshold, we can simply choose the one that maximizes the F1 score. The formula for computing the F1 score is F1 = 2 · P · R / (P + R), where P is precision and R is recall. Implement this idea, and select the best threshold based on the F1 metric.

- We've seen that precision and recall are better metrics for evaluating classification models than accuracy because they don't rely on false positives, the amount of which could be high in imbalanced datasets. Yet, we saw later that AUC does actually use false positives in FPR. For very highly imbalanced cases (say, 1,000 negatives to 1 positive), AUC may become problematic as well. Another metric works better in such cases: area under the precision-recall curve, or AU PR. The precision-recall curve is similar to ROC, but instead of plotting FPR versus TPR, we plot recall on the x-axis and precision on the y-axis. Like for the ROC curve, we can also calculate the area under the PR curve and use it as a metric for evaluating different models. Try plotting the PR curves for our models, calculating the AU PR scores, and comparing them with those of the random model as well as the ideal model.

- We covered K-fold cross-validation, and we used it to understand what the distribution of AUC scores could look like on a test dataset. When K = 10, we get 10 observations, which under some circumstances might not be enough. However, the idea can be extended to repeated K-fold cross-validation steps. The process is simple: we repeat the K-fold cross-validation process multiple times, each time shuffling the dataset differently by selecting a different random seed at each iteration. Implement repeated cross-validation and perform 10-fold cross-validation 10 times to see what the distribution of scores looks like.

4.5.2   *Other projects*

You can also continue with the other self-study projects from the previous chapter: the lead scoring project and the default prediction project. Try the following:

- Calculate all the metrics that we covered in this chapter: the confusion table, precision and recall, and AUC. Also try to calculate the scores from the exercises: the F1 score as well as AU PR (the area under the precision-recall curve).
- Use K-fold cross-validation to select the best parameter C for the model.

Summary

- A metric is a single number that can be used for evaluating the performance of a machine learning model. Once we choose a metric, we can use it to compare multiple machine learning models with each other and select the best one.
- Accuracy is the simplest binary classification metric: it tells us the percentage of correctly classified observations in the validation set. It's easy to understand and compute, but it can be misleading when a dataset is imbalanced.

- When a binary classification model makes a prediction, we have only four possible outcomes: true positive and true negative (correct answers) and false positive and false negative (incorrect answers). The confusion table arranges these outcomes visually so it's easy to understand them. It gives us the foundation for many other binary classification metrics.

- Precision is the fraction of correct answers among observations for which our prediction is True. If we use the churn model to send promotional messages, precision tells us the percentage of customers who really were going to churn among everybody who received the message. The higher the precision, the fewer non-churning users we incorrectly classify as churning.

- Recall is the fraction of correct answers among all positive observations. It tells us the percentage of churning customers who we correctly identified as churning. The higher the recall, the fewer churning customers we fail to identify.

- The ROC curve analyzes binary classification models at all the thresholds at once. The area under the ROC curve (AUC) tells us how well a model separates positive observations from negative ones. Because of its interpretability and wide applicability, AUC has become the default metric for evaluating binary classification models.

- K-fold cross-validation gives us a way to use all the training data for model validation: we split the data into K folds and use each fold in turn as a validation set, and the remaining K – 1 folds are used for training. As a result, instead of a single number, we have K values, one for each fold. We can use these numbers to understand the performance of a model on average as well as to estimate how volatile it is across different folds.

- K-fold cross-validation is the best way of tuning parameters and selecting the best model: it gives us a reliable estimate of the metric across multiple folds.

In the next chapter we look into deploying our model into a production environment.

Answers to exercises

- Exercise 4.1 B) A customer for whom we predicted "churn," but they didn't churn.

- Exercise 4.2 B) The percent of customers who actually churned among the customers who we predicted as churning.

- Exercise 4.3 A) The percent of correctly identified churned customers among all churned customers.

- Exercise 4.4 A) The ideal ranking model always scores churning customers higher than non-churning ones.

Deploying machine learning models

This chapter covers

- Saving models with Pickle
- Serving models with Flask
- Managing dependencies with Pipenv
- Making the service self-contained with Docker
- Deploying it to the cloud using AWS Elastic Beanstalk

As we continue to work with machine learning techniques, we'll keep using the project we already started: churn prediction. In chapter 3, we used Scikit-learn to build a model for identifying churning customers. After that, in chapter 4, we evaluated the quality of this model and selected the best parameter C using cross-validation.

We already have a model that lives in our Jupyter Notebook. Now we need to put this model into production, so other services can use the model to make decisions based on the output of our model.

In this chapter, we cover *model deployment*: the process of putting models to use. In particular, we see how to package a model inside a web service, so other services can use it. We also see how to deploy the web service to a production-ready environment.

5.1   *Churn-prediction model*

To get started with deployment we use the model we trained previously. First, in this section, we review how we can use the model for making predictions, and then we see how to save it with Pickle.

5.1.1   *Using the model*

To make it easier, we can continue the same Jupyter Notebook we used for chapters 3 and 4.

Let's use this model to calculate the probability of churning for the following customer:

```
customer = {
    'customerid': '8879-zkjof',
    'gender': 'female',
    'seniorcitizen': 0,
    'partner': 'no',
    'dependents': 'no',
    'tenure': 41,
    'phoneservice': 'yes',
    'multiplelines': 'no',
    'internetservice': 'dsl',
    'onlinesecurity': 'yes',
    'onlinebackup': 'no',
    'deviceprotection': 'yes',
    'techsupport': 'yes',
    'streamingtv': 'yes',
    'streamingmovies': 'yes',
    'contract': 'one_year',
    'paperlessbilling': 'yes',
    'paymentmethod': 'bank_transfer_(automatic)',
    'monthlycharges': 79.85,
    'totalcharges': 3320.75,
}
```

To predict whether this customer is going to churn, we can use the `predict` function we wrote in the previous chapter:

```
df = pd.DataFrame([customer])
y_pred = predict(df, dv, model)
y_pred[0]
```

This function needs a dataframe, so first we create a dataframe with one row — our customer. Next, we put it into the `predict` function. The result is a NumPy array with a single element — the predicted probability of churn for this customer:

```
0.059605
```

This means that this customer has a 6% probability of churning.

Now let's take a look at the `predict` function, which we wrote previously for apply-ing the model to the customers in the validation set:

```
def predict(df, dv, model):
    cat = df[categorical + numerical].to_dict(orient='rows')
    X = dv.transform(cat)
    y_pred = model.predict_proba(X)[:, 1]
    return y_pred
```

Using it for one customer seems inefficient and unnecessary: we create a dataframe from a single customer only to convert this dataframe back to a dictionary later inside `predict`.

To avoid doing this unnecessary conversion, we can create a separate function for predicting the probability of churn for a single customer only. Let's call this function `predict_single`:

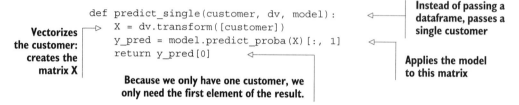

Vectorizes the customer: creates the matrix X

Instead of passing a dataframe, passes a single customer

Applies the model to this matrix

Because we only have one customer, we only need the first element of the result.

Using it becomes simpler — we simply invoke it with our customer (a dictionary):

```
predict_single(customer, dv, model)
```

The result is the same: this customer has a 6% probability of churning.

We trained our model inside the Jupyter Notebook we started in chapter 3. This model lives there, and once we stop the Jupyter Notebook, the trained model will disappear. This means that now we can use it only inside the notebook and nowhere else. Next, we see how to address it.

5.1.2   *Using Pickle to save and load the model*

To be able to use it outside of our notebook, we need to save it, and then later, another process can load and use it (figure 5.1).

Pickle is a serialization/deserialization module that's already built into Python: using it, we can save an arbitrary Python object (with a few exceptions) to a file. Once we have a file, we can load the model from there in a different process.

NOTE   "Pickle" can also be used as a verb: *pickling* an object in Python means saving it using the Pickle module.

SAVING THE MODEL

To save the model, we first import the Pickle module, and then use the `dump` function:

```
import pickle

with open('churn-model.bin', 'wb') as f_out:
    pickle.dump(model, f_out)
```

Specifies the file where we want to save

Saves the model to file with Pickle

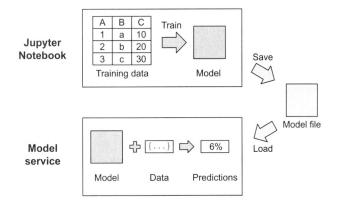

Figure 5.1 We train a model in a Jupyter Notebook. To use it, we first need to save it and then load it in a different process.

To save the model, we use the `open` function, which takes two arguments:

- The name of the file that we want to open. For us, it's churn-model.bin.
- The mode with which we open the file. For us, it's `wb`, which means we want to write to the file (`w`), and the file is binary (`b`) and not text — Pickle uses binary format for writing to files.

The `open` function returns `f_out` — the file descriptor we can use to write to the file. Next, we use the `dump` function from Pickle. It also takes two arguments:

- The object we want to save. For us, it's `model`.
- The file descriptor, pointing to the output file, which is `f_out` for us.

Finally, we use the `with` construction in this code. When we open a file with `open`, we need to close it after we finish writing. When using `with`, it happens automatically. Without `with`, our code would look like this:

```
f_out = open('churn-model.bin', 'wb')
pickle.dump(model, f_out)
f_out.close()
```

In our case, however, saving just the model is not enough: we also have a `DictVectorizer` that we "trained" together with the model. We need to save both.

The simplest way of doing this is to put both of them in a tuple when pickling:

```
with open('churn-model.bin', 'wb') as f_out:
    pickle.dump((dv, model), f_out)
```
The object we save is a tuple with two elements.

LOADING THE MODEL

To load the model, we use the `load` function from Pickle. We can test it in the same Jupyter Notebook:

```
with open('churn-model.bin', 'rb') as f_in:          Opens the file in read mode
    dv, model = pickle.load(f_in)          Loads the tuple and unpacks it
```

We again use the `open` function, but this time, with a different mode: rb, which means we open it for reading (r), and the file is binary (b).

> **WARNING** Be careful when specifying the mode. Accidentally specifying an incorrect mode may result in data loss: if you open an existing file with the w mode instead of r, it will overwrite the content.

Because we saved a tuple, we unpack it when loading, so we get both the vectorizer and the model at the same time.

> **WARNING** Unpickling objects found on the internet is not secure: it can execute arbitrary code on your machine. Use it only for things you trust and things you saved yourself.

Let's create a simple Python script that loads the model and applies it to a customer.

We will call this file churn_serving.py. (In the book's GitHub repository, this file is called churn_serving_simple.py.) It contains

- The `predict_single` function that we wrote earlier
- The code for loading the model
- The code for applying the model to a customer

You can refer to appendix B to learn more about creating Python scripts.

First, we start with imports. For this script, we need to import Pickle and NumPy:

```
import pickle
import numpy as np
```

Next, let's put the `predict_single` function there:

```
def predict_single(customer, dv, model):
    X = dv.transform([customer])
    y_pred = model.predict_proba(X)[:, 1]
    return y_pred[0]
```

Now we can load our model:

```
with open('churn-model.bin', 'rb') as f_in:
    dv, model = pickle.load(f_in)
```

And apply it:

```
customer = {
    'customerid': '8879-zkjof',
    'gender': 'female',
```

```
    'seniorcitizen': 0,
    'partner': 'no',
    'dependents': 'no',
    'tenure': 41,
    'phoneservice': 'yes',
    'multiplelines': 'no',
    'internetservice': 'dsl',
    'onlinesecurity': 'yes',
    'onlinebackup': 'no',
    'deviceprotection': 'yes',
    'techsupport': 'yes',
    'streamingtv': 'yes',
    'streamingmovies': 'yes',
    'contract': 'one_year',
    'paperlessbilling': 'yes',
    'paymentmethod': 'bank_transfer_(automatic)',
    'monthlycharges': 79.85,
    'totalcharges': 3320.75,
}

prediction = predict_single(customer, dv, model)
```

Finally, let's display the results:

```
print('prediction: %.3f' % prediction)

if prediction >= 0.5:
    print('verdict: Churn')
else:
    print('verdict: Not churn')
```

After saving the file, we can run this script with Python:

```
python churn_serving.py
```

We should immediately see the results:

```
prediction: 0.059
verdict: Not churn
```

This way, we can load the model and apply it to the customer we specified in the script.

Of course, we aren't going to manually put the information about customers in the script. In the next section, we cover a more practical approach: putting the model into a web service.

5.2 Model serving

We already know how to load a trained model in a different process. Now we need to *serve* this model — make it available for others to use.

In practice, this usually means that a model is deployed as a web service, so other services can communicate with it, ask for predictions, and use the results to make their own decisions.

In this section, we see how to do it in Python with Flask — a Python framework for creating web services. First, we take a look at why we need to use a web service for it.

5.2.1 *Web services*

We already know how to use a model to make a prediction, but so far, we have simply hardcoded the features of a customer as a Python dictionary. Let's try to imagine how our model will be used in practice.

Suppose we have a service for running marketing campaigns. For each customer, it needs to determine the probability of churn, and if it's high enough, it will send a promotional email with discounts. Of course, this service needs to use our model to decide whether it should send an email.

One possible way of achieving this is to modify the code of the campaign service: load the model, and score the customers right in the service. This approach is good, but the campaign service needs to be in Python, and we need to have full control over its code.

Unfortunately, this situation is not always the case: it may be written in some other language, or a different team might be in charge of this project, which means we won't have the control we need.

The typical solution for this problem is putting a model inside a web service — a small service (a *microservice*) that only takes care of scoring customers.

So, we need to create a churn service — a service in Python that will serve the churn model. Given the features of a customer, it will respond with the probability of churn for this customer. For each customer, the campaign service will ask the churn service for the probability of churn, and if it's high enough, then we send a promotional email (figure 5.2).

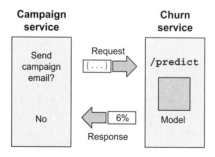

Figure 5.2   The churn service takes care of serving the churn-prediction model, making it possible for other services to use it.

This gives us another advantage: separation of concerns. If the model is created by data scientists, then they can take ownership of the service and maintain it, while the other team takes care of the campaign service.

One of the most popular frameworks for creating web services in Python is Flask, which we cover next.

5.2.2 *Flask*

The easiest way to implement a web service in Python is to use Flask. It's quite lightweight, requires little code to get started, and hides most of the complexity of dealing with HTTP requests and responses.

Before we put our model inside a web service, let's cover the basics of using Flask. For that, we'll create a simple function and make it available as a web service. After covering the basics, we'll take care of the model.

Suppose we have a simple Python function called `ping`:

```
def ping():
    return 'PONG'
```

It doesn't do much: when invoked, it simply responds with PONG. Let's use Flask to turn this function into a web service.

Anaconda comes with Flask preinstalled, but if you use a different Python distribution, you'll need to install it:

```
pip install flask
```

We will put this code in a Python file and will call it flask_test.py.

To be able to use Flask, we first need to import it:

```
from flask import Flask
```

Now we create a Flask app — the central object for registering functions that need to be exposed in the web service. We'll call our app test:

```
app = Flask('test')
```

Next, we need to specify how to reach the function by assigning it to an address, or a *route* in Flask terms. In our case, we want to use the /ping address:

```
@app.route('/ping', methods=['GET'])    ◁─┐  Registers the /ping route, and
def ping():                                │  assigns it to the ping function
    return 'PONG'
```

This code uses decorators — an advanced Python feature that we don't cover in this book. We don't need to understand how it works in detail; it's enough to know that by putting `@app.route` on top of the function definition, we assign the /ping address of the web service to the `ping` function.

To run it, we only need one last bit:

```
if __name__ == '__main__':
    app.run(debug=True, host='0.0.0.0', port=9696)
```

The run method of app starts the service. We specify three parameters:

- debug=True. Restarts our application automatically when there are changes in the code.
- host='0.0.0.0'. Makes the web service public; otherwise, it won't be possible to reach it when it's hosted on a remote machine (e.g., in AWS).
- port=9696. The port that we use to access the application.

We're ready to start our service now. Let's do it:

```
python flask_test.py
```

When we run it, we should see the following:

```
* Serving Flask app "test" (lazy loading)
* Environment: production
  WARNING: This is a development server. Do not use it in a production
    deployment.
  Use a production WSGI server instead.
* Debug mode: on
* Running on http://0.0.0.0:9696/ (Press CTRL+C to quit)
* Restarting with stat
* Debugger is active!
* Debugger PIN: 162-129-136
```

This means that our Flask app is now running and ready to get requests. To test it, we can use our browser: open it and type localhost:9696/ping in the address bar. If you run it on a remote server, you should replace localhost with the address of the server. (For AWS EC2, use the public DNS hostname. Make sure that the port 9696 is open in the security group of your EC2 instance: go to the security group, and add a custom TCP rule with the port 9696 and the source 0.0.0.0/0.) The browser should respond with PONG (figure 5.3).

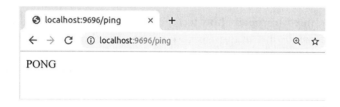

Figure 5.3   The easiest way to check if our application works is to use a web browser.

Flask logs all the requests it receives, so we should see a line indicating that there was a GET request on the /ping route:

```
127.0.0.1 - - [02/Apr/2020 21:59:09] "GET /ping HTTP/1.1" 200 -
```

As we can see, Flask is quite simple: with fewer than 10 lines of code, we created a web service.

Next, we'll see how to adjust our script for churn prediction and also turn it into a web service.

5.2.3 *Serving churn model with Flask*

We've learned a bit of Flask, so now we can come back to our script and convert it to a Flask application.

To score a customer, our model needs to get the features, which means that we need a way of transferring some data from one service (the campaign service) to another (the churn service).

As a data exchange format, web services typically use JSON (Javascript Object Notation). It's similar to the way we define dictionaries in Python:

```
{
    "customerid": "8879-zkjof",
    "gender": "female",
    "seniorcitizen": 0,
    "partner": "no",
    "dependents": "no",
    ...
}
```

To send data, we use POST requests, not GET: POST requests can include the data in the request, whereas GET cannot.

Thus, to make it possible for the campaign service to get predictions from the churn service, we need to create a /predict route that accepts POST requests. The churn service will parse JSON data about a customer and respond in JSON as well (figure 5.4).

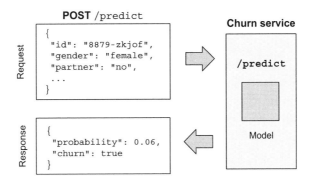

Figure 5.4   To get predictions, we POST the data about a customer in JSON to the /predict route and get the probability of churn in response.

Now we know what we want to do, so let's start modifying the churn_serving.py file.

First, we add a few more imports at the top of the file:

```
from flask import Flask, request, jsonify
```

Although previously we imported only `Flask`, now we need to import two more things:

- `request`: To get the content of a POST request
- `jsonsify`: To respond with JSON

Next, create the Flask app. Let's call it churn:

```
app = Flask('churn')
```

Now we need to create a function that

- Gets the customer data in a request
- Invokes `predict_simple` to score the customer
- Responds with the probability of churn in JSON

We'll call this function `predict` and assign it to the `/predict` route:

```
@app.route('/predict', methods=['POST'])         Assigns the /predict route
def predict():                                    to the predict function
    customer = request.get_json()                 Gets the content
                                                  of the request in
    prediction = predict_single(customer, dv, model)    JSON
    churn = prediction >= 0.5
                                                  Scores the
    result = {                                    customer
        'churn_probability': float(prediction),
        'churn': bool(churn),
    }                          Converts the
                               response to JSON
    return jsonify(result)
```

Prepares the response

To assign the route to the function, we use the `@app.route` decorator, where we also tell Flask to expect POST requests only.

The core content of the `predict` function is similar to what we did in the script previously: it takes a customer, passes it to `predict_single`, and does some work with the result.

Finally, let's add the last two lines for running the Flask app:

```
if __name__ == '__main__':
    app.run(debug=True, host='0.0.0.0', port=9696)
```

We're ready to run it:

```
python churn_serving.py
```

After running it, we should see a message saying that the app started and is now waiting for incoming requests:

```
* Serving Flask app "churn" (lazy loading)
* Environment: production
  WARNING: This is a development server. Do not use it in a production
    deployment.
  Use a production WSGI server instead.
* Debug mode: on
* Running on http://0.0.0.0:9696/ (Press CTRL+C to quit)
* Restarting with stat
* Debugger is active!
```

Testing this code is a bit more difficult than previously: this time, we need to use POST requests and include the customer we want to score in the body of the request.

The simplest way of doing this is to use the requests library in Python. It also comes preinstalled in Anaconda, but if you use a different distribution, you can install it with `pip`:

```
pip install requests
```

We can open the same Jupyter Notebook that we used previously and test the web service from there.

First, import requests:

```
import requests
```

Now, make a POST request to our service

```
url = 'http://localhost:9696/predict'
response = requests.post(url, json=customer)
result = response.json()
```

The URL where
the service lives

Sends the customer
(as JSON) in the
POST request

Parses the
response as JSON

The `results` variable contains the response from the churn service:

```
{'churn': False, 'churn_probability': 0.05960590758316391}
```

This is the same information we previously saw in the terminal, but now we got it as a response from a web service.

> **NOTE** Some tools, like Postman (https://www.postman.com/), make it easier to test web services. We don't cover Postman in this book, but you're free to give it a try.

If the campaign service used Python, this is exactly how it could communicate with the churn service and decide who should get promotional emails.

With just a few lines of code, we created a working web service that runs on our laptop. In the next section, we'll see how to manage dependencies in our service and prepare it for deployment.

5.3   *Managing dependencies*

For local development, Anaconda is a perfect tool: it has almost all the libraries we may ever need. This, however, also has a downside: it takes up 4 GB when unpacked, which is too large. For production, we prefer to have only the libraries we actually need.

Additionally, different services have different requirements. Often, these requirements conflict, so we cannot use the same environment for running multiple services at the same time.

In this section, we see how to manage dependencies of our application in an isolated way that doesn't interfere with other services. We cover two tools for this: Pipenv, for managing Python libraries, and Docker, for managing the system dependencies such as the operating system and the system libraries.

5.3.1   *Pipenv*

To serve the churn model, we only need a few libraries: NumPy, Scikit-learn, and Flask. So, instead of bringing in the entire Anaconda distribution with all its libraries, we can get a fresh Python installation and install only the libraries we need with `pip`:

```
pip install numpy scikit-learn flask
```

Before we do that, let's think for a moment about what happens when we use `pip` to install a library:

- We run `pip install library` to install a Python package called Library (let's suppose it exists).
- Pip goes to PyPI.org (the Python package index — a repository with Python packages), and gets and installs the latest version of this library. Let's say, it's version 1.0.0.

After installing it, we develop and test our service using this particular version. Everything works great. Later, our colleagues want to help us with the project, so they also run `pip install` to set up everything on their machine — except this time, the latest version turns out to be 1.3.1.

If we're unlucky, versions 1.0.0 and 1.3.1 might not be compatible with each other, meaning that the code we wrote for version 1.0.0 won't work for version 1.3.1.

It's possible to solve this problem by specifying the exact version of the library when installing it with `pip`:

```
pip install library==1.0.0
```

Unfortunately, a different problem may appear: what if some of our colleagues already have version 1.3.1 installed, and they already used it for some other services?

In this case, they cannot go back to using version 1.0.0: it could cause their code to stop working.

We can solve these problems by creating a *virtual environment* for each project — a separate Python distribution with nothing else but libraries required for this particular project.

Pipenv is a tool that makes managing virtual environments easier. We can install it with pip:

```
pip install pipenv
```

After that, we use `pipenv` instead of `pip` for installing dependencies:

```
pipenv install numpy scikit-learn flask
```

When running it, we'll see that first, it configures the virtual environment, and then it installs the libraries:

```
Running virtualenv with interpreter .../bin/python3
✓ Successfully created virtual environment!
Virtualenv location: ...
Creating a Pipfile for this project…
Installing numpy…
Adding numpy to Pipfile's [packages]…
✓ Installation Succeeded
Installing scikit-learn…
Adding scikit-learn to Pipfile's [packages]…
✓ Installation Succeeded
Installing flask…
Adding flask to Pipfile's [packages]…
✓ Installation Succeeded
Pipfile.lock not found, creating…
Locking [dev-packages] dependencies…
Locking [packages] dependencies…
⠋ Locking...
```

After finishing the installation, it creates two files: Pipenv and Pipenv.lock.

The Pipenv file looks pretty simple:

```
[[source]]
name = "pypi"
url = "https://pypi.org/simple"
verify_ssl = true

[dev-packages]

[packages]
numpy = "*"
scikit-learn = "*"
flask = "*"

[requires]
python_version = "3.7"
```

We see that this file contains a list of libraries as well as the version of Python we use.

The other file — Pipenv.lock — contains the specific versions of the libraries that we used for the project. The file is too large to show in its entirety here, but let's take a look at one of the entries in the file:

```
"flask": {
    "hashes": [
        "sha256:4efa1ae2d7c9865af48986de8aeb8504...",
        "sha256:8a4fdd8936eba2512e9c85df320a37e6..."
    ],
    "index": "pypi",
    "version": "==1.1.2"
}
```

As we can see, it records the exact version of the library that was used during installation. To make sure the library doesn't change, it also saves the hashes — the checksums that can be used to validate that in the future we download the exact same version of the library. This way, we "lock" the dependencies to specific versions. By doing this, we make sure that in the future we will not have surprises with two incompatible versions of the same library.

If somebody needs to work on our project, they simply need to run the `install` command:

```
pipenv install
```

This step will first create a virtual environment and then install all the required libraries from Pipenv.lock.

> **IMPORTANT** Locking the version of a library is important for reproducibility in the future and helps us avoid having unpleasant surprises with code incompatibility.

After all the libraries are installed, we need to activate the virtual environment — this way, our application will use the correct versions of the libraries. We do it by running the `shell` command:

```
pipenv shell
```

It tells us that it's running in a virtual environment:

```
Launching subshell in virtual environment…
```

Now we can run our script for serving:

```
python churn_serving.py
```

Alternatively, instead of first explicitly entering the virtual environment and then running the script, we can perform these two steps with just one command:

```
pipenv run python churn_serving.py
```

The `run` command in Pipenv simply runs the specified program in the virtual environment.

Regardless of the way we run it, we should see exactly the same output as previously:

```
* Serving Flask app "churn" (lazy loading)
* Environment: production
  WARNING: This is a development server. Do not use it in a production
    deployment.
  Use a production WSGI server instead.
* Debug mode: on
* Running on http://0.0.0.0:9696/ (Press CTRL+C to quit)
```

When we test it with requests, we see the same output:

```
{'churn': False, 'churn_probability': 0.05960590758316391}
```

You most likely also noticed the following warning in the console:

```
* Environment: production
  WARNING: This is a development server. Do not use it in a production
    deployment.
  Use a production WSGI server instead.
```

The built-in Flask web server is indeed for development only: it's very easy to use for testing our application, but it won't work reliably under load. We should use a proper WSGI server instead, as the warning suggests.

WSGI stands for *web server gateway interface*, which is a specification describing how Python applications should handle HTTP requests. The details of WSGI are not important for the purposes of this book, so we won't cover it in detail.

We will, however, address the warning by installing a production WSGI server. We have multiple possible options in Python, and we'll use Gunicorn.

> **NOTE** Gunicorn doesn't work on Windows: it relies on features specific to Linux and Unix (which includes MacOS). A good alternative that also works on Windows is Waitress. Later, we will use Docker, which will solve this problem — it runs Linux inside a container.

Let's install it with Pipenv:

```
pipenv install gunicorn
```

This command installs the library and includes it as a dependency in the project by adding it to the Pipenv and Pipenv.lock files.

Let's run our application with Gunicorn:

```
pipenv run gunicorn --bind 0.0.0.0:9696 churn_serving:app
```

If everything goes well, we should see the following messages in the terminal:

```
[2020-04-13 22:58:44 +0200]  [15705]  [INFO]  Starting gunicorn 20.0.4
[2020-04-13 22:58:44 +0200]  [15705]  [INFO]  Listening at: http://0.0.0.0:9696
(15705)
[2020-04-13 22:58:44 +0200]  [15705]  [INFO]  Using worker: sync
[2020-04-13 22:58:44 +0200]  [16541]  [INFO]  Booting worker with pid: 16541
```

Unlike the Flask built-in web server, Gunicorn is ready for production, so it will not have any problems under load when we start using it.

If we test it with the same code as previously, we see the same answer:

```
{'churn': False, 'churn_probability': 0.05960590758316391}
```

Pipenv is a great tool for managing dependencies: it isolates the required libraries into a separate environment, thus helping us avoid conflicts between different versions of the same package.

In the next section, we look at Docker, which allows us to isolate our application even further and ensure it runs smoothly anywhere.

5.3.2 *Docker*

We have learned how to manage Python dependencies with Pipenv. However, some of the dependencies live outside of Python. Most importantly, these dependencies include the operating system (OS) as well as the system libraries.

For example, we might use Ubuntu version 16.04 for developing our service, but if some of our colleagues use Ubuntu version 20.04, they may run into trouble when trying to execute the service on their laptop.

Docker solves this "but it works on my machine" problem by also packaging the OS and the system libraries into a *Docker container* — a self-contained environment that works anywhere where Docker is installed (figure 5.5).

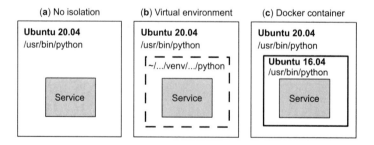

Figure 5.5   In case of no isolation (a), the service runs with system Python. In virtual environments (b), we isolate the dependencies of our service inside the environment. In Docker containers (c), we isolate the entire environment of the service, including the OS and system libraries.

Once the service is packaged into a Docker container, we can run it on the *host machine* — our laptop (regardless of the OS) or any public cloud provider.

Let's see how to use it for our project. We assume you already have Docker installed. Please refer to appendix A for details on how to install it.

First, we need to create a *Docker image* — the description of our service that includes all the settings and dependencies. Docker will later use the image to create a container. To do it, we need a Dockerfile — a file with instructions on how the image should be created (figure 5.6).

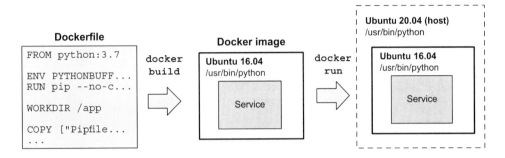

Figure 5.6 **We build an image using instructions from Dockerfile. Then we can run this image on a host machine.**

Let's create a file with name Dockerfile and the following content (note that the file shouldn't include the annotations):

```
FROM python:3.7.5-slim         ◁———— Specifies the base image

ENV PYTHONUNBUFFERED=TRUE       ◁——┐ Sets a special Python settings
                                    │ for being able to see logs

RUN pip --no-cache-dir install pipenv   ◁———— Installs Pipenv

WORKDIR /app      ◁———— Sets the working directory to /app

COPY ["Pipfile", "Pipfile.lock", "./"]   ◁———— Copies the Pipenv files

RUN pipenv install --deploy --system && \    │ Installs the dependencies from
    rm -rf /root/.cache                      │ the Pipenv files

COPY ["*.py", "churn-model.bin", "./"]    ◁———— Copies our code as well as the model

EXPOSE 9696    ◁———— Opens the port that our web service uses

ENTRYPOINT ["gunicorn", "--bind", "0.0.0.0:9696", "churn_serving:app"]   ◁──┐
                                    Specifies how the service should be started │
```

That's a lot of information to unpack, especially if you have never seen Dockerfiles previously. Let's go line by line.

First, we specify the base Docker image:

```
FROM python:3.7.5-slim
```

We use this image as the starting point and build our own image on top of that. Typically, the base image already contains the OS and the system libraries like Python itself, so we need to install only the dependencies of our project. In our case, we use `python:3.7.5-slim`, which is based on Debian 10.2 and contains Python version 3.7.5 and pip. You can read more about the Python base image in Docker hub (https://hub.docker.com/_/python) — the service for sharing Docker images.

All Dockerfiles should start with the `FROM` statement.

Next, we set the `PYTHONUNBUFFERED` environmental variable to `TRUE`:

```
ENV PYTHONUNBUFFERED=TRUE
```

Without this setting, we won't be able to see the logs when running Python scripts inside Docker.

Then, we use `pip` to install Pipenv:

```
RUN pip --no-cache-dir install pipenv
```

The `RUN` instruction in Docker simply runs a shell command. By default, `pip` saves the libraries to a cache, so later they can be installed faster. We don't need that in a Docker container, so we use the `--no-cache-dir` setting.

Then, we specify the working directory:

```
WORKDIR /app
```

This is roughly equivalent to the `cd` command in Linux (change directory), so everything we will run after that will be executed in the /app folder.

Then, we copy the Pipenv files to the current working directory (i.e., /app):

```
COPY ["Pipfile", "Pipfile.lock", "./"]
```

We use these files for installing the dependencies with Pipenv:

```
RUN pipenv install --deploy --system && \
    rm -rf /root/.cache
```

Previously, we simply used `pipenv install` for doing this. Here, we include two extra parameters: `--deploy` and `--system`. Inside Docker, we don't need to create a virtual environment — our Docker container is already isolated from the rest of the system. Setting these parameters allows us to skip creating a virtual environment and use the system Python for installing all the dependencies.

After installing the libraries, we clean the cache to make sure our Docker image doesn't grow too big.

Then, we copy our project files as well as the pickled model:

```
COPY ["*.py", "churn-model.bin", "./"]
```

Next, we specify which port our application will use. In our case, it's 9696:

```
EXPOSE 9696
```

Finally, we tell Docker how our application should be started:

```
ENTRYPOINT ["gunicorn", "--bind", "0.0.0.0:9696", "churn_serving:app"]
```

This is the same command we used previously when running Gunicorn locally.

Let's build the image. We do it by running the `build` command in Docker:

```
docker build -t churn-prediction .
```

The `-t` flag lets us set the tag name for the image, and the final parameter — the dot — specifies the directory with the Dockerfile. In our case, it means that we use the current directory.

When we run it, the first thing Docker does is download the base image:

```
Sending build context to Docker daemon   51.71kB
Step 1/11 : FROM python:3.7.5-slim
3.7.5-slim: Pulling from library/python
000eee12ec04: Downloading  24.84MB/27.09MB
ddc2d83f8229: Download complete
735b0bee82a3: Downloading  19.56MB/28.02MB
8c69dcedfc84: Download complete
495e1cccc7f9: Download complete
```

Then it executes each line of the Dockerfile one by one:

```
Step 2/9 : ENV PYTHONUNBUFFERED=TRUE
 ---> Running in d263b412618b
Removing intermediate container d263b412618b
 ---> 7987e3cf611f
Step 3/9 : RUN pip --no-cache-dir install pipenv
 ---> Running in e8e9d329ed07
Collecting pipenv
 ...
```

At the end, Docker tells us that it successfully built an image and tagged it as churn-prediction:latest:

```
Successfully built d9c50e4619a1
Successfully tagged churn-prediction:latest
```

We're ready to use this image to start a Docker container. Use the `run` command for that:

```
docker run -it -p 9696:9696 churn-prediction:latest
```

We specify a few parameters here:

- The `-it` flag tells Docker that we run it from our terminal and we need to see the results.
- The `-p` parameter specifies the port mapping. `9696:9696` means to map the port 9696 on the container to the port 9696 on the host machine.
- Finally, we need the image name and tag, which in our case is `churn-prediction:latest`.

Now our service is running inside a Docker container, and we can connect to it using port 9696 (figure 5.7). This is the same port we used for our application previously.

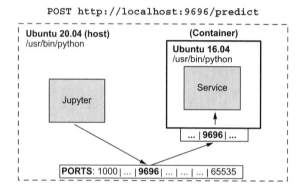

Figure 5.7   **The 9696 port on the host machine is mapped to the 9696 port of the container, so when we send a request to** `localhost:9696`**, it's handled by our service in Docker.**

Let's test it using the same code. When we run it, we'll see the same response:

```
{'churn': False, 'churn_probability': 0.05960590758316391}
```

Docker makes it easy to run services in a reproducible way. With Docker, the environment inside the container always stays the same. This means that if we can run our service on a laptop, it will work anywhere else.

We already tested our application on our laptop, so now let's see how to run it on a public cloud and deploy it to AWS.

5.4 Deployment

We don't run production services on our laptops; we need special servers for that.

In this section, we'll cover one possible option for that: Amazon Web Services, or AWS. We decided to choose AWS for its popularity — we're not affiliated with Amazon or AWS.

Other popular public clouds include Google Cloud, Microsoft Azure, and Digital Ocean. We don't cover them in this book, but you should be able to find similar instructions online and deploy a model to your favourite cloud provider.

This section is optional, so you can safely skip it. To follow the instructions in this section, you need to have an AWS account and configure the AWS command-line tool (CLI). Please refer to appendix A to see how to set it up.

5.4.1 *AWS Elastic Beanstalk*

AWS provides a lot of services, and we have many possible ways of deploying a web service there. For example, you can rent an EC2 machine (a server in AWS) and manually set up a service on it, use a "serverless" approach with AWS Lambda, or use a range of other services.

In this section, we'll use AWS Elastic Beanstalk, which is one of the simplest ways of deploying a model to AWS. Additionally, our service is simple enough, so it's possible to stay within the free-tier limits. In other words, we can use it for free for the first year.

Elastic Beanstalk automatically takes care of many things that we typically need in production, including

- Deploying our service to EC2 instances
- Scaling up: adding more instances to handle the load during peak hours
- Scaling down: removing these instances when the load goes away
- Restarting the service if it crashes for any reason
- Balancing the load between instances

We'll also need a special utility — Elastic Beanstalk command-line interface (CLI) — to use Elastic Beanstalk. The CLI is written in Python, so we can install it with `pip`, like any other Python tool.

However, because we use Pipenv, we can add it as a development dependency. This way, we'll install it only for our project and not systemwide.

```
pipenv install awsebcli --dev
```

> **NOTE** Development dependencies are the tools and libraries that we use for developing our application. Usually, we need them only locally and don't need them in the actual package deployed to production.

After installing Elastic Beanstalk, we can enter the virtual environment of our project:

```
pipenv shell
```

Now the CLI should be available. Let's check it:

```
eb --version
```

It should print the version:

```
EB CLI 3.18.0 (Python 3.7.7)
```

Next, we run the initialization command:

```
eb init -p docker churn-serving
```

Note that we use -p docker: this way, we specify that this is a Docker-based project.

If everything is fine, it creates a couple of files, including a config.yml file in .elasticbeanstalk folder.

Now we can test our application locally by using local run command:

```
eb local run --port 9696
```

This should work in the same way as in the previous section with Docker: it'll first build an image and then run the container.

To test it, we can use the same code as previously and get the same answer:

```
{'churn': False, 'churn_probability': 0.05960590758316391}
```

After verifying that it works well locally, we're ready to deploy it to AWS. We can do that with one command:

```
eb create churn-serving-env
```

This simple command takes care of setting up everything we need, from the EC2 instances to auto-scaling rules:

```
Creating application version archive "app-200418_120347".
Uploading churn-serving/app-200418_120347.zip to S3. This may take a while.
Upload Complete.
Environment details for: churn-serving-env
  Application name: churn-serving
  Region: us-west-2
  Deployed Version: app-200418_120347
  Environment ID: e-3xkqdzdjbq
  Platform: arn:aws:elasticbeanstalk:us-west-2::platform/Docker running on
    64bit Amazon Linux 2/3.0.0
  Tier: WebServer-Standard-1.0
  CNAME: UNKNOWN
  Updated: 2020-04-18 10:03:52.276000+00:00
Printing Status:
2020-04-18 10:03:51    INFO    createEnvironment is starting.
 -- Events -- (safe to Ctrl+C)
```

It'll take a few minutes to create everything. We can monitor the process and see what it's doing in the terminal.

When it's ready, we should see the following information:

```
2020-04-18 10:06:53    INFO    Application available at churn-serving-
env.5w9pp7bkmj.us-west-2.elasticbeanstalk.com.
2020-04-18 10:06:53    INFO    Successfully launched environment: churn-
serving-env
```

The URL (churn-serving-env.5w9pp7bkmj.us-west-2.elasticbeanstalk.com) in the logs is important: this is how we reach our application. Now we can use this URL to make predictions (figure 5.8).

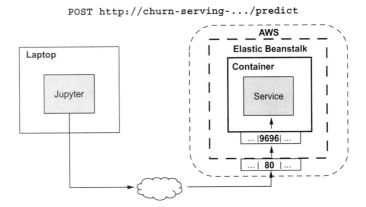

Figure 5.8 Our service is deployed inside a container on AWS Elastic Beanstalk. To reach it, we use its public URL.

Let's test it:

```
host = 'churn-serving-env.5w9pp7bkmj.us-west-2.elasticbeanstalk.com'
url = 'http://%s/predict' % host
response = requests.post(url, json=customer)
result = response.json()
result
```

As previously, we should see the same response:

```
{'churn': False, 'churn_probability': 0.05960590758316393}
```

That's all! We have a running service.

> **WARNING** This is a toy example, and the service we created is accessible by anyone in the world. If you do it inside an organization, the access should be restricted as much as possible. It's not difficult to extend this example to be secure, but it's outside the scope of this book. Consult the security department at your company before doing it at work.

We can do everything from the terminal using the CLI, but it's also possible to manage it from the AWS Console. To do so, we find Elastic Beanstalk there and select the environment we just created (figure 5.9).

To turn it off, choose Terminate deployment in the Environment actions menu using the AWS Console.

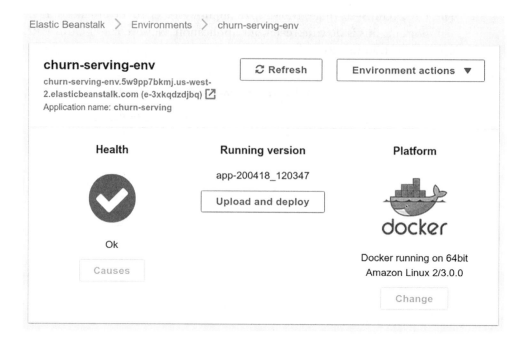

Figure 5.9   We can manage the Elastic Beanstalk environment in the AWS Console.

WARNING   Even though Elastic Beanstalk is free-tier eligible, we should always be careful and turn it off as soon as we no longer need it.

Alternatively, we use the CLI to do it:

```
eb terminate churn-serving-env
```

After a few minutes, the deployment will be removed from AWS and the URL will no longer be accessible.

AWS Elastic Beanstalk is a great tool for getting started with serving machine learning models. More advanced ways of doing it involve container orchestration systems like AWS ECS or Kubernetes or "serverless" with AWS Lambda. We will come back to this topic in chapters 8 and 9 when covering the deployment of deep learning models.

5.5   Next steps

We've learned about Pipenv and Docker and deployed our model to AWS Elastic Beanstalk. Try these other things to expand your skills on your own.

5.5.1 *Exercises*

Try the following exercises to further explore the topics of model deployment:

- If you don't use AWS, try to repeat the steps from section 5.4 on any other cloud provider. For example, you could try Google Cloud, Microsoft Azure, Heroku, or Digital Ocean.
- Flask is not the only way of creating web services in Python. You can try alternative frameworks like FastAPI (https://fastapi.tiangolo.com/), Bottle (https://github.com/bottlepy/bottle), or Falcon (https://github.com/falconry/falcon).

5.5.2 *Other projects*

You can continue other projects from the previous chapters and make them available as a web service as well. For example:

- The car-price prediction model we created in chapter 2
- The self-study projects from chapter 3: the lead scoring project and the default prediction project.

Summary

- Pickle is a serialization/deserialization library that comes built into Python. We can use it to save a model we trained in Jupyter Notebook and load it in a Python script.
- The simplest way of making a model available for others is wrapping it into a Flask web service.
- Pipenv is a tool for managing Python dependencies by creating virtual environments, so dependencies of one Python project don't interfere with dependencies of another Python project.
- Docker makes it possible to isolate the service completely from other services by packaging into a Docker container not only the Python dependencies but also the system dependencies, as well as the operational system itself.
- AWS Elastic Beanstalk is a simple way to deploy a web service. It takes care of managing EC2 instances, scaling the service up and down, and restarting if something fails.

In the next chapter, we continue learning about classification but with a different type of model — decision trees.

Decision trees
and ensemble learning

6

This chapter covers

- Decision trees and the decision tree learning algorithm
- Random forests: putting multiple trees together into one model
- Gradient boosting as an alternative way of combining decision trees

In chapter 3, we described the binary classification problem and used the logistic regression model to predict if a customer is going to churn.

In this chapter, we also solve a binary classification problem, but we use a different family of machine learning models: tree-based models. Decision trees, the simplest tree-based model, are nothing but a sequence of if-then-else rules put together. We can combine multiple decision trees into an ensemble to achieve better performance. We cover two tree-based ensemble models: random forest and gradient boosting.

The project we prepared for this chapter is default prediction: we predict whether or not a customer will fail to pay back a loan. We learn how to train decision trees and random forest models with Scikit-learn and explore XGBoost — a library for implementing gradient boosting models.

6.1 Credit risk scoring project

Imagine that we work at a bank. When we receive a loan application, we need to make sure that if we give the money, the customer will be able to pay it back. Every application carries a risk of *default* — the failure to return the money.

We'd like to minimize this risk: before agreeing to give a loan, we want to score the customer and assess the chances of default. If it's too high, we reject the application. This process is called "credit risk scoring."

Machine learning can be used for calculating the risk. For that, we need a dataset with loans, where for each application, we know whether or not it was paid back successfully. Using this data, we can build a model for predicting the probability of default, and we can use this model to assess the risk of future borrowers not repaying the money.

This is what we do in this chapter: use machine learning to calculate the risk of default. The plan for the project is the following:

- First, we get the data and do some initial preprocessing.
- Next, we train a decision tree model from Scikit-learn for predicting the probability of default.
- After that, we explain how decision trees work and which parameters the model has and show how to adjust these parameters to get the best performance.
- Then we combine multiple decision trees into one model — a random forest. We look at its parameters and tune them to achieve the best predictive performance.
- Finally, we explore a different way of combining decision trees — gradient boosting. We use XGBoost, a highly efficient library that implements gradient boosting. We'll train a model and tune its parameters.

Credit risk scoring is a binary classification problem: the target is positive ("1") if the customer defaults and negative ("0") otherwise. For evaluating our solution, we'll use AUC (area under the ROC curve), which we covered in chapter 4. AUC describes how well our model can separate the cases into positive and negative ones.

The code for this project is available in the book's GitHub repository at https://github.com/alexeygrigorev/mlbookcamp-code (in the chapter-06-trees folder).

6.1.1 Credit scoring dataset

For this project, we use a dataset from a data mining course at the Polytechnic University of Catalonia (https://www.cs.upc.edu/~belanche/Docencia/mineria/mineria.html). The dataset describes the customers (seniority, age, marital status, income, and other characteristics), the loan (the requested amount, the price of the item), and its status (paid back or not).

We use a copy of this dataset available on GitHub at https://github.com/gastonstat/CreditScoring/. Let's download it.

First, create a folder for our project (e.g., chapter-06-credit-risk), and then use wget to get it:

```
wget https://github.com/gastonstat/CreditScoring/raw/master/CreditScoring.csv
```

Alternatively, you can enter the link to your browser and save it to the project folder.

Next, start a Jupyter Notebook server if it's not started yet:

```
jupyter notebook
```

Go to the project folder, and create a new notebook (e.g., chapter-06-credit-risk).

As usual, we begin by importing Pandas, NumPy, Seaborn, and Matplotlib:

```
import pandas as pd
import numpy as np

import seaborn as sns
from matplotlib import pyplot as plt
%matplotlib inline
```

After we press Ctrl-Enter, the libraries are imported and we're ready to read the data with Pandas:

```
df = pd.read_csv('CreditScoring.csv')
```

Now the data is loaded, so let's take an initial look at it and see if we need to do any preprocessing before we can use it.

6.1.2   Data cleaning

To use a dataset for our task, we need to look for any issues in the data and fix them.

Let's start by looking at the first rows of the DataFrame, generated by the df.head() function (figure 6.1).

```
df.head()
```

	Status	Seniority	Home	Time	Age	Marital	Records	Job	Expenses	Income	Assets	Debt	Amount	Price
0	1	9	1	60	30	2	1	3	73	129	0	0	800	846
1	1	17	1	60	58	3	1	1	48	131	0	0	1000	1658
2	2	10	2	36	46	2	2	3	90	200	3000	0	2000	2985
3	1	0	1	60	24	1	1	1	63	182	2500	0	900	1325
4	1	0	1	36	26	1	1	1	46	107	0	0	310	910

Figure 6.1   The first five rows of the credit scoring dataset

First, we can see that all the column names start with a capital letter. Before doing anything else, let's lowercase all the column names and make it consistent with other projects (figure 6.2):

```
df.columns = df.columns.str.lower()
```

```
df.columns = df.columns.str.lower()
df.head()
```

	status	seniority	home	time	age	marital	records	job	expenses	income	assets	debt	amount	price
0	1	9	1	60	30	2	1	3	73	129	0	0	800	846
1	1	17	1	60	58	3	1	1	48	131	0	0	1000	1658
2	2	10	2	36	46	2	2	3	90	200	3000	0	2000	2985
3	1	0	1	60	24	1	1	1	63	182	2500	0	900	1325
4	1	0	1	36	26	1	1	1	46	107	0	0	310	910

Figure 6.2 The DataFrame with lowercase column names

We can see that the DataFrame has the following columns:

- status: whether the customer managed to pay back the loan (1) or not (2)
- seniority: job experience in years
- home: type of homeownership: renting (1), a homeowner (2), and others
- time: period planned for the loan (in months)
- age: age of the client
- marital [status]: single (1), married (2), and others
- records: whether the client has any previous records: no (1), yes (2) (It's not clear from the dataset description what kind of records we have in this column. For the purposes of this project, we may assume that it's about records in the bank's database.)
- job: type of job: full-time (1), part-time (2), and others
- expenses: how much the client spends per month
- income: how much the client earns per month
- assets: total worth of all the assets of the client
- debt: amount of credit debt
- amount: requested amount of the loan
- price: price of an item the client wants to buy

Although most of the columns are numerical, some are categorical: status, home, marital [status], records, and job. The values we see in the DataFrame, however, are numbers, not strings. This means that we need to translate them to their actual names. In the GitHub repository with the dataset is a script that decodes the numbers to categories (https://github.com/gastonstat/CreditScoring/blob/master/Part1_CredScoring_Processing.R). Originally, this script was written in R, so we need to translate it to Pandas.

We start with the status column. The value "1" means "OK," the value "2" means "default," and "0" means that the value is missing — let's replace it with "unk" (short for "unknown").

In Pandas, we can use `map` for converting the numbers to strings. For that, we first define the dictionary with mapping from the current value (number) to the desired value (string):

```
status_values = {
    1: 'ok',
    2: 'default',
    0: 'unk'
}
```

Now we can use this dictionary to do the mapping:

```
df.status = df.status.map(status_values)
```

It creates a new series, which we immediately write back to the DataFrame. As a result, the values in the status column are overwritten and look more meaningful (figure 6.3).

```
status_values = {
    1: 'ok',
    2: 'default',
    0: 'unk'
}

df.status = df.status.map(status_values)
df.head()
```

	status	seniority	home	time	age	marital	records	job	expenses	income	assets	debt	amount	price
0	ok	9	1	60	30	2	1	3	73	129	0	0	800	846
1	ok	17	1	60	58	3	1	1	48	131	0	0	1000	1658
2	default	10	2	36	46	2	2	3	90	200	3000	0	2000	2985
3	ok	0	1	60	24	1	1	1	63	182	2500	0	900	1325
4	ok	0	1	36	26	1	1	1	46	107	0	0	310	910

Figure 6.3   To translate the original values in the status column (numbers) to a more meaningful representation (strings), we use the `map` method.

We repeat the same procedure for all the other columns. First, we'll do it for the home column:

```
home_values = {
    1: 'rent',
    2: 'owner',
    3: 'private',
    4: 'ignore',
    5: 'parents',
    6: 'other',
```

```
        0: 'unk'
}

df.home = df.home.map(home_values)
```

Next, let's do it for the marital, records, and job columns:

```
marital_values = {
    1: 'single',
    2: 'married',
    3: 'widow',
    4: 'separated',
    5: 'divorced',
    0: 'unk'
}

df.marital = df.marital.map(marital_values)


records_values = {
    1: 'no',
    2: 'yes',
    0: 'unk'
}

df.records = df.records.map(records_values)


job_values = {
    1: 'fixed',
    2: 'parttime',
    3: 'freelance',
    4: 'others',
    0: 'unk'
}

df.job = df.job.map(job_values)
```

After these transformations, the columns with categorical variables contain the actual values, not numbers (figure 6.4).

```
df.head()
```

	status	seniority	home	time	age	marital	records	job	expenses	income	assets	debt	amount	price
0	ok	9	rent	60	30	married	no	freelance	73	129	0	0	800	846
1	ok	17	rent	60	58	widow	no	fixed	48	131	0	0	1000	1658
2	default	10	owner	36	46	married	yes	freelance	90	200	3000	0	2000	2985
3	ok	0	rent	60	24	single	no	fixed	63	182	2500	0	900	1325
4	ok	0	rent	36	26	single	no	fixed	46	107	0	0	310	910

Figure 6.4 The values of categorical variables are translated from integers to strings.

As the next step, let's take a look at numerical columns. First, let's check the summary statistics for each of the columns: min, mean, max, and others. To do so, we can use the describe method of the DataFrame:

```
df.describe().round()
```

> **NOTE** The output of describe may be confusing. In our case, there are values in scientific notation like 1.000000e+08 or 8.703625e+06. To force Pandas to use a different notation, we use round: it removes the fractional part of a number and rounds it to the closest integer.

It gives us an idea of how the distribution of the values in each column looks (figure 6.5).

```
df.describe().round()
```

	seniority	time	age	expenses	income	assets	debt	amount	price
count	4455.0	4455.0	4455.0	4455.0	4455.0	4455.0	4455.0	4455.0	4455.0
mean	8.0	46.0	37.0	56.0	763317.0	1060341.0	404382.0	1039.0	1463.0
std	8.0	15.0	11.0	20.0	8703625.0	10217569.0	6344253.0	475.0	628.0
min	0.0	6.0	18.0	35.0	0.0	0.0	0.0	100.0	105.0
25%	2.0	36.0	28.0	35.0	80.0	0.0	0.0	700.0	1118.0
50%	5.0	48.0	36.0	51.0	120.0	3500.0	0.0	1000.0	1400.0
75%	12.0	60.0	45.0	72.0	166.0	6000.0	0.0	1300.0	1692.0
max	48.0	72.0	68.0	180.0	99999999.0	99999999.0	99999999.0	5000.0	11140.0

Figure 6.5   **The summary of all numerical columns of the dataframe. We notice that some of them have 99999999 as the max value.**

One thing we notice immediately is that the max value is 99999999 in some cases. This is quite suspicious. As it turns out, it's an artificial value — this is how missing values are encoded in this dataset.

Three columns have this problem: income, assets, and debt. Let's replace this big number with NaN for these columns:

```
for c in ['income', 'assets', 'debt']:
    df[c] = df[c].replace(to_replace=99999999, value=np.nan)
```

We use the replace method, which takes two values:

- to_replace: the original value ("99999999," in our case)
- value: the target value ("NaN," in our case)

After this transformation, no more suspicious numbers appear in the summary (figure 6.6).

```
df.describe().round()
```

	seniority	time	age	expenses	income	assets	debt	amount	price
count	4455.0	4455.0	4455.0	4455.0	4421.0	4408.0	4437.0	4455.0	4455.0
mean	8.0	46.0	37.0	56.0	131.0	5403.0	343.0	1039.0	1463.0
std	8.0	15.0	11.0	20.0	86.0	11573.0	1246.0	475.0	628.0
min	0.0	6.0	18.0	35.0	0.0	0.0	0.0	100.0	105.0
25%	2.0	36.0	28.0	35.0	80.0	0.0	0.0	700.0	1118.0
50%	5.0	48.0	36.0	51.0	120.0	3000.0	0.0	1000.0	1400.0
75%	12.0	60.0	45.0	72.0	165.0	6000.0	0.0	1300.0	1692.0
max	48.0	72.0	68.0	180.0	959.0	300000.0	30000.0	5000.0	11140.0

Figure 6.6 The summary statistics after replacing large values with NaN

Before we finish with the dataset preparation, let's look at our target variable `status`:

```
df.status.value_counts()
```

The output of `value_counts` shows the count of each value:

```
ok          3200
default     1254
unk            1
Name: status, dtype: int64
```

Notice that there's one row with "unknown" status: we don't know whether or not this client managed to pay back the loan. For our project, this row is not useful, so let's remove it from the dataset:

```
df = df[df.status != 'unk']
```

In this case, we don't really "remove" it: we create a new DataFrame where we don't have records with "unknown" status.

By looking at the data, we have identified a few important issues in the data and addressed them.

For this project, we skip a more detailed exploratory data analysis like we did for chapter 2 (the car-price prediction project) and chapter 3 (churn prediction project), but you're free to repeat the steps we covered there for this project as well.

6.1.3 Dataset preparation

Now our dataset is cleaned, and we're almost ready to use it for model training. Before we can do that, we need to do a few more steps:

- Split the dataset into train, validation, and test.
- Handle missing values.

- Use one-hot encoding to encode categorical variables.
- Create the feature matrix X and the target variable y.

Let's start by splitting the data. We will split the data into three parts:

- Training data (60% of the original dataset)
- Validation data (20%)
- Test data (20%)

Like previously, we'll use `train_test_split` from Scikit-learn for that. Because we cannot split it into three datasets at once, we'll need to split two times (figure 6.7). First we'll hold out 20% of data for testing, and then split the remaining 80% into training and validation:

```
from sklearn.model_selection import train_test_split

df_train_full, df_test = train_test_split(df, test_size=0.2, random_state=11)
df_train, df_val = train_test_split(df_train_full, test_size=0.25,
    random_state=11)
```

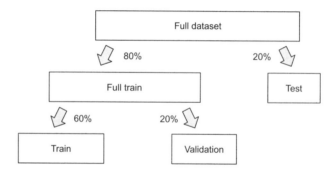

Figure 6.7   Because `train_test_split` can split a dataset into only two parts, but we need three, we perform the split two times.

When splitting for the second time, we put aside 25% of data instead of 20% (`test_size=0.25`). Because `df_train_full` contains 80% of records, one-quarter (i.e., 25%) of 80% corresponds to 20% of the original dataset.

To check the size of our datasets, we can use the `len` function:

```
len(df_train), len(df_val), len(df_test)
```

When running it, we get the following output:

```
(2672, 891, 891)
```

So, for training, we will use approximately 2,700 examples and almost 900 for validation and testing.

The outcome we want to predict is status. We will use it to train a model, so it's our *y* — the target variable. Because our objective is to determine if somebody fails to pay back their loan, the positive class is default. This means that *y* is "1" if the client defaulted and "0" otherwise. It's quite simple to implement:

```
y_train = (df_train.status == 'default').values
y_val = (df_val.status == 'default').values
```

Now we need to remove status from the DataFrames. If we don't do it, we may accidentally use this variable for training. For that, we use the del operator:

```
del df_train['status']
del df_val['status']
```

Next, we'll take care of *X* — the feature matrix.

From the initial analysis, we know our data contains missing values — we added these NaNs ourselves. We can replace the missing values with zero:

```
df_train = df_train.fillna(0)
df_val = df_val.fillna(0)
```

To use categorical variables, we need to encode them. In chapter 3, we applied the one-hot encoding technique for that. In one-hot encoding, each value is encoded as "1" if it's present ("hot") or "0" if it's absent ("cold"). To implement it, we used Dict-Vectorizer from Scikit-learn.

DictVectorizer needs a list of dictionaries, so we first need to convert the Data-Frames into this format:

```
dict_train = df_train.to_dict(orient='records')
dict_val = df_val.to_dict(orient='records')
```

Each dictionary in the result represents a row from the DataFrame. For example, the first record in dict_train looks like this:

```
{'seniority': 10,
 'home': 'owner',
 'time': 36,
 'age': 36,
 'marital': 'married',
 'records': 'no',
 'job': 'freelance',
 'expenses': 75,
 'income': 0.0,
 'assets': 10000.0,
 'debt': 0.0,
 'amount': 1000,
 'price': 1400}
```

This list of dictionaries now can be used as input to DictVectorizer:

```
from sklearn.feature_extraction import DictVectorizer

dv = DictVectorizer(sparse=False)

X_train = dv.fit_transform(dict_train)
X_val = dv.transform(dict_val)
```

As a result, we have feature matrices for both train and validation datasets. Please refer to chapter 3 for more details on doing one-hot encoding with Scikit-learn.

Now we're ready to train a model! In the next section, we cover the simplest tree model: decision tree.

6.2   *Decision trees*

A *decision tree* is a data structure that encodes a series of if-then-else rules. Each node in a tree contains a condition. If the condition is satisfied, we go to the right side of the tree; otherwise, we go to the left. In the end we arrive at the final decision (figure 6.8).

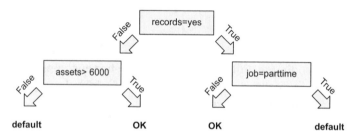

Figure 6.8   A decision tree consists of nodes with conditions. If the condition in a node is satisfied, we go right; otherwise, we go left.

It's quite easy to represent a decision tree as a set of if-else statements in Python. For example:

```
def assess_risk(client):
    if client['records'] == 'yes':
        if client['job'] == 'parttime':
            return 'default'
        else:
            return 'ok'
    else:
        if client['assets'] > 6000:
            return 'ok'
        else:
            return 'default'
```

With machine learning, we can extract these rules from data automatically. Let's see how we can do it.

6.2.1 *Decision tree classifier*

We'll use Scikit-learn for training a decision tree. Because we're solving a classification problem, we need to use `DecisionTreeClassifier` from the `tree` package. Let's import it:

```
from sklearn.tree import DecisionTreeClassifier
```

Training the model is as simple as invoking the `fit` method:

```
dt = DecisionTreeClassifier()
dt.fit(X_train, y_train)
```

To check if the result is good, we need to evaluate the predictive performance of the model on the validation set. Let's use AUC (area under the ROC curve) for that.

Credit risk scoring is a binary classification problem, and for cases like that, AUC is one of the best evaluation metrics. As you may recall from our discussion in chapter 4, AUC shows how well a model separates positive examples from negative examples. It has a nice interpretation: it describes the probability that a randomly chosen positive example ("default") has a higher score than a randomly chosen negative example ("OK"). This is a relevant metric for the project: we want risky clients to have higher scores than nonrisky ones. For more details on AUC, refer to chapter 4.

Like previously, we'll use an implementation from Scikit-learn, so let's import it:

```
from sklearn.metrics import roc_auc_score
```

First, we evaluate the performance on the training set. Because we chose AUC as the evaluation metric, we need scores, not hard predictions. As we know from chapter 3, we need to use the `predict_proba` method for that:

```
y_pred = dt.predict_proba(X_train)[:, 1]
roc_auc_score(y_train, y_pred)
```

When we execute it, we see that the score is 100% — the perfect score. Does it mean that we can predict default without errors? Let's check the score on validation before jumping to conclusions:

```
y_pred = dt.predict_proba(X_val)[:, 1]
roc_auc_score(y_val, y_pred)
```

After running, we see that AUC on validation is only 65%.

We just observed a case of *overfitting*. The tree learned the training data so well that it simply memorized the outcome for each customer. However, when we applied it to the validation set, the model failed. The rules it extracted from the data turned out to be too specific to the training set, so it worked poorly for customers it didn't see during training. In such cases, we say that the model cannot *generalize*.

Overfitting happens when we have a complex model with enough power to remember all the training data. If we force the model to be simpler, we can make it less powerful and improve the model's ability to generalize.

We have multiple ways to control the complexity of a tree. One option is to restrict its size: we can specify the max_depth parameter, which controls the maximum number of levels. The more levels a tree has, the more complex rules it can learn (figure 6.9).

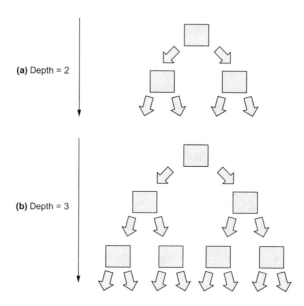

Figure 6.9   A tree with more levels can learn more complex rules. A tree with two levels is less complex than a tree with three levels and, thus, less prone to overfitting.

The default value for the max_depth parameter is None, which means that the tree can grow as large as possible. We can try a smaller value and compare the results.

For example, we can change it to 2:

```
dt = DecisionTreeClassifier(max_depth=2)
dt.fit(X_train, y_train)
```

To visualize the tree we just learned, we can use the export_text function from the tree package:

```
from sklearn.tree import export_text

tree_text = export_text(dt, feature_names=dv.feature_names_)
print(tree_text)
```

We only need to specify the names of features using the feature_names parameter. We can get it from the DictVectorizer. When we print it, we get the following:

```
|--- records=no <= 0.50
|    |--- seniority <= 6.50
|    |    |--- class: True
|    |--- seniority >  6.50
|    |    |--- class: False
|--- records=no >  0.50
|    |--- job=parttime <= 0.50
|    |    |--- class: False
|    |--- job=parttime >  0.50
|    |    |--- class: True
```

Each line in the output corresponds to a node with a condition. If the condition is true, we go inside and repeat the process until we arrive at the final decision. At the end, if class is True, then the decision is "default," and otherwise it's "OK."

The condition records=no > 0.50 means that a customer has no records. Recall that we use one-hot encoding to represent records with two features: records=yes and records=no. For a customer with no records, records=no is set to "1" and records=yes to "0." Thus, "records=no > 0.50 is true when the value for records is no (figure 6.10).

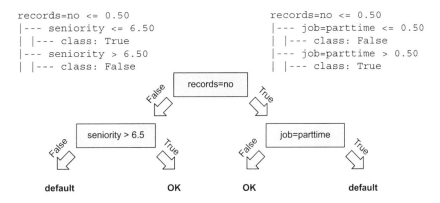

Figure 6.10   The tree we learned with max_depth set to 2

Let's check the score:

```
y_pred = dt.predict_proba(X_train)[:, 1]
auc = roc_auc_score(y_train, y_pred)
print('train auc', auc)

y_pred = dt.predict_proba(X_val)[:, 1]
auc = roc_auc_score(y_val, y_pred)
print('validation auc', auc)
```

We see that the score on train dropped:

```
train auc: 0.705
val auc: 0.669
```

Previously, the performance on the training set was 100%, but now it's only 70.5%. It means that the model can no longer memorize all the outcomes from the training set.

However, the score on the validation set is better: it's 66.9%, which is an improvement over the previous result (65%). By making it less complex, we improved the ability of our model to generalize. Now it's better at predicting the outcomes for customers it hasn't seen previously.

However, this tree has another problem — it's too simple. To make it better, we need to tune the model: try different parameters, and see which ones lead to the best AUC. In addition to max_depth, we can control other parameters. To understand what these parameters mean and how they influence the model, let's take a step back and look at how decision trees learn rules from data.

6.2.2   *Decision tree learning algorithm*

To understand how a decision tree learns from data, let's simplify the problem. First, we'll use a much smaller dataset with just one feature: assets (figure 6.11).

	assets	status
0	8000	default
1	2000	OK
2	0	OK
3	6000	OK
4	6000	default
5	9000	default

Figure 6.11   **A smaller dataset with one feature: assets. The target variable is status.**

Second, we'll grow a very small tree, with a single node.

The only feature we have in the dataset is assets. This is why the condition in the node will be assets > T, where *T* is a threshold value that we need to determine. If the condition is true, we'll predict "OK," and if it's false, our prediction will be "default" (figure 6.12).

The condition assets > T is called a *split*. It splits the dataset into two groups: the data points that satisfy the condition and the data points that do not.

If T is 4000, then we have customers with more than $4,000 in assets (on the right) and the customers with less than $4,000 in assets (on the left) (figure 6.13).

Figure 6.12   A simple decision tree with only one node. The node contains a condition `assets > T`. We need to find the best value for *T*.

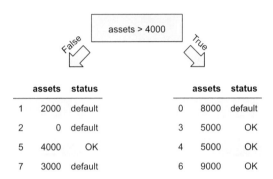

Figure 6.13   The condition in a node splits the dataset into two parts: data points that satisfy the condition (on the right) and data points that don't (on the left).

Now we turn these groups into *leaves* — the decision nodes — by taking the most frequent status in each group and using it as the final decision. In our example, "default" is the most frequent outcome in the left group and "OK" in the right (figure 6.14).

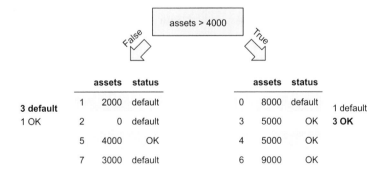

Figure 6.14   The most frequent outcome on the left is "default." For the group on the right, it's "OK."

Thus, if a customer has more than $4,000 in assets, our decision is "OK," and, otherwise, it's "default" `assets > 4000` (figure 6.15).

Figure 6.15   By taking the most frequent outcome in each group and assigning it to leaves, we get the final decision tree

IMPURITY

These groups should be as homogeneous as possible. Ideally, each group should contain only observations of one class. In this case, we call these groups *pure*.

For example, if we have a group of four customers with outcomes ["default," "default," "default," "default"], it's pure: it contains only customers who defaulted. But a group ["default," "default," "default," "OK"] is impure: there's one customer who didn't default.

When training a decision tree model, we want to find such T that the *impurity* of both groups is minimal.

So, the algorithm for finding T is quite simple:

- Try all possible values of T.
- For each T, split the dataset into left and right groups and measure their impurity.
- Select T that has the lowest degree of impurity.

We can use different criteria for measuring impurity. The easiest one to understand is the *misclassification rate*, which says how many observations in a group don't belong to the majority class.

> **NOTE** Scikit-learn uses more advanced split criteria such as entropy and the Gini impurity. We do not cover them in this book, but the idea is the same: they measure the degree of impurity of the split.

Let's calculate the misclassification rate for the split $T = 4000$ (figure 6.16):

- For the left group, the majority class is "default." There are four data points in total, and one doesn't belong to "default." The misclassification rate is 25% (1/4).
- For the right group, "OK" is the majority class, and there's one "default." Thus, the misclassification rate is also 25% (1/4).
- To calculate the overall impurity of the split, we can take the average across both groups. In this case, the average is 25%.

> **NOTE** In reality, instead of taking the simple average across both groups, we take a weighted average — we weight each group proportionally to its size. To simplify calculations, we use the simple average in this chapter.

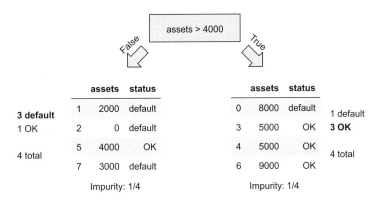

Figure 6.16 For `assets > 4000`, the misclassification rate for both groups is one-quarter.

$T = 4000$ is not the only possible split for `assets`. Let's try other values for T such as 2000, 3000, and 5000 (figure 6.17):

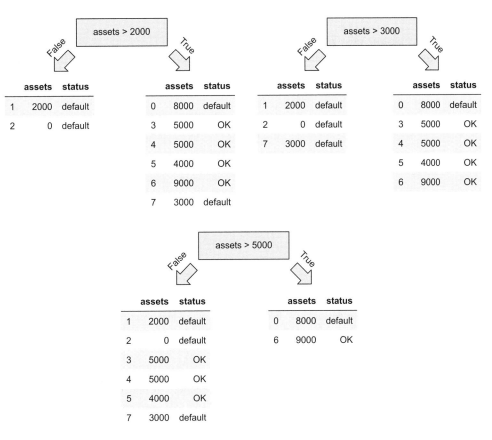

Figure 6.17 In addition to `assets > 4000`, we can try other values of T, such as 2000, 3000, and 5000.

- For $T = 2000$, we have 0% impurity on the left (0/2, all are "default") and 33.3% impurity on the right (2/6, 2 out of 6 are "default," the rest are "OK"). The average is 16.6%.
- For $T = 3000$, 0% on the left and 20% (1/5) on the right. The average is 10%.
- For $T = 5000$, 50% (3/6) on the left and 50% (1/2) on the right. The average is 50%.

The best average impurity is 10% for $T = 3000$: we got zero mistakes for the left tree and only one (out of five rows) for the right. So, we should select 3000 as the threshold for our final model (figure 6.18).

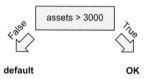

Figure 6.18   The best split for this dataset is `assets > 3000`.

SELECTING THE BEST FEATURE FOR SPLITTING

Now let's make the problem a bit more complex and add another feature to the dataset: `debt` (figure 6.19).

	assets	debt	status
0	8000	3000	default
1	2000	1000	default
2	0	1000	default
3	5000	1000	OK
4	5000	1000	OK
5	4000	1000	OK
6	9000	500	OK
7	3000	2000	default

Figure 6.19   A dataset with two features: `assets` and `debt`. The target variable is `status`.

Previously we had only one feature: `assets`. We knew for sure that it would be used for splitting the data. Now we have two features, so in addition to selecting the best threshold for splitting, we need to figure out which feature to use.

The solution is simple: we try all the features, and for each feature select the best threshold.

Let's modify the training algorithm to include this change:

- For each feature, try all possible thresholds.
- For each threshold value T, measure the impurity of the split.
- Select the feature and the threshold with the lowest impurity possible.

Let's apply this algorithm to our dataset:

- We already identified that for `assets`, the best T is 3000. The average impurity of this split is 10%.
- For `debt`, the best T is 1000. In this case, the average impurity is 17%.

So, the best split is `asset > 3000` (figure 6.20).

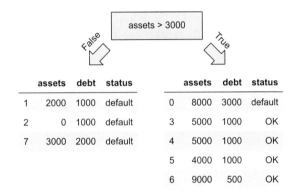

Figure 6.20   The best split is `assets > 3000`, which has the average impurity of 10%.

The group on the left is already pure, but the group on the right is not. We can make it less impure by repeating the process: split it again!

When we apply the same algorithm to the dataset on the right, we find that the best split condition is `debt > 1000`. We have two levels in the tree now — or we can say that the depth of this tree is 2 (figure 6.21).

Before the decision tree is ready, we need to do the last step: convert the groups into decision nodes. For that, we take the most frequent status in each group. This way, we get a decision tree (figure 6.22).

STOPPING CRITERIA

When training a decision tree, we can keep splitting the data until all the groups are pure. This is exactly what happens when we don't put any restrictions on the trees in Scikit-learn. As we've seen, the resulting model becomes too complex, which leads to overfitting.

We solved this problem by using the `max_depth` parameter — we restricted the tree size and didn't let it grow too big.

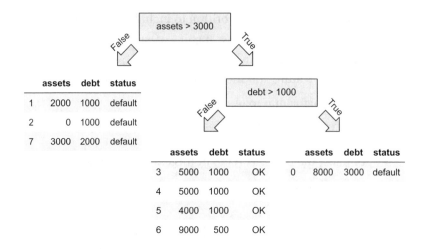

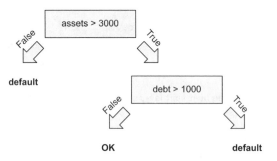

Figure 6.21   By repeating the algorithm recursively to the group on the right, we get a tree with two levels.

Figure 6.22   The groups are already pure, so the most frequent status is the only status each group has. We take this status as the final decision in each leaf.

To decide if we want to continue splitting the data, we use *stopping criteria* — criteria that describe if we should add another split in the tree or stop.

The most common stopping criteria are

- The group is already pure.
- The tree reached the depth limit (controlled by the max_depth parameter).
- The group is too small to continue splitting (controlled by the min_samples_ leaf parameter).

By using these criteria to stop earlier, we force our model to be less complex and, therefore, reduce the risk of overfitting.

Let's use this information to adjust the training algorithm:

- Find the best split:
  - For each feature try all possible threshold values.
  - Use the one with the lowest impurity.
- If the maximum allowed depth is reached, stop.
- If the group on the left is sufficiently large and it's not pure yet, repeat on the left.
- If the group on the right is sufficiently large and it's not pure yet, repeat on the right.

Even though this is a simplified version of the decision tree learning algorithm, it should provide you enough intuition about the internals of the learning process.

Most important, we know two parameters control the complexity of the model. By changing these parameters, we can improve the performance of the model.

Exercise 6.1

We have a dataset with 10 features and need to add another feature to this dataset. What happens with the speed of training?

a With one more feature, training takes longer.

b The number of features does not affect the speed of training.

6.2.3 *Parameter tuning for decision tree*

The process of finding the best set of parameters is called *parameter tuning*. We usually do it by changing the model and checking its score on the validation dataset. In the end, we use the model with the best validation score.

As we have just learned, we can tune two parameters:

- `max_depth`
- `min_leaf_size`

These two are the most important ones, so we will adjust only them. You can check the other parameters in the official documentation (https://scikit-learn.org/stable/modules/generated/sklearn.tree.DecisionTreeClassifier.html).

When we trained our model previously, we restricted the depth of the tree to 2, but we didn't touch `min_leaf_size`. With this, we got an AUC of 66% on the validation set.

Let's find the best parameters.

We start by tuning max_depth. For that, we iterate over a few reasonable values and see what works best:

```
for depth in [1, 2, 3, 4, 5, 6, 10, 15, 20, None]:
    dt = DecisionTreeClassifier(max_depth=depth)
```

```
dt.fit(X_train, y_train)
y_pred = dt.predict_proba(X_val)[:, 1]
auc = roc_auc_score(y_val, y_pred)
print('%4s -> %.3f' % (depth, auc))
```

The value `None` means that there's no restriction on depth, so the tree will grow as large as it can.

When we run this code, we see that `max_depth` of 5 gives the best AUC (76.6%), followed by 4 and 6 (figure 6.23).

```
    1 -> 0.606
    2 -> 0.669
    3 -> 0.739
    4 -> 0.761 ⎤ Optimal values
    5 -> 0.766 ⎥ for max_depth
    6 -> 0.754 ⎦
   10 -> 0.685
   15 -> 0.671
   20 -> 0.657
 None -> 0.657
```

Figure 6.23   The optimal value for depth is 5 (76.6%) followed by 4 (76.1%) and 6 (75.4%).

Next, we tune `min_leaf_size`. For that, we iterate over the three best parameters of `max_depth`, and for each, go over different values of `min_leaf_size`:

```
for m in [4, 5, 6]:
    print('depth: %s' % m)

    for s in [1, 5, 10, 15, 20, 50, 100, 200]:
        dt = DecisionTreeClassifier(max_depth=m, min_samples_leaf=s)
        dt.fit(X_train, y_train)
        y_pred = dt.predict_proba(X_val)[:, 1]
        auc = roc_auc_score(y_val, y_pred)
        print('%s -> %.3f' % (s, auc))

    print()
```

After running it, we see that the best AUC is 78.5% with parameters `min_sample_leaf=15` and `max_depth=6` (table 6.1).

> **NOTE**   As we see, the value we use for `min_leaf_size` influences the best value of `max_depth`. You can experiment with a wider range of values for `max_depth` to tweak the performance further.

Table 6.1 AUC on validation set for different values of `min_leaf_size` **(rows) and** `max_depth` **(columns)**

	depth=4	depth=5	depth=6
1	0.761	0.766	0.754
5	0.761	0.768	0.760
10	0.761	0.762	0.778
15	0.764	0.772	**0.785**
20	0.761	0.774	0.774
50	0.753	0.768	0.770
100	0.756	0.763	0.776
200	0.747	0.759	0.768

We have found the best parameters, so let's use them to train the final model:

```
dt = DecisionTreeClassifier(max_depth=6, min_samples_leaf=15)
dt.fit(X_train, y_train)
```

Decision trees are simple and effective models, but they become even more powerful when we combine many trees together. Next, we'll see how we can do it to achieve even better predictive performance.

6.3   *Random forest*

For a moment, let's suppose that we don't have a machine learning algorithm to help us with credit risk scoring. Instead, we have a group of experts.

Each expert can independently decide if we should approve a loan application or reject it. An individual expert may make a mistake. However, it's less likely that all the experts together decide to accept the application, but the customer fails to pay the money back.

Thus, we can ask all the experts independently and then combine their verdicts into the final decision, for example, by using the majority vote (figure 6.24).

This idea also applies to machine learning. One model individually may be wrong, but if we combine the output of multiple models into one, the chance of an incorrect answer is smaller. This concept is called *ensemble learning*, and a combination of models is called an *ensemble*.

For this to work, the models need to be different. If we train the same decision tree model 10 times, they will all predict the same output, so it's not useful at all.

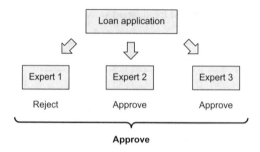

Figure 6.24 **A group of experts can make a decision better than a single expert individually.**

The easiest way to have different models is to train each tree on a different subset of features. For example, suppose we have three features: assets, debts, and price. We can train three models:

- The first will use assets and debts.
- The second will use debts and price.
- The last one will use assets and price.

With this approach, we'll have different trees, each making its own decisions (figure 6.25). But when we put their predictions together, their mistakes average out, and combined, they have more predictive power.

This way of putting together multiple decision trees into an ensemble is called a *random forest.* To train a random forest, we can do this (figure 6.26):

- Train *N* independent decision tree models.
- For each model, select a random subset of features, and use only them for training.
- When predicting, combine the output of *N* models into one.

NOTE This is a very simplified version of the algorithm. It's enough to illustrate the main idea, but in reality, it's more complex.

Scikit-learn contains an implementation of a random forest, so we can use it for solving our problem. Let's do it.

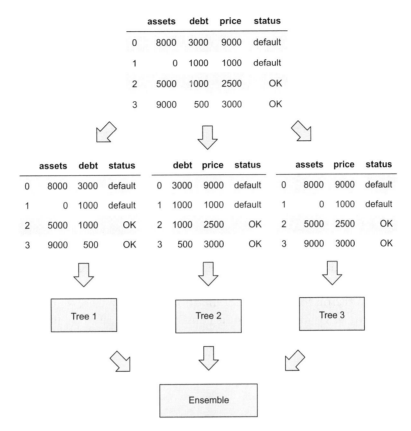

	assets	debt	price	status
0	8000	3000	9000	default
1	0	1000	1000	default
2	5000	1000	2500	OK
3	9000	500	3000	OK

	assets	debt	status
0	8000	3000	default
1	0	1000	default
2	5000	1000	OK
3	9000	500	OK

	debt	price	status
0	3000	9000	default
1	1000	1000	default
2	1000	2500	OK
3	500	3000	OK

	assets	price	status
0	8000	9000	default
1	0	1000	default
2	5000	2500	OK
3	9000	3000	OK

Tree 1   Tree 2   Tree 3

Ensemble

Figure 6.25 Models we want to combine in an ensemble should not be the same. We can make sure they are different by training each tree on a different subset of features.

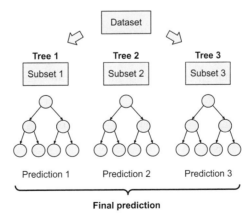

Dataset

Tree 1 Subset 1
Tree 2 Subset 2
Tree 3 Subset 3

Prediction 1   Prediction 2   Prediction 3

Final prediction

Figure 6.26 Training a random forest model: for training each tree, randomly select a subset of features. When making the final prediction, combine all the predictions into one.

6.3.1   *Training a random forest*

To use random forest in Scikit-learn, we need to import `RandomForestClassifier` from the ensemble package:

```
from sklearn.ensemble import RandomForestClassifier
```

When training a model, the first thing we need to specify is the number of trees we want to have in the ensemble. We do it with the `n_estimators` parameter:

```
rf = RandomForestClassifier(n_estimators=10)
rf.fit(X_train, y_train)
```

After training finishes, we can evaluate the performance of the result:

```
y_pred = rf.predict_proba(X_val)[:, 1]
roc_auc_score(y_val, y_pred)
```

It shows 77.9%. However, the number you see may be different. Every time we retrain the model, the score changes: it varies from 77% to 80%.

The reason for this is randomization: to train a tree, we randomly select a subset of features. To make the results consistent, we need to fix the seed for the random-number generator by assigning some value to the `random_state` parameter:

```
rf = RandomForestClassifier(n_estimators=10, random_state=3)
rf.fit(X_train, y_train)
```

Now we can evaluate it:

```
y_pred = rf.predict_proba(X_val)[:, 1]
roc_auc_score(y_val, y_pred)
```

This time, we get an AUC of 78%. This score doesn't change, no matter how many times we retrain the model.

The number of trees in the ensemble is an important parameter, and it influences the performance of the model. Usually, a model with more trees is better than a model with fewer trees. On the other hand, adding too many trees is not always helpful.

To see how many trees we need, we can iterate over different values for `n_estimators` and see its effect on AUC:

```
aucs = []         ◁———— Creates a list with AUC results

for i in range(10, 201, 10):                                          Trains progressively
    rf = RandomForestClassifier(n_estimators=i, random_state=3)       more trees in each
    rf.fit(X_train, y_train)                                          iteration

    y_pred = rf.predict_proba(X_val)[:, 1]      Evaluates
    auc = roc_auc_score(y_val, y_pred)          the score
    print('%s -> %.3f' % (i, auc))
                                                Adds the score to the
    aucs.append(auc)   ◁────────────────────    list with other scores
```

In this code, we try different numbers of trees: from 10 to 200, going by steps of 10 (10, 20, 30, …). Each time we train a model, we calculate its AUC on the validation set and record it.

After we finish, we can plot the results:

```
plt.plot(range(10, 201, 10), aucs)
```

In figure 6.27, we can see the results.

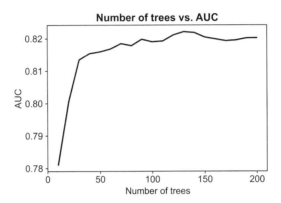

Figure 6.27   The performance of the random forest model with different values for the `n_estimators` parameter

The performance grows rapidly for the first 25–30 trees; then the growth slows down. After 130, adding more trees is not helpful anymore: the performance stays approximately at the level of 82%.

The number of trees is not the only parameter we can change to get better performance. Next, we see which other parameters we should also tune to improve the model.

6.3.2   *Parameter tuning for random forest*

A random forest ensemble consists of multiple decision trees, so the most important parameters we need to tune for random forest are the same:

- `max_depth`
- `min_leaf_size`

We can change other parameters, but we won't cover them in detail in this chapter. Refer to the official documentation for more information (https://scikit-learn.org/stable/modules/generated/sklearn.ensemble.RandomForestClassifier.html).

Let's start with `max_depth`. We already know that this parameter significantly affects the performance of a decision tree. This is also the case for random forest: larger trees tend to overfit more than smaller trees.

Let's test a few values for max_depth and see how AUC evolves as the number of trees grows:

```
all_aucs = {}                          Creates a dictionary with AUC results

for depth in [5, 10, 20]:              Iterates over different depth values
    print('depth: %s' % depth)
    aucs = []                          Creates a list with AUC results
                                       for the current depth level
    for i in range(10, 201, 10):
        rf = RandomForestClassifier(n_estimators=i, max_depth=depth,
        random_state=1)                Iterates over different
        rf.fit(X_train, y_train)       n_estimator values
        y_pred = rf.predict_proba(X_val)[:, 1]
        auc = roc_auc_score(y_val, y_pred)
        print('%s -> %.3f' % (i, auc))  Evaluates
        aucs.append(auc)                the model

    all_aucs[depth] = aucs             Save the AUCs for the current
    print()                            depth level in the dictionary
```

Now for each value of max_depth, we have a series of AUC scores. We can plot them now:

```
num_trees = list(range(10, 201, 10))
plt.plot(num_trees, all_aucs[5], label='depth=5')
plt.plot(num_trees, all_aucs[10], label='depth=10')
plt.plot(num_trees, all_aucs[20], label='depth=20')
plt.legend()
```

In figure 6.28 we see the result.

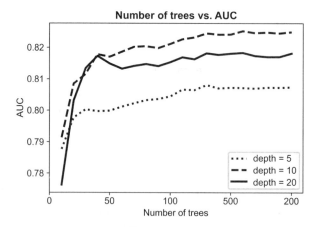

Figure 6.28 **The performance of random forest with different values of the** max_depth **parameter**

With `max_depth=10`, AUC goes over 82%, whereas for other values it performs worse.

Now let's tune `min_samples_leaf`. We set the value for the `max_depth` parameter from the previous step and then follow the same approach as previously for determining the best value for `min_samples_leaf`:

```
all_aucs = {}

for m in [3, 5, 10]:
    print('min_samples_leaf: %s' % m)
    aucs = []

    for i in range(10, 201, 20):
        rf = RandomForestClassifier(n_estimators=i, max_depth=10,
    min_samples_leaf=m, random_state=1)
        rf.fit(X_train, y_train)
        y_pred = rf.predict_proba(X_val)[:, 1]
        auc = roc_auc_score(y_val, y_pred)
        print('%s -> %.3f' % (i, auc))
        aucs.append(auc)

    all_aucs[m] = aucs
    print()
```

Let's plot it:

```
num_trees = list(range(10, 201, 20))
plt.plot(num_trees, all_aucs[3], label='min_samples_leaf=3')
plt.plot(num_trees, all_aucs[5], label='min_samples_leaf=5')
plt.plot(num_trees, all_aucs[10], label='min_samples_leaf=10')
plt.legend()
```

Then review the results (figure 6.29).

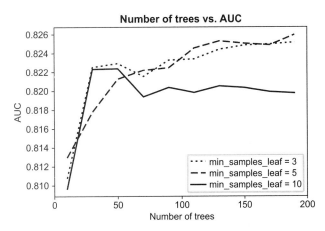

Figure 6.29 **The performance of random forest with different values of `min_samples_leaf` (with `max_depth=10`)**

We see that AUC is slightly better for small values of `min_samples_leaf` and the best value is 5.

Thus, the best parameters for random forest for our problem are

- `max_depth=10`
- `min_samples_leaf=5`

We achieved the best AUC with 200 trees, so we should set the `n_estimators` parameter to 200.

Let's train the final model:

```
rf = RandomForestClassifier(n_estimators=200, max_depth=10,
    min_samples_leaf=5, random_state=1)
```

Random forest is not the only way to combine multiple decision trees. There's a different approach: gradient boosting. We cover that next.

Exercise 6.2

To make an ensemble useful, trees in a random forest should be different from each other. This is done by

   a Selecting different parameters for each individual tree
   b Randomly selecting a different subset of features for each tree
   c Randomly selecting values for splitting

6.4 *Gradient boosting*

In a random forest, each tree is independent: it's trained on a different set of features. After individual trees are trained, we combine all their decisions together to get the final decision.

It's not the only way to combine multiple models together in one ensemble, however. Alternatively, we can train models sequentially — each next model tries to fix errors from the previous one:

- Train the first model.
- Look at the errors it makes.
- Train another model that fixes these errors.
- Look at the errors again; repeat sequentially.

This way of combining models is called *boosting*. *Gradient boosting* is a particular variation of this approach that works especially well with trees (figure 6.30).

Let's have a look at how we can use it for solving our problem.

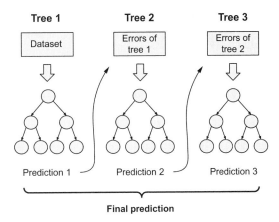

Figure 6.30 In gradient boosting, we train the models sequentially, and each next tree fixes the errors of the previous one.

6.4.1 XGBoost: Extreme gradient boosting

We have many good implementations of the gradient boosting model: `Gradient-BoostingClassifier` from Scikit-learn, XGBoost, LightGBM and CatBoost. In this chapter, we use XGBoost (short for "Extreme Gradient Boosting"), which is the most popular implementation.

XGBoost doesn't come with Anaconda, so to use it, we need to install it. The easiest way is to install it with `pip`:

```
pip install xgboost
```

Next, open the notebook with our project and import it:

```
import xgboost as xgb
```

> **NOTE** In some cases, importing XGBoost may give you a warning like `YMLLoadWarning`. You shouldn't worry about it; the library will work without problems.

Using the alias `xgb` when importing XGBoost is a convention, just like with other popular machine learning packages in Python.

Before we can train an XGBoost model, we need to wrap our data into `DMatrix` — a special data structure for finding splits efficiently. Let's do it:

```
dtrain = xgb.DMatrix(X_train, label=y_train, feature_names=dv.feature_names_)
```

When creating an instance of `DMatrix`, we pass three parameters:

- `X_train`: the feature matrix
- `y_train`: the target variable
- `feature_names`: the names of features in `X_train`

Let's do the same for the validation dataset:

```
dval = xgb.DMatrix(X_val, label=y_val, feature_names=dv.feature_names_)
```

The next step is specifying the parameters for training. We're using only a small subset of the default parameters of XGBoost (check the official documentation for the entire list of parameter: https://xgboost.readthedocs.io/en/latest/parameter.html):

```
xgb_params = {
    'eta': 0.3,
    'max_depth': 6,
    'min_child_weight': 1,

    'objective': 'binary:logistic',
    'nthread': 8,
    'seed': 1,
    'silent': 1
}
```

For us, the most important parameter now is `objective`: it specifies the learning task. We're solving a binary classification problem — that's why we need to choose `binary:logistic`. We cover the rest of these parameters later in this section.

For training an XGBoost model, we use the `train` function. Let's start with 10 trees:

```
model = xgb.train(xgb_params, dtrain, num_boost_round=10)
```

We provide three arguments to `train`:

- xgb_params: the parameters for training
- dtrain: the dataset for training (an instance of `DMatrix`)
- num_boost_round=10: the number of trees to train

After a few seconds, we get a model. To evaluate it, we need to make a prediction on the validation dataset. For that, use the `predict` method with the validation data wrapped in `DMatrix`:

```
y_pred = model.predict(dval)
```

The result, `y_pred`, is a one-dimensional NumPy array with predictions: the risk score for each customer in the validation dataset (figure 6.31).

```
y_pred = model.predict(dval)
y_pred[:10]
```
```
array([0.08926772, 0.0468099 , 0.09692743, 0.17261842, 0.05435968,
       0.12576081, 0.08033007, 0.61870354, 0.486538  , 0.04056795],
      dtype=float32)
```

Figure 6.31   The predictions of XGBoost

Next, we calculate AUC using the same approach as previously:

```
roc_auc_score(y_val, y_pred)
```

After executing it, we get 81.5%. This is quite a good result, but it's still slightly worse than our best random forest model (82.5%).

Training an XGBoost model is simpler when we can see how its performance changes when the number of trees grows. We see how to do it next.

6.4.2 Model performance monitoring

To get an idea of how AUC changes as the number of trees grows, we can use a watchlist — a built-in feature in XGBoost for monitoring model performance.

A watchlist is a Python list with tuples. Each tuple contains a DMatrix and its name. This is how we typically do it:

```
watchlist = [(dtrain, 'train'), (dval, 'val')]
```

Additionally, we modify the list of parameters for training: we need to specify the metric we use for evaluation. In our case, it's the AUC:

```
xgb_params = {
    'eta': 0.3,
    'max_depth': 6,
    'min_child_weight': 1,

    'objective': 'binary:logistic',
    'eval_metric': 'auc',          ◁───┐  Sets the evaluation
    'nthread': 8,                       │  metric to the AUC
    'seed': 1,
    'silent': 1
}
```

To use the watchlist during training, we need to specify two extra arguments for the train function:

- `evals`: the watchlist.
- `verbose_eval`: how often we print the metric. If we set it to "10," we see the result after each 10th step.

Let's train it:

```
model = xgb.train(xgb_params, dtrain,
                  num_boost_round=100,
                  evals=watchlist, verbose_eval=10)
```

While training, XGBoost prints the scores to the output:

```
[0]   train-auc:0.862996   val-auc:0.768179
[10]  train-auc:0.950021   val-auc:0.815577
[20]  train-auc:0.973165   val-auc:0.817748
```

```
[30] train-auc:0.987718   val-auc:0.817875
[40] train-auc:0.994562   val-auc:0.813873
[50] train-auc:0.996881   val-auc:0.811282
[60] train-auc:0.998887   val-auc:0.808006
[70] train-auc:0.999439   val-auc:0.807316
[80] train-auc:0.999847   val-auc:0.806771
[90] train-auc:0.999915   val-auc:0.806371
[99] train-auc:0.999975   val-auc:0.805457
```

As the number of trees grows, the score on the training set goes up (figure 6.32).

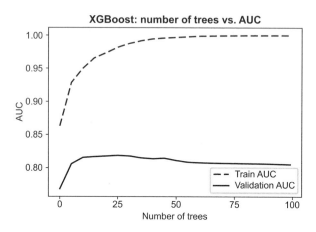

**Figure 6.32   The effect of the number of trees on the AUC from train and validation sets.
To see how to plot these values, check the notebook in the book's GitHub repository.**

This behavior is expected: in boosting, every next model tries to fix the mistakes from the previous step, so the score is always improving.

For the validation score, however, this is not the case. It goes up initially but then starts to decrease. This is the effect of overfitting: our model becomes more and more complex until it simply memorizes the entire training set. It's not helpful for predicting the outcome for the customers outside of the training set, and the validation score reflects that.

We get the best AUC on the 30th iteration (81.7%), but it's not so different from the score we got on the 10th iteration (81.5%).

Next, we'll see how to get the best out of XGBoost by tuning its parameters.

6.4.3   *Parameter tuning for XGBoost*

Previously, we used a subset of default parameters for training a model:

```
xgb_params = {
    'eta': 0.3,
    'max_depth': 6,
    'min_child_weight': 1,
```

```
    'objective': 'binary:logistic',
    'eval_metric': 'auc',
    'nthread': 8,
    'seed': 1,
    'silent': 1
}
```

We're mostly interested in the first three parameters. These parameters control the training process:

- `eta`: Learning rate. Decision trees and random forest don't have this parameter. We cover it later in this section when we tune it.
- `max_depth`: The maximum allowed depth of each tree; the same as `max_depth` in `DecisionTreeClassifier` from Scikit-learn.
- `min_child_weight`: The minimal number of observations in each group; the same as `min_leaf_size` in `DecisionTreeClassifier` from Scikit-learn.

Other parameters:

- `objective`: The type of task we want to solve. For classification, it should be `binary:logistic`.
- `eval_metric`: The metric we use for evaluation. For this project, it's "AUC."
- `nthread`: The number of threads we use for training the model. XGBoost is very good at parallelizing training, so set it to the number of cores your computer has.
- `seed`: The seed for the random-number generator; we need to set it to make sure the results are reproducible.
- `silent`: The verbosity of the output. When we set it to "1," it outputs only warnings.

This is not the full list of parameters, only the basic ones. You can learn more about all the parameters in the official documentation (https://xgboost.readthedocs.io/en/latest/parameter.html).

We already know `max_depth` and `min_child_weight` (`min_leaf_size`), but we haven't previously come across `eta` — the learning rate parameter. Let's talk about it and see how we can optimize it.

LEARNING RATE

In boosting, each tree tries to correct the mistakes from the previous iterations. Learning rate determines the weight of this correction. If we have a large value for `eta`, the correction overweights the previous predictions significantly. On the other hand, if the value is small, only a small fraction of this correction is used.

In practice it means

- If `eta` is too large, the model starts to overfit quite early without realizing its full potential.
- If it's too small, we need to train too many trees before it can produce good results.

The default value of 0.3 is reasonably good for large datasets, but for smaller datasets like ours, we should try smaller values like 0.1 or even 0.05.

Let's do it and see if it helps to improve the performance:

```
xgb_params = {
    'eta': 0.1,                          Changes eta from
    'max_depth': 6,                      0.3 to 0.1
    'min_child_weight': 1,

    'objective': 'binary:logistic',
    'eval_metric': 'auc',
    'nthread': 8,
    'seed': 1,
    'silent': 1
}
```

Because now we can use a watchlist to monitor the performance of our model, we can train for as many iterations as we want. Previously we used 100 iterations, but this may be not enough for smaller eta. So let's use 500 rounds for training:

```
model = xgb.train(xgb_params, dtrain,
                  num_boost_round=500, verbose_eval=10,
                  evals=watchlist)
```

When running it, we see that the best validation score is 82.4%:

```
[60] train-auc:0.976407   val-auc:0.824456
```

Previously, we could achieve AUC of 81.7% when eta was set to the default value of 0.3. Let's compare these two models (figure 6.33).

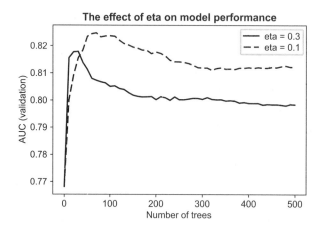

Figure 6.33   The effect of the eta **parameter on the validation score**

When eta is 0.3, we get the best AUC pretty quickly, but then it starts to overfit. After the 30th iteration, the performance on the validation set goes down.

When eta is 0.1, AUC grows more slowly but peaks at a higher value. For a smaller learning rate, it takes more trees to reach the peak, but we could achieve better performance.

For comparison, we can also try other values of eta (figure 6.34):

- For 0.05, the best AUC is 82.2% (after 120 iterations).
- For 0.01, the best AUC is 82.1% (after 500 iterations).

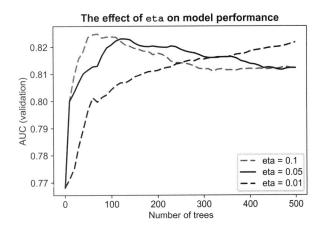

Figure 6.34   The model requires more trees when eta is small.

When eta is 0.05, the performance is similar to 0.1, but it takes 60 more iterations to reach the peak.

For eta of 0.01, it grows too slowly, and even after 500 iterations, it hasn't reached the peak. If we tried it for more iterations, it could potentially get to the same level of AUC as other values. Even if it was the case, it's not practical: it becomes computationally expensive to evaluate all these trees during prediction time.

Thus, we use the value of 0.1 for eta. Next, let's tune other parameters.

Exercise 6.3

We have a gradient boosting model with eta=0.1. It needs 60 trees to get the peak performance. If we increase eta to 0.5, what will happen?

- a The number of trees will not change.
- b The model will need more trees to reach its peak performance.
- c The model will need fewer trees to reach its peak performance.

TUNING OTHER PARAMETERS

The next parameter we tune is `max_depth`. The default value is 6, so we can try

- A lower value; for example, 3
- A higher value; for example, 10

The outcome should give us an idea if the best value for `max_depth` is between 3 and 6 or between 6 and 10.

First, check 3:

```
xgb_params = {
    'eta': 0.1,                          Changes max_depth
    'max_depth': 3,        ◁——          from 6 to 3
    'min_child_weight': 1,

    'objective': 'binary:logistic',
    'eval_metric': 'auc',
    'nthread': 8,
    'seed': 1,
    'silent': 1
}
```

The best AUC we get with it is 83.6%.

Next, try 10. In this case, the best value is 81.1%.

This means that the optimal parameter of `max_depth` should be between 3 and 6. When we try 4, however, we see that the best AUC is 83%, which is slightly worse than the AUC we got with the depth of 3 (figure 6.35).

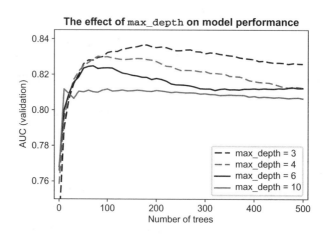

Figure 6.35 The optimal value for `max_depth` is 4: with it, we can achieve an AUC of 83.6%.

The next parameter we tune is `min_child_weight`. It's the same as `min_leaf_size` in decision trees from Scikit-learn: it controls the minimal number of observations a tree can have in a leaf.

Let's try a range of values and see which one works best. In addition to the default value (1), we can try 10 and 30 (figure 6.36).

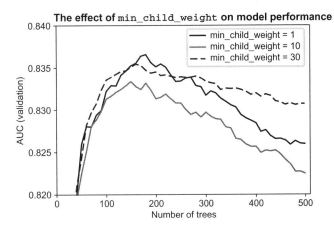

Figure 6.36 **The optimal value for** `min_child_weight` **is 1, but it's not drastically different from other values for this parameter.**

From figure 6.36 we see that

- For `min_child_weight=1`, AUC is 83.6%.
- For `min_child_weight=10`, AUC is 83.3%.
- For `min_child_weight=30`, AUC is 83.5%.

The difference between these options is not significant, so we'll leave the default value.

The parameters for our final model are

```
xgb_params = {
    'eta': 0.1,
    'max_depth': 3,
    'min_child_weight': 1,

    'objective': 'binary:logistic',
    'eval_metric': 'auc',
    'nthread': 8,
    'seed': 1,
    'silent': 1
}
```

We need to do one last step before we can finish the model: we need to select the optimal number of trees. It's quite simple: look at the iteration when the validation score peaked and use this number.

In our case, we need to train 180 trees for the final model (figure 6.37):

```
[160] train-auc:0.935513    val-auc:0.835536
[170] train-auc:0.937885    val-auc:0.836384
```

```
[180] train-auc:0.93971    val-auc:0.836565 <- best
[190] train-auc:0.942029   val-auc:0.835621
[200] train-auc:0.943343   val-auc:0.835124
```

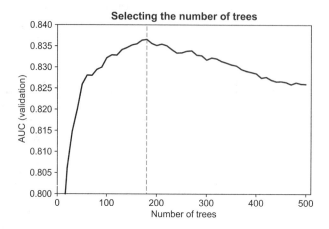

Figure 6.37   The optimal number of trees for the final model is 180.

The best the random forest model was able to get 82.5% AUC, whereas the best the gradient boosting model could get was 1% more (83.6%).

This is the best model, so let's use it as our final model — and we should use it for scoring loan applications.

6.4.4   *Testing the final model*

We're almost ready to use it for risk scoring. We still need to do two things before we can use it:

- Retrain the final model on both train and validation datasets combined. We no longer need the validation dataset, so we can use more data for training, which will make the model slightly better.
- Test the model on the test set. This is the part of data we kept aside from the beginning. Now we use it to make sure the model didn't overfit and performs well on completely unseen data.

The next steps are:

- Apply the same preprocessing to df_full_train and df_test as we did to df_train and df_val. As a result, we get the feature matrices X_train and X_test as well as our target variables y_train and y_test.
- Train a model on the combined dataset with the parameters we selected previously.
- Apply the model to the test data to get the test predictions.
- Verify that the model performs well and doesn't overfit.

Let's do it. First, create the target variable:

```
y_train = (df_train_full.status == 'default').values
y_test = (df_test.status == 'default').values
```

Because we use the entire DataFrame for creating the feature matrix, we need to remote the target variable:

```
del df_train_full['status']
del df_test['status']
```

Next, we convert DataFrames into lists of dictionaries and then use one-hot encoding to get the feature matrices:

```
dict_train = df_train_full.fillna(0).to_dict(orient='records')
dict_test = df_test.fillna(0).to_dict(orient='records')

dv = DictVectorizer(sparse=False)
X_train = dv.fit_transform(dict_train)
X_test = dv.transform(dict_test)
```

Finally, we train the XGBoost model using this data and the optimal parameters we determined previously:

```
dtrain = xgb.DMatrix(X_train, label=y_train, feature_names=dv.feature_names_)
dtest = xgb.DMatrix(X_test, label=y_test, feature_names=dv.feature_names_)

xgb_params = {
    'eta': 0.1,
    'max_depth': 3,
    'min_child_weight': 1,

    'objective': 'binary:logistic',
    'eval_metric': 'auc',
    'nthread': 8,
    'seed': 1,
    'silent': 1
}

num_trees = 160

model = xgb.train(xgb_params, dtrain, num_boost_round=num_trees)
```

Then evaluate its performance on the test set:

```
y_pred_xgb = model.predict(dtest)
roc_auc_score(y_test, y_pred_xgb)
```

The output is 83.2%, which is comparable to 83.6% — the performance on the validation set. It means that our model doesn't overfit and can work well with customers it hasn't seen.

Exercise 6.4

The main difference between random forest and gradient boosting is

  a Trees in gradient boosting are trained sequentially, and each next tree improves the previous one. In a random forest, all trees are trained independently.

  b Gradient boosting is a lot faster than using a random forest.

  c Trees in a random forest are trained sequentially, and each next tree improves the previous one. In gradient boosting, all trees are trained independently.

6.5   Next steps

We've learned the basics about decision trees, random forest, and gradient boosting. We've learned a lot, but there's much more than we could fit in this chapter. You can explore this topic further by doing the exercises.

6.5.1   Exercises

- Feature engineering is the process of creating new features out of existing ones. For this project, we haven't created any features; we simply used the ones provided in the dataset. Adding more features should help improve the performance of our model. For example, we can add the ratio of requested money to the total price of the item. Experiment with engineering more features.

- When training a random forest, we get different models by selecting a random subset of features for each tree. To control the size of the subset, we use the `max_features` parameter. Try adjusting this parameter, and see if it changes the AUC on validation.

- Extreme randomized trees (or extra trees, for short) is a variation of a random forest where the idea of randomization is taken to the extreme. Instead of finding the best possible split, it picks a splitting condition randomly. This approach has a few advantages: extra trees are faster to train, and they are less prone to overfitting. On the other hand, they require more trees to have adequate performance. In Scikit-learn, `ExtraTreesClassifier` from the `ensemble` package implements it. Experiment with it for this project.

- In XGBoost, the `colsample_bytree` parameter controls the number of features we select for each tree — it's similar to `max_features` from the random forest. Experiment with this parameter, and see if it improves the performance: try values from 0.1 to 1.0 with a step of 0.1. Usually the optimal values are between 0.6 and 0.8, but sometimes 1.0 gives the best result.

- In addition to randomly selecting columns (features), we can also select a subset of rows (customers). This is called *subsampling*, and it helps to prevent overfitting. In XGBoost, the `subsample` parameter controls the fraction of examples we select for training each tree in the ensemble. Try values from 0.4 to 1.0 with a step of 0.1. Usually the optimal values are between 0.6 and 0.8.

6.5.2   *Other projects*

- All tree-based models can solve the regression problem — predict a number. In Scikit-learn, DecisionTreeRegressor, and RandomForestRegressor, implement the regression variation of the models. In XGBoost, we need to change the objective to `reg:squarederror`. Use these models for predicting the price of the car, and try to solve other regression problems as well.

Summary

- Decision tree is a model that represents a sequence of if-then-else decisions. It's easy to understand, and it also performs quite well in practice.
- We train decision trees by selecting the best split using impurity measures. The main parameters that we control are the depth of the tree and the maximum number of samples in each leaf.
- A random forest is a way to combine many decision trees into one model. Like a team of experts, individual trees can make mistakes, but together, they are less likely to reach an incorrect decision.
- A random forest should have a diverse set of models to make good predictions. That's why each tree in the model uses a different set of features for training.
- The main parameters we need to change for random forest are the same as for decision trees: the depth and the maximum number of samples in each leaf. Additionally, we need to select the number of trees we want to have in the ensemble.
- While in a random forest the trees are independent, in gradient boosting, the trees are sequential, and each next model corrects the mistakes of the previous one. In some cases, this leads to better predictive performance.
- The parameters we need to tune for gradient boosting are similar for a random forest: the depth, the maximum number of observations in the leaf, and the number of trees. In addition to that, we have `eta` — the learning rate. It specifies the contribution of each individual tree to the ensemble.

Tree-based models are easy to interpret and understand, and often they perform quite well. Gradient boosting is great and often achieves the best possible performance on structured data (data in tabular format).

In the next chapter, we look at neural nets: a different type of model, which, in contrast, achieves best performance on unstructured data, such as images.

Answers to exercises

- Exercise 6.1 A) With one more feature, training takes longer.
- Exercise 6.3 C) The model will need fewer trees to reach its peak performance.
- Exercise 6.2 B) Randomly selecting a different subset of features for each tree.
- Exercise 6.4 A) Trees in gradient boosting are trained sequentially. In a random forest, trees are trained independently.

Neural networks
and deep learning

This chapter covers

- Convolutional neural networks for image classification
- TensorFlow and Keras — frameworks for building neural networks
- Using pretrained neural networks
- Internals of a convolutional neural network
- Training a model with transfer learning
- Data augmentations — the process of generating more training data

Previously, we only dealt with tabular data — data in CSV files. In this chapter, we'll work with a completely different type of data — images.

The project we prepared for this chapter is classification of clothes. We will predict if an image of clothing is a T-shirt, a shirt, a skirt, a dress, or something else.

This is an image classification problem. To solve it, we will learn how to train a deep neural network using TensorFlow and Keras to recognize the types of clothes. The materials of this chapter will help you start using neural networks and perform any similar image classification project.

Let's start!

7.1   Fashion classification

Imagine that we work at an online fashion marketplace. Our users upload thousands of images every day to sell their clothes. We want to help our users create listings faster by automatically recommending the right category for their clothes.

To do it, we need a model for classifying images. Previously, we covered multiple models for classification: logistic regression, decision trees, random forests, and gradient boosting. These models work great with tabular data, but it's quite difficult to use them for images.

To solve our problem, we need a different type of model: a convolutional neural network, a special model used for images. These neural networks consist of many layers, and that's why they are often called "deep." Deep learning is a part of machine learning that deals with deep neural networks.

The frameworks for training these models are also different from what we saw previously, so in this chapter we use TensorFlow and Keras instead of Scikit-learn.

The plan for our project is

- First, we download the dataset and use a pretrained model to classify images.
- Then, we talk about neural networks, and see how they work internally.
- After that, we adjust the pretrained neural network for solving our tasks.
- Finally, we expand our dataset by generating many more images from the images we have.

For evaluating the quality of our models, let's use accuracy: the percentage of items we classified correctly.

It's not possible to cover all the theory behind deep learning in just one chapter. In this book, we focus on the most fundamental parts, which is enough for completing the project of this chapter and other similar projects about image classification. When we come across concepts that are nonessential for completing this project, for details, we refer to CS231n — a course about neural networks from Stanford University. The course notes are available online at cs231n.github.io.

The code for this project is available in the book's GitHub repository at https://github.com/alexeygrigorev/mlbookcamp-code, in the folder chapter-07-neural-nets. There are multiple notebooks in this folder. For most of the chapter, we need 07-neural-nets-train.ipynb. For section 7.5, we use 07-neural-nets-test.ipynb.

7.1.1   GPU vs. CPU

Training a neural network is a computationally demanding process, and it requires powerful hardware to make it faster. To speed up training, we usually use GPUs — graphical processing units, or, simply, graphic cards.

For this chapter, a GPU is not required. You can do everything on your laptop, but without a GPU, it will be approximately eight times slower than with a GPU.

If you have a GPU card, you need to install special drivers from TensorFlow to use it. (Check the official documentation of TensorFlow for more details: https://www .tensorflow.org/install/gpu.) Alternatively, you can rent a preconfigured GPU server. For example, we can use AWS SageMaker to rent a Jupyter Notebook instance with everything already set up. Refer to appendix E for details on how to use SageMaker. Other cloud providers also have servers with GPU, but we do not cover them in this book. Regardless of the environment you use, the code works anywhere, as long as you can install Python and TensorFlow there.

After deciding where to run the code, we can go to the next step: downloading the dataset.

7.1.2   *Downloading the clothing dataset*

First, let's create a folder for this project and call it 07-neural-nets.

For this project, we need a dataset of clothes. We will use a subset of the clothing dataset (for more information, check https://github.com/alexeygrigorev/clothing-dataset), which contains around 3,800 images of 10 different classes. The data is available in a GitHub repository. Let's clone it:

```
git clone https://github.com/alexeygrigorev/clothing-dataset-small.git
```

If you're doing this in AWS SageMaker, you can execute this command in a cell of the notebook. Just add the exclamation sign ("!") before the command (figure 7.1).

```
!git clone https://github.com/alexeygrigorev/clothing-dataset-small.git

Cloning into 'clothing-dataset-small'...
remote: Enumerating objects: 3839, done.
remote: Counting objects: 100% (400/400), done.
remote: Compressing objects: 100% (400/400), done.
remote: Total 3839 (delta 9), reused 384 (delta 0), pack-reused 3439
Receiving objects: 100% (3839/3839), 100.58 MiB | 1.21 MiB/s, done.
Resolving deltas: 100% (10/10), done.
Checking out files: 100% (3783/3783), done.
```

Figure 7.1   Executing a shell script command in Jupyter: simply add the exclamation sign ("!") in front of the command.

The dataset is already split into folders (figure 7.2):

- train: Images for training a model (3,068 images)
- validation: Images for validating (341 image)
- test: Images for testing (372 images)

Figure 7.2   The dataset is already split into train, validation, and test.

Each of these folders has 10 subfolders: one subfolder for each type of clothing (figure 7.3).

Figure 7.3 Images in the dataset are organized in subfolders.

As we see, this dataset contains 10 classes of clothes, from dresses and hats, to shorts and shoes.

Each subfolder contains images of only one class (figure 7.4).

Figure 7.4 The content of the pants folder

In these pictures, the clothing items have different colors and the background is different. Some items are on the floor, some are spread out on a bed or a table, and some are hung in front of a neutral background.

With this variety of images, it's not possible to use the methods we previously covered. We need a special type of model: neural networks. This model also requires different tools, and we cover them next.

7.1.3 *TensorFlow and Keras*

If you use AWS SageMaker, you don't need to install anything: it already has all the required libraries.

But if you use your laptop with Anaconda, or run the code somewhere else, you need to install TensorFlow — a library for building neural networks.

Use `pip` to do it:

```
pip install tensorflow
```

TensorFlow is a low-level framework, and it's not always easy to use. In this chapter, we use Keras — a higher-level library built on top of TensorFlow. Keras makes training neural networks a lot simpler. It comes preinstalled together with TensorFlow, so we don't need to install anything extra.

> **NOTE** Previously, Keras was not a part of TensorFlow, and you can find many examples on the internet where it's still a separate library. However, the interface of Keras hasn't changed significantly, so most of the examples you may discover still work in the new Keras.

At the time of writing, the latest version of TensorFlow was 2.3.0 and AWS SageMaker used TensorFlow version 2.1.0. The difference in versions is not a problem; the code from this chapter works for both versions, and it will most likely work for all TensorFlow 2 versions.

We're ready to start and create a new notebook called chapter-07-neural-nets. As usual, we begin by importing NumPy and MatplotLib:

```
import numpy as np
import matplotlib.pyplot as plt
%matplotlib inline
```

Next, import TensorFlow and Keras:

```
import tensorflow as tf
from tensorflow import keras
```

The preparation work is done, and now we can take a look at the images we have.

7.1.4 *Loading images*

Keras offers a special function for loading images called `load_img`. Let's import it:

```
from tensorflow.keras.preprocessing.image import load_img
```

> **NOTE** When Keras was a separate package, the imports looked like this:
>
> ```
> from keras.preprocessing.image import load_img
> ```

If you find some old Keras code on the internet and want to use it with the latest versions of TensorFlow, simply add `tensorflow.` at the beginning when importing it. Most likely, it will be enough to make it work.

Let's use this function to take a look at one of the images:

```
path = './clothing-dataset-small/train/t-shirt'
name = '5f0a3fa0-6a3d-4b68-b213-72766a643de7.jpg'
fullname = path + '/' + name
load_img(fullname)
```

After executing the cell, we should see an image of a T-shirt (figure 7.5).

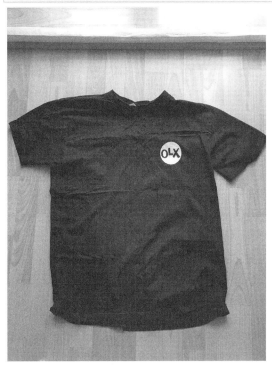

Figure 7.5   An image of a T-shirt from the train set

To use this image in a neural network, we need to resize it because the models always expect images of a certain size. For example, the network we use in this chapter requires a 150×150 image or an 299×299 image.

To resize the image, specify the `target_size` parameter:

```
load_img(fullname, target_size=(299, 299))
```

As a result, the image becomes square and a bit squashed (figure 7.6).

```
load_img(fullname, target_size=(299, 299))
```

Figure 7.6   To resize an image, use the `target_size` parameter.

Let's now use a neural network to classify this image.

7.2   Convolutional neural networks

Neural networks are a class of machine learning models for solving classification and regression problems. Our problem is a classification problem — we need to determine the category of an image.

However, our problem is special: we're dealing with images. This is why we need a special type of neural network — a convolutional neural network, which can extract visual patterns from an image and use them to make predictions.

Pre-trained neural networks are available on the internet, so let's see how we can use one of them for this project.

7.2.1   Using a pretrained model

Training a convolutional neural network from scratch is a time-consuming process and requires a lot of data and powerful hardware. It may take weeks of nonstop training for large datasets like ImageNet with 14 million images. (Check image-net.org for more information.)

Luckily, we don't need to do it ourselves: we can use pretrained models. Usually, these models are trained on ImageNet and can be used for general-purpose image classification.

It's very simple, and we don't even need to download anything ourselves — Keras will take care of it automatically. We can use many different types of models (called *architectures*). You can find a good summary of available pretrained models in the official Keras documentation (https://keras.io/api/applications/).

For this chapter, we'll use Xception, a relatively small model that has good performance. First, we need to import the model itself and some helpful functions:

```
from tensorflow.keras.applications.xception import Xception
from tensorflow.keras.applications.xception import preprocess_input
from tensorflow.keras.applications.xception import decode_predictions
```

We imported three things:

- `Xception`: the actual model
- `preprocess_input`: a function for preparing the image to be used by the model
- `decode_prediction`: a function for decoding the model's prediction

Let's load this model:

```
model = Xception(
    weights='imagenet',
    input_shape=(299, 299, 3)
)
```

We specify two parameters here:

- `weights`: We want to use a pretrained model from ImageNet.
- `imput_shape`: The size of the input images: height, width, and the number of channels. We resize the images to 299 × 299, and each image has three channels: red, green and blue.

When we load it for the first time, it downloads the actual model from the internet. After it's done, we can use it.

Let's test it on the image we saw previously. First, we load it using the `load_img` function:

```
img = load_img(fullname, target_size=(299, 299))
```

The `img` variable is an `Image` object, which we need to convert to a NumPy array. It's easy to do:

```
x = np.array(img)
```

This array should have the same shape as the image. Let's check it:

```
x.shape
```

We see `(299, 299, 3)`. It contains three dimensions (figure 7.7):

- The width of the image: 299
- The height of the image: 299
- The number of channels: red, green, blue

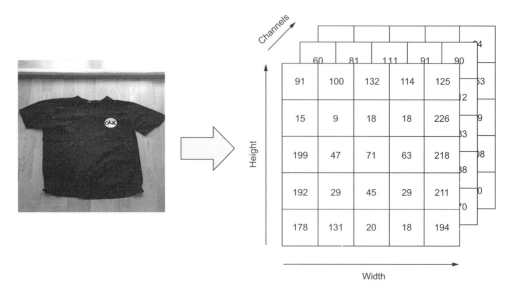

Figure 7.7   After converting, an image becomes a NumPy array of shape width × height × number of channels.

This matches the input shape we specified when loading the neural network. However, the model doesn't expect to get just a single image. It gets a *batch* of images — several images put together in one array. This array should have four dimensions:

- The number of images
- The width
- The height
- The number of channels

For example, for 10 images, the shape is `(10, 299, 299, 3)`. Because we have just one image, we need to create a batch with this single image:

```
X = np.array([x])
```

> **NOTE**   If we had several images, for example, x, y and z, we'd write
>
> ```
> X = np.array([x, y, z])
> ```

Let's check its shape:

```
X.shape
```

As we see, it's `(1, 299, 299, 3)` — it's one image of size 299×299 with three channels.

Before we can apply the model to our image, we need to prepare it with the preprocess_input function:

```
X = preprocess_input(X)
```

This function converts the integers between 0 and 255 in the original array to numbers between −1 and 1.

Now, we're ready to use the model.

7.2.2 Getting predictions

To apply the model, use the `predict` method:

```
pred = model.predict(X)
```

Let's take a look at this array:

```
pred.shape
```

This array is quite large — it contains 1,000 elements (figure 7.8).

```
pred = model.predict(X)
```

```
pred.shape
```
```
(1, 1000)
```

```
pred[0, :10]
```
```
array([0.0003238 , 0.00015736, 0.00021406, 0.00015296, 0.00024657,
       0.00030446, 0.00032349, 0.00014726, 0.00020487, 0.00014866],
      dtype=float32)
```

Figure 7.8   The output of the pretrained Xception model

This Xception model predicts whether an image belongs to one of 1,000 classes, so each element in the prediction array is the probability of belonging to one of these classes.

We don't know what these classes are, so it's difficult to make sense from this prediction just by looking at the numbers. Luckily, we can use a function, `decode_predictions`, that decodes the prediction into meaningful class names:

```
decode_predictions(pred)
```

It shows the top five most likely classes for this image:

```
[[('n02667093', 'abaya', 0.028757658),
  ('n04418357', 'theater_curtain', 0.020734021),
  ('n01930112', 'nematode', 0.015735716),
  ('n03691459', 'loudspeaker', 0.013871926),
  ('n03196217', 'digital_clock', 0.012909736)]]
```

Not quite the result we expected. Most likely, images like this T-shirt are not common in ImageNet, and that's why the result isn't useful for our problem.

Even though these results aren't particularly helpful for us, we can use this neural network as a base model for solving our problem.

To understand how we can do it, we should first get a feeling for how convolutional neural networks work. Let's see what happens inside the model when we invoke the `predict` method.

7.3   *Internals of the model*

All neural networks are organized in layers. We take an image, pass it through all the layers, and, at the end, get the predictions (figure 7.9).

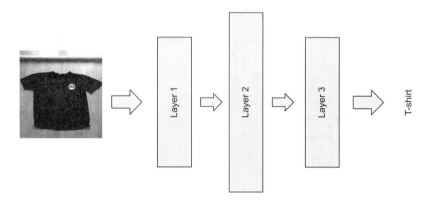

Figure 7.9   A neural network consists of multiple layers.

Usually, a model has a lot of layers. For example, the Xception model we use here has 71 layers. That's why these neural networks are called "deep" neural networks — because they have many layers.

For a convolutional neural network, the most important layers are

- Convolutional layers
- Dense layers

First, let's take a look at convolutional layers.

7.3.1   *Convolutional layers*

Even though "convolutional layer" sounds complicated, it's nothing more than a set of *filters* — small "images" with simple shapes like stripes (figure 7.10).

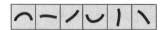

Figure 7.10   Examples of filters for a convolutional layer (not from a real network)

The filters in a convolutional layer are learned by the model during training. However, because we are using a pretrained neural network, we don't need to worry about it; we already have the filters.

To apply a convolutional layer to a picture, we slide each filter across this image. For example, we can slide it from left to right and from top to bottom (figure 7.11).

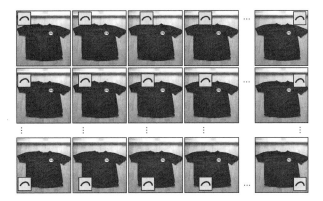

Figure 7.11   To apply a filter, we slide it over an image.

While sliding, we compare the content of the filter with the content of the image under the filter. For each comparison, we record the degree of similarity. This way, we get a *feature map* — an array with numbers, where a large number means a match between the filter and the image, and a low number means no match (figure 7.12).

So, a feature map tells us where on the image we can find the shape from the filter.

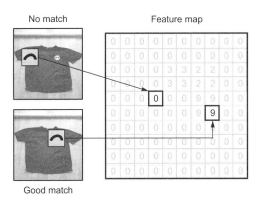

Figure 7.12   A feature map is a result of applying a filter to an image. A high value in the map corresponds to areas with a high degree of similarity between the image and the filter.

One convolutional layer consists of many filters, so we actually get multiple feature maps — one for each filter (figure 7.13).

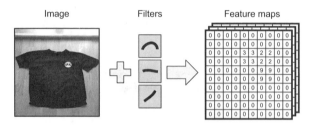

Figure 7.13   Each convolutional layer contains many filters, so we get a set of feature maps: one for each filter that we use.

Now we can take the output of one convolutional layer and use it as the input to the next layer.

From the previous layer we know the location of different stripes and other simple shapes. When two simple shapes occur in the same location, they form more complex patterns — crosses, angles, or circles.

That's what the filters of the next layer do: they combine shapes from the previous layer into more complex structures. The deeper we go down the network, the more complex patterns the network can recognize (figure 7.14).

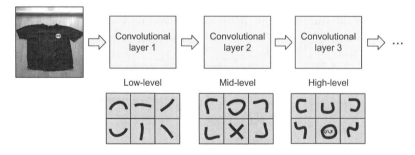

Figure 7.14   Deeper convolutional layers can detect progressively more complex features of the image.

We repeat this process to detect more and more complex shapes. This way, the network "learns" some distinctive features of the image. For clothes, it can be short or long sleeves or the type of neck. For animals, it can be pointy or floppy ears or the presence of whiskers.

At the end, we get a vector representation of an image: a one-dimensional array, where each position corresponds to some high-level visual features. Some parts of the array may correspond to sleeves, whereas other parts represent ears and whiskers. At this level, it's usually difficult to make sense from these features, but they have enough discriminative power to distinguish between a T-shirt and pants or between a cat and a dog.

Now we need to use this vector representation to combine these high-level features and arrive at the final decision. For that, we use a different kind of layers — dense layers.

7.3.2 *Dense layers*

Dense layers process the vector representation of an image and translate these visual features to the actual class — T-shirt, dress, jacket, or other class (figure 7.15).

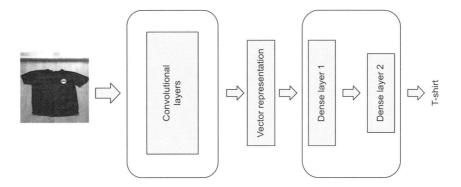

Figure 7.15 **Convolutional layers transform an image into its vector representation, and dense layers translate the vector representation into the actual label.**

To understand how it works, let's take a step back and think how we could use logistic regression for classifying images.

Suppose we want to build a binary classification model for predicting whether an image is a T-shirt. In this case, the input to logistic regression is the vector representation of an image — a feature vector x.

From chapter 3, we know that to make the prediction, we need to combine the features in x with the weights vector w and then apply the sigmoid function to get the final prediction:

$$\text{sigmoid}(x^T w)$$

We can show it visually by taking all the components of the vector x and connecting them to the output — the probability of being a T-shirt (figure 7.16).

What if we need to make predictions for multiple classes? For example, we may want to know if we have an image of a T-shirt, shirt, or dress. In this case, we can build multiple logistic regressions — one for each class (figure 7.17).

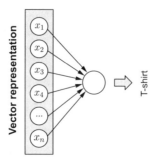

Figure 7.16   Logistic regression: we take all the components of the feature vector *x* and combine them to get the prediction.

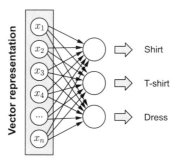

Figure 7.17   To predict multiple classes, we train multiple logistic regression models.

By putting together multiple logistic regression models, we just created a small neural network!

To make it visually simpler, we can combine the outputs into one layer — the output layer (figure 7.18).

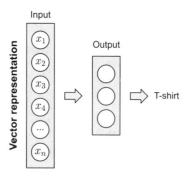

Figure 7.18   Multiple logistic regressions put together form a small neural network.

When we have 10 classes we want to predict, we have 10 elements in the output layer. To make a prediction, we look at each element of the output layer and take the one with the highest score.

In this case, we have a network with one layer: the layer that converts the input to the output.

This layer is called a *dense layer*. It's "dense" because it connects each element of the input with all the elements of its output. For this reason, these layers are sometimes called "fully connected" (figure 7.19).

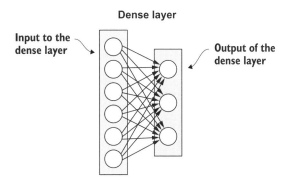

Figure 7.19 A dense layer connects every element of its input with every element of its output.

However, we don't have to stop at just one output layer. We can add more layers between the input and the final output (figure 7.20).

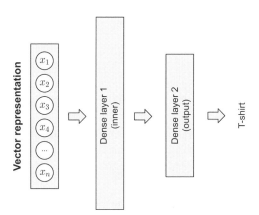

Figure 7.20 A neural network with two layers: one inner layer and one output layer

So, when we invoke `predict`, the image first goes through a series of convolutional layers. This way, we extract the vector representation of this image. Next, this vector representation goes through a series of dense layers, and we get the final prediction (figure 7.21).

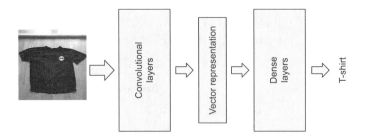

Figure 7.21   In a convolutional neural network, an image first goes through a series of convolutional layers, and then through a series of dense layers.

NOTE   In this book, we give a simplified and high-level overview of the internals of convolutional neural networks. Many other layers exist in addition to convolutional layers and dense layers. For a more in-depth introduction to this topic, check the CS231n notes (cs231n.github.io/convolutional-networks).

Now let's get back to code and see how we can adjust a pretrained neural network for our project.

7.4   Training the model

Training a convolutional neural network takes a lot of time and requires a lot of data. But there's a shortcut: we can use *transfer learning*, an approach where we adapt a pretrained model to our problem.

7.4.1   Transfer learning

The difficulty in training usually comes from convolutional layers. To be able to extract a good vector representation from an image, the filters need to learn good patterns. For that, the network has to see many different images — the more, the better. But once we have a good vector representation, training dense layers is relatively easy.

This means that we can take a neural network pretrained on ImageNet and use it for solving our problem. This model has already learned good filters. So, we take this model and keep the convolutional layers, but drop the dense layers and instead train new ones (figure 7.22).

In this section, we do exactly that. But before we can start training, we need to get our dataset ready.

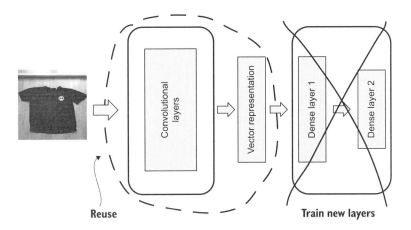

Figure 7.22 To adapt a pretrained model to a new domain, we keep the old convolutional layers but train new dense layers.

7.4.2 *Loading the data*

In previous chapters, we loaded the entire dataset into memory and used it to get X — the matrix with features. With images, it's more difficult: we may not have enough memory to keep all the images.

Keras comes with a solution — `ImageDataGenerator`. Instead of loading the entire dataset into memory, it loads the images from disk in small batches. Let's use it:

```
from tensorflow.keras.preprocessing.image import ImageDataGenerator

train_gen = ImageDataGenerator(
    preprocessing_function=preprocess_input          ◁─┤  Applies the preprocess_input
)                                                        function to each image
```

We already know that images need to be preprocessed using the `preprocess_input` function. That's why we need to tell `ImageDataGenerator` how the data should be prepared.

We have a generator now, so we just need to point it to the directory with the data. For that, use the `flow_from_directory` method:

```
train_ds = train_gen.flow_from_directory(            ┌  Loads all the images
    "clothing-dataset-small/train",        ◁─┤         from the train directory
    target_size=(150, 150),         ◁─────────────┐  Resizes the images
    batch_size=32,      ◁─┐                           to 150 × 150
)                          Loads the images in
                           batches of 32 images
```

For our initial experiments, we use small images of size 150×150. This way, it's faster to train the model. Also, the small size makes it possible to use a laptop for training.

We have 10 classes of clothing in our dataset, and images of each class are stored in a separate directory. For example, all T-shirts are stored in the t-shirt folder. The generator can use the folder structure to infer the label for each image.

When we execute the cell, it informs us how many images there are in the train dataset and how many classes:

```
Found 3068 images belonging to 10 classes.
```

Now we repeat the same process for the validation dataset:

```
validation_gen = ImageDataGenerator(
    preprocessing_function=preprocess_input
)

val_ds = validation_gen.flow_from_directory(
    "clothing-dataset-small/validation",
    target_size=image_size,
    batch_size=batch_size,
)
```

Like previously, we use the train dataset for training the model and the validation dataset for selecting the best parameters.

We have loaded the data, and now we're ready to train a model.

7.4.3 *Creating the model*

First, we need to load the base model — this is the pretrained model that we're using for extracting the vector representation from images. Like previously, we also use Xception, but this time, we include only the part with pretrained convolutional layers. After that, we add our own dense layers.

So, let's create the base model:

```
base_model = Xception(
    weights='imagenet',              Uses the model
                                     pretrained on ImageNet
    include_top=False
    input_shape=(150, 150, 3),       Keeps only the
)                                    convolutional layers
        Images should be 150 ×
        150 with three channels.
```

Note the include_top parameter: this way, we explicitly specify that we're not interested in the dense layers of the pretrained neural network, only in the convolutional layers. In Keras terminology, the "top" is the set of final layers of the network (figure 7.23).

We don't want to train the base model; attempting to do so will destroy all the filters. So, we "freeze" the base model by setting the trainable parameter to False:

```
base_model.trainable = False
```

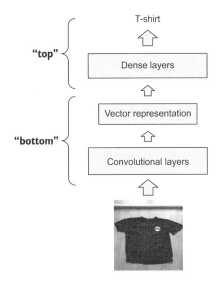

Figure 7.23 In Keras, the input to the network is on the bottom and the output is on the top, so `include_top=False` **means "don't include the final dense layers."**

Now let's build the clothing classification model:

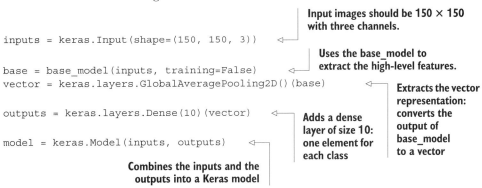

```
inputs = keras.Input(shape=(150, 150, 3))
```
Input images should be 150 × 150 with three channels.

```
base = base_model(inputs, training=False)
vector = keras.layers.GlobalAveragePooling2D()(base)
```
Uses the base_model to extract the high-level features.

Extracts the vector representation: converts the output of base_model to a vector

```
outputs = keras.layers.Dense(10)(vector)
```
Adds a dense layer of size 10: one element for each class

```
model = keras.Model(inputs, outputs)
```
Combines the inputs and the outputs into a Keras model

The way we build the model is called the "functional style." It may be confusing at first, so let's take a look at each line individually.

First, we specify the input and the size of the arrays we expect:

```
inputs = keras.Input(shape=(150, 150, 3))
```

Next, we create the base model:

```
base = base_model(inputs, training=False)
```

Even though `base_model` is already a model, we use it as a function and give it two parameters — inputs, and `training=False`:

- The first parameter says what will be the input to `base_model`. It will come from inputs.
- The second parameter (`training=False`) is optional and says that we don't want to train the base model.

The result is base, which is a *functional component* (like `base_model`) that we can combine with other components. We use it as the input to the next layer:

```
vector = keras.layers.GlobalAveragePooling2D()(base)
```

Here, we create a pooling layer — a special construction that allows us to convert the output of a convolutional layer (a 3-D array) into a vector (a one-dimensional array).

After creating it, we immediately invoke it with base as the argument. This way, we say that the input to this layer comes from base.

This may be a bit confusing because we create a layer and immediately connect it to base. We can rewrite it to make it simpler to understand:

```
pooling = keras.layers.GlobalAveragePooling2D()      ⟵─┐  Creates a pooling
vector = pooling(base)    ⟵─┐                          │  layer first
                             └ Connects it to base
```

As a result, we get vector. This is another functional component that we connect to the next layer — a dense layer:

```
outputs = keras.layers.Dense(10)(vector)
```

Similarly, we first create the layer, and then connect it to vector. For now, we create a network with only one dense layer. It's enough to get started.

Now the result is outputs — the final result that we want to get out of the network.

So, in our case, the data comes into inputs and goes out of outputs. We just need to do one final step — wrap both inputs and outputs into a Model class:

```
model = keras.Model(inputs, outputs)
```

We need to specify two parameters here:

- What the model will get as input, which is inputs in our case
- What the output of the model is, which is outputs

Let's take a step back and look at the model definition code again, following the flow of data from inputs to outputs (figure 7.24).

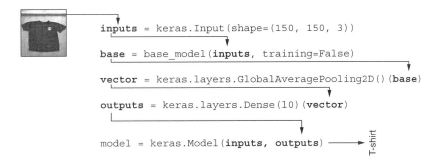

Figure 7.24 The flow of data: an image goes to `inputs`**, then** `base_model` **converts it to** `base`**, then pooling converts it to** `vector`**, and then a dense layer converts it to** `output`**. At the end,** `inputs` **and** `outputs` **go to a Keras model.**

To make it easier to visualize, we can think of every line of code as a block, which gets the data from the previous block, transforms it, and passes to the next block (figure 7.25).

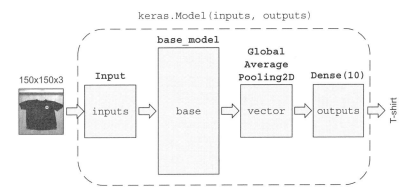

Figure 7.25 The flow of data: each line of Keras code as a block

So, we have created a model that can take in an image, get the vector representation using the base model, and make the final prediction with a dense layer.

Let's train it now.

7.4.4 Training the model

We have specified the model: the input, the elements of the model (the base model, the pooling layer), and the final output layer.

Now we need to train it. For that, we need an *optimizer*, which adjusts the weights of a network to make it better at doing its task.

We won't cover the details of how optimizers work — that's beyond the scope for this book, and it's not required to finish the project. But if you'd like to learn more about them, check the CS231n notes (https://cs231n.github.io/neural-networks-3/). You can see the list of available optimizers in the official documentation for Keras (https://keras.io/api/optimizers/).

For our project, we will use the Adam optimization algorithm — a good default choice, and in most cases, using it is sufficient.

Let's create it:

```
learning_rate = 0.01
optimizer = keras.optimizers.Adam(learning_rate)
```

Adam requires one parameter: the learning rate, which specifies how fast our network learns.

The learning rate may significantly affect the quality of our network. If we set it too high, the network learns too fast and may accidentally skip some important details. In this case, the predictive performance is not optimal. If we set it too low, the network takes too long to train, so the training process is highly ineffective.

We will later adjust this parameter. For now, we set it to 0.01 — a good default value to start with.

To train a model, the optimizer needs to know whether the model is doing well. For that, it uses a loss function, which becomes smaller as the network becomes better. The goal of the optimizer is to minimize this loss.

The `keras.losses` package offers many different losses. Here's a list of the most important ones:

- `BinaryCrossentropy`: For training a binary classifier
- `CategoricalCrossentropy`: For training a classification model with multiple classes
- `MeanSquaredError`: For training a regression model

Because we need to classify clothing into 10 different classes, we use the categorical cross-entropy loss:

```
loss = keras.losses.CategoricalCrossentropy(from_logits=True)
```

For this loss, we specify one parameter: `from_logits=True`. We need to do this because the last layer of our network outputs raw scores (called "logits"), not probabilities. The official documentation recommends doing this for numerical stability (https://www.tensorflow.org/api_docs/python/tf/keras/losses/CategoricalCrossentropy).

NOTE   Alternatively, we could define the last layer of the network like this:

```
outputs = keras.layers.Dense(10, activation='softmax')(vector)
```

In this case, we explicitly tell the network to output probabilities: softmax is similar to sigmoid but for multiple classes. Then the output is not "logits" anymore, so we can drop this parameter:

```
loss = keras.losses.CategoricalCrossentropy()
```

Now let's put the optimizer and the loss together. For that, we use the `compile` method of our model:

```
model.compile(
    optimizer=optimizer,
    loss=loss,
    metrics=["accuracy"]
)
```

In addition to the optimizer and the loss, we also specify metrics we want to track during training. We're interested in accuracy: the percentage of images with correct predictions.

Our model is ready for training! To do it, use the `fit` method:

```
model.fit(train_ds, epochs=10, validation_data=val_ds)
```

We specify three parameters:

- `train_ds`: The dataset for training
- `epochs`: The number of times it will go over the training data
- `validation_data`: The dataset for evaluation

One iteration over the entire training dataset is called an *epoch*. The more iterations we do, the better the network learns the training dataset.

At some point, it can learn the dataset so well that it starts overfitting. To know when this happens, we need to monitor the performance of our model on the validation dataset. That's why we specify the `validation_data` parameter.

When we start training, Keras informs us about the progress:

```
Train for 96 steps, validate for 11 steps
Epoch 1/10
96/96 [==============================] - 22s 227ms/step - loss: 1.2372 -
    accuracy: 0.6734 - val_loss: 0.8453 - val_accuracy: 0.7713
Epoch 2/10
96/96 [==============================] - 16s 163ms/step - loss: 0.6023 -
    accuracy: 0.8194 - val_loss: 0.7928 - val_accuracy: 0.7859
...
Epoch 10/10
96/96 [==============================] - 16s 165ms/step - loss: 0.0274 -
    accuracy: 0.9961 - val_loss: 0.9342 - val_accuracy: 0.8065
```

From that we can see

- The speed of training: how long each epoch takes.
- The accuracy on the train and validation datasets. We should monitor the accuracy on the validation set to make sure the model doesn't start overfitting. For

example, if the validation accuracy decreases for multiple epochs, it's a sign of overfitting.

- The loss on training and validation. We're not interested in loss — it's less intuitive and the values are harder to interpret.

NOTE   Your results will likely be different. The overall predictive performance of the model should be similar, but the exact numbers will not be the same. With neural networks, it's a lot more difficult to ensure perfect reproducibility, even with fixing random seeds.

As you can see, the model quickly becomes 99% accurate on the train dataset, but the score on validation stays around 80% for all the epochs (figure 7.26).

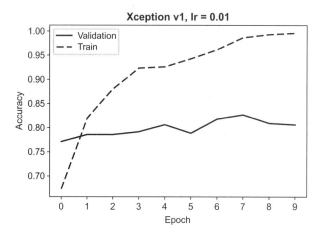

Figure 7.26   The accuracy on the train and validation datasets evaluated after each epoch

The perfect accuracy on the train data doesn't necessarily mean that our model overfits, but it's a good sign that we should adjust the learning rate parameter. We have previously mentioned that it's an important parameter, so let's tune it now.

Exercise 7.1

Transfer learning is the process of using a pretrained model (a base model) for converting an image to its vector representation and then training another model on top of it.

- a   True
- b   False

7.4.5 Adjusting the learning rate

We have started with a learning rate of 0.01. It's a good starting point, but it's not necessarily the best rate: we have seen that our model learns too fast and after a few epochs predicts the train set with 100% accuracy.

Let's experiment and try other values for this parameter.

First, to make it easier, we should put the logic for model creating in a separate function. This function takes learning rate as a parameter.

> **Listing 7.1 A function for creating a model**

```
def make_model(learning_rate):
    base_model = Xception(
        weights='imagenet',
        input_shape=(150, 150, 3),
        include_top=False
    )

    base_model.trainable = False

    inputs = keras.Input(shape=(150, 150, 3))

    base = base_model(inputs, training=False)
    vector = keras.layers.GlobalAveragePooling2D()(base)

    outputs = keras.layers.Dense(10)(vector)

    model = keras.Model(inputs, outputs)

    optimizer = keras.optimizers.Adam(learning_rate)
    loss = keras.losses.CategoricalCrossentropy(from_logits=True)

    model.compile(
        optimizer=optimizer,
        loss=loss,
        metrics=["accuracy"],
    )

    return model
```

We've tried 0.01, so let's try 0.001:

```
model = make_model(learning_rate=0.001)
model.fit(train_ds, epochs=10, validation_data=val_ds)
```

We can also try an even smaller value of 0.0001:

```
model = make_model(learning_rate=0.0001)
model.fit(train_ds, epochs=10, validation_data=val_ds)
```

As we see (figure 7.27), for 0.001, the training accuracy doesn't go up as fast as with 0.01, but with 0.0001 it goes up very slowly. The network in this case learns too slow — it *underfits*.

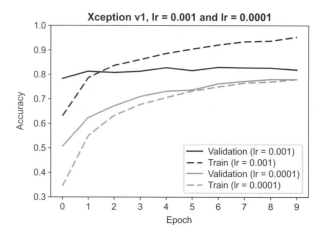

Figure 7.27   The performance of our model with learning rates of 0.001 and 0.0001

If we look at validation scores for all the learning rates (figure 7.28), we see that the learning rate of 0.001 is the best one.

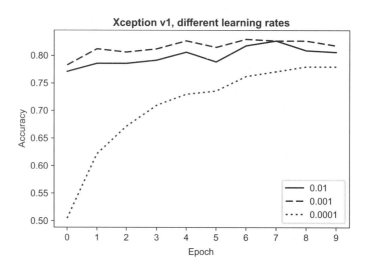

Figure 7.28   The accuracy of our model on the validation set for three different learning rates

For the learning rate of 0.001, the best accuracy is 83% (table 7.1).

Table 7.1   The validation accuracy with different values of dropout rate

Learning rate	0.01	0.001	0.0001
Validation accuracy	82.7%	83.0%	78.0%

NOTE Your numbers may be slightly different. It's also possible that in your experiments, the learning rate of 0.01 achieves slightly better results than 0.001.

The difference between 0.01 and 0.001 is not significant. But if we look at the accuracy on the training data, with 0.01, it overfits the training data a lot faster. At some point, it even achieves an accuracy of 100%. When the discrepancy between the performance on train and validation sets is high, the risk of overfitting is also high. So, we should prefer the learning rate of 0.001.

After training is done, we need to save the model. Now we'll see how to do it.

7.4.6 *Saving the model and checkpointing*

Once the model is trained, we can save it using the `save_weights` method:

```
model.save_weights('xception_v1_model.h5', save_format='h5')
```

We need to specify the following:

- The output file: `'xception_v1_model.h5'`
- The format: h5, which is a format for saving binary data

You may have noticed that while training, the performance of our model on the validation set jumps up and down. This way, after 10 iterations, we don't necessarily have the best model — maybe the best performance was achieved on iteration 5 or 6.

We can save the model after each iteration, but it generates too much data. And if we rent a server in the cloud, it can quickly take all the available space.

Instead, we can save the model only when it's better than the previous best score on validation. For example, if the previous best accuracy is 0.8, but we have improved it to 0.91, we save the model. Otherwise, we continue the training process without saving the model.

This process is called *model checkpointing*. Keras has a special class for doing it: `ModelCheckpoint`. Let's use it:

```
checkpoint = keras.callbacks.ModelCheckpoint(
    "xception_v1_{epoch:02d}_{val_accuracy:.3f}.h5",
    save_best_only=True,
    monitor="val_accuracy"
)
```

Specifies the filename template for saving the models

Saves the model only when it's better than previous iterations

Uses the accuracy on validation for selecting the best model

The first parameter is a template for the filename. Let's take a look at it again:

```
"xception_v1_{epoch:02d}_{val_accuracy:.3f}.h5"
```

It has two parameters inside:

- `{epoch:02d}` is replaced by the number of the epoch.
- `{val_accuracy:.3f}` is replaced by the validation accuracy.

Because we set `save_best_only` to `True`, `ModelCheckpoint` keeps track of the best accuracy and saves the results to disk each time the accuracy improves.

We implement `ModelCheckpoint` as a callback — a way to execute anything after each epoch finishes. In this particular case, the callback evaluates the model and saves the result if the accuracy gets better.

We can use it by passing it to the `callbacks` argument of the `fit` method:

```
model = make_model(learning_rate=0.001)        ◁──┐  Creates a
                                                   │  new model

model.fit(
    train_ds,
    epochs=10,                      ┐ Specifies the list of
    validation_data=val_ds,         │ callbacks to be used
    callbacks=[checkpoint]      ◁───┘ during training
)
```

After a few iterations, we already have some models saved to disk (figure 7.29).

☐ 0 ▾ ▰ /		Name ↓	Last Modified	File size
☐ ▢ clothing-dataset-small			2 days ago	
☐ ▰ chapter-07-neural-nets.ipynb		Running	seconds ago	549 kB
☐ ▢ xception_v1_01_0.765.h5			2 minutes ago	84 MB
☐ ▢ xception_v1_02_0.789.h5			2 minutes ago	84 MB
☐ ▢ xception_v1_03_0.809.h5			2 minutes ago	84 MB
☐ ▢ xception_v1_06_0.830.h5			a minute ago	84 MB

Figure 7.29   Because the `ModelCheckpoint` callback saves the model only when it improves, we only have 4 files with our model, not 10.

We've learned how to store the best model. Now let's improve our model by adding more layers to the network.

7.4.7   Adding more layers

Previously, we trained a model with one dense layer:

```
inputs = keras.Input(shape=(150, 150, 3))

base = base_model(inputs, training=False)
vector = keras.layers.GlobalAveragePooling2D()(base)

outputs = keras.layers.Dense(10)(vector)

model = keras.Model(inputs, outputs)
```

We don't have to restrict ourselves to just one layer, so let's add another layer between the base model and the last layer with predictions (figure 7.30).

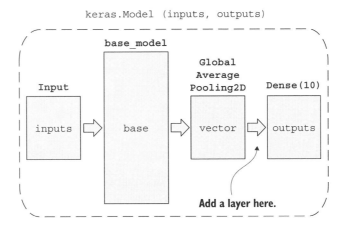

Figure 7.30 **We add another dense layer between the vector representation and the output.**

For example, we can add a dense layer of size 100:

```
inputs = keras.Input(shape=(150, 150, 3))
base = base_model(inputs, training=False)
vector = keras.layers.GlobalAveragePooling2D()(base)

inner = keras.layers.Dense(100, activation='relu')(vector)

outputs = keras.layers.Dense(10)(inner)

model = keras.Model(inputs, outputs)
```

Adds another dense layer of size 100

Instead of connecting outputs to vector, connects it to inner

> **NOTE** There's no particular reason for selecting the size of 100 for the inner dense layer. We should treat it as a parameter: as with the learning rate, we can try different values and see which one leads to better performance on validation. In this chapter, we will not experiment with changing the size of the inner layer, but feel free to do so.

This way, we added a layer between the base model and the outputs (figure 7.31). Let's take another look at the line with the new dense layer:

```
inner = keras.layers.Dense(100, activation='relu')(vector)
```

Here, we set the activation parameter to relu.

Remember that we get a neural network by putting together multiple logistic regressions. In logistic regression, sigmoid is used for converting the raw score to probability.

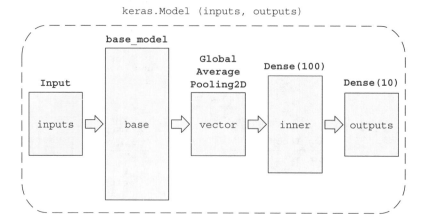

Figure 7.31   A new inner layer added between `vector` and `outputs`

But for inner layers, we don't need probabilities, and we can replace sigmoid with other functions. These functions are called *activation functions*. ReLU (Rectified Linear Unit) is one of them, and for inner layers, it's a better choice than sigmoid.

The sigmoid function suffers from the vanishing gradient problem, which makes training deep neural networks impossible. ReLU solves this problem. To read more about this problem, and about activation functions in general, please refer to the CS231n notes (https://cs231n.github.io/neural-networks-1/).

With another layer, our chances of overfitting increase significantly. To avoid that, we need to add regularization to our model. Next, we'll see how to do it.

7.4.8   *Regularization and dropout*

Dropout is a special technique for fighting overfitting in neural networks. The main idea behind dropout is freezing a part of a dense layer when training. At each iteration, the part to freeze is chosen randomly. Only the unfrozen part is trained, and the frozen part is not touched at all.

If some parts of the network are ignored, the model overall is less likely to overfit. When the network goes over a batch of images, the frozen part of a layer doesn't see this data — it's turned off. This way, it's more difficult for the network to memorize the images (figure 7.32).

For every batch, the part to freeze is selected randomly, so the network learns to extract patterns from incomplete information, which makes it more robust and less likely to overfit.

We can control the strength of dropout by setting the dropout rate — the fraction of elements in a layer to be frozen at each step.

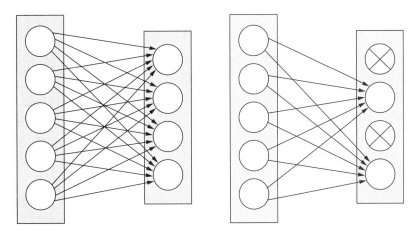

(A) Two dense layers without dropout   **(B) Two dense layers with dropout**

Figure 7.32   **With dropout, the connections to frozen nodes are dropped out.**

To do this in Keras, we add a `Dropout` layer after the first `Dense` layer and set up the dropout rate:

```
inputs = keras.Input(shape=(150, 150, 3))
base = base_model(inputs, training=False)
vector = keras.layers.GlobalAveragePooling2D()(base)

inner = keras.layers.Dense(100, activation='relu')(vector)
drop = keras.layers.Dropout(0.2)(inner)
outputs = keras.layers.Dense(10)(drop)

model = keras.Model(inputs, outputs)
```

This way, we add another block in the network — the dropout block (figure 7.33).

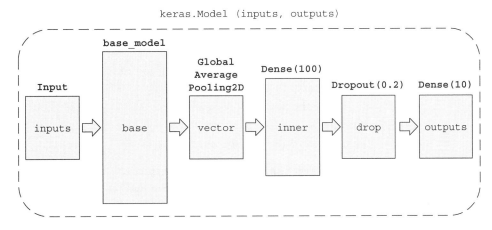

Figure 7.33   **Dropout is another block between the `inner` layer and the `outputs` layer.**

Let's train this model. To make it easier, we first need to update the `make_model` function and add another parameter there for controlling the dropout rate.

Listing 7.2 A function for creating a model with dropout

```
def make_model(learning_rate, droprate):
    base_model = Xception(
        weights='imagenet',
        input_shape=(150, 150, 3),
        include_top=False
    )

    base_model.trainable = False

    inputs = keras.Input(shape=(150, 150, 3))
    base = base_model(inputs, training=False)
    vector = keras.layers.GlobalAveragePooling2D()(base)

    inner = keras.layers.Dense(100, activation='relu')(vector)
    drop = keras.layers.Dropout(droprate)(inner)

    outputs = keras.layers.Dense(10)(drop)

    model = keras.Model(inputs, outputs)

    optimizer = keras.optimizers.Adam(learning_rate)
    loss = keras.losses.CategoricalCrossentropy(from_logits=True)

    model.compile(
        optimizer=optimizer,
        loss=loss,
        metrics=["accuracy"],
    )

    return model
```

Let's try four different values for the `droprate` parameter to see how the performance of our model changes:

- 0.0: Nothing gets frozen, so this is equivalent to not including the dropout layer at all.
- 0.2: Only 20% of the layer gets frozen,
- 0.5: Half of the layer is frozen.
- 0.8: Most of the layer (80%) is frozen.

With dropout, it takes more time to train a model: at each step, only a part of our network learns, so we need to make more steps. This means that we should increase the number of epochs when training.

So, let's train it:

```
model = make_model(learning_rate=0.001, droprate=0.0)
model.fit(train_ds, epochs=30, validation_data=val_ds)
```

Modifies droprate
to experiment with
different values

Trains a model for more epochs than previously

When it finishes, repeat this for other values of the `droprate` parameter by copying the code to another cell and changing the value to 0.2, 0.5, and 0.8.

From the results on the validation dataset, we see that there's no significant difference between 0.0, 0.2, and 0.5. However, 0.8 is worse — we made it really difficult for the network to learn anything (figure 7.34).

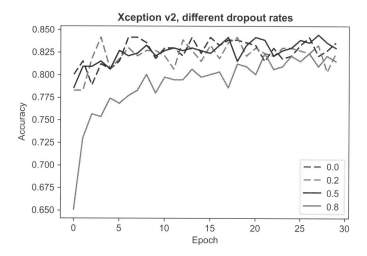

Figure 7.34   The accuracy on the validation set is similar for dropout rates of 0.0, 0.2, and 0.5. However, it's worse for 0.8.

The best accuracy we could achieve is 84.5% for the dropout rate of 0.5 (table 7.2).

Table 7.2   The validation accuracy with different values of dropout rate

Dropout rate	0.0	0.2	0.5	0.8
Validation accuracy	84.2%	84.2%	84.5%	82.4%

> **NOTE**   You may have different results, and it's possible that a different value for dropout rate achieves the best accuracy.

In cases like this, when there's no visible difference between accuracy on the validation dataset, it's useful to look at the accuracy on the train set as well (figure 7.35).

With no dropout, the model quickly memorizes the entire train dataset, and after 10 epochs, it becomes 99.9% accurate. With a dropout rate of 0.2, it needs more time

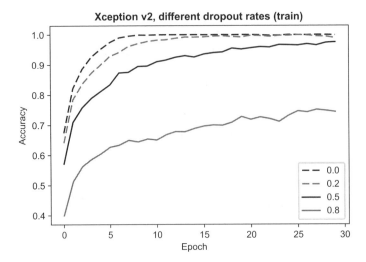

Figure 7.35   With a dropout rate of 0.0, the network overfits quickly, whereas the rate of 0.8 makes it really difficult to learn.

to overfit the training dataset, whereas for 0.5, it hasn't reached the perfect accuracy, even after 30 iterations. By setting the rate to 0.8, we make it really difficult for the network to learn anything, so the accuracy is low even on the training dataset.

We can see that with a dropout rate of 0.5, the network doesn't overfit as fast as others, while maintaining the same level of accuracy on the validation dataset as 0.0 and 0.2. Thus, we should prefer the model we trained with the dropout rate of 0.5 to other models.

By adding another layer and dropout, we have increased the accuracy from 83% to 84%. Even though this increase is not significant for this particular case, dropout is a powerful tool for fighting overfitting, and we should use it when making our models more complex.

In addition to dropout, we can use other ways to fight overfitting. For example, we can generate more data. In the next section, we'll see how to do it.

Exercise 7.2

In dropout, we

a   Remove a part of a model completely
b   Freeze a random part of a model, so it doesn't get updated during one iteration of training
c   Freeze a random part of a model, so it doesn't get used during the entire training process

7.4.9 Data augmentation

Getting more data is always a good idea, and it's usually the best thing we can do to improve the quality of our model. Unfortunately, it's not always possible to get more data.

For images, however, we can generate more data from existing images. For example:

- Flip an image vertically and horizontally.
- Rotate an image.
- Zoom in or out a bit.
- Change an image in other ways.

The process of generating more data from an existing dataset is called *data augmentation* (figure 7.36).

Figure 7.36   We can generate more training data by modifying existing images.

The easiest way to create a new image from an existing one is to flip it horizontally, vertically, or both (figure 7.37).

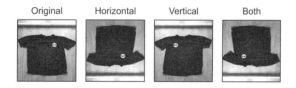

Figure 7.37   Flipping an image horizontally and vertically

In our case, horizontal flipping might not make much sense, but vertical flipping should be useful.

> **NOTE**   If you're curious how these images are generated, check the notebook 07-augmentations.ipynb in the GitHub repository for this book.

Rotating is another image-manipulation strategy that we can use: we can generate a new image by rotating an existing one by some degree (figure 7.38).

rotation = –30   rotation = –15   rotation = 0   rotation = 15   rotation = 30

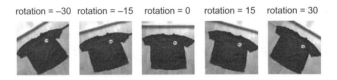

Figure 7.38   Rotating an image. If the rotation degree is negative, the image is rotated counterclockwise.

Shear is another possible transformation. It skews the image by "pulling" it by one of its sides. When the shear is positive, we pull the right side down, and when it's negative, we pull the right side up (figure 7.39).

shear = –20   shear = –10   shear = 0   shear = 10   shear = 20

Figure 7.39   The shear transformation. We pull the image up or down by its right side.

At first glance, the effect of shear and rotation may look similar, but actually, they are quite different. Shear changes the geometrical shape of an image, but rotation doesn't: it only rotates an image (figure 7.40).

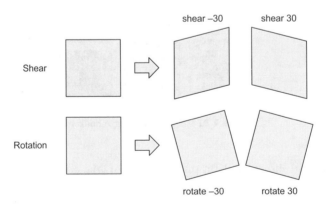

Figure 7.40   Shear changes the geometrical shape of an image by pulling it, so a square becomes a parallelogram. Rotation doesn't change the shape, so a square remains a square.

Next, we can shift an image horizontally (figure 7.41) or vertically (figure 7.42).

Figure 7.41 **Shifting an image horizontally. Positive values shift the image to the left, whereas negative values shift it to the right.**

Figure 7.42 **Shifting an image vertically. Positive values shift the image to the top, whereas negative values shift it to the bottom.**

Finally, we can zoom an image in or out (figure 7.43).

Figure 7.43 **Zooming in or out. When the zoom factor is smaller than 1, we zoom in. If it's larger than 1, we zoom out.**

What is more, we can combine multiple data augmentation strategies. For example, we can take an image, flip it horizontally, zoom out, and then rotate it.

By applying different augmentations to the same image, we can generate many more new images (figure 7.44).

Keras provides a built-in way of augmenting a dataset. It's based on `ImageData-Generator`, which we have already used for reading the images.

The generator takes in many arguments. Previously, we used only `preprocessing_function` — it's needed to preprocess the images. Others are available, and many of them are responsible for augmenting the dataset.

Figure 7.44   10 new images generated from the same image

For example, we can create a new generator:

```
train_gen = ImageDataGenerator(
    rotation_range=30,
    width_shift_range=30.0,
    height_shift_range=30.0,
    shear_range=10.0,
    zoom_range=0.2,
    horizontal_flip=True,
    vertical_flip=False,
    preprocessing_function=preprocess_input
)
```

Let's take a closer look at these parameters:

- `rotation_range=30`: Rotate an image by a random degree between –30 and 30.
- `width_shift_range=30`: Shift an image horizontally by a value between –30 and 30 pixels.
- `height_shift_range=30`: Shift an image vertically by a value between –30 and 30 pixels.
- `shear_range=10`: Apply the shear transformation by a value between –10 and 10 (also in pixels).
- `zoom_range=0.2`: Apply the zoom transformation using the zoom factor between 0.8 and 1.2 (1 – 0.2 and 1 + 0.2).
- `horizontal_flip=True`: Randomly flip an image horizontally.
- `vertical_flip=False`: Don't flip an image vertically.

For our project, let's take a small set of these augmentations:

```
train_gen = ImageDataGenerator(
    shear_range=10.0,
    zoom_range=0.1,
    horizontal_flip=True,
```

```
    preprocessing_function=preprocess_input,
)
```

Next, we use the generator in the same way as previously:

```
train_ds = train_gen.flow_from_directory(
    "clothing-dataset-small/train",
    target_size=(150, 150),
    batch_size=32,
)
```

We need to apply augmentations only to training data. We don't use it for validation: we want to make our evaluation consistent and be able to compare a model trained on the augmented dataset with a model trained without augmentations.

So, we load the validation dataset using exactly the same code as before:

```
validation_gen = ImageDataGenerator(
    preprocessing_function=preprocess_input
)

val_ds = validation_gen.flow_from_directory(
    "clothing-dataset-small/validation",
    target_size=image_size,
    batch_size=batch_size,
)
```

We're ready to train a new model now:

```
model = make_model(learning_rate=0.001, droprate=0.2)
model.fit(train_ds, epochs=50, validation_data=val_ds)
```

> **NOTE** We omit the code for model checkpointing here for brevity. Add it if you want to save the best model.

To train this model, we need even more epochs than previously. Data augmentation is also a regularization strategy. Instead of training on the same image over and over again, the network sees a different variation of the same image for every epoch. This makes it more difficult for the model to memorize the data, and it decreases the chances of overfitting.

After training this model, we managed to improve the accuracy by 1%, from 84% to 85%.

This improvement is not really significant. But we have experimented a lot, and we could do this relatively quickly because we used small images of size 150×150. Now we can apply everything we have learned so far to larger images.

Exercise 7.3
Data augmentation helps fight overfitting because

    a The model doesn't get to see the same images over and over again.

    b It adds a lot of variety into the dataset — rotations and other image transformations.

    c It generates examples of images that may exist, but the model overwise wouldn't have seen.

    d All of the above.

7.4.10 *Training a larger model*

Even for people it may be challenging to understand what kind of item is in a small 150×150 image. It's also difficult for a computer: it's not easy to see the important details, so the model may confuse pants and shorts or T-shirts and shirts.

By increasing the size of images from 150×150 to 299×299, it'll be easier for the network to see more details and, therefore, achieve greater accuracy.

> **NOTE** Training a model on larger images takes approximately four times longer than on small images. If you don't have access to a computer with a GPU, you don't have to run the code in this section. Conceptually, the process is the same, and the only difference is the input size.

So, let's modify our function for creating a model. For that, we need to take the code of make_model (listing 7.2) and adjust it in two places:

- The input_shape argument of Xception
- The C argument for input

In both these cases, we need to replace (150, 150, 3) with (299, 299, 3).

Next, we need to adjust the target_size parameter for the train and validation generators. We replace (150, 150) by (299, 299), and everything else stays the same.

Now we're ready to train a model!

```
model = make_model(learning_rate=0.001, droprate=0.2)
model.fit(train_ds, epochs=20, validation_data=val_ds)
```

> **NOTE** To save the model, add checkpointing.

This model achieves accuracy of around 89% on the validation data. This is a considerable improvement over the previous model.

We have trained a model, so now it's time to use it.

7.5   Using the model

Previously, we trained multiple models. The best one is the model we trained on large images — it has 89% accuracy. The second-best model has an accuracy of 85%.

Let's now use these models to make predictions. To use a model, we first need to load it.

7.5.1   Loading the model

You can either use the model you trained yourself or download the model we trained for the book and use it.

To download them, go to the releases section of the book's GitHub repository and look for Models for Chapter 7: Deep learning (figure 7.45). Alternatively, go to this URL: https://github.com/alexeygrigorev/mlbookcamp-code/releases/tag/chapter7-model.

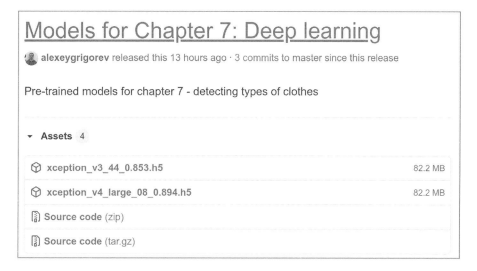

Figure 7.45   You can download the models we trained for this chapter from the book's GitHub repository.

Then download the large model trained on 299 × 299 images (xception_v4_large). To use it, load the model using the `load_model` function from the `models` package:

```
model = keras.models.load_model('xception_v4_large_08_0.894.h5')
```

We have already used both the train and validation datasets. We have finished the training process, so now it's time to evaluate this model on test data.

7.5.2   *Evaluating the model*

To load the test data, we follow the same approach: we use `ImageDataGenerator` but point to the test directory. Let's do it:

```
test_gen = ImageDataGenerator(
    preprocessing_function=preprocess_input
)

test_ds = test_gen.flow_from_directory(
    "clothing-dataset-small/test",
    shuffle=False,
    target_size=(299, 299),          ◁──┐ Use (150, 150) if
    batch_size=32,                       │ you're using the
)                                        │ small model.
```

Evaluating a model in Keras is as simple as invoking the `evaluate` method:

```
model.evaluate(test_ds)
```

It applies the model to all the data in the test folder and shows the evaluation metrics of loss and accuracy:

```
12/12 [==============================] - 70s 6s/step - loss: 0.2493 -
    accuracy: 0.9032
```

Our model shows 90% accuracy on the test dataset, which is comparable with the performance on the validation dataset (89%).

If we repeat the same process for the small dataset, we see that the performance is worse:

```
12/12 [==============================] - 15s 1s/step - loss: 0.6931 -
    accuracy: 0.8199
```

The accuracy is 82%, whereas on the validation it's 85%. The model performed worse on the test dataset.

It may be because of random fluctuations: the size of validation and test sets are not large, only 300 examples. So the model could get lucky on validation and unlucky on test.

However, it could be a sign of overfitting. By repeatedly evaluating the model on the validation dataset, we picked the model that got very lucky. Maybe this luck is not generalizable, and that's why the model performs worse on the data it hasn't seen previously.

Now let's see how we can apply the model to individual images to get predictions.

7.5.3 *Getting the predictions*

If we want to apply the model to a single image, we need to do the same thing `Image-DataGenerator` performs internally:

- Load an image.
- Preprocess it.

We already know how to load an image. We can use `load_img` for that:

```
path = 'clothing-dataset-small/test/pants/c8d21106-bbdb-4e8d-83e4-
    bf3d14e54c16.jpg'
img = load_img(path, target_size=(299, 299))
```

It's a picture of pants (figure 7.46).

Figure 7.46   An image of pants from the train dataset

Next, we preprocess the image:

```
x = np.array(img)
X = np.array([x])
X = preprocess_input(X)
```

And, finally, we get the predictions:

```
pred = model.predict(X)
```

We can see the predictions for the image by checking the first row of predictions: `pred[0]` (figure 7.47).

```
pred = model.predict(X)
pred[0]
```

```
array([-2.8609202, -4.234048 , -1.5732546, -1.907885 , 10.247051 ,
       -2.2489133, -4.297381 ,  4.43905  , -4.4588056, -3.9616938],
      dtype=float32)
```

Figure 7.47   The predictions of our model. It's an array with 10 elements, one for each class.

The result is an array with 10 elements, where each element contains the score. The higher the score, the more likely the image is to belong to the respective class.

To get the element with the highest score, we can use the `argmax` method. It returns the index of the element with the highest score (figure 7.48).

```
pred[0].argmax()
```
4

Figure 7.48   The `argmax` function returns the element with the highest score.

To know which label corresponds to class 4, we need to get the mapping. It can be extracted from a data generator. But let's put it manually to a dictionary:

```
labels = {
    0: 'dress',
    1: 'hat',
    2: 'longsleeve',
    3: 'outwear',
    4: 'pants',
    5: 'shirt',
    6: 'shoes',
    7: 'shorts',
    8: 'skirt',
    9: 't-shirt'
}
```

To get the label, simply look it up in the dictionary:

```
labels[pred[0].argmax()]
```

As we see, the label is "pants," which is correct. Also note that the label "shorts" has a high positive score: pants and shorts are quite similar visually. But "pants" is clearly the winner.

We will use this code in the next chapter, where we will productionize our model.

7.6 Next steps

We've learned the basics we need for training a classification model for predicting the type of clothes. We've covered a lot of material, but there is a lot more to learn than we could fit into this chapter. You can explore this topic more by doing the exercises.

7.6.1 Exercises

- For deep learning, the more data we have, the better. But the dataset we used for this project is not large: we trained our model on only 3,068 images. To make it better, we can add more training data. You can find more pictures of clothes in other data sources; for example, at https://www.kaggle.com/dqmonn/zalando-store-crawl, https://www.kaggle.com/paramaggarwal/fashion-product-images-dataset, or https://www.kaggle.com/c/imaterialist-fashion-2019-FGVC6. Try adding more pictures to the training data, and see if it improves the accuracy on the validation dataset.
- Augmentations help us train better models. In this chapter, we used only the most basic augmentation strategies. You can further explore this topic and try other kinds of image modifications. For example, add rotations and shifting, and see if it helps the model achieve better performance.
- In addition to the built-in way of augmenting the dataset, we have special libraries for doing this. One of them is Albumentations (https://github.com/albumentations-team/albumentations), which contains many more image manipulation algorithms. You can also experiment with it and see which augmentations work well for this problem.
- Many different pretrained models are available. We used Xception, but many others are out there. You can try them and see if they give a better performance. With Keras, it's quite simple to use a different model: just import from a different package. For example, you can try ResNet50 and compare it with the results from Xception. Check the documentation for more information (https://keras.io/api/applications/).

7.6.2 Other projects

There are many image classification projects that you can do:

- Cats or dogs (https://www.kaggle.com/c/dogs-vs-cats)
- Hotdog or not hotdog (https://www.kaggle.com/dansbecker/hot-dog-not-hot-dog)
- Predicting the category of images from Avito's dataset (online classifieds) (https://www.kaggle.com/c/avito-duplicate-ads-detection). Note that many duplicates appear in this dataset, so be careful when splitting the data for validation. It might be a good idea to use the train/test split that the organizators prepared and do a bit of extra cleaning to make sure there are no duplicate images.

Summary

- TensorFlow is a framework for building and using neural networks. Keras is a library on top of TensorFlow that makes training models simpler.
- For image processing, we need a special kind of neural network: a convolutional neural network. It consists of a series of convolutional layers followed by a series of dense layers.
- The convolutional layers in a neural network convert an image to its vector representation. This representation contains high-level features. The dense layers use these features to make the prediction.
- We don't need to train a convolutional neural network from scratch. We can use pretrained models on ImageNet for general-purpose classification.
- Transfer learning is the process of adjusting a pretrained model to our problem. We keep the original convolutional layers but create new dense layers. This significantly reduces the time we need to train a model.
- We use dropout to prevent overfitting. At each iteration, it freezes a random part of the network, so only the other part can be used for training. This allows the network to generalize better.
- We can create more training data from existing images by rotating them, flipping them vertically and horizontally, and doing other transformations. This process is called data augmentation, and it adds more variability to the data and reduces the risk of overfitting.

In this chapter, we have trained a convolutional neural network for classifying images of clothing. We can save it, load it, and use it inside a Jupyter Notebook. This is not enough to use it in production.

In the next chapter, we show how to use it in production and talk about two ways of productionizing deep learning models: TensorFlow Lite in AWS Lambda and Tensor-Flow Serving in Kubernetes.

Answers to exercises

- Exercise 7.1 A) True
- Exercise 7.2 B) Freeze a random part of a model, so it doesn't get updated during one iteration of training.
- Exercise 7.3 D) All of the above

Serverless deep learning

This chapter covers

- Serving models with TensorFlow Lite —
  a lightweight environment for applying
  TensorFlow models
- Deploying deep learning models with AWS
  Lambda
- Exposing the lambda function as a web service
  via API Gateway

In the previous chapter, we trained a deep learning model for categorizing images of clothing. Now we need to deploy it, making the model available for other services.

We have many possible ways of doing this. We have already covered the basics of model deployment in chapter 5, where we talked about using Flask, Docker, and AWS Elastic Beanstalk for deploying a logistic regression model.

In this chapter, we'll talk about the serverless approach for deploying models — we'll use AWS Lambda.

8.1   *Serverless: AWS Lambda*

AWS Lambda is a service from Amazon. Its main promise is that you can "run code without thinking about servers."

It lives up to the promise: in AWS Lambda, we just need to upload some code. The service takes care of running it and scales it up and down according to the load.

Additionally, you only need to pay for the time when the function is actually used. When nobody uses the model and invokes our service, you don't pay for anything.

In this chapter, we use AWS Lambda for deploying the model we trained previously. For doing that, we'll also use TensorFlow Lite — a lightweight version of Tensor-Flow that has only the most essential functions.

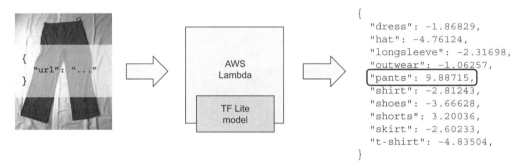

Figure 8.1   Overview of the service: it gets the URL of an image, applies the model, and returns the predictions.

We want to build a web service that

- Gets the URL in the request
- Loads the image from this URL
- Uses TensorFlow Lite to apply the model to the image and get the predictions
- Responds with the results (figure 8.1)

To create this service, we will need to

- Convert the model from Keras to the TensorFlow Lite format
- Preprocess the images — resize them and apply the preprocessing function
- Package the code in a Docker image, and upload it to ECR (the Docker registry from AWS)
- Create and test the lambda function on AWS
- Make the lambda function available to everyone with AWS API Gateway

We assume you have an AWS account and have configured the AWS CLI tool. For details, please refer to appendix A.

NOTE At the time of writing, AWS Lambda is covered by the AWS free tier. This means that it's possible to do all the experiments in this chapter for free. To check the conditions, refer to the AWS documentation (https:// aws.amazon.com/free/).

We use AWS here, but this approach also works for other serverless platforms.

The code for this chapter is available in the book's GitHub repository (https:// github.com/alexeygrigorev/mlbookcamp-code/) in the chapter-08-serverless folder.

Let's start by discussing TensorFlow Lite.

8.1.1 *TensorFlow Lite*

TensorFlow is a great framework with a rich set of features. However, most of these features are not needed for model deployment, and they take up a lot of space: when compressed, TensorFlow takes up more than 1.5 GB of space.

TensorFlow Lite (usually abbreviated as "TF Lite"), on the other hand, takes up only 50 MB of space. It's optimized for mobile devices and contains only the essential parts. With TF Lite, you can use the model only for making predictions and nothing else, including training new models.

Even though it was originally created for mobile devices, it's applicable for more cases. We can use it whenever we have a TensorFlow model but can't afford to take the entire TensorFlow package with us.

NOTE The TF Lite library is under active development and changes rather quickly. It's possible that the way you install this library has changed since the book was published. Please refer to the official documentation for up-to-date instructions (https://www.tensorflow.org/lite/guide/python).

Let's install the library now. We can do so with `pip`:

```
pip install --extra-index-url https://google-coral.github.io/py-repo/
    tflite_runtime
```

When running `pip install`, we add the `extra-index-url` parameter. The library we install is not available in the central repository with Python packages, but it's available in a different repository. We need to point to this repository.

NOTE For non-Debian-based Linux distributions, like CentOS, Fedora, or Amazon Linux, the library installed this way might not work: you might get an error when trying to import the library. If that's the case, you need to compile this library yourself. Refer to the instructions here for more details: https:// github.com/alexeygrigorev/serverless-deep-learning. For MacOS and Windows, it should work as expected.

TF Lite uses a special optimized format for storing models. To use our model with TF Lite, we need to convert our model to this format. We'll do that next.

8.1.2   *Converting the model to TF Lite format*

We used the h5 format for saving the model from the previous chapter. This format is suitable for storing Keras models, but it won't work for TF Lite. So, we need to convert our model to TF-Lite format.

If you don't have the model from the previous chapter, go ahead and download it:

```
wget https://github.com/alexeygrigorev/mlbookcamp-code/releases/download/
    chapter7-model/xception_v4_large_08_0.894.h5
```

Now let's create a simple script for converting this model — convert.py.

First, start with imports:

```
import tensorflow as tf
from tensorflow import keras
```

Next, load the Keras model:

```
model = keras.models.load_model('xception_v4_large_08_0.894.h5')
```

And finally, convert it to TF Lite:

```
converter = tf.lite.TFLiteConverter.from_keras_model(model)

tflite_model = converter.convert()

with tf.io.gfile.GFile('clothing-model-v4.tflite', 'wb') as f:
    f.write(tflite_model)
```

Let's run it:

```
python convert.py
```

After running it, we should have a file named clothing-model-v4.tflite in our directory.

We're ready to use this model now for image classification, applying the model to images of clothing to understand if a given image is a T-shirt, pants, a skirt, or something else. However, remember that before we can use a model for classifying an image, the image needs to be preprocessed. We'll see how to do that next.

8.1.3   *Preparing the images*

Previously, when testing the model in Keras, we preprocessed each image using the preprocess_input function. This is how we imported it in the previous chapter:

```
from tensorflow.keras.applications.xception import preprocess_input
```

And then we applied this function to images before we put them into models.

However, we can't use the same function when deploying our model. This function is a part of the TensorFlow package, and there's no equivalent in TF Lite. We don't want to depend on TensorFlow just for this simple preprocessing function.

Instead, we can use a special library that has only the code we need: `keras_image_helper`. This library was written to simplify the explanation in this book. If you want to know how images are pre-processed in more detail, check the source code. It's available at https://github.com/alexeygrigorev/keras-image-helper. This library can load an image, resize it, and apply other preprocessing transformations that Keras models require.

Let's install it with `pip`:

```
pip install keras_image_helper
```

Next, open Jupyter, and create a notebook called chapter-08-model-test.

We start by importing the `create_preprocessor` function from the library:

```
from keras_image_helper import create_preprocessor
```

The function `create_preprocessor` takes two arguments:

- `name`: The name of the model. You can see the list of available models at https://keras.io/api/applications/.
- `target_size`: The size of the image that the neural network expects to get.

We used the Xception model, and it expects an image of size 299 × 299. Let's create a preprocessor for our model:

```
preprocessor = create_preprocessor('xception', target_size=(299, 299))
```

Now let's get a picture of pants (figure 8.2), and prepare it:

```
image_url = 'http://bit.ly/mlbookcamp-pants'
X = preprocessor.from_url(image_url)
```

Figure 8.2   The picture of pants that we use for testing

The result is a NumPy array of shape (1, 299, 299, 3):

- It's a batch of one image only.
- 299 × 299 is the size of the image.
- There are three channels: red, green, and blue.

We have prepared the image, and we're ready to use the model for classifying it. Let's see how we can do this with TF Lite.

8.1.4   *Using the TensorFlow Lite model*

We have the array X from the previous step, and now we can use TF Lite for classifying it.

First, import TF Lite:

```
import tflite_runtime.interpreter as tflite
```

Load the model we previously converted:

Creates the TF Lite interpreter

```
interpreter = tflite.Interpreter(model_path='clothing-model-v4.tflite')   ◁
interpreter.allocate_tensors()   ◁
```
Initializes the interpreter with the model

To be able to use the model, we need to get its input (where X will go) and the output (where we get the predictions from):

```
input_details = interpreter.get_input_details()
input_index = input_details[0]['index']
```
Gets the input: the part of the network that takes in the array X

```
output_details = interpreter.get_output_details()
output_index = output_details[0]['index']
```
Gets the output: the part of the network with final predictions

To apply the model, take the X we previously prepared, put it into the input, invoke the interpreter, and get the results from the output:

```
interpreter.set_tensor(input_index, X)   ◁
interpreter.invoke()   ◁
```
Puts X into the input

Runs the model to get predictions

```
preds = interpreter.get_tensor(output_index)   ◁
```
Gets the predictions from the output

The preds array contains the predictions:

```
array([[-1.8682897, -4.7612453, -2.316984 , -1.0625705,  9.887156 ,
         -2.8124316, -3.6662838,  3.2003622, -2.6023388, -4.8350453]],
       dtype=float32)
```

Now we can do the same thing with it as previously — assign the label to each element of this array:

```
labels = [
    'dress',
    'hat',
    'longsleeve',
    'outwear',
    'pants',
    'shirt',
    'shoes',
    'shorts',
    'skirt',
    't-shirt'
]

results = dict(zip(labels, preds[0]))
```

It's done! We have the predictions in the `results` variable:

```
{'dress': -1.8682897,
 'hat': -4.7612453,
 'longsleeve': -2.316984,
 'outwear': -1.0625705,
 'pants': 9.887156,
 'shirt': -2.8124316,
 'shoes': -3.6662838,
 'shorts': 3.2003622,
 'skirt': -2.6023388,
 't-shirt': -4.8350453}
```

We see that the `pants` label has the highest score, so this must be a picture of pants.

Let's now use this code for our future AWS Lambda function!

8.1.5   *Code for the lambda function*

In the previous section, we wrote all the code we need for the lambda function. Let's put it together in a single script — lambda_function.py.

As usual, start with imports:

```
import tflite_runtime.interpreter as tflite
from keras_image_helper import create_preprocessor
```

Then, create the preprocessor:

```
preprocessor = create_preprocessor('xception', target_size=(299, 299))
```

Next, load the model, and get the output and input:

```
interpreter = tflite.Interpreter(model_path='clothing-model-v4.tflite')
interpreter.allocate_tensors()

input_details = interpreter.get_input_details()
input_index = input_details[0]['index']
```

```
output_details = interpreter.get_output_details()
output_index = output_details[0]['index']
```

To make it a bit cleaner, we can put all the code for making a prediction together in one function:

```
def predict(X):
    interpreter.set_tensor(input_index, X)
    interpreter.invoke()
    preds = interpreter.get_tensor(output_index)
    return preds[0]
```

Next, let's make another function for preparing the results:

```
labels = [
    'dress',
    'hat',
    'longsleeve',
    'outwear',
    'pants',
    'shirt',
    'shoes',
    'shorts',
    'skirt',
    't-shirt'
]

def decode_predictions(pred):
    result = {c: float(p) for c, p in zip(labels, pred)}
    return result
```

Finally, put everything together in one function — `lambda_handler` — which is the function invoked by the AWS Lambda environment. It will use all the things we defined previously:

```
def lambda_handler(event, context):
    url = event['url']
    X = preprocessor.from_url(url)
    preds = predict(X)
    results = decode_predictions(preds)
    return results
```

In this case, the `event` parameter contains all the information we pass to the lambda function in our request (figure 8.3). The `context` parameter is typically not used.

We're ready to test it now! To do it locally, we need to put this code into the Python Docker container for AWS Lambda.

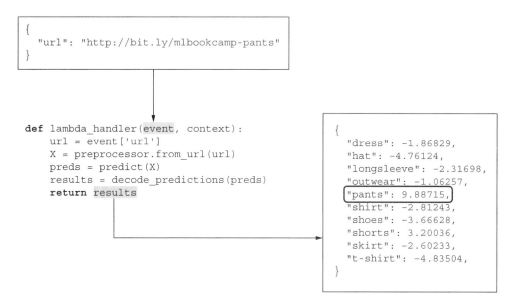

Figure 8.3 The input and the output of the lambda function: the input goes to the `event` parameter, and the predictions are returned as the output.

8.1.6 Preparing the Docker image

First, create a file named Dockerfile:

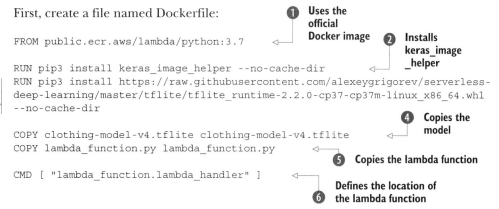

Let's take a look at each line of the file. First ❶, we use the official Python 3.7 Docker image for Lambda from AWS. You can see other available images here: https://gallery.ecr.aws/. Then ❷, we install the keras_image_helper library.

Next ❸, we install a special version of TF Lite that was compiled to work with Amazon Linux. The installation instructions we used in this chapter earlier don't work for Amazon Linux, only for Ubuntu (and other Debian-based distributions). That's why we need to use a special version. You can read more about it here: https://github.com/alexeygrigorev/serverless-deep-learning.

Then ❹, we copy the model to the image. When we do so, the model becomes a part of the image. This way, it's simpler to deploy the model. We could use an alternative approach — the model can be put to S3 and loaded when the script starts. It's more complex but also more flexible. For the book, we went with the simpler approach.

Then ❺, we copy the code of the lambda function we prepared earlier.

Finally ❻, we tell the `lambda` environment that it needs to look for the file named lambda_function and look for the function `lambda_handler` inside this function. This is the function we prepared in the previous section.

Let's build this image:

```
docker build -t tf-lite-lambda .
```

Next, we need to check that the lambda function works. Let's run the image:

```
docker run --rm -p 8080:8080 tf-lite-lambda
```

It's running! We can test it now.

We can continue using the Jupyter Notebook we created earlier, or we can create a separate Python file named test.py. It should have the following content — and you'll note it's very similar to the code we wrote in chapter 5 for testing our web service:

```
import requests                     ❶ Prepares
                                       the request
data = {
    "url": "http://bit.ly/mlbookcamp-pants"
}
                                                    Specifies the URL ❷
url = "http://localhost:8080/2015-03-31/functions/function/invocations"

results = requests.post(url, json=data).json()   ❸ Sends a POST request
print(results)                                       to the service
```

First, we define the `data` variable in ❶ — this is our request. Then we specify the URL of the service in ❷ — this is the location where the function is currently deployed. Finally, in ❸, we use the POST method to submit the request and get back the predictions in the `results` variable.

When we run it, we get the following response:

```
{
  "dress": -1.86829,
  "hat": -4.76124,
  "longsleeve": -2.31698,
  "outwear": -1.06257,
  "pants": 9.88715,
  "shirt": -2.81243,
  "shoes": -3.66628,
  "shorts": 3.20036,
```

```
  "skirt": -2.60233,
  "t-shirt": -4.83504
}
```

The model works!

We're almost ready to deploy it to AWS. To do that, we first need to publish this image to ECR — the Docker container registry from AWS.

8.1.7 Pushing the image to AWS ECR

To publish this Docker image to AWS, we first need to create a registry using the AWS CLI tool:

```
aws ecr create-repository --repository-name lambda-images
```

It will return back an URL that looks like this:

```
<ACCOUNT_ID>.dkr.ecr.<REGION>.amazonaws.com/lambda-images
```

You'll need this URL.

Alternatively, it's possible to create the registry using the AWS Console.

Once the registry is created, we need to push the image there. Because this registry belongs to our account, we first need to authenticate our Docker client. On Linux and MacOS, you can do this:

```
$(aws ecr get-login --no-include-email)
```

On Windows, run `aws ecr get-login --no-include-email`, copy the output, enter it into the terminal, and execute it manually.

Now let's use the registry URL to push the image to ECR:

```
REGION=eu-west-1                                              Specify the region and
ACCOUNT=XXXXXXXXXXXX                                          your AWS account ID.
REMOTE_NAME=${ACCOUNT}.dkr.ecr.${REGION}.amazonaws.com/lambda-images:tf-lite-
    lambda
docker tag tf-lite-lambda ${REMOTE_NAME}
docker push ${REMOTE_NAME}
```

Now it's pushed, and we can use it to create a lambda function in AWS.

8.1.8 Creating the lambda function

This step is easier to do with the AWS Console, so open it, go to services, and select Lambda.

Next, click Create Function. Select Container Image (figure 8.4).

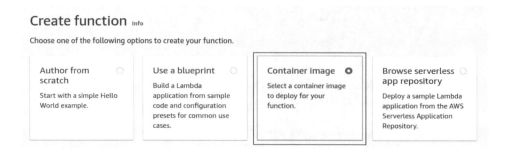

Figure 8.4   When creating a `lambda` function, select Container Image.

After that, fill in the details (figure 8.5).

Basic information

Function name
Enter a name that describes the purpose of your function.

> clothes-classification|

Use only letters, numbers, hyphens, or underscores with no spaces.

Container image URI   Info
The location of the container image to use for your function.

> <ACCOUNT>.dkr.ecr.<REGION>.amazonaws.com/lambda-images:tf-lite-lambda

Requires a valid Amazon ECR image URI.

> **Browse images**

Figure 8.5   Enter the function name and the container image URI.

The container image URI should be the image we created earlier and pushed to ECR:

```
<ACCOUNT>.dkr.ecr.<REGION>.amazonaws.com/lambda-images:tf-lite-lambda
```

You can use the Browse Images button to find it (figure 8.5). Keep the rest unchanged, and click Create Function. The function is created!

Now we need to give our function more memory and let it run for a longer time without timing out. For that, select the Configuration tab, choose General Configuration, and then click Edit (figure 8.6).

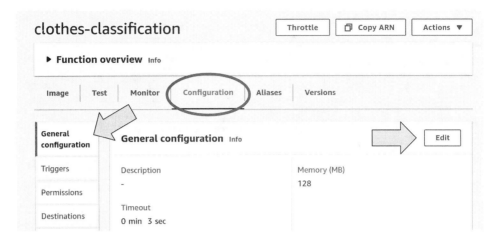

Figure 8.6 **The default settings of a lambda function: the default amount of memory (128 MB) is not enough, so we need to increase it. Click Edit to do so.**

The default settings are not good for deep learning models. We need to configure this function to give it more RAM and allow it to take more time.

For that, click the Edit button, give it 1024 MB of RAM, and set the timeout to 30 seconds (figure 8.7).

Figure 8.7 **Increase the amount of memory to 1024 MB and set the timeout to 30 seconds.**

Save it.

It's ready! To test it, go to the Test tab (figure 8.8).

It'll suggest creating a test event. Give it a name (for example, test), and put the following content in the request body:

```
{
    "url": "http://bit.ly/mlbookcamp-pants"
}
```

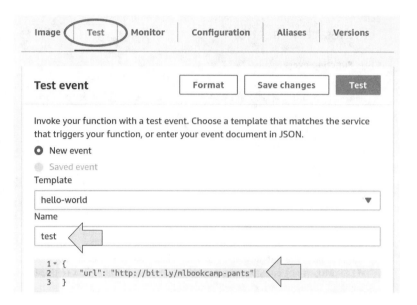

Figure 8.8   **The Test button is located at the top of the screen. Click it to test the function.**

Save it and click the Test button again. After approximately 15 seconds, you should see "Execution results: succeeded" (figure 8.9).

Figure 8.9   **The predictions of our model. The prediction for `pants` has the highest score.**

When we run the test for the first time, it needs to pull the image from ECR, load all the libraries in memory, and do some other things to "warm up." But once it's done it, the consequent invocations take less time — approximately two seconds for this model.

We have successfully deployed our model to AWS Lambda, and it's working!

Also, remember that you pay only when the function is invoked, so you don't need to worry about deleting this function if it's not used. And you don't need to worry about managing EC2 instances at all — AWS Lambda takes care of everything for us.

It's already possible to use this model for many things: AWS Lambda integrates well with a lot of other services from AWS. But if we want to use it as a web service and send requests over HTTP, we need to expose it through API Gateway.

We'll see how to do this next.

8.1.9   *Creating the API Gateway*

In the AWS Console, find the API Gateway service. Create a new API: select REST API, and click Build.

Then select New API, and call it clothes-classification (figure 8.10). Click Create API.

Create new API

In Amazon API Gateway, a REST API refers to a collection of resources and methods that can be invoked through HTTPS endpoints.

⦿ **New API**   ◯ **Import from Swagger or Open API 3**   ◯ **Example API**

Settings

Choose a friendly name and description for your API.

API name*	clothes-classifiication
Description	expose lambda as a web service
Endpoint Type	Regional ⌄ ❶

Figure 8.10   Creating a new REST API Gateway in AWS

Next, click the Actions button and select Resource. Then, create a resource predict (figure 8.11).

> **NOTE**   The name predict doesn't follow the REST naming standards: usually resources should be nouns. However, it's common to name endpoints for predictions as predict; that's why we don't follow the REST convention.

Configure as ☐ proxy resource   ☐ ❶

Resource Name*   Predict endpoint

Resource Path*   /   predict

You can add path parameters using brackets. For example, the
resource path **{username}** represents a path parameter called
'username'. Configuring /{proxy+} as a proxy resource catches
all requests to its sub-resources. For example, it works for a
GET request to /foo. To handle requests to /, add a new ANY
method on the / resource.

Enable API Gateway CORS   ☐ ❶

Figure 8.11   Creating a predict resource

After creating the resource, create a POST method for it (figure 8.12):

1   Click Predict.
2   Click Actions.
3   Select Create Method.
4   Choose POST from the list.
5   Click the tick button.

Figure 8.12   Create a POST method for the predict resource.

We're almost ready!

Now select Lambda Function as the integration type and enter the name of your
lambda function (figure 8.13).

NOTE   Make sure you don't use proxy integration — this checkbox should
remain unchecked. If you use this option, API Gateway adds some extra information to the request, and we would need to adjust the lambda function.

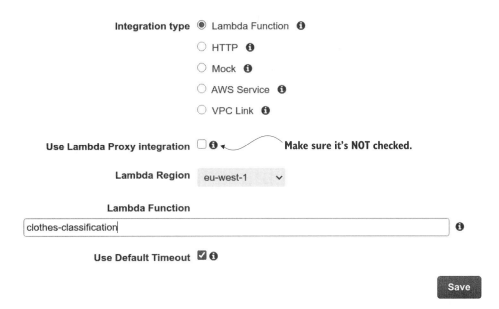

Figure 8.13 **Configuring the POST action for the predict resource. Make sure Proxy Integration is not checked.**

After doing this, we should see the integration (figure 8.14).

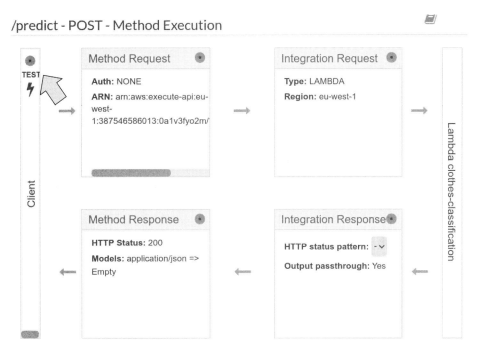

Figure 8.14 **Deploying the API**

Let's test it. Click TEST, and put the same request in the request body as previously:

```
{
    "url": "http://bit.ly/mlbookcamp-pants"
}
```

The response is the same: the predicted class is pants (figure 8.15).

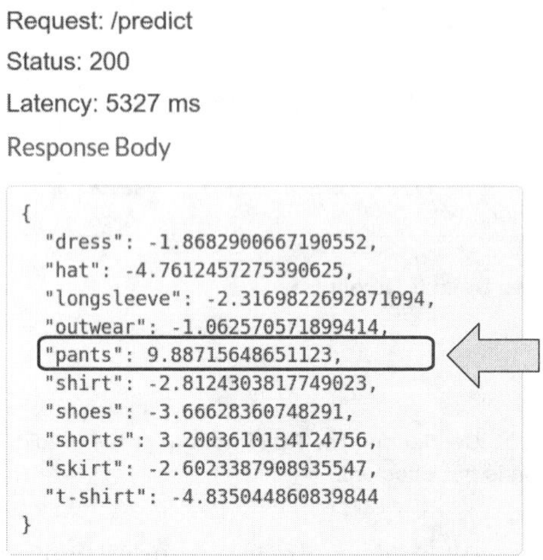

Request: /predict

Status: 200

Latency: 5327 ms

Response Body

```
{
    "dress": -1.8682900667190552,
    "hat": -4.7612457275390625,
    "longsleeve": -2.3169822692871094,
    "outwear": -1.062570571899414,
    "pants": 9.88715648651123,
    "shirt": -2.8124303817749023,
    "shoes": -3.66628360748291,
    "shorts": 3.2003610134124756,
    "skirt": -2.6023387908935547,
    "t-shirt": -4.835044860839844
}
```

Figure 8.15   **The response from the lambda function. The pants category has the highest score.**

To use it externally, we need to deploy the API. Select Deploy API from the list of actions (figure 8.16).

Next, create a new stage test (figure 8.17).

By clicking Deploy, we deploy the API. Now find the Invoke URL field. It should look like this:

https://0a1v3fyo2m.execute-api.eu-west-1.amazonaws.com/test

All we need to do now to invoke the lambda function is to add "/predict" at the end of this URL.

Let's take the test.py script we created previously and replace the URL there:

```
import requests

data = {
    "url": "http://bit.ly/mlbookcamp-pants"
}
url = "https://0a1v3fyo2m.execute-api.eu-west-1.amazonaws.com/test/predict"

results = requests.post(url, json=data).json()

print(results)
```

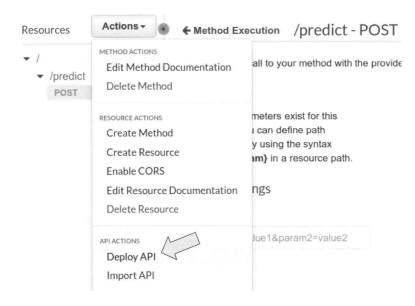

Figure 8.16 The function `clothes-classification` is now connected to the POST method of the predict resource in the API Gateway. The TEST button helps with verifying that the connection with lambda works.

Deploy API ●

Choose a stage where your API will be deployed. For example, a test version of your API could be deployed to a stage named beta.

Deployment stage	[New Stage] ⌄
Stage name*	test
Stage description	Testing the API
Deployment description	

Cancel   **Deploy**

Figure 8.17 Configuring the stage for the API

Run it:

```
python test.py
```

The response is the same as previously:

```
{
  "dress": -1.86829,
  "hat": -4.76124,
  "longsleeve": -2.31698,
  "outwear": -1.06257,
  "pants": 9.88715,
  "shirt": -2.81243,
  "shoes": -3.66628,
  "shorts": 3.20036,
  "skirt": -2.60233,
  "t-shirt": -4.83504
}
```

Now our model is exposed with a web service that we can use from anywhere.

8.2   Next steps

8.2.1   Exercises

Try the following to further explore the topics of serverless model deployment:

- AWS Lambda is not the only serverless environment. You can also experiment with cloud functions in Google Cloud and Azure functions on Azure.
- SAM (Serverless Application Model) is a tool from AWS for making the process of creating AWS Lambda functions easier (https://aws.amazon.com/serverless/sam/). You can use it to reimplement the project from this chapter.
- Serverless (https://www.serverless.com/) is a framework similar to SAM. It's not specific to AWS and works for other cloud providers. You can experiment with it and deploy the project from this chapter.

8.2.2   Other projects

You can do many other projects:

- AWS Lambda is a convenient platform for hosting machine learning models. In this chapter, we deployed a deep learning model. You can also experiment with it more and deploy the models we trained in the previous chapters as well as the models you developed as a part of the exercises.

Summary

- TensorFlow Lite is a lightweight alternative to "full" TensorFlow. It contains only the most important parts that are needed for using deep learning models. Using it makes the process of deploying models with AWS Lambda faster and simpler.

- Lambda functions can be run locally using Docker. This way, we can test our code without deploying it to AWS.
- To deploy a lambda function, we need to put its code in Docker, publish the Docker image to ECR, and then use the URI of the image when creating a lambda function.
- To expose the lambda function, we use API Gateway. This way, we make the lambda function available as a web service, so it could be used by anyone.

In this chapter, we've used AWS Lambda — the serverless approach for deploying deep learning models. We didn't want to worry about servers and let the environment worry about it instead.

In the next chapter, we actually think about servers, and we use a Kubernetes cluster for deploying a model.

Serving models with Kubernetes and Kubeflow

This chapter covers

- Understanding different methods of deploying and serving models in the cloud
- Serving Keras and TensorFlow models with TensorFlowServing
- Deploying TensorFlow Serving to Kubernetes
- Using Kubeflow and KFServing for simplifying the deployment process

In the previous chapter, we talked about model deployment with AWS Lambda and TensorFlow Lite.

In this chapter, we discuss the "serverful" approach to model deployment: we serve the clothing classification model with TensorFlow Serving on Kubernetes. Also, we talk about Kubeflow, an extension for Kubernetes that makes model deployment easier.

We're going to cover a lot of material in this chapter, but Kubernetes is so complex that it's simply not possible to go deep into detail. Because of that, we often refer to external resources for a more in-depth coverage of some topics. But don't worry; you will learn enough to feel comfortable deploying your own models with it.

9.1 Kubernetes and Kubeflow

Kubernetes is a container orchestration platform. It sounds complex, but it's nothing other than a place where we can deploy Docker containers. It takes care of exposing these containers as web services and scales these services up and down as the amount of requests we receive changes.

Kubernetes is not the easiest tool to learn, but it's very powerful. It's likely that you will need to use it at some point. That's why we decided to cover it in this book.

Kubeflow is another popular tool built on top of Kubernetes. It makes it easier to use Kubernetes to deploy machine learning models. In this chapter, we cover both Kubernetes and Kubeflow.

In the first part, we talk about TensorFlow Serving and plain Kubernetes. We discuss how we can use these technologies for model deployment. The plan for the first part is

- First, we convert the Keras model into the special format used by TensorFlow Serving.
- Then we use TensorFlow Serving to run the model locally.
- After that, we create a service for preprocessing images and communicating with TensorFlow Serving.
- Finally, we deploy both the model and the preprocessing service with Kubernetes.

NOTE This chapter doesn't attempt to cover Kubernetes in depth. We show only how to use Kubernetes for deploying models and often refer to more specialized sources that cover it in more detail.

In the second part, we use Kubeflow, a tool on top of Kubernetes that makes deployment easier:

- We use the same model we've prepared for TensorFlow Serving and deploy it with KFServing — the part of Kubeflow that takes care of serving.
- Then we create a transformer for preprocessing the images and postprocessing the predictions.

The code for this chapter is available in the book's GitHub repository (https://github.com/alexeygrigorev/mlbookcamp-code/) in the chapter-09-kubernetes and chapter-09-kubeflow folders.

Let's get started!

9.2 Serving models with TensorFlow Serving

In chapter 7, we used Keras for predicting the classes of images. In chapter 8, we converted the model to TF Lite and used it for making predictions from AWS Lambda. In this chapter, we do this with TensorFlow Serving.

TensorFlow Serving, usually abbreviated as "TF Serving," is a system designed for serving TensorFlow models. Unlike TF Lite, which is made for mobile devices, TF Serving focuses on servers. Often, the servers have GPUs, and TF Serving knows how to make use of them.

AWS Lambda is great for experimenting and for dealing with small amounts of images — fewer than one million per day. But when we grow past that amount and get more images, AWS Lambda becomes expensive. Then deploying models with Kubernetes and TF Serving is a better option.

Just using TF Serving for deploying models is not sufficient, however. We also need another service for preparing the images. Next, we'll discuss the architecture of the system that we will build.

9.2.1   Overview of the serving architecture

TF Serving focuses on only one thing — serving the model. It expects that the data it receives is already prepared: images are resized, preprocessed, and sent in the right format.

This is why simply putting the model into TF Serving is not enough. We need an additional service that takes care of preprocessing the data.

We need two components for a system for serving a deep learning model (figure 9.1):

- Gateway: The preprocessing part. It gets the URL for which we need to make the prediction, prepares it, and sends it further to the model. We will use Flask for creating this service.
- Model: The part with the actual model. We will use TF Serving for this.

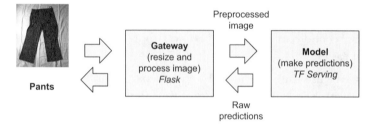

Figure 9.1   The two-tier architecture of our system. The gateway gets the user requests and prepares the data, and TF Serving uses the data to make the predictions.

Creating a system with two components instead of one may seem like an unnecessary complication. In the previous chapter, we didn't need to do it. We had only one part — the lambda function.

In principle, we could take the code from that lambda function, put it in Flask, and use it for serving the model. This approach will indeed work, but it won't be the most effective one. If we need to process millions of images, being able to properly utilize the resources is important.

Having two separate components instead of a single one makes it easier to select the right resource for each part:

- The gateway spends a lot of time downloading the images in addition to doing preprocessing. It doesn't need a powerful computer for that.
- The TF Serving component requires a more powerful machine, often with a GPU. It would be wasteful to use this powerful machine for downloading images.
- We might require many gateway instances and only a few TF Serving instances. By separating them into different components, we can scale each independently.

We will start with the second component — TF Serving.

In chapter 7, we trained a Keras model. To use it with TF Serving, we need to convert it to the special format used by TF Serving, which is called *saved_model*. We do this next.

9.2.2 *The saved_model format*

The Keras model we trained previously was saved in the h5 format. TF Serving cannot read h5: it expects models to be in the saved_model format. In this section, we convert the h5 model to a saved_model file.

In case you don't have the model from chapter 7, you can download it with wget:

```
wget https://github.com/alexeygrigorev/mlbookcamp-
code/releases/download/chapter7-model/xception_v4_large_08_0.894.h5
```

Now let's convert it. We can do this from a Jupyter Notebook or from a Python script.
In either case, we start with imports:

```
import tensorflow as tf
from tensorflow import keras
```

Then load the model:

```
model = keras.models.load_model('xception_v4_large_08_0.894.h5')
```

And, finally, save it in the saved_model format:

```
tf.saved_model.save(model, 'clothing-model')
```

That's it. After running this code, we have the model saved in the clothing-model folder.
To be able to use this model later, we need to know a few things:

- The name of the model signature. The model signature describes the model's inputs and outputs. You can read more about model signatures here: https://www.tensorflow.org/tfx/serving/signature_defs.
- The name of the input layer.
- The name of the output layer.

When using Keras, we didn't need to worry about it, but TF Serving requires us to have this information.

TensorFlow comes with a special utility for analyzing the models in the saved_model format — saved_model_cli. We don't need to install anything extra. We will use the show command from this utility:

```
saved_model_cli show --dir clothing-model --all
```

Let's take a look at the output:

```
MetaGraphDef with tag-set: 'serve' contains the following SignatureDefs:

...                                          The signature definition —
                                             serving_default
signature_def['serving_default']:        ◄─┘
  The given SavedModel SignatureDef contains the following input(s):
    inputs['input_8'] tensor_info:    ◄
      dtype: DT_FLOAT                       The input name —
      shape: (-1, 299, 299, 3)             input_8
      name: serving_default_input_8:0
  The given SavedModel SignatureDef contains the following output(s):
    outputs['dense_7'] tensor_info:   ◄
      dtype: DT_FLOAT                       The output name —
      shape: (-1, 10)                      dense_7
      name: StatefulPartitionedCall:0
  Method name is: tensorflow/serving/predict
```

In this output, we're interested in three things:

- The signature definition (signature_def) of the model. In this case, it's serving_default.
- The input (input_8). The name of the input of the model.
- The output (dense_7). tThe name of the output layer of the model.

NOTE   Take note of these names — we'll need them later when invoking this model.

The model is converted, and now we're ready to serve it with TF Serving.

9.2.3   *Running TensorFlow Serving locally*

One of the easiest ways of running TF Serving locally is to use Docker. You can read more about it in the official documentation: https://www.tensorflow.org/tfx/serving/docker. Refer to chapter 5 for more information about Docker.

All we need to do is invoke the docker run command specifying the path to the model and its name:

```
docker run -it --rm \                    ❶ Opens port 8500
  -p 8500:8500 \                            for serving
  -v "$(pwd)/clothing-model:/models/clothing-model/1" \    ❷ Mounts
  -e MODEL_NAME=clothing-model \                              our model
  tensorflow/serving:2.3.0
```

❸ Specifies the name of the model

❹ Uses the TensorFlow Serving image, version 2.3.0

When running it, we use three parameters:

- -p: To map port 8500 on the host machine (the computer where we run Docker) to port 8500 inside the container ❶.
- -v: To put the model files inside the Docker image ❷. The model is put in /models/clothing-model/1, where clothing-model is the name of the model and 1 is the version.
- -e: To set the MODEL_NAME variable to clothing-model ❸, which is the directory name from ❷.

To learn more about the docker run command, refer to the official Docker documentation (https://docs.docker.com/engine/reference/run/).

After running this command, we should see logs in the terminal:

```
2020-12-26 22:56:37.315629: I tensorflow_serving/core/loader_harness.cc:87]
Successfully loaded servable version {name: clothing-model version: 1}
2020-12-26 22:56:37.321376: I tensorflow_serving/model_servers/server.cc:371]
Running gRPC ModelServer at 0.0.0.0:8500 ...
[evhttp_server.cc : 238] NET_LOG: Entering the event loop ...
```

The Entering the event loop message tells us that TF Serving has started successfully and is ready to receive requests.

But we cannot use it yet. To prepare a request, we need to load an image, preprocess it, and convert it to a special binary format. Next, we'll see how we can do it.

9.2.4 *Invoking the TF Serving model from Jupyter*

For communication, TF Serving uses gRPC — a special protocol designed for high-performance communication. This protocol relies on protobuf, a format for effective data transfer. Unlike JSON, it's binary, which makes the requests significantly more compact.

To understand how to use it, let's first experiment with these technologies from a Jupyter Notebook. We connect to our model deployed with TF Serving using gRPC and protobuf. After that, we can put this code into a Flask application in the next section.

Let's start. We need to install a couple of libraries:

- grpcio: For gRPC support in Python
- tensorflow-serving-api: For using TF Serving from Python

Install them with pip:

```
pip install grpcio==1.32.0 tensorflow-serving-api==2.3.0
```

We also need the keras_image_helper library for preprocessing the images. We already used this library in chapter 8. If you haven't installed it yet, use pip for that:

```
pip install keras_image_helper==0.0.1
```

Next, create a Jupyter Notebook. We can call it chapter-09-image-preparation. As usual, we start with imports:

```
import grpc
import tensorflow as tf

from tensorflow_serving.apis import predict_pb2
from tensorflow_serving.apis import prediction_service_pb2_grpc
```

We imported three things:

- gRPC: for communicating with TF Serving
- TensorFlow: for protobuf definitions (We'll see later how it's used.)
- A couple of functions from TensorFlow Serving

Now we need to define the connection to our service:

```
host = 'localhost:8500'
channel = grpc.insecure_channel(host)
stub = prediction_service_pb2_grpc.PredictionServiceStub(channel)
```

NOTE We use an insecure channel — a channel that requires no authentication. All the communication between the services in this chapter happens inside the same network. This network is closed to the outside world, so using an insecure channel does not cause any security vulnerabilities. Setting a secure channel is possible but outside the scope of this book.

For preprocessing the images, we use the keras_image_helper library, like previously:

```
from keras_image_helper import create_preprocessor

preprocessor = create_preprocessor('xception', target_size=(299, 299))
```

Let's use the same image of pants we used in chapter 8 (figure 9.2).

Figure 9.2   The picture of pants that we use for testing

Let's convert it to a NumPy array:

```
url = "http://bit.ly/mlbookcamp-pants"
X = preprocessor.from_url(url)
```

We have a NumPy array in X, but we can't use it as is. For gRPC, we need to convert it to protobuf. TensorFlow has a special function for that: `tf.make_tensor_proto`.

This is how we use it:

```
def np_to_protobuf(data):
    return tf.make_tensor_proto(data, shape=data.shape)
```

This function takes two arguments:

- A NumPy array: `data`,
- The dimensions of this array: `data.shape`

> **NOTE** In this example, we use TensorFlow for converting a NumPy array to protobuf. TensorFlow is a large library, so depending on it for just one small function is unreasonable. In this chapter, we do it for simplicity, but you shouldn't do it in production, because using Docker with big images can create problems: it takes more time to download the image and they occupy more space. Check this repository to see what you can do instead: https://github.com/alexeygrigorev/tensorflow-protobuf.

Now we can use the `np_to_protobuf` function to prepare a gRPC request:

```
pb_request = predict_pb2.PredictRequest()        ◁──┐  ❶ If there is one item,
                                                       bringing in the one item

pb_request.model_spec.name = 'clothing-model'    ◁──┐  ❷ Sets the model name
                                                       to clothing-model
pb_request.model_spec.signature_name = 'serving_default'
pb_request.inputs['input_8'].CopyFrom(np_to_protobuf(X))    ◁──┘

        Specifies the signature              Converts X to protobuf,
    ❸   name: serving_default               and assigns it to input_8  ❹
```

Let's take a look at each line. First, in ❶, we create a request object. TF Serving uses the information from this object to determine how to process the request.

In ❷, we specify the name of the model. Recall that when running TF Serving in Docker, we specified the MODEL_NAME parameter — we set it to `clothing-model`. Here we say that we want to send the request to that model.

In ❸, we specify which signature we want to query. When we analyzed the saved_model file, the signature name was `serving_default`, so this is what we use here. You can read more about signatures in the official TF Serving documentation (https://www.tensorflow.org/tfx/serving/signature_defs).

In ❹, we do two things. First, we convert X to protobuf. Then, we set the results to the input named `input_8`. This name also comes from our analysis of the saved_-model file.

Let's execute it:

```
pb_result = stub.Predict(pb_request, timeout=20.0)
```

This sends a request to the TF Serving instance. Then TF Serving applies the model to the request and sends back the results. The results are saved to the `pb_result` variable. To get the predictions from there, we need to access one of the outputs:

```
pred = pb_result.outputs['dense_7'].float_val
```

Note that we need to refer to a specific output by name — `dense_7`. When analyzing the signatures of the saved_model file, we also took a note of it — and now used it to get the predictions.

The `pred` variable is a list of floats — the predictions:

```
[-1.868, -4.761, -2.316, -1.062, 9.887, -2.812, -3.666, 3.200, -2.602, -4.835]
```

We need to turn this list of numbers into something that we can understand — we need to connect it to the labels. We use the same approach as in the previous chapters:

```
labels = [
    'dress',
    'hat',
    'longsleeve',
    'outwear',
    'pants',
    'shirt',
    'shoes',
    'shorts',
    'skirt',
    't-shirt'
]

result = {c: p for c, p in zip(labels, pred)}
```

This gives us the final result:

```
{'dress': -1.868,
 'hat': -4.761,
 'longsleeve': -2.316,
 'outwear': -1.062,
 'pants': 9.887,
 'shirt': -2.812,
 'shoes': -3.666,
 'shorts': 3.200,
 'skirt': -2.602,
 't-shirt': -4.835}
```

We see that the pants label has the highest score.

We successfully managed to connect to the TF Serving instance from a Jupyter Notebook, and we used gRPC and protobuf for that. Now let's put this code into a web service.

9.2.5 *Creating the Gateway service*

We already have all the code we need for communicating with our model deployed with TF Serving.

This code, however, is not convenient to use. The users of our model shouldn't need to worry about downloading the image, doing the preprocessing, converting it to protobuf, and all other things we did. They should be able to send an URL of an image and get back the predictions.

To make it easier for our users, we'll put all this code into a web service. The users will interact with the service, and the service will talk to TF Serving. So, the service will act as a gateway to our model. This is why we can simply call it "Gateway" (figure 9.3).

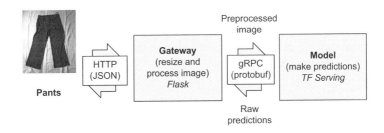

Figure 9.3   The Gateway service is a Flask app that gets an URL to the image and prepares it. Then it uses gRPC and protobuf to communicate with TF Serving.

We use Flask to create this service. We already used Flask previously; you can refer to chapter 5 for more details.

The Gateway service needs to do these things:

- Take the URL of an image in the request.
- Download the image, preprocess it, and convert it to a NumPy array.
- Convert the NumPy array to protobuf, and use gRPC to communicate with TF Serving.
- Postprocess the results — convert the raw list with numbers to human-understandable form.

So, let's create it! Start by creating a file model_server.py — we'll put all this logic there.

First, we get the same imports as we have in the notebook:

```
import grpc
import tensorflow as tf
from tensorflow_serving.apis import predict_pb2
from tensorflow_serving.apis import prediction_service_pb2_grpc

from keras_image_helper import create_preprocessor
```

Now we need to add Flask imports:

```
from flask import Flask, request, jsonify
```

Next, create the connection gRPC stub:

```
host = os.getenv('TF_SERVING_HOST', 'localhost:8500')     ⊲──┤  Makes the TF Serving
channel = grpc.insecure_channel(host)                            URL configurable
stub = prediction_service_pb2_grpc.PredictionServiceStub(channel)
```

Instead of simply hardcoding the URL of the TF Serving instance, we make it configurable via the environment variable TF_SERVING_HOST. If the variable is not set, we use the default value 'localhost:8500'.

Now let's create the preprocessor:

```
preprocessor = create_preprocessor('xception', target_size=(299, 299))
```

Also, we need to define the names of our classes:

```
labels = [
    'dress',
    'hat',
    'longsleeve',
    'outwear',
    'pants',
    'shirt',
    'shoes',
    'shorts',
    'skirt',
    't-shirt'
]
```

Instead of simply copying and pasting the code from the notebook, we can make the code more organized and put it into two functions:

- make_request: For creating a gRPC request from a NumPy array
- process_response: For attaching the class labels to the predictions

Let's start with make_request:

```
def np_to_protobuf(data):
    return tf.make_tensor_proto(data, shape=data.shape)

def make_request(X):
    pb_request = predict_pb2.PredictRequest()
```

```
pb_request.model_spec.name = 'clothing-model'
pb_request.model_spec.signature_name = 'serving_default'
pb_request.inputs['input_8'].CopyFrom(np_to_protobuf(X))
return pb_request
```

Next, create process_response:

```
def process_response(pb_result):
    pred = pb_result.outputs['dense_7'].float_val
    result = {c: p for c, p in zip(labels, pred)}
    return result
```

And finally, let's put everything together:

```
def apply_model(url):
    X = preprocessor.from_url(url)          ⟵── Preprocesses an image from the provided URL
    pb_request = make_request(X)            ⟶
    pb_result = stub.Predict(pb_request, timeout=20.0)   ⟵── Executes the request
    return process_response(pb_result)      ⟵─
```

Converts the NumPy array into a gRPC request

Processes the response, and attaches the labels to predictions

All the code is ready. We only need to do one last thing: create a Flask app and the predict function. Let's do it:

```
app = Flask('clothing-model')

@app.route('/predict', methods=['POST'])
def predict():
    url = request.get_json()
    result = apply_model(url['url'])
    return jsonify(result)

if __name__ == "__main__":
    app.run(debug=True, host='0.0.0.0', port=9696)
```

Now we're ready to run the service. Execute this command in the terminal:

```
python model_server.py
```

Wait until it's ready. We should see the following in the terminal:

```
 * Running on http://0.0.0.0:9696/ (Press CTRL+C to quit)
```

Let's test it! Like in chapter 5, we use the requests library for that. You can open any Jupyter Notebook. For example, you can continue in the same notebook where we experimented with connecting to TF Serving with gRPC.

We need to send a request with a URL and show the response. This is how we do it with requests:

```
import requests

req = {
    "url": "http://bit.ly/mlbookcamp-pants"
}

url = 'http://localhost:9696/predict'

response = requests.post(url, json=req)
response.json()
```

Here, we send a POST request to our service and display the results. The response is the same as previously:

```
{'dress': -1.868,
 'hat': -4.761,
 'longsleeve': -2.316,
 'outwear': -1.062,
 'pants': 9.887,
 'shirt': -2.812,
 'shoes': -3.666,
 'shorts': 3.200,
 'skirt': -2.602,
 't-shirt': -4.835}
```

The service is ready and it works locally. Let's deploy it with Kubernetes!

9.3   *Model deployment with Kubernetes*

Kubernetes is an orchestration system for automating container deployment. We can use it to host any Docker containers. In this section, we'll see how we can use Kubernetes to deploy our application.

First, we'll start by going over some Kubernetes basics.

9.3.1   *Introduction to Kubernetes*

The main unit of abstraction in Kubernetes is a *pod*. A pod contains a single Docker image, and when we want to serve something, pods do the actual job.

Pods live on a *node* — this is an actual machine. A node usually contains one or more pods.

To deploy an application, we define a *deployment*. We specify how many pods the application should have and which image should be used. When our application starts to get more requests, sometimes we want to add more pods to our deployment to handle the increase in traffic. This can also happen automatically — this process is called *horizontal autoscaling*.

A *service* is the entry point to the pods in a deployment. The clients interact with the service, not individual pods. When a service gets a request, it routes it to one of the pods in the deployment.

Clients outside of the Kubernetes cluster interact with the services inside the cluster through *ingress*.

Suppose we have a service — Gateway. For this service, we have a deployment (Gateway Deployment) with three pods — pod A, pod B on Node 1, and pod D on Node 2 (figure 9.4). When a client wants to send a request to the service, it's first processed by the ingress, and then the service routes the request to one of the pods. In this example, it's pod A deployed on node 1. The service on pod A processes the request, and the client receives the response.

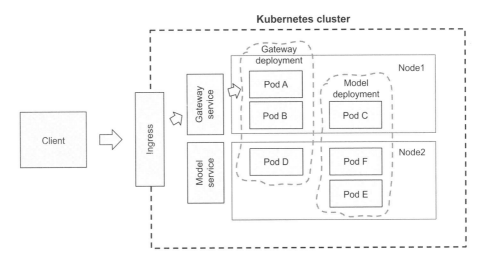

Figure 9.4   The anatomy of a Kubernetes cluster. Pods are instances of our application. They live on nodes — the actual machines. Pods that belong to the same application are grouped in a deployment. The client communicates to services, and the services route the request to one of the pods in a deployment.

This is a very short introduction to the key vocabulary of Kubernetes, but it should be sufficient to get started. To learn more about Kubernetes, refer to the official documentation (https://kubernetes.io/).

In the next section, we'll see how we can create our own Kubernetes cluster on AWS.

9.3.2   Creating a Kubernetes cluster on AWS

To be able to deploy our services to a Kubernetes cluster, we need to have one. We have multiple options:

- You can create a cluster in the cloud. All the major cloud providers make it possible to set up a Kubernetes cluster in the cloud.
- You can set it up locally using Minikube or MicroK8S. You can read more about it here: https://mlbookcamp.com/article/local-k8s.html.

In this section, we use EKS from AWS. EKS, which stands for Elastic Kubernetes Service, is a service from AWS that lets us create a Kubernetes cluster with a minimal amount of effort. Alternatives are GKE (Google Kubernetes Engine) from Google Cloud and AKS (Azure Kubernetes Service) from Azure.

For this section, you need to use three command-line tools:

- AWS CLI: Manages AWS resources. Refer to appendix A for more information.
- eksctl: Manages EKS clusters (https://docs.aws.amazon.com/eks/latest/ userguide eksctl.html).
- kubectl: Manages resources in a Kubernetes cluster (https://kubernetes.io/ docs/tasks/tools/install-kubectl/). It works for any cluster, not just EKS.

The official documentation is sufficient for installing these tools, but you can also refer to the book's website for more information (https://mlbookcamp.com/article/eks).

If you don't use AWS but do use a different cloud provider, you need to use their tools for setting up a Kubernetes cluster. Because Kubernetes is not tied to any particular vendor, most of the instructions in this chapter will work, regardless of where you have the cluster.

Once you have installed eksctl and AWS CLI, we can create an EKS cluster.

First, prepare a file with the cluster configuration. Create a file in your project directory and call it cluster.yaml:

```
apiVersion: eksctl.io/v1alpha5
kind: ClusterConfig

metadata:
  name: ml-bookcamp-eks
  region: eu-west-1
  version: "1.18"

nodeGroups:
  - name: ng
    desiredCapacity: 2
    instanceType: m5.xlarge
```

After creating the config file, we can use eksctl for spinning up a cluster:

```
eksctl create cluster -f cluster.yaml
```

> **NOTE** Creating a cluster takes 15–20 minutes, so be patient.

With this configuration, we create a cluster with Kuberbetes version 1.18 deployed in the eu-west-1 region. The name of the cluster is ml-bookcamp-eks. If you want to deploy it to a different region, you can change it. This cluster will use two m5.xlarge machines. You can read more about this type of instance here: https://aws.amazon .com/ec2/instance-types/m5/. This is sufficient for the experiments we need to do in this chapter for both Kubernetes and Kubeflow.

> **NOTE** EKS is not covered by the AWS free tier. You can learn more about the costs in the official documentation of AWS (https://aws.amazon.com/ eks/pr-icing/).

Once it's created, we need to configure `kubectl` to be able to access it. For AWS, we do this with the AWS CLI:

```
aws eks --region eu-west-1 update-kubeconfig --name ml-bookcamp-eks
```

This command should generate a `kubectl` config file in the default location. On Linux and MacOS, this location is ~/.kube/config.

Now let's check that everything works, and that we can connect to our cluster using `kubectl`:

```
kubectl get service
```

This command returns the list of currently running services. We haven't deployed anything, so we expect to see only one service — Kubernetes itself. This is the result you should see:

```
NAME         TYPE        CLUSTER-IP    EXTERNAL-IP   PORT(S)    AGE
kubernetes   ClusterIP   10.100.0.1    <none>        443/TCP    6m17s
```

The connection works, and now we can deploy a service. To do that, we first need to prepare a Docker image with the actual service. Let's do that next.

9.3.3 *Preparing the Docker images*

In the previous sections, we created two components of the serving system:

- TF-Serving: The component with the actual model
- Gateway: The component for image preprocessing that communicates with TF Serving

Now we deploy them. We start first with deploying the TF Serving image.

THE TENSORFLOW SERVING IMAGE

As in chapter 8, we first need to publish our image to ECR — the Docker registry of AWS. Let's create a registry called model-serving:

```
aws ecr create-repository --repository-name model-serving
```

It should return a path like this:

```
<ACCOUNT>.dkr.ecr.<REGION>.amazonaws.com/model-serving
```

IMPORTANT Take note — we'll need this path later.

When running a Docker image of TF Serving locally, we used this command (you don't need to run it now):

```
docker run -it --rm \
    -p 8500:8500 \
    -v "$(pwd)/clothing-model:/models/clothing-model/1" \
```

```
-e MODEL_NAME=clothing-model \
tensorflow/serving:2.3.0
```

We used the `-v` parameter to mount the model from the `clothing-model` to the /models/clothing-model/1 directory within the image.

It's also possible to do it with Kubernetes, but in this chapter, we follow a simpler approach and include the model into the image itself, similar to what we did in chapter 8.

Let's create a Dockerfile for that. We can name it tf-serving.dockerfile:

```
FROM tensorflow/serving:2.3.0          ◁──────┐  Uses the Tensorflow
                                          ❶   Serving image as its base
ENV MODEL_NAME clothing-model
COPY clothing-model /models/clothing-model/1   ◁──┐  Copies the model to
                                               ❸   /models/clothing-model/1
Sets the MODEL_NAME
❷  variable to clothing-model
```

We base our image on the TensorFlow Serving image in ❶. Next, in ❷, we set the environment variable `MODEL_NAME` to `clothing-model`, which is the equivalent of the `-e` parameter. Next, we copy the model to /models/clothing-model/1 in ❸, which is the equivalent of using the `-v` parameter.

> **NOTE** If you want to use a computer with a GPU, use the tensorflow/serving :2.3.0-gpu image (commented as ❶ in the Dockerfile).

Let's build it:

```
IMAGE_SERVING_LOCAL="tf-serving-clothing-model"
docker build -t ${IMAGE_SERVING_LOCAL} -f tf-serving.dockerfile .
```

Next, we need to publish this image to ECR. First, we need to authenticate with ECR using AWS CLI:

```
$(aws ecr get-login --no-include-email)
```

> **NOTE** You need to include the "$" when typing the command. The command inside the parentheses returns another command. Using the "$()", we execute this command.

Next, tag the image with the remote URI:

```
ACCOUNT=XXXXXXXXXXXX
REGION=eu-west-1
REGISTRY=${ACCOUNT}.dkr.ecr.${REGION}.amazonaws.com/model-serving
IMAGE_SERVING_REMOTE=${REGISTRY}:${IMAGE_SERVING_LOCAL}
docker tag ${IMAGE_SERVING_LOCAL} ${IMAGE_SERVING_REMOTE}
```

Be sure to change the `ACCOUNT` and `REGION` variables.

Now we're ready to push the image to ECR:

```
docker push ${IMAGE_SERVING_REMOTE}
```

It's pushed! Now we need to do the same with the Gateway component.

THE GATEWAY IMAGE

Now let's prepare the image for the Gateway component. Gateway is a web service, and it relies on a number of Python libraries:

- Flask and Gunicorn
- keras_image_helper
- grpcio
- TensorFlow
- TensorFlow-Serving-API

Remember that in chapter 5, we used Pipenv for managing dependencies. Let's use it here as well:

```
pipenv install flask gunicorn \
    keras_image_helper==0.0.1 \
    grpcio==1.32.0 \
    tensorflow==2.3.0 \
    tensorflow-serving-api==2.3.0
```

Running this command creates two files: Pipfile and Pipfile.lock.

> **WARNING** Even though we already mentioned it, it's important enough to repeat it. Here, we rely on TensorFlow for only one function. In a production environment, it's better not to install TensorFlow. In this chapter, we do it for simplicity. Instead of depending on TensorFlow, we can take only the protobuf files we need and reduce the size of our Docker image significantly. Refer to this repository for instructions: https://github.com/alexeygrigorev/tensorflow-protobuf.

Now let's create a Docker image. Start with creating a Dockerfile named gateway.dockerfile with the following content:

```
FROM python:3.7.5-slim

ENV PYTHONUNBUFFERED=TRUE

RUN pip --no-cache-dir install pipenv

WORKDIR /app

COPY ["Pipfile", "Pipfile.lock", "./"]
RUN pipenv install --deploy --system && \
    rm -rf /root/.cache
```

```
COPY "model_server.py" "model_server.py"

EXPOSE 9696

ENTRYPOINT ["gunicorn", "--bind", "0.0.0.0:9696", "model_server:app"]
```

This Dockerfile is very similar to the file we had previously. Refer to chapter 5 for more information about it.

Let's build this image now:

```
IMAGE_GATEWAY_LOCAL="serving-gateway"
docker build -t ${IMAGE_GATEWAY_LOCAL} -f gateway.dockerfile .
```

And push it to ECR:

```
IMAGE_GATEWAY_REMOTE=${REGISTRY}:${IMAGE_GATEWAY_LOCAL}
docker tag ${IMAGE_GATEWAY_LOCAL} ${IMAGE_GATEWAY_REMOTE}

docker push ${IMAGE_GATEWAY_REMOTE}
```

> **NOTE**   For verifying that these images work well together locally, you need to use Docker Compose (https://docs.docker.com/compose/). This is a very useful tool, and we recommend that you spend time learning it, but we will not cover it here.

We have published both images to ECR, and now we're ready to deploy the services to Kubernetes! We'll do that next.

9.3.4   *Deploying to Kubernetes*

Before we deploy, let's revisit the basics of Kubernetes. We have the following objects living inside a cluster:

- Pod: The smallest unit in Kubernetes. It's a single process, and we have one Docker container in one pod.
- Deployment: A group of multiple related pods.
- Service: What sits in front of a deployment and routes the requests to individual pods.

To deploy an application to Kubernetes, we need to configure two things:

- A deployment: It specifies how the pods of this deployment will look.
- A service: Specifies how to access the service and how the service connects to the pods.

Let's start with configuring the deployment for TF Serving.

DEPLOYMENT FOR TF SERVING

In Kubernetes, we usually configure everything with YAML files. For configuring a deployment, we create a file named tf-serving-clothing-model-deployment.yaml in our project directory with the following content:

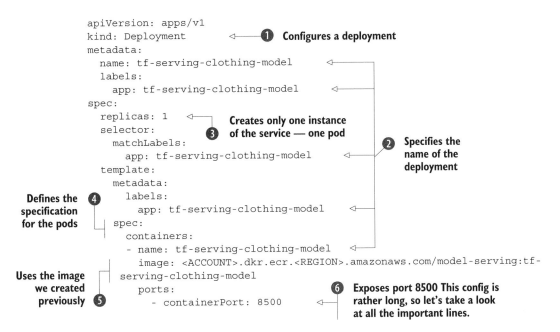

In ❶, we specify the type of the Kubernetes object we want to configure in this YAML file — it's a deployment.

In ❷, we define the name of the deployment as well as set some metadata information. We need to repeat it multiple times: one time for setting the name of the deployment ("name") and a few more times ("labels: app") for the service that we'll configure later.

In ❸, we set the number of instances — pods — we want to have in the deployment.

In ❹, we specify the configuration for the pods — we set the parameters that all of the pods will have.

In ❺, we set the URI for the Docker image. The pod will use this image. Don't forget to put your account ID there as well as the correct region.

Finally, in ❻, we open port 8500 on the pods of this deployment. This is the port that TF Serving uses.

To learn more about configuring deployments in Kubernetes, check the official documentation (https://kubernetes.io/docs/concepts/workloads/controllers/deployment).

We have a config. Now we need to use it to create a Kubernetes object — a deployment in our case. We do it by using the apply command from kubectl:

```
kubectl apply -f tf-serving-clothing-model-deployment.yaml
```

The -f parameter tells kubectl that it needs to read the configuration from the config file.

To verify that it's working, we need to check if a new deployment appeared. This is how we can get the list of all active deployments:

```
kubectl get deployments
```

The output should look similar to this:

```
NAME                         READY  UP-TO-DATE  AVAILABLE  AGE
tf-serving-clothing-model    1/1    1           1          41s
```

We see that our deployment is there. Also, we can get the list of pods. It's quite similar to getting the list of all deployments:

```
kubectl get pods
```

We should see something like that in the output:

```
NAME                                           READY  STATUS   RESTARTS  AGE
tf-serving-clothing-model-56bc84678d-b6n4r     1/1    Running  0         108s
```

Now we need to create a service on top of this deployment.

SERVICE FOR TF SERVING

We want to invoke TF Serving from Gateway. For that, we need to create a service in front of the TF Serving deployment.

Like with a deployment, we start by creating a configuration file for the service. It's also a YAML file. Create a file called tf-serving-clothing-model-service.yaml with the following content:

```
apiVersion: v1
kind: Service
metadata:
  name: tf-serving-clothing-model        ◁──┐  Configures the name of
  labels:                                    │  the service
    app: tf-serving-clothing-model     ◁─────┘
spec:                         ◁──┐
  ports:                         │  Specification of the service —
    - port: 8500                 │  the port that will be used
      targetPort: 8500    ───────┘
      protocol: TCP
      name: http
  selector:                           │  Connects the service to the deployment by
    app: tf-serving-clothing-model    │  specifying the label of the deployment
```

We apply it in the same way — by using the `apply` command:

```
kubectl apply -f tf-serving-clothing-model-service.yaml
```

To check that it works, we can get the list of all services and see if our service is there:

```
kubectl get services
```

We should see something like

```
NAME                TYPE          CLUSTER-IP        EXTERNAL-IP    PORT(S)     AGE
kubernetes          ClusterIP     10.100.0.1        <none>         443/TCP     84m
tf-serving-         ClusterIP     10.100.111.165    <none>         8500/TCP    19s
clothing-model
```

In addition to the default Kubernetes service, we also have tf-serving-clothing-model, which is the service we just created.

To access this service, we need to get its URL. The internal URLs typically follow this pattern:

```
<service-name>.<namespace-name>.svc.cluster.local
```

The `<service-name>` part is tf-serving-clothing-model.

We haven't used any specific namespace for this service, so Kubernetes automatically put the service in the "default" namespace. We won't cover namespaces here, but you can read more about them in the official documentation (https://kubernetes.io/docs/concepts/overview/working-with-objects/namespaces/).

This is the URL for the service we just created:

```
tf-serving-clothing-model.default.svc.cluster.local
```

We'll need this URL later, when configuring Gateway.

We've created a deployment for TF Serving as well as a service. Now let's create a deployment for Gateway.

DEPLOYMENT FOR GATEWAY

Like previously, we start by creating a YAML file with configuration. Create a file named serving-gateway-deployment.yaml:

```yaml
apiVersion: apps/v1
kind: Deployment
metadata:
  name: serving-gateway
  labels:
    app: serving-gateway
spec:
  replicas: 1
  selector:
    matchLabels:
      app: serving-gateway
  template:
    metadata:
      labels:
        app: serving-gateway
    spec:
      containers:
      - name: serving-gateway
        image: <ACCOUNT>.dkr.ecr.<REGION>.amazonaws.com/model-
    serving:serving-gateway
```

```
        ports:
        - containerPort: 9696
        env:
        - name: TF_SERVING_HOST
          value: "tf-serving-clothing-model.default.svc.cluster.local:8500"
```

Sets the value for the TF_SERVING_HOST environment variable

Replace <ACCOUNT> and <REGION> in the image URL with your values.

The configuration of this deployment is very similar to the deployment of TF Serving, with one important difference: we specify the value of the TF_SERVING_HOST variable by setting it to the URL of the service with our model (shown in bold in the listing).

Let's apply this configuration:

```
kubectl apply -f serving-gateway-deployment.yaml
```

This should create a new pod and a new deployment. Let's take a look at the list of pods:

```
kubectl get pod
```

Indeed, a new pod is there:

```
NAME                                      READY   STATUS    RESTARTS   AGE
tf-serving-clothing-model-56bc84678d-b6n4r   1/1   Running   0          1h
serving-gateway-5f84d67b59-lx8tq             1/1   Running   0          30s
```

> **WARNING**   Gateway uses gRPC to communicate with TF Serving. When deploying multiple instances of TF Serving, you may run into a problem with distributing the load between these instances (https://kubernetes.io/blog/2018/11/07/grpc-load-balancing-on-kubernetes-without-tears/). To solve it, you will need to install a service mesh tool like Linkerd, Istio, or something similar. Talk to your operations team to see how you can do it at your company.

We've created a deployment for Gateway. Now we need to configure the service for. We do it next.

SERVICE FOR GATEWAY

We've created a deployment for Gateway, and now we need to create a service. This service is different from the service we created for TF Serving — it needs to be publicly accessible, so services outside of our Kubernetes cluster can use it. For that, we need to use a special type of service — LoadBalancer. It creates an external load balancer, which is available outside of the Kubernetes cluster. In the case of AWS, it uses ELB, the Elastic Load Balancing service.

Let's create a config file named serving-gateway-service.yaml:

```
apiVersion: v1
kind: Service
metadata:
  name: serving-gateway
```

```
labels:
  app: serving-gateway
spec:
  type: LoadBalancer        ①  Uses the
  ports:                        LoadBalancer type
    - port: 80            ②  Maps port 9696 in the pod
      targetPort: 9696        to port 80 n the service
      protocol: TCP
      name: http
  selector:
    app: serving-gateway
```

In ①, we specify the type of the service — LoadBalancer.

In ②, we connect port 80 in the service to port 9696 in pods. This way, we don't need to specify the port when connecting to the service — it will use the default HTTP port, which is 80.

Let's apply this config:

```
kubectl apply -f serving-gateway-service.yaml
```

To see the external URL of the service, use the `describe` command:

```
kubectl describe service serving-gateway
```

It will output some information about the service:

```
Name:                     serving-gateway
Namespace:                default
Labels:                   <none>
Annotations:              <none>
Selector:                 app=serving-gateway
Type:                     LoadBalancer
IP Families:              <none>
IP:                       10.100.100.24
IPs:                      <none>
LoadBalancer Ingress:     ad1fad0c1302141989ed8ee449332e39-117019527.eu-west-
    1.elb.amazonaws.com
Port:                     http  80/TCP
TargetPort:               9696/TCP
NodePort:                 http  32196/TCP
Endpoints:                <none>
Session Affinity:         None
External Traffic Policy:  Cluster
Events:
  Type    Reason                 Age   From                 Message
  ----    ------                 ----  ----                 -------
  Normal  EnsuringLoadBalancer   4s    service-controller   Ensuring load
                                                            balancer
  Normal  EnsuredLoadBalancer    2s    service-controller   Ensured load
                                                            balancer
```

We're interested in the line with `LoadBalancer Ingress`. This is the URL we need to use to access the Gateway service. In our case, this is the URL:

```
ad1fad0c1302141989ed8ee449332e39-117019527.eu-west-1.elb.amazonaws.com
```

The Gateway service is ready to use. Let's do it!

9.3.5 *Testing the service*

When running TF Serving and Gateway locally, we prepared a simple snippet of Python code for testing our service. Let's reuse it. Go to the same notebook, and replace the local IP address by the URL we got from the previous section:

```
import requests

req = {
    "url": "http://bit.ly/mlbookcamp-pants"
}

url = 'http://ad1fad0c1302141989ed8ee449332e39-117019527.eu-west-
    1.elb.amazonaws.com/predict'

response = requests.post(url, json=req)
response.json()
```

Run it. As a result, we get the same predictions as previously:

```
{'dress': -1.86829,
 'hat': -4.76124,
 'longsleeve': -2.31698,
 'outwear': -1.06257,
 'pants': 9.88716,
 'shirt': -2.81243,
 'shoes': -3.66628,
 'shorts': 3.20036,
 'skirt': -2.60233,
 't-shirt': -4.83504}
```

It's working — and it means we just successfully deployed our deep learning model with TF Serving and Kubernetes!

> **IMPORTANT** If you finished experimenting with EKS, don't forget to shut down the cluster. If you don't turn it off, you'll need to pay for it, even if it's idle and you don't use it. You will find the instructions for that at the end of this chapter.

In this example, we covered Kubernetes from the user's perspective only, not from an operational standpoint. We haven't talked about autoscaling, monitoring, alerting, and other important topics required for productionizing machine learning models.

For more details about these topics, consult a Kubernetes book or the official documentation of Kubernetes.

You probably noticed that we needed to do quite a lot of things for deploying a single model: create a Docker image, push it to ECR, create a deployment, create a service. Doing this for a couple of models is not a problem, but if you need to do it for tens or hundreds of models, it becomes problematic and repetitive.

There's a solution — Kubeflow. It makes deployment easier. In the next section, we'll see how we can use it for serving Keras models.

9.4 Model deployment with Kubeflow

Kubeflow is a project that aims to simplify the deployment of machine learning services on Kubernetes.

It consists of a set of tools, each of which aims at solving a particular problem. For example:

- Kubeflow Notebooks Server: Makes it easier to centrally host Jupyter Notebooks
- Kubeflow Pipelines: Automates the training process
- Katib: Selects the best parameters for the model
- Kubeflow Serving (abbreviated as "KFServing"): Deploys machine learning models

And many others. You can read more about its components here: https://www.kubeflow .org/docs/components/.

In this chapter, we focus on model deployment, so we'll need to use only one component of Kubeflow — KFServing.

If you want to install the entire Kubeflow project, refer to the official documentation. It has the installation instructions for the major cloud providers such as Google Cloud Platform, Microsoft Azure, and AWS (https://www.kubeflow.org/docs/aws/aws-e2e/).

For the instructions about installing only KFServing without the rest of Kubeflow on AWS, refer to the book's website: https://mlbookcamp.com/article/kfserving-eks-install. We used this article for setting up the environment for the rest of this chapter, but the code here should work with any Kubeflow installation with minor changes.

> **NOTE** The installation may be nontrivial for you, especially if you haven't done anything similar in the past. If you are not sure about some things, ask somebody from the operations team to help you set it up.

9.4.1 Preparing the model: Uploading it to S3

To deploy a Keras model with KFServing, we first need to convert it to the saved_ model format. We already did this previously, so we can just use the converted files.

Next, we need to create a bucket in S3, where we will put our models. Let's call it mlbookcamp-models-<NAME>, where <NAME> could be anything — for example, your name. Bucket names must be unique across the entire AWS. That's why we need to add some suffix to the name of the bucket. It should be in the same region as our EKS cluster. In our case, it's eu-west-1.

We can create it with the AWS CLI:

```
aws s3api create-bucket \
    --bucket mlbookcamp-models-alexey \
    --region eu-west-1 \
    --create-bucket-configuration LocationConstraint=eu-west-1
```

After creating a bucket, we need to upload the model there. Use the AWS CLI for that:

```
aws s3 cp --recursive clothing-model s3://mlbookcamp-models-alexey/clothing-
    model/0001/
```

Note that there's "0001" at the end. This is important — KFServing, like TF Serving, needs a version of the model. We don't have any previous versions of this model, so we add "0001" at the end.

Now we're ready to deploy this model.

9.4.2 *Deploying TensorFlow models with KFServing*

Previously, when deploying our model with plain Kubernetes, we needed to configure a deployment and then a service. Instead of doing it, KFServing defines a special kind of Kubernetes object — InferenceService. We need to configure it only once, and it will take care of creating all other Kubernetes objects — including a service and a deployment — automatically.

First, create another YAML file (tf-clothes.yaml) with the following content:

```
apiVersion: "serving.kubeflow.org/v1beta1"
kind: "InferenceService"
metadata:
  name: "clothing-model"                    ❶ Uses serviceAccountName
spec:                                           to access S3
  default:
    predictor:                              ❷ Specifies the location
      serviceAccountName: sa    ◁              in S3 with the model
      tensorflow:                   ◁
        storageUri: "s3://mlbookcamp-models-alexey/clothing-model"
```

When accessing a model from S3, we need to specify the service account name to be able to get the model. This tells KFServing how to access the S3 bucket — and we specify it in ❶. The article about installing KFServing on EKS covers this as well (https://mlbookcamp.com/article/kfserving-eks-install).

Like with usual Kubernetes, we use kubectl to apply this config:

```
kubectl apply -f tf-clothing.yaml
```

Because it creates an InferenceService object, we need to get the list of such objects using the get command from kubectl:

```
kubectl get inferenceservice
```

We should see something like this:

```
NAME                URL                          READY     AGE
clothing-model      http://clothing-model...     True  ... 97s
```

If our service READY is not yet True, we need to wait a bit before it becomes ready. It may take 1–2 minutes.

Now take note of the URL and the name of the model:

- The URL: https://clothing-model.default.kubeflow.mlbookcamp.com/v1/ models/clothing-model. In your configuration, the host will be different, so the entire URL will also be different.
- The model name: clothing-model.

NOTE It may take some time for the URL to become reachable from our laptop. Changes in DNS may need some time to propagate.

9.4.3 Accessing the model

The model is deployed. Let's use it! For that, we can start a Jupyter Notebook or create a Python script file.

KFServing uses HTTP and JSON, so we use the requests library for communicating with it. So let's start by importing it:

```
import requests
```

Next, we need to use the image preprocessor for preparing the images. It's the same one we used previously:

```
from keras_image_helper import create_preprocessor

preprocessor = create_preprocessor('xception', target_size=(299, 299))
```

Now, we need an image for testing. We use the same image of pants as in the previous section and use the same code for getting it and preprocessing it:

```
image_url = "http://bit.ly/mlbookcamp-pants"
X = preprocessor.from_url(image_url)
```

The X variable contains a NumPy array. We need to convert it to a list before we can send the data to KFServing:

```
data = {
    "instances": X.tolist()
}
```

We have the request. As the next step, we need to define the URL where we will send this request. We already have it from the previous section, but we need to modify it slightly:

- Use HTTPS instead of HTTP.
- Add ":predict" at the end of the URL.

With these changes, this is how the URL appears:

```
url = 'https://clothing-model.default.kubeflow.mlbookcamp.com/v1/models/
    clothing-model:predict'
```

We're ready to post the request:

```
resp = requests.post(url, json=data)
results = resp.json()
```

Let's take a look at the results:

```
{'predictions': [[-1.86828923,
    -4.76124525,
    -2.31698346,
    -1.06257045,
    9.88715553,
    -2.81243205,
    -3.66628242,
    3.20036,
    -2.60233665,
    -4.83504581]]}
```

Like we did previously, we need to translate the predictions into human-readable form. We do it by assigning a label to each element of the result:

```
pred = results['predictions'][0]

labels = [
    'dress',
    'hat',
    'longsleeve',
    'outwear',
    'pants',
    'shirt',
    'shoes',
    'shorts',
    'skirt',
    't-shirt'
]

result = {c: p for c, p in zip(labels, pred)}
```

Here's the result:

```
{'dress': -1.86828923,
 'hat': -4.76124525,
 'longsleeve': -2.31698346,
 'outwear': -1.06257045,
 'pants': 9.88715553,
 'shirt': -2.81243205,
 'shoes': -3.66628242,
 'shorts': 3.20036,
 'skirt': -2.60233665,
 't-shirt': -4.83504581}
```

We have deployed our model, and it can be used.

But we cannot expect that the people who use our model will be happy about having to prepare the images themselves. In the next section, we'll talk about transformers — they can take away the burden of preprocessing the images.

9.4.4 KFServing transformers

In the previous section, we introduced the Gateway service. It was sitting between the client and the model, and it took care of transforming the requests from the clients to the format the model expects (figure 9.5).

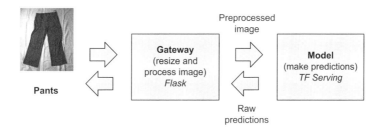

Figure 9.5 The Gateway service takes care of preprocessing the image, so the clients of our applications don't need to do it.

Fortunately for us, we don't have to introduce another Gateway service for KFServing. Instead, we can use a *transformer*.

Transformers take care of

- Preprocessing the request coming from the client and converting it to the format our model expects
- Postprocessing the output of the model — converting it to the format the client needs

We can put all the preprocessing code from the previous section into a transformer (figure 9.6).

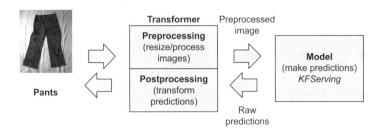

Figure 9.6   The KFServing transformer can download the image and prepare it in the preprocessing step, as well as attach labels to the output of the model in the postprocessing step.

Like the Gateway service we created manually, transformers in KFServing are deployed separately from the model. This means that they can scale up and down independently. It's a good thing — they perform a different kind of work:

- Transformers are doing I/O work (downloading the image).
- Models are doing CPU-intensive work (applying the neural network to make predictions).

To create a transformer, we need to install the KFServing library for Python and create a class that extends the KFModel class.

It looks like this:

```
class ImageTransformer(kfserving.KFModel):
    def preprocess(self, inputs):
        # implement pre-processing logic

    def postprocess(self, inputs):
        # implement post-processing logic
```

We will not go into details about building your own transformer, but if you'd like to know how to do it, check out this article: https://mlbookcamp.com/article/kfserving-transformers. Instead, for this book, we've prepared a transformer that uses the keras_image_helper library. You can check its source code here: https://github.com/alexeygrigorev/kfserving-keras-transformer.

Let's use it. First, we need to delete the old inference service:

```
kubectl delete -f tf-clothes.yaml
```

Then, update the config file (tf-clothes.yaml), and include the transformer section (in bold) there:

```
apiVersion: "serving.kubeflow.org/v1alpha2"
kind: "InferenceService"
metadata:
  name: "clothing-model"
```

```
spec:
  default:                    ┌─  Defines the model in
    predictor:            ◁──┘   the predictor section
      serviceAccountName: sa
      tensorflow:
        storageUri: "s3://mlbookcamp-models-alexey/clothing-model"
    transformer:         ◁──┐  Defines the transformer in
      custom:               │  the transformer section
        container:
          image: "agrigorev/kfserving-keras-transformer:0.0.1"  ◁─┐ Sets the
          name: user-container                                    │ image for the
          env:                                                    │ transformer
            - name: MODEL_INPUT_SIZE
              value: "299,299"
            - name: KERAS_MODEL_NAME
              value: "xception"
            - name: MODEL_LABELS
              value: "dress,hat,longsleeve,outwear,pants,
          shirt,shoes,shorts,skirt,t-shirt"
```

Sets the image for the transformer

Configures it — specifies input size, model name, and labels

In addition to the "predictor" section, which we had previously, we add another one — "transformer." The transformer we use is a publicly available image at agrigorev/kfserving-keras-transformer:0.0.1.

It relies on the keras_image_helper library to do the transformation. For that, we need to set three parameters:

- MODEL_INPUT_SIZE: The size of the input that the model expects: 299 x 299
- KERAS_MODEL_NAME: The name of the architecture from Keras applications (https://keras.io/api/applications/) that we used for training the model
- MODEL_LABELS: The classes that we want to predict

Let's apply this config:

```
kubectl apply -f tf-clothes.yaml
```

Wait a couple of minutes before it becomes ready — use kubectl get inferenceservice to check the status.

After it's deployed (READY is True), we can test it. We'll do that next.

9.4.5 *Testing the transformer*

With a transformer, we don't need to worry about preparing the image: it's enough to just send the URL of an image. The code becomes much simpler.

This is how it looks:

```
import requests

data = {
    "instances": [
        {"url": "http://bit.ly/mlbookcamp-pants"},
    ]
}
```

```
url = 'https://clothing-model.default.kubeflow.mlbookcamp.com/v1/models/
    clothing-model:predict'
result = requests.post(url, json=data).json()
```

The URL of the service stays the same. The result contains the predictions:

```
{'predictions': [{'dress': -1.8682, 'hat': -4.7612, 'longsleeve': -2.3169,
'outwear': -1.0625, 'pants': 9.8871, 'shirt': -2.8124, 'shoes': -3.6662,
'shorts': 3.2003, 'skirt': -2.6023, 't-shirt': -4.8350}]}
```

And that's all! Now we can use the model.

9.4.6 Deleting the EKS cluster

After experimenting with EKS, don't forget to shut down the cluster. Use `eksctl` for that:

```
eksctl delete cluster --name ml-bookcamp-eks
```

To verify that the cluster was removed, you can check the EKS service page in AWS Console.

9.5   Next steps

You've learned the basics you need for training a classification model for predicting the type of clothes. We've covered a lot of material, but there is a lot more to learn than we could fit in this chapter. You can explore this topic more by doing the exercises.

9.5.1 Exercises

- Docker Compose is a tool for running applications with multiple containers. In our example, Gateway needs to communicate with the TF Serving model; that is why we need to be able to link them. Docker Compose can help with that. Experiment with it for running TF Serving and Gateway locally.
- In this chapter, we used EKS from AWS. For learning Kubernetes, it's beneficial to experiment with Kubernetes locally. Use Minikube or Microk8s to reproduce the example with TF Serving and Gateway locally.
- For all experiments in this chapter, we used the default Kubernetes namespace. In practice, we typically use different namespaces for different groups of applications. Learn more about namespaces in Kubernetes and then deploy our services in a different namespace. For example, you can call it "models."
- KFServing transformers are a powerful tool for preprocessing the data. We haven't discussed how we can implement them ourselves and instead used an already-implemented transformer. To learn more about them, implement this transformer yourself.

9.5.2 Other projects

There are many projects that you can do to learn Kubernetes and Kubeflow better:

- In this chapter, we covered a deep learning model. It's quite complex, and we ended up creating two services. Other models we developed before chapter 7 are less complex and only require a simple Flask app for hosting them. You can deploy the models from chapters 2, 3, and 6 using Flask and Kubernetes.
- KFServing can be used for deploying other types of models, not just Tensor-Flow. Use it for deploying the Scikit-learn models from chapters 3 and 6.

Summary

- TensorFlow-Serving is a system for deploying Keras and TensorFlow models. It uses gRPC and protobuf for communication, and it's highly optimized for serving.
- When using TensorFlow Serving, we typically need a component for preparing the user request into the format the model expects. This component hides the complexity of interacting with TensorFlow Serving and makes it easier for the clients to use the model.
- To deploy something on Kubernetes, we need to create a deployment and a service. The deployment describes what should be deployed: the Docker image and its configuration. The service sits in front of a deployment and routes requests to individual containers.
- Kubeflow and KFServing make the deployment process simpler: we need to specify only the location to the model, and they take care of creating a deployment, a service, and other important things automatically.
- KFServing transformers make it easier to preprocess data coming to the model and postprocess the results. With transformers, we don't need to create a special Gateway service for preprocessing.

appendix A
Preparing the environment

A.1 Installing Python and Anaconda

For the projects in this book, we will use Anaconda, a Python distribution that comes with most of the required machine learning packages that you'll need to use: NumPy, SciPy, Scikit-learn, Pandas, and many more.

A.1.1 Installing Python and Anaconda on Linux

The instructions in this section will work regardless of whether you're installing Anaconda on a remote machine or your laptop. Although we tested it only on Ubuntu 18.04 LTS and 20.04 LTS, this process should work fine for most Linux distributions.

> **NOTE** Using Ubuntu Linux is recommended for the examples in this book. It's not a strict requirement, however, and you should not have problems running the examples in other operating systems. If you don't have a computer with Ubuntu, it's possible to rent one online in the cloud. Please refer to the "Renting a server on AWS" section for more detailed instructions.

Almost every Linux distribution comes with a Python interpreter installed, but it's always a good idea to have a separate installation of Python to avoid trouble with the system Python. Using Anaconda is a great option: it's installed in the user directory and it doesn't interfere with the system Python.

To install Anaconda, you first need to download it. Go to https://www.anaconda .com and click Get Starter. Then select Download Anaconda Installer. This should take you to https://www.anaconda.com/products/individual.

Select 64-Bit (x86) installer and the latest available version — 3.8 at the moment of writing (figure A.1).

Next, copy the link to the installation package. In our case it was https://repo.anaconda.com/archive/Anaconda3-2021.05-Linux-x86_64.sh.

Windows ⊞	MacOS	Linux △
Python 3.8	Python 3.8	Python 3.8
64-Bit Graphical Installer (477 MB)	64-Bit Graphical Installer (440 MB)	64-Bit (x86) Installer (544 MB)
32-Bit Graphical Installer (409 MB)	64-Bit Command Line Installer (433 MB)	64-Bit (Power8 and Power9) Installer (285 MB)
		64-Bit (AWS Graviton2 / ARM64) Installer (413 M)
		64-bit (Linux on IBM Z & LinuxONE) Installer (292 M)

Figure A.1   Downloading the Linux Installer for Anaconda

NOTE   If a newer version of Anaconda is available, you should install it instead. All the code will work on newer versions without problems.

Now go to the terminal to download it:

```
wget  https://repo.anaconda.com/archive/Anaconda3-2021.05-Linux-x86_64.sh
```

Then install it:

```
bash Anaconda3-2021.05-Linux-x86_64.sh
```

Read the agreement, type "yes" if you accept it, and then select the location where you want to install Anaconda. You can use the default location, but you don't have to.

During the installation, you'll be asked if you want to initialize Anaconda. Type "yes," and it will do everything automatically:

```
Do you wish the installer to initialize Anaconda3
by running conda init? [yes|no]
[no] >>> yes
```

If you don't want to let the installer initialize it, you can do it manually by adding the location with Anaconda's binaries to the PATH variable. Open the .bashrc file in the home directory and add this line at the end:

```
export PATH=~/anaconda3/bin:$PATH
```

After the installation has completed, you can delete the installer:

```
rm Anaconda3-2021.05-Linux-x86_64.sh
```

Next, open a new terminal shell. If you're using a remote machine, you can simply exit the current session by pressing Ctrl-D and then log in again using the same `ssh` command as previously.

Now everything should work. You can test that your system picks the right binary by using the `which` command:

```
which python
```

If you're running on an EC2 instance from AWS, you should see something similar to this:

```
/home/ubuntu/anaconda3/bin/python
```

Of course, the path may be different, but it should be the path to the Anaconda installation.

Now you're ready to use Python and Anaconda.

A.1.2   Installing Python and Anaconda on Windows

LINUX SUBSYSTEM FOR WINDOWS

The recommended way to install Anaconda on Windows is to use the Linux Subsystem for Windows.

To install Ubuntu on Windows, open the Microsoft Store and look for ubuntu in the search box; then select Ubuntu 18.04 LTS (figure A.2).

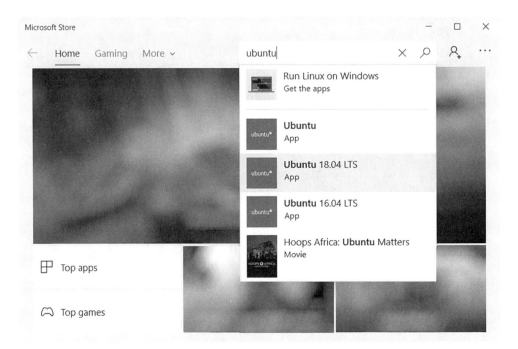

Figure A.2   Use Microsoft Store to install Ubuntu on Windows.

To install it, simply click Get in the next window (figure A.3).

Figure A.3   To install Ubuntu 18.04 for Windows, click Get.

Once it's installed, we can use it by clicking the Launch button (figure A.4).

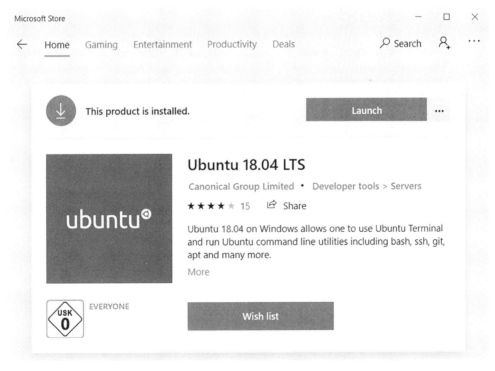

Figure A.4   Click Launch to run the Ubuntu terminal.

When running it for the first time, it will ask you to specify the username and password (figure A.5). After that, the terminal is ready to use.

```
ml@LAPTOP-GV0371AS: ~                                        —    □    ×
Installing, this may take a few minutes...
Please create a default UNIX user account. The username does not need to
match your Windows username.
For more information vitis: https://aka.ms/wslusers
Enter new UNIX username: ml
Enter new UNIX password:
Retype new UNIX password:
passwd: password updated successfully
Installation successful!
To run a command as administrator (user "root"), use "sudo <command>".
See "man sudo_root" for details.

ml@LAPTOP-GV0371AS:~$ whoami
ml
ml@LAPTOP-GV0371AS:~$ _
```

Figure A.5   The Ubuntu Terminal running on Windows

Now you can use the Ubuntu Terminal and follow the instructions for Linux to install Anaconda.

ANACONDA WINDOWS INSTALLER

Alternatively, we can use the Windows Installer for Anaconda. First, we need to download it from https://anaconda.com/distribution (figure A.6). Navigate to the Windows Installer section and download the 64-Bit Graphical Installer (or the 32-bit version, if you're using an older computer).

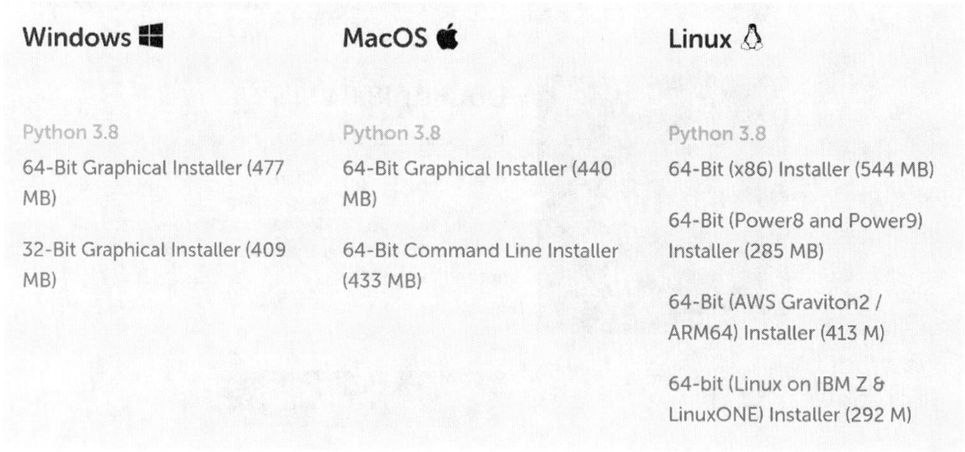

Windows ▦	MacOS	Linux △
Python 3.8	Python 3.8	Python 3.8
64-Bit Graphical Installer (477 MB)	64-Bit Graphical Installer (440 MB)	64-Bit (x86) Installer (544 MB)
32-Bit Graphical Installer (409 MB)	64-Bit Command Line Installer (433 MB)	64-Bit (Power8 and Power9) Installer (285 MB)
		64-Bit (AWS Graviton2 / ARM64) Installer (413 M)
		64-bit (Linux on IBM Z & LinuxONE) Installer (292 M)

Figure A.6   Downloading the Windows Installer for Anaconda

Once you've downloaded the installer, simply run it and follow the setup guide (figure A.7).

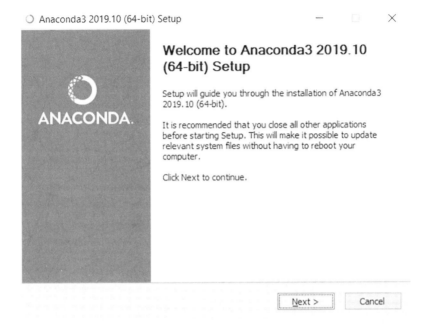

Figure A.7 The installer for Anaconda

It's pretty straightforward and you should have no problems running it. After the installation is successful, you should be able to run it by choosing Anaconda Navigator from the start menu.

A.1.3 Installing Python and Anaconda on macOS

The instructions for macOS should be similar to Linux and Windows: select the installer with the latest version of Python and execute it.

A.2 Running Jupyter

A.2.1 Running Jupyter on Linux

Once Anaconda is installed, you can run Jupyter. First, you need to create a directory that Jupyter will use for all the notebooks:

```
mkdir notebooks
```

Then cd to this directory to run Jupyter from there:

```
cd notebooks
```

It will use this directory for creating notebooks. Now let's run Jupyter:

```
jupyter notebook
```

This should be enough if you want to run Jupyter on a local computer. If you want to run it on a remote server, such as an EC2 instance from AWS, you need to add a few extra command-line options:

```
jupyter notebook --ip=0.0.0.0 --no-browser
```

In this case, you must specify two things:

- The IP address Jupyter will use to accept incoming HTTP requests (--ip=0.0.0.0). By default it uses localhost, meaning that it's possible to access the Notebook service only from within the computer.
- The --no-browser parameter, so Jupyter won't attempt to use the default web browser to open the URL with the notebooks. Of course, there's no web browser on the remote machine, only a terminal.

> **NOTE** In the case of EC2 instances on AWS, you will also need to configure the security rules to allow the instance to receive requests on the port 8888. Please refer to the "Renting a server on AWS" section for more details.

When you run this command, you should see something similar to this:

```
[C 04:50:30.099 NotebookApp]

    To access the notebook, open this file in a browser:
        file:///run/user/1000/jupyter/nbserver-3510-open.html
    Or copy and paste one of these URLs:
        http://(ip-172-31-21-255 or 127.0.0.1):8888/
     ?token=670dfec7558c9a84689e4c3cdbb473e158d3328a40bf6bba
```

When starting, Jupyter generates a random token. You need this token to access the web page. This is for security purposes, so no one can access the Notebook service but you.

Copy the URL from the terminal, and replace (ip-172-31-21-255 or 127.0.0.1) with the instance URL. You should end up with something like this:

http://ec2-18-217-172-167.us-east-2.compute.amazonaws.com:8888/ ?token=f04317713e74e65289fe5a43dac43d5bf164c144d05ce613

This URL consists of three parts:

- The DNS name of the instance: if you use AWS, you can get it from the AWS console or by using the AWS CLI.
- The port (8888, which is the default port for the Jupyter notebooks service).
- The token you just copied from the terminal.

After that, you should be able to see the Jupyter Notebooks service and create a new notebook (figure A.8).

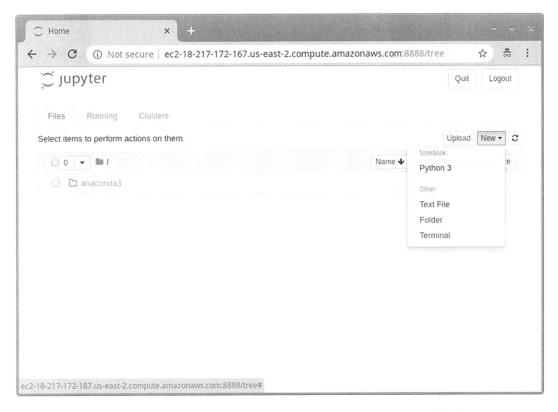

Figure A.8 The Jupyter Notebook service. Now you can create a new notebook.

If you're using a remote machine, when you exit the SSH session the Jupyter Notebook service will stop working. The internal process is attached to the SSH session, and it will be terminated. To avoid this, you can run the service inside screen, a tool for managing multiple virtual terminals:

```
screen -R jupyter
```

This command will attempt to connect to a screen with the name jupyter, but if no such screen exists, it will create one.

Then, inside the screen, you can type the same command for starting Jupyter Notebook:

```
jupyter notebook --ip=0.0.0.0 --no-browser
```

Check that it's working by trying to access it from your web browser. After verifying that it works, you can detach the screen by pressing Ctrl-A followed by D: first press

Ctrl-A, wait a bit, and then press D (for macOS, first press Ctrl-A and then press Ctrl-D). Anything running inside the screen is not attached to the current SSH session, so when you detach the screen and exit the session, the Jupyter process will keep running.

You can now disconnect from SSH (by pressing Ctrl-D) and verify that the Jupyter URL is still working.

A.2.2   *Running Jupyter on Windows*

As with Python and Anaconda, if you use the Linux Subsystem for Windows to install Jupyter, the instructions for Linux should work for Windows too.

By default, there's no browser configured to run in the Linux Subsystem. So we need to use the following command for launching Jupyter:

```
jupyter notebook --no-browser
```

Alternatively, we can set the BROWSER variable to point it to a browser from Windows:

```
export BROWSER='/mnt/c/Windows/explorer.exe'
```

However, if you didn't use the Linux Subsystem and installed Anaconda using the Windows Installer, starting the Jupyter Notebook service is different.

First, we need to open the Anaconda Navigator in the start menu. Once it's open, find Jupyter in the Applications tab and click Launch (figure A.9).

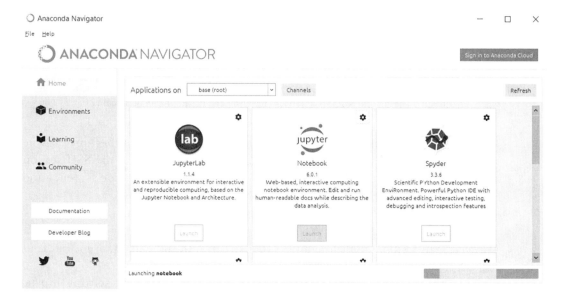

Figure A.9   To run the Jupyter Notebook service, find Jupyter in the applications tab and click Launch.

After the service launches successfully, the browser with Jupyter should open automatically (figure A.10).

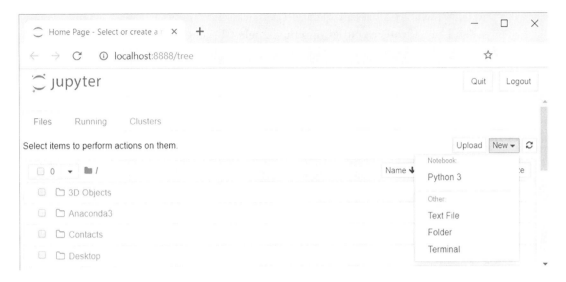

Figure A.10   The Jupyter Notebook service launched using Anaconda Navigator

A.2.3   Running Jupyter on MacOS

The instructions for Linux should also work for macOS, with no additional changes.

A.3   Installing the Kaggle CLI

The Kaggle CLI is the command-line interface for accessing the Kaggle platform, which includes data from Kaggle competitions and Kaggle datasets.

You can install it using pip:

```
pip install kaggle --upgrade
```

Then you need to configure it. First, you need to get credentials from Kaggle. For that, go to your Kaggle profile (create one if you don't have one yet), located at https://www.kaggle.com/<username>/account. The URL will be something like https://www.kaggle.com/agrigorev/account.

In the API section, click Create New API Token (figure A.11).

API

Using Kaggle's beta API, you can interact with Competitions and Datasets to download data, make submissions, and more via the command line. Read the docs

Create New API Token   Expire API Token

Figure A.11   To generate an API token to use from the Kaggle CLI, click Create New API Token on your Kaggle account page.

This will download a file called kaggle.json, which is a JSON file with two fields: user-name and key. If you're configuring the Kaggle CLI on the same computer you used to download the file, you should simply move this file to the location where the Kaggle CLI expects it:

```
mkdir ~/.kaggle
mv kaggle.json ~/.kaggle/kaggle.json
```

If you're configuring it on a remote machine, such as an EC2 instance, you need to copy the content of this file and paste it into the terminal. Open the file using nano (this will create the file if it doesn't exist):

```
mkdir ~/.kaggle
nano ~/.kaggle/kaggle.json
```

Paste in the content of the kaggle.json file you downloaded. Save the file by pressing Ctrl-O and exit nano by pressing Ctrl-X.

Now test that it's working by trying to list the available datasets:

```
kaggle datasets list
```

You can also test that it can download datasets by trying the dataset from chapter 2:

```
kaggle datasets download -d CooperUnion/cardataset
```

It should download a file called cardataset.zip.

A.4 *Accessing the source code*

We've stored the source code for this book on GitHub, a platform for hosting source code. You can see it here: https://github.com/alexeygrigorev/mlbookcamp-code.

GitHub uses Git to manage code, so you'll need a Git client to access the code for this book.

Git comes preinstalled in all the major Linux distributions. For example, the AMI we used for creating an instance with Ubuntu on AWS already has it.

If your distribution doesn't have Git, it's easy to install it. For example, for Debian-based distributions (such as Ubuntu), you need to run the following command:

```
sudo apt-get install git
```

On macOS, to use Git you need to install Command Line Tools or, alternatively, download the installer at https://sourceforge.net/projects/git-osx-installer/.

For Windows, you can download Git at https://git-scm.com/download/win.

Once you have Git installed, you can use it to get the book's code. To access it, you need to run the following command:

```
git clone https://github.com/alexeygrigorev/mlbookcamp-code.git
```

Now you can run Jupyter Notebook:

```
cd mlbookcamp-code
jupyter notebook
```

If you don't have Git and don't want to install it, it's also possible to access the code without it. You can download the latest code in a zip archive and unpack it. On Linux, you can do that by executing these commands:

```
wget -O mlbookcamp-code.zip \
    https://github.com/alexeygrigorev/mlbookcamp-code/archive/master.zip
unzip mlbookcamp-code.zip
rm mlbookcamp-code.zip
```

You can also just use your web browser: type the URL, download the zip archive, and extract the content.

A.5 Installing Docker

In chapter 5, we use Docker to package our application in an isolated container. It's quite easy to install.

A.5.1 Installing Docker on Linux

These steps are based on the official instructions for Ubuntu from the Docker website (https://docs.docker.com/engine/install/ubuntu/).

First, we need to install all the prerequisites:

```
sudo apt-get update
sudo apt-get install apt-transport-https ca-certificates curl software-
    properties-common
```

Next, we add the repository with the Docker binaries:

```
curl -fsSL https://download.docker.com/linux/ubuntu/gpg | sudo apt-key add -
sudo add-apt-repository "deb [arch=amd64] https://download.docker.com/linux/
    ubuntu $(lsb_release -cs) stable"
```

Now we can install it:

```
sudo apt-get update
sudo apt-get install docker-ce
```

Finally, if we want to execute Docker commands without sudo, we need to add our user to the docker user group:

```
sudo adduser $(whoami) docker
```

Now you'll need to reboot your system. In the case of EC2 or another remote machine, just logging off and on is enough.

To test that everything works fine, run the `hello-world` container:

```
docker run hello-world
```

You should see a message saying that everything works:

```
Hello from Docker!
This message shows that your installation appears to be working correctly.
```

A.5.2 *Installing Docker on Windows*

To install Docker on Windows, you need to download the installer from the official website (https://hub.docker.com/editions/community/docker-ce-desktop-windows/) and simply follow the instructions.

A.5.3 *Installing Docker on MacOS*

Like with Windows, installing Docker on MacOS is simple: first, download the installer from the official website (https://hub.docker.com/editions/community/docker-ce-desktop-mac/), and then follow the instructions.

A.6 *Renting a server on AWS*

Using a cloud service is the easiest way of getting a remote machine that you can use for following the examples in the book.

There are quite a few options nowadays, including cloud computing providers like Amazon Web Services (AWS), Google Cloud Platform, Microsoft Azure, and Digital Ocean. Rather than having to rent a server for a long time, in the cloud you can use it for a short period and typically pay per hour, per minute, or even per second. You can select the best machine for your needs in terms of computing power (number of CPUs or GPUs) and RAM.

It's also possible to rent a dedicated server for a longer time and pay per month. If you intend to use the server for a long time — say, six months or more — renting a dedicated server will be cheaper. Hetzner.com might be a good option in this case. They also offer servers with GPUs.

To make it easier for you to set up the environment with all the required libraries for the book, we provide instructions here for setting up an EC2 (Elastic Compute Cloud) machine on AWS. EC2 is part of AWS and allows you to rent a server of any configuration for any duration of time.

> **NOTE** We're not affiliated with Amazon or AWS. We chose to use it in this book because at the time of writing it's the most commonly used cloud provider.

If you don't have an AWS account or only recently created it, you're eligible for the free tier: you have a 12-month trial period in which to check out most of the AWS products for free. We try to use the free tier whenever possible, and we will specifically mention if something isn't covered by this tier.

Note that the instructions in this section are optional, and you don't have to use AWS or any other cloud. The code should work on any Linux machine, so if you have a laptop with Linux, it should be enough to work through the book. A Mac or Windows computer should also be fine, but we haven't tested the code thoroughly on these platforms.

A.6.1 Registering on AWS

The first thing you need to do is create an account. To do this, go to https://aws .amazon.com and click the Create an AWS Account button (see figure A.12).

Figure A.12 To create an account, click Create an AWS Account on the main AWS page.

NOTE This appendix was written in October 2019 and the screenshots were taken at that time. Please be aware that content on the AWS web site and the appearance of the management console could change.

Follow the instructions and fill in the required details. It should be a straightforward process, similar to the process of registering on any website.

NOTE Please be aware that AWS will ask you to provide the details of a bank card during the registration process.

Once you've completed the registration and verified your account, you should see the main page — the AWS Management Console (figure A.13).

Congratulations! You've just created a root account. However, it's not advisable to use the root account for anything: it has very broad permissions that allow you to do

AWS Management Console

AWS services

Find Services
You can enter names, keywords or acronyms.

Q *Example: Relational Database Service, database, RDS*

▶ All services

Build a solution
Get started with simple wizards and automated workflows.

Figure A.13   The AWS Management Console is the starting page for AWS.

anything and everything on your AWS acount. Typically, you use the root account to create less powerful accounts and then use them for your day-to-day tasks.

To create such an account, type "IAM" in the Find Services box and click on that item in the drop-down list. Select Users in the menu on the left, and click Add User (see figure A.14).

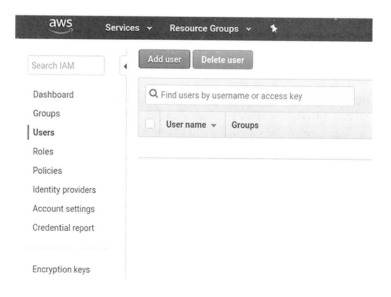

Figure A.14   Adding a user in the AWS Identity and Access Management (IAM) service

Now you just need to follow the instructions and answer the questions. At some point, it will ask about an access type: you'll need to select both Programmatic Access and AWS Management Console Access (see figure A.15). We will use both the command-line interface (CLI) and the web interface for working with AWS.

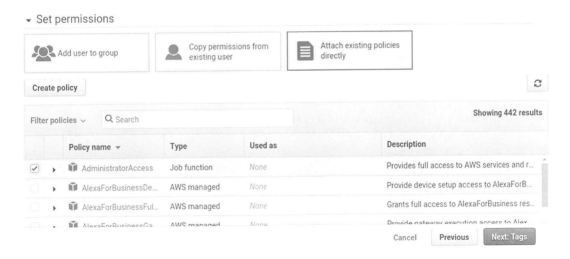

Figure A.15   We will use both the web interface and the command-line interface for working with AWS, so you need to select both access types.

In the Set Permissions step, you specify what this new user will be able to do. You want the user to have full privileges, so select Attach Existing Policies Directly at the top and choose AdministratorAccess in the list of policies (see figure A.16).

Figure A.16   Select the AdministratorAccess policy to enable the new user to access everything on AWS.

As the next step, the system will ask you about tags — you can safely ignore these for now. Tags are needed for companies where multiple people work on the same AWS account, mostly for expense-management purposes, so they shouldn't be a concern for the projects you'll do in this book.

At the end, when you've successfully created the new user, the wizard will suggest that you download the credentials (figure A.17). Download them and keep them safe; you'll need to use them later when configuring the AWS CLI.

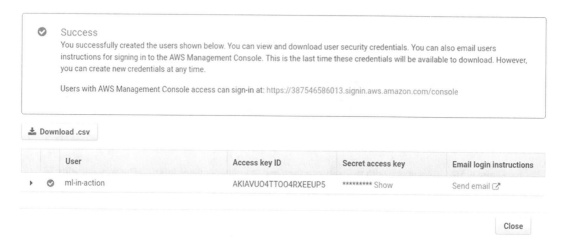

Figure A.17   The details for the newly created user. You can see the sign-in URL and download the credentials for programmatic access.

To access the management console, you can use the link AWS has generated for you. It appears in the Success box and follows this pattern:

https://<accountid>.signin.aws.amazon.com/console

It might be a good idea to bookmark this link. Once AWS has validated the account (which can take a little while), you can use it to log in: simply provide the username and password you specified when creating the user.

You can now start using the services of AWS. Most importantly, you can create an EC2 machine.

A.6.2   Accessing billing information

When using a cloud service provider, you are typically charged per second: for every second you use a particular AWS service, you pay a pre-defined rate. At the end of each month you get a bill, which is typically processed automatically. The money is withdrawn from the bank card you linked to the AWS account.

IMPORTANT   Even though we use the free tier to follow most of the examples in the book, you should periodically check the billing page to make sure you're not accidentally using billable services.

To understand how much you will need to pay at the end of the month, you can access the billing page of AWS.

If you use the root account (the account you created first), simply type "Billing" on the homepage of the AWS console to navigate to the billing page (figure A.18).

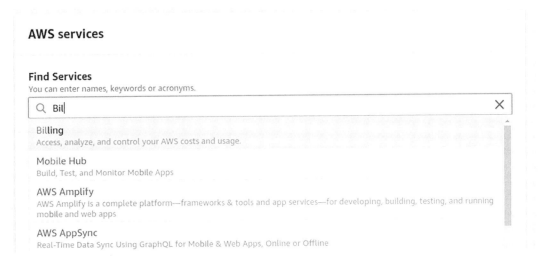

Figure A.18   To get to the billing page, type in "Billing" in the quick access search box.

If you try to access the same page from the user account (or IAM user — the one we created after creating the root account), you will notice that this is not allowed. To fix that, you need to

- Allow the billing page to be accessed by all IAM users, and
- Give the AMI user permissions to access the billing page.

Allowing all the IAM users access the billing page is simple: go to My Account (figure A.19 A), go to the IAM User and Role Access to Billing Information section and click Edit (figure A.19 B), and then select the Activate IAM Access option and click Update (figure A.19 C).

(A) To allow AMI users to access the billing info, click on My Account.

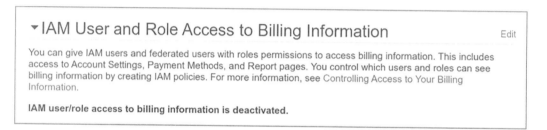

(B) In the My Account settings, find the IAM User and Role Access to Billing Information section and click Edit.

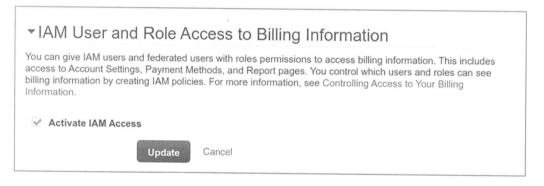

(C) Enable the Activate IAM Access option and click Update.

Figure A.19   Enabling access to billing information to IAM users

After that, go to the IAM service, find the IAM user we previously created, and click on it. Next, click on the Add permissions button (figure A.20).

Then attach the existing Billing policy to the user (figure A.21).

After that, the IAM user should be able to access the billing information page.

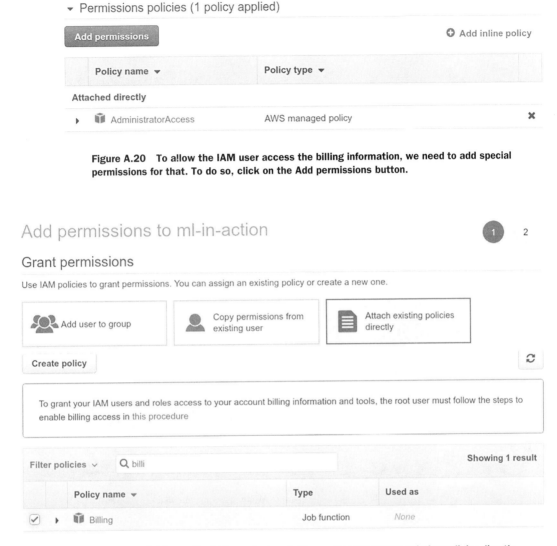

Figure A.20   To allow the IAM user access the billing information, we need to add special permissions for that. To do so, click on the Add permissions button.

Add permissions to ml-in-action

Grant permissions

Use IAM policies to grant permissions. You can assign an existing policy or create a new one.

Add user to group

Copy permissions from existing user

Attach existing policies directly

Create policy

To grant your IAM users and roles access to your account billing information and tools, the root user must follow the steps to enable billing access in this procedure

Policy name ▼	Type	Used as
☑ ▸ 📦 Billing	Job function	None

Filter policies ∨   🔍 billi   Showing 1 result

Figure A.21   After clicking on the Add permissions button, select the Attach existing policies directly option and select Billing in the list.

A.6.3   Creating an EC2 instance

EC2 is a service for renting a machine from AWS. You can use it to create a Linux machine to use for the projects in this book. To do this, first go to the EC2 page in AWS. The easiest way to do this is by typing "EC2" in the Find Services box on the home page of the AWS Management Console; then select EC2 from the drop-down list and press Enter (figure A.22).

AWS services

Find Services
You can enter names, keywords or acronyms.

> 🔍 EC2| ✕
>
> EC2
> Virtual Servers in the Cloud
>
> ECS
> Run and Manage Docker Containers
>
> EFS
> Managed File Storage for EC2
>
> GuardDuty
> Intelligent Threat Detection to Protect Your AWS Accounts and Workloads

Figure A.22   To go to the EC2 service's page, type EC2 in the Find Services box on the main page of the AWS Management Console and press Enter.

On the EC2 page, choose Instances from the menu on the left and then click Launch Instance (figure A.23).

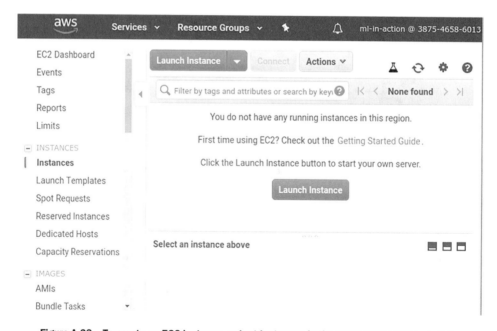

Figure A.23   To create an EC2 instance, select Instances in the menu on the left and click Launch Instance.

This brings you to a six-step form. The first step is to specify the AMI (Amazon Machine Image) you'll use for the instance. We recommend Ubuntu: it's one of the most popular Linux distributions, and we used it for all the examples in this book. Other images should also work fine, but we haven't tested them.

At the time of writing, Ubuntu Server 20.04 LTS is available (figure A.24), so use that one. Find it in the list and then click Select.

Figure A.24 Your instance will be based on Ubuntu Server 18.04 LTS.

You should take note of the AMI's ID: in this example it's ami-0a8e758f5e873d1c1, but it might be different for you, depending on your AWS region and version of Ubuntu.

> **NOTE** This AMI is free-tier eligible, which means that if you use the free tier for testing AWS, you won't be charged for using this AMI.

After that you need to select the instance type. There are many options, with different numbers of CPU cores and different amounts of RAM. If you want to stay within the free tier, select t2.micro (figure A.25). It's a rather small machine: it has only 1 CPU and 1 GB RAM. Of course, it's not the best instance in terms of computing power, but it should be enough for many projects in this book.

The next step is where you configure the instance details. You don't need to change anything here and can simply go on to the next step: adding storage (figure A.26).

Here, you specify how much space you need on the instance. The default suggestion of 8GB is not enough, so select 18GB. This should be good enough for most of the projects we'll do in this book. After changing it, click Next: Add Tags.

In the next step, you add tags to your new instance. The only tag you should add is Name, which allows you to give an instance a human-readable name. Add the key

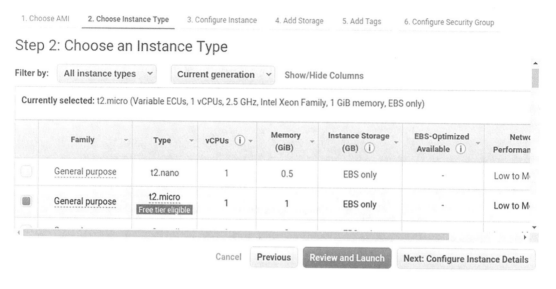

Figure A.25   The t2.micro is a rather small instance with only 1 CPU and 1 GB RAM, but it can be used for free.

1. Choose AMI   2. Choose Instance Type   3. Configure Instance   **4. Add Storage**   5. Add Tags   6. Configure Security Group

Step 4: Add Storage

Your instance will be launched with the following storage device settings. You can attach additional EBS volumes and instance store volumes to your instance, or edit the settings of the root volume. You can also attach additional EBS volumes after launching an instance, but not instance store volumes. Learn more about storage options in Amazon EC2.

Volume Type ⓘ	Device ⓘ	Snapshot ⓘ	Size (GiB) ⓘ	Volume Type ⓘ	IOPS ⓘ	Throughput (MB/s) ⓘ
Root	/dev/sda1	snap-03d99c0b3ce00a9c3	16	General Purpose SSD (gp2)	100 / 3000	N/A

Add New Volume

> Free tier eligible customers can get up to 30 GB of EBS General Purpose (SSD) or Magnetic storage. Learn more about free usage tier eligibility and usage restrictions.

Cancel   Previous   Review and Launch   Next: Add Tags

Figure A.26   The fourth step of creating an EC2 instance in AWS: adding storage. Change the size to 16GB.

Name and the value ml-bookcamp-instance (or any other name you prefer), as seen in figure A.27.

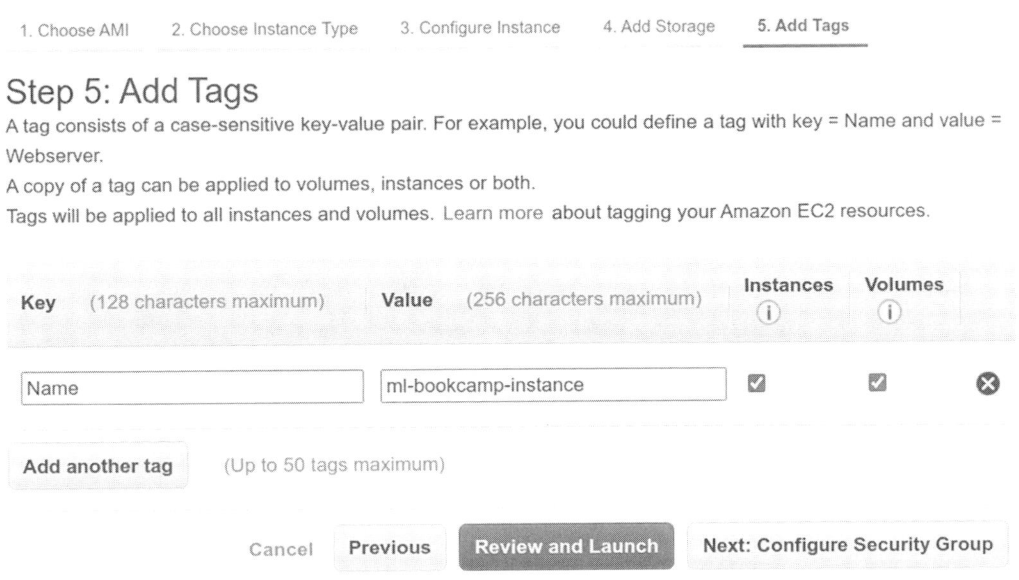

1. Choose AMI   2. Choose Instance Type   3. Configure Instance   4. Add Storage   **5. Add Tags**

Step 5: Add Tags

A tag consists of a case-sensitive key-value pair. For example, you could define a tag with key = Name and value = Webserver.

A copy of a tag can be applied to volumes, instances or both.

Tags will be applied to all instances and volumes. Learn more about tagging your Amazon EC2 resources.

Key (128 characters maximum)	Value (256 characters maximum)	Instances ⓘ	Volumes ⓘ	
Name	ml-bookcamp-instance	☑	☑	✕

Add another tag (Up to 50 tags maximum)

Cancel   **Previous**   **Review and Launch**   **Next: Configure Security Group**

Figure A.27 The only tag you may want to specify in step 5 is "Name": it allows you to give a human-readable name to the instance.

The next step is quite an important one: choosing the security group. This allows you to configure the network firewall and specify how the instance can be accessed and which ports are open. You'll want to host Jupyter Notebook on the instance, so you need to make sure its port is open and you can log in to the remote machine.

Because you don't yet have any security groups in your AWS account, you'll need to create a new one now: choose Create a New Security Group and give it the name jupyter (figure A.28). You'll want to use SSH to connect to the instance from your computers, so you need to make sure SSH connections are allowed. To enable this, select SSH in the Type drop-down list in the first row.

Typically the Jupyter Notebook service runs on port 8888, so you need to add a custom TCP rule that port 8888 can be accessed from anywhere on the internet.

When you do this, you may see a warning telling you that this might not be safe (figure A.29). It's not a problem for us because we are not running anything critical on the instances. Implementing proper security is not trivial and is out of scope for this book.

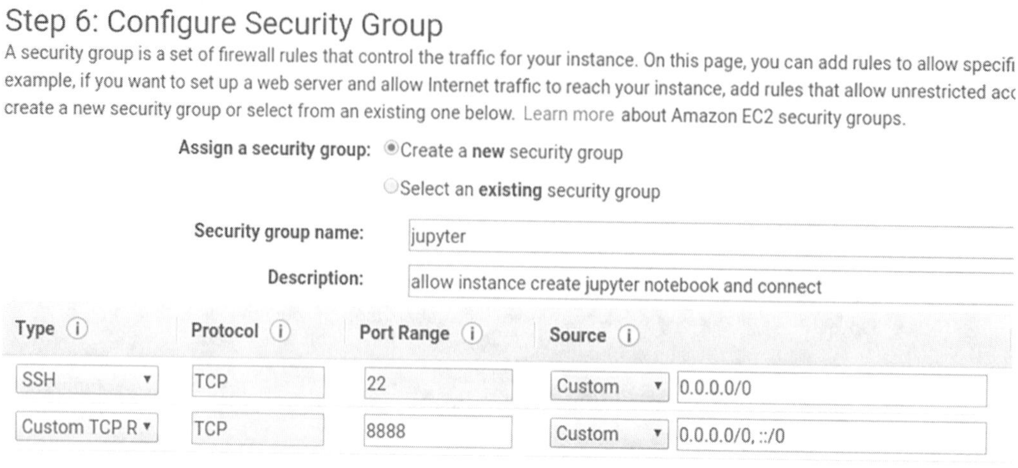

Step 6: Configure Security Group

A security group is a set of firewall rules that control the traffic for your instance. On this page, you can add rules to allow specifi example, if you want to set up a web server and allow Internet traffic to reach your instance, add rules that allow unrestricted acc create a new security group or select from an existing one below. Learn more about Amazon EC2 security groups.

Assign a security group: ◉ Create a **new** security group

○ Select an **existing** security group

Security group name: | jupyter

Description: | allow instance create jupyter notebook and connect

Type ⓘ	Protocol ⓘ	Port Range ⓘ	Source ⓘ	
SSH ▾	TCP	22	Custom ▾	0.0.0.0/0
Custom TCP R ▾	TCP	8888	Custom ▾	0.0.0.0/0, ::/0

Figure A.28   Creating a security group for running Jupyter Notebook on EC2 instances

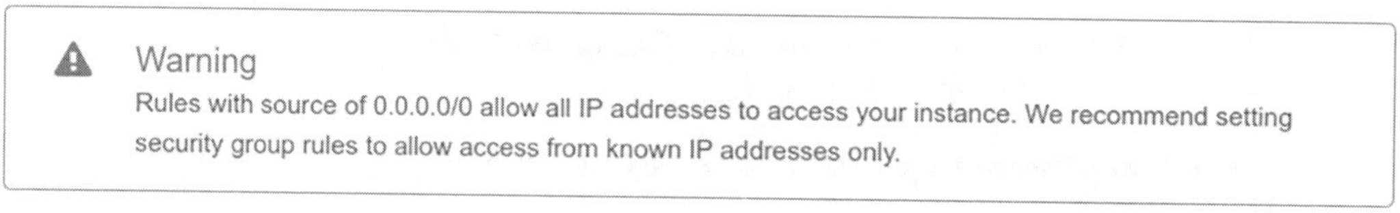

⚠ Warning

Rules with source of 0.0.0.0/0 allow all IP addresses to access your instance. We recommend setting security group rules to allow access from known IP addresses only.

Figure A.29   AWS warns us that the rules we added are not strict. For our case it's not a problem and we can safely ignore the warning.

The next time you create an instance, you'll be able to reuse this security group instead of creating a new one. Choose Select an Existing Security Group and select it from the list (figure A.30).

Configuring the security group is the last step. Verify that everything is fine, and click Review and Launch.

AWS won't let you launch the instance yet: you still need to configure the SSH keys for logging into the instance. Because your AWS account is still fresh and doesn't have keys yet, you need to create a new key pair. Choose Create a New Key Pair from the drop-down list and give it the name jupyter (figure A.31).

Click Download Key Pair and save the file somewhere on your computer. Make sure you can access this file later; it's important for being able to connect to the instance.

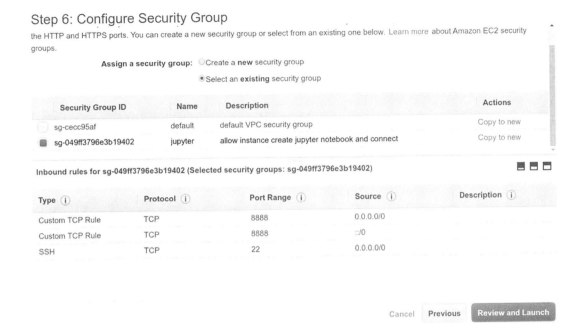

Step 6: Configure Security Group

the HTTP and HTTPS ports. You can create a new security group or select from an existing one below. Learn more about Amazon EC2 security groups.

Assign a security group: ○ Create a **new** security group

● Select an **existing** security group

	Security Group ID	Name	Description	Actions
☐	sg-cecc95af	default	default VPC security group	Copy to new
☑	sg-049ff3796e3b19402	jupyter	allow instance create jupyter notebook and connect	Copy to new

Inbound rules for sg-049ff3796e3b19402 (Selected security groups: sg-049ff3796e3b19402)

Type ⓘ	Protocol ⓘ	Port Range ⓘ	Source ⓘ	Description ⓘ
Custom TCP Rule	TCP	8888	0.0.0.0/0	
Custom TCP Rule	TCP	8888	::/0	
SSH	TCP	22	0.0.0.0/0	

Cancel Previous Review and Launch

Figure A.30 When creating an instance, it's also possible to assign an existing security group to the instance.

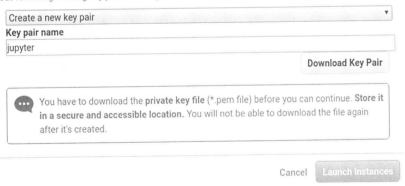

A key pair consists of a **public key** that AWS stores, and a **private key file** that you store. Together, they allow you to connect to your instance securely. For Windows AMIs, the private key file is required to obtain the password used to log into your instance. For Linux AMIs, the private key file allows you to securely SSH into your instance.

Note: The selected key pair will be added to the set of keys authorized for this instance. Learn more about removing existing key pairs from a public AMI.

Create a new key pair ▼

Key pair name

jupyter

Download Key Pair

You have to download the **private key file** (*.pem file) before you can continue. **Store it in a secure and accessible location.** You will not be able to download the file again after it's created.

Cancel Launch Instances

Figure A.31 To be able to use SSH to log in to the instance, you need to create a key pair.

The next time you create an instance, you can reuse this key. Select Choose an Existing Key Pair in the first drop-down list, choose the key you want to use, and click the checkbox to confirm that you still have the key (figure A.32).

Figure A.32   You can also use an existing key when creating an instance.

Now you can launch the instance by clicking Launch Instances. You should see a confirmation that everything is good and the instance is launching (figure A.33).

Figure A.33   AWS tells us that everything went well and now the instance is launching.

In this message, you can see the ID of the instance. In our case, it's i-0b1a64d4d20997aff. You can click on it now to see the details of the instance (figure A.34). Because you want to use SSH to connect to your instance, you need to get the public DNS name to do it. You can find this on the Description tab.

A.6.4   Connecting to the instance

In the previous section you created an instance on EC2. Now you need to log in to this instance to install all the required software. You will use SSH for this.

CONNECTING TO THE INSTANCE ON LINUX

You already know the public DNS name of your instance. In our example, it's ec2-18-191-156-172.us-east-2.compute.amazonaws.com. In your case the name will be different: the first part of the name (ec2-18-191-156-172) depends on the IP that the instance gets and the second (us-east-2) on the region where it's running. To use SSH to enter the instance, you will need this name.

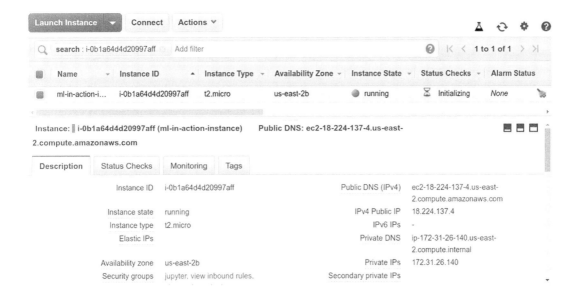

Figure A.34   The details of the newly created instance. To use SSH to connect to it, you need the public DNS name.

When using the key you downloaded from AWS for the first time, you need to make sure the permissions on the file are set correctly. Execute this command:

```
chmod 400 jupyter.pem
```

Now you can use the key to log in to the instance:

```
ssh -i "jupyter.pem" \
    ubuntu@ec2-18-191-156-172.us-east-2.compute.amazonaws.com
```

Of course, you should replace the DNS name shown here with the one you copied from the instance description.

Before allowing you to enter the machine, the SSH client will ask you to confirm that you trust the remote instance:

```
The authenticity of host 'ec2-18-191-156-172.us-east-2.compute.amazonaws.com
    (18.191.156.172)' can't be established.
ECDSA key fingerprint is SHA256:S5doTJOGwXVF3i1IFjB10RuHufaVSe+EDqKbGpIN0wI.
Are you sure you want to continue connecting (yes/no)?
```

Type "yes" to confirm.

Now you should be able to log in to the instance and see the welcome message (figure A.35).

Now it's possible to do anything you want with the machine.

```
Welcome to Ubuntu 18.04.2 LTS (GNU/Linux 4.15.0-1032-aws x86_64)

 * Documentation:  https://help.ubuntu.com
 * Management:     https://landscape.canonical.com
 * Support:        https://ubuntu.com/advantage

System information as of Wed Jun  5 06:01:51 UTC 2019

System load:    0.02              Processes:        86
Usage of /:     13.6% of 7.69GB   Users logged in: 0
Memory usage:   14%               IP address for eth0: 172.31.46.216
Swap usage:     0%

0 packages can be updated.
0 updates are security updates.

The programs included with the Ubuntu system are free software;
the exact distribution terms for each program are described in the
individual files in /usr/share/doc/*/copyright.

Ubuntu comes with ABSOLUTELY NO WARRANTY, to the extent permitted by
applicable law.

To run a command as administrator (user "root"), use "sudo <command>".
See "man sudo_root" for details.

ubuntu@ip-172-31-46-216:~$
```

Figure A.35   After successfully logging into the EC2 instance, you should see the welcome message.

CONNECTING TO THE INSTANCE ON WINDOWS

Using the Linux subsystem on Windows is the easiest way for connecting to the EC2 instance: you can use SSH there and follow the same instructions as for Linux.

Alternatively, you can use Putty (https://www.putty.org) for connecting to EC2 instances from Windows.

CONNECTING TO THE INSTANCE ON MACOS

SSH is built in on macOS, so the steps for Linux should work on a Mac.

A.6.5   Shutting down the instance

After you've finished working with the instance, you should turn it off.

> **IMPORTANT**   It's very important to turn off the instance after the work is finished. For each second you use the instance, you get billed, even if you no longer need the machine and it's idle. That doesn't apply in the first 12 months of using AWS if the requested instance is free-tier eligible, but nonetheless, it's good to develop the habit of periodically checking your account status and disabling unneeded services.

You can do this from the terminal:

```
sudo shutdown now
```

It's also possible to do it from the web interface: select the instance you want to turn off, go to Actions, and select Instance State > Stop (figure A.36).

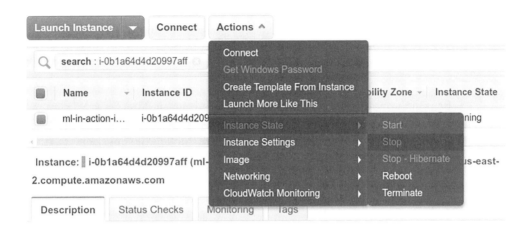

Figure A.36 Stopping the instance from the AWS console

Once the instance has been stopped, you can start it again by choosing Start from the same submenu. It's also possible to completely remove the instance: for this you need to use the Terminate option.

A.6.6 Configuring AWS CLI

AWS CLI is the command line interface for AWS. For most of the things we need, using the AWS Console is sufficient, but in some cases, we need the command line tool. For example, in chapter 5, we deploy a model to Elastic Beanstalk, and we need to configure the CLI.

To use the CLI, you need to have Python. If you use Linux or macOS, you should already have a Python distribution built in. Alternatively, you can install Anaconda using the instructions in the next section.

Just having Python is not enough; you also need to install the AWS CLI itself. You can do this by running the following command in the terminal:

```
pip install awscli
```

If you already have it, it's a good idea to update it:

```
pip install -U awscli
```

After the installation finishes you need to configure the tool, specifying the access token and secret you downloaded earlier when creating a user.

One way to do this is to use the `configure` command:

```
aws configure
```

It will ask you for the keys, which we downloaded, when creating a user:

```
$ aws configure
AWS Access Key ID [None]: <ENTER_ACCESS_KEY>
AWS Secret Access Key [None]: <ENTER_SECRET_KEY>
Default region name [None]: us-east-2
Default output format [None]:
```

The region name used here is us-east-2, which is located in Ohio.

When you're finished configuring the tool, verify that it works. You can ask the CLI to return your identity, which should match the details of your user:

```
$ aws sts get-caller-identity
{
    "UserId": "AIDAVUO4TTOO55WN6WHZ4",
    "Account": "XXXXXXXXXXXX",
    "Arn": "arn:aws:iam::XXXXXXXXXXXX:user/ml-bookcamp"
}
```

appendix B
Introduction to Python

Python is currently the most popular language for building machine learning projects, and this is why we use it for doing the projects in this book.

In case you're not familiar with Python, this appendix covers the basics: the syntax and the language features we use in the book. It's not meant to be an in-depth tutorial, but it should give you enough information to start using Python immediately after finishing the appendix. Note that it's brief, and it's aimed at people who already know how to program in any other programming language.

To get the best of this appendix, create a jupyter notebook, give it a name like appendix-b-python, and use it to execute the code from the appendix. Let's start.

B.1   *Variables*

Python is a dynamic language — so you don't need to declare types like in Java or C++. For example, to create a variable with integer or string, we only need to do a simple assignment:

```
a = 10          ⟵⌐   a is an integer.
b = 'string_b'
c = "string_c"       b and c are strings.
d = 0.999       ⟵⌐
                     d is a float.
```

To print something to standard output, we can use the `print` function:

```
print(a, b, c, d)
```

It prints

```
10 string_b string_c 0.999
```

357

To execute the code, you can put each code snippet in a separate jupyter notebook cell and then execute it. For executing the code in the cell, you can press the Run button, or use the Shift+Enter hotkey (figure B.1).

```
In [1]:  a = 10
         b = 'string_b'
         c = "string_c"
         d = 0.999

In [2]:  print(a, b, c, d)

         10 string_b string_c 0.999
```

Figure B.1   Code executed in Jupyter Notebook cells. You can see the output immediately after executing the code.

When we pass multiple arguments to print, like in the previous example, it adds a space between the arguments when printing.

We can put multiple variables together with a special construction called *tuple*:

```
t = (a, b)
```

When we print t, we get the following:

```
(10, 'string_b')
```

To unwrap a tuple into multiple variables we use *tuple assignment*:

```
(c, d) = t
```

Now c and d contain the first value of the tuple, as well as the second one:

```
print(c, d)
```

It prints

```
10 string_b
```

We can drop the parentheses when using the tuple assignment:

```
c, d = t
```

This produces the same result.

Tuple assignment is quite useful and can make the code shorter. For example, we can use it to swap the content of two variables:

```
a = 10
b = 20
a, b = b, a          ⟵  Replace a with
print("a =", a)          b and b with a.
print("b =", b)
```

It will print

```
a = 20
b = 10
```

When printing, we can have nicely formatted strings using the % operator:

```
print("a = %s" % a)          Replace %s with
print("b = %s" % b)          the content of a.

                             Replace %s with
                             the content of b.
```

It will produce the same output:

```
a = 20
b = 10
```

Here %s is a placeholder: in this case, it means that we want to format the passed argument as a string. Other commonly used options are

- %d to format it as a number
- %f to format it as a floating-point number

We can pass in multiple arguments to the format operator in a tuple:

```
print("a = %s, b = %s" % (a, b))
```

The first occurrence of the placeholder %s will be replaced by a, and the second by b, so it will produce the following:

```
a = 20, b = 10
```

Finally, if we have a floating-point number, we can use special formatting for it:

```
n = 0.0099999999
print("n = %.2f" % n)
```

This will round the float to the second decimal point when formatting the string, so we will see 0.01 when executing the code.

There are many options for formatting strings, and also other ways of formatting. For example, there's also the so-called "new" way of formatting using the string.format method, which we won't cover in this appendix. You can read more about these formatting options at https://pyformat.info or in the official documentation.

B.1.1   *Control flow*

There are three control-flow statements in Python: if, for and while. Let's take a look at each of them.

CONDITIONS

A simple way to control the execution flow of a program is the `if` statement. In Python the syntax for `if` is the following:

```python
a = 10

if a >= 5:
    print('the statement is true')
else:
    print('the statement is false')
```

This will print the first statement:

```
the statement is true
```

Note that in Python we use indentation for grouping the code after the `if` statement. We can chain multiple `if` statements together using `elif`, which is a shortening for `else-if`:

```python
a = 3

if a >= 5:
    print('the first statement is true')
elif a >= 0:
    print('the second statement is true')
else:
    print('both statements are false')
```

This code will print the second statement:

```
the second statement is true
```

FOR LOOP

When we want to repeat the same piece of code multiple times, we use loops. The traditional `for` loop in Python looks like this:

```python
for i in range(10):
    print(i)
```

This code will print numbers from 0 to 9, and 10 is not included:

```
0
1
2
3
4
5
6
7
8
9
```

When specifying the range, we can set the starting number, the end number, and the increment step:

```
for i in range(10, 100, 5):
    print(i)
```

This code will print numbers from 10 to 100 (excluded) with step 5: 10, 15, 20, ..., 95.

To exit the loop earlier, we can use the break statement:

```
for i in range(10):
    print(i)
    if i > 5:
        break
```

This code will print numbers between 0 and 6. When i is 6, it will break the loop, so it will not print any numbers after 6:

```
0
1
2
3
4
5
6
```

To skip an iteration of the loop, we use the continue statement:

```
for i in range(10):
    if i <= 5:
        continue
    print(i)
```

This code will skip the iterations when i is 5 or less, so it will print only numbers starting from 6:

```
6
7
8
9
```

WHILE LOOP

The while loop is also available in Python. It executes while a certain condition is True. For example:

```
cnt = 0

while cnt <= 5:
    print(cnt)
    cnt = cnt + 1
```

In this code, we repeat the loop while the condition `cnt <= 5` is `True`. Once this condition is no longer `True`, the execution stops. This code will print numbers between 0 and 5, including 5:

```
0
1
2
3
4
5
```

We can use the `break` and `continue` statements in `while` loops as well.

B.1.2   Collections

Collections are special containers that allow keeping multiple elements in them. We will look at four types of collections: lists, tuples, sets, and dictionaries.

Lists

A *list* is an ordered collection with the possibility to access an element by index. To create a list, we can simply put elements inside squared brackets:

```
numbers = [1, 2, 3, 5, 7, 11, 13]
```

To get an element by its index, we can use the brackets notation:

```
el = numbers[1]
print(el)
```

Indexing starts at 0 in Python, so when we ask for the element at index 1, we get 2.

We can also change the values in the list:

```
numbers[1] = -2
```

To access the elements from the end, we can use negative indices. For example, `-1` will get the last element, `-2` — the one before the last and so on:

```
print(numbers[-1], numbers[-2])
```

As we expect, it prints 13 11.

To add elements to the list, use the `append` function. It will append the element to the end of the list:

```
numbers.append(17)
```

To iterate over the elements of a list, we use a `for` loop:

```
for n in numbers:
    print(n)
```

When we execute it, we see all the elements printed:

```
1
-2
3
5
7
11
13
17
```

This is also known as a `for-each` loop in other languages: we execute the body of the loop for each element of the collection. It doesn't include the indices, only the elements themselves. If we also need to have access to the index of each element, we can use `range`, as we did previously:

```
for i in range(len(numbers)):
    n = numbers[i]
    print("numbers[%d] = %d" % (i, n))
```

The function `len` returns the length of the list, so this code is roughly equivalent to the traditional way of traversing an array in C or Java and accessing each element by its index. When we execute it, the code prints the following:

```
numbers[0] = 1
numbers[1] = -2
numbers[2] = 3
numbers[3] = 5
numbers[4] = 7
numbers[5] = 11
numbers[6] = 13
numbers[7] = 17
```

A more "pythonic" (more common and idiomatic in the Python world) way of achieving the same thing is using the `enumerate` function:

```
for i, n in enumerate(numbers):
    print("numbers[%d] = %d" % (i, n))
```

In this code, the `i` variable will get the index, and the `n` variable, the respective element from the list. This code will produce the exact same output as the previous loop.

To concatenate multiple lists into one, we can use the plus operator. For example, consider two lists:

```
list1 = [1, 2, 3, 5]
list2 = [7, 11, 13, 17]
```

We can create a third list that contains all the elements from `list1` followed by the elements from `list2` by concatenating the two lists:

```
new_list = list1 + list2
```

This will produce the following list:

```
[1, 2, 3, 5, 7, 11, 13, 17]
```

Finally, it's also possible to create a list of lists: a list whose elements are lists as well. To show that, let's first create three lists with numbers:

```
list1 = [1, 2, 3, 5]
list2 = [7, 11, 13, 17]
list3 = [19, 23, 27, 29]
```

Now let's put them together in another list:

```
lists = [list1, list2, list3]
```

Now `lists` is a list of lists. When we iterate over it with a `for` loop, at each iteration we get a list:

```
for l in lists:
    print(l)
```

This will produce the following output:

```
[1, 2, 3, 5]
[7, 11, 13, 17]
[19, 23, 27, 29]
```

SLICING

Another useful concept in Python is *slicing*— it's used for getting a part of the list. For example, let's consider the list of numbers again:

```
numbers = [1, 2, 3, 5, 7]
```

If we want to select a sublist with the first three elements, we can use the colon operator (`:`) for specifying the range for selection:

```
top3 = numbers[0:3]
```

In this case, `0:3` means "select elements starting from index 0 till index 3 (exclusive)." The result contains the first three elements: `[1, 2, 3]`. Note that it selects elements at the indices 0, 1, and 2, so 3 is not included.

If we want to include the beginning of the list, we don't need to specify the first number in the range:

```
top3 = numbers[:3]
```

If we don't specify the second number in the range, we get everything until the end of the list:

```
last3 = numbers[2:]
```

The list `last3` will contain the last three elements: `[3, 5, 7]` (figure B.2).

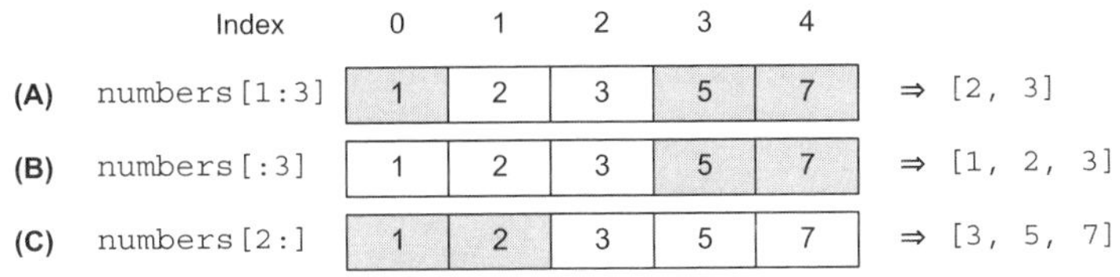

Figure B.2 Using the colon operator to select a sublist of a list

TUPLES

We already met tuples previously in the Variables section. Tuples are also collections; they are quite similar to lists. The only difference is that they are immutable: once you create a tuple, you cannot change the content of the tuple.

To create a tuple we use parentheses:

```
numbers = (1, 2, 3, 5, 7, 11, 13)
```

Like with lists, we can get the value by index:

```
el = numbers[1]
print(el)
```

However, we cannot update the values in the tuple. When we try to do it, we get an error:

```
numbers[1] = -2
```

If we try to execute this code, we get

```
---------------------------------------------------------------------
TypeError                                 Traceback (most recent call last)
<ipython-input-15-9166360b9018> in <module>
----> 1 numbers[1] = -2

TypeError: 'tuple' object does not support item assignment
```

Likewise, we cannot append a new element to the tuple. However, we can use concatenation to achieve the same result:

```
numbers = numbers + (17,)
```

Here we create a new tuple that contains the old numbers, and we concatenate it with another tuple that contains only one number: 17. Note that we need to add a comma to make a tuple; otherwise Python will treat it as a simple number.

Effectively, the expression on the previous page is the same as writing

```
numbers = (1, 2, 3, 5, 7, 11, 13) + (17,)
```

After doing this, we get a new tuple that contains a new element, so when printing it, we get

```
(1, 2, 3, 5, 7, 11, 13, 17)
```

SET

Another useful collection is a *set*: it's an unordered collection that keeps only unique elements. Unlike lists, it cannot contain duplicates, and it's also not possible to access an individual element of a set by index.

To create a set, we use curly braces:

```
numbers = {1, 2, 3, 5, 7, 11, 13}
```

> **NOTE**   To create an empty set, we need to use set:
>
> ```
> empty_set = set()
> ```

Simply putting empty curly braces will create a dictionary — a collection that we cover later in this appendix:

```
empty_dict = {}
```

Sets are faster than lists for checking if the collection contains an element. We use the in operator for checking it:

```
print(1 in numbers)
```

Since "1" is in the numbers set, this line of code will print True.

To add an element to the set, we use the add method:

```
numbers.add(17)
```

To iterate over all the elements of the set we again use a for loop:

```
for n in numbers:
    print(n)
```

When we execute it, it prints

```
1
2
3
5
7
11
13
17
```

DICTIONARIES

Dictionary is another extremely useful collection in Python: we use it to build a key-value map. To create a dictionary, we use curly braces, and to separate the keys and values we use colons (:):

```
words_to_numbers = {
    'one': 1,
    'two': 2,
    'three': 3,
}
```

To retrieve the value by the key, we use brackets:

```
print(words_to_numbers['one'])
```

If something is not in the dictionary, Python raises an exception:

```
print(words_to_numbers['five'])
```

When we try to execute it, we get the following error:

```
-------------------------------------------------------------------------
KeyError                                    Traceback (most recent call last)
<ipython-input-38-66a309b8feb5> in <module>
----> 1 print(words_to_numbers['five'])

KeyError: 'five'
```

To avoid it, we can first check if the key is in the dictionary before attempting to get the value. We can use the in statement for checking it:

```
if 'five' in words_to_numbers:
    print(words_to_numbers['five'])
else:
    print('not in the dictionary')
```

When running this code, we'll see not in the dictionary in the output.

Another option is to use the get method. It doesn't raise an exception, but returns None if the key is not present in the dictionary:

```
value = words_to_numbers.get('five')
print(value)
```

It will print None. When using get, we can specify the default value in case the key is not present in the dictionary:

```
value = words_to_numbers.get('five', -1)
print(value)
```

In this situation, we'll get -1.

To iterate over all the keys of a dictionary, we use a `for` loop over the results from the `keys` method:

```
for k in words_to_numbers.keys():
    v = words_to_numbers[k]
    print("%s: %d" % (k, v))
```

It will print

```
one: 1
two: 2
three: 3
```

Alternatively, we can directly iterate over the key-value pairs in the dictionary using the `items` method:

```
for k, v in words_to_numbers.items():
    print("%s: %d" % (k, v))
```

It produces exactly the same output as the previous code.

LIST COMPREHENSION

List comprehension is a special syntax for creating and filtering lists in Python. Let's again consider a list with numbers:

```
numbers = [1, 2, 3, 5, 7]
```

Suppose we want to create another list where all the elements of the original list are squared. For that we can use a `for` loop:

```
squared = []

for n in numbers:
    s = n * n
    squared.append(s)
```

We can concisely rewrite this code into one single line using list comprehension:

```
squared = [n * n for n in numbers]
```

It's also possible to add an `if` condition inside to process only the elements that meet the condition:

```
squared = [n * n for n in numbers if n > 3]
```

It translates to the following code:

```
squared = []

for n in numbers:
    if n > 3:
        s = n * n
        squared.append(s)
```

If all we need is to apply the filter and leave the elements as is, we can do that as well:

```
filtered = [n for n in numbers if n > 3]
```

This translates to

```
filtered = []

for n in numbers:
    if n > 3:
        filtered.append(n)
```

It's also possible to use list comprehension for creating other collections with a slightly different syntax. For example, for dictionaries we put curly braces around the expression and use a colon to separate keys with values:

```
result = {k: v * 10 for (k, v) in words_to_numbers.items() if v % 2 == 0}
```

This is a shortcut for the following code:

```
result = {}

for (k, v) in words_to_numbers.items():
    if v % 2 == 0:
        result[k] = v * 10
```

> **WARNING** When learning about list comprehension, it might be tempting to start using it everywhere. Typically it fits best for simple cases, but for more complex situations, `for` loops should be preferred over list comprehension for better code readability. If in doubt, use `for` loops.

B.1.3 *Code reusability*

At some point, when we write a lot of code, we need to think about how to organize it better. We can achieve that by putting small reusable pieces of code inside functions or classes. Let's take a look at how to do it.

FUNCTIONS

To create a function, we use the `def` keyword:

```
def function_name(arg1, arg2):
    # body of the function
    return 0
```

When we want to exit the function and return some value, we use the `return` statement. If we simply put `return` without any value or don't include `return` in the body of the function, the function will return `None`.

For example, we can write a function that prints values from 0 up to a specified number:

```
def print_numbers(max):
    for i in range(max + 1):
        print(i)
```

Create a function with one argument: max.

Use the max argument inside the function.

To call this function, simply add the arguments in parentheses after the name:

```
print_numbers(10)
```

It's also possible to provide the names of the arguments when invoking the function:

```
print_numbers(max=10)
```

CLASSES

Classes provide higher-level abstraction than functions: they can have an internal state and methods that operate on this state. Let's consider a class, NumberPrinter, that does the same thing as the function from the previous section — it prints numbers.

```
class NumberPrinter:

    def __init__(self, max):
        self.max = max

    def print_numbers(self):
        for i in range(self.max + 1):
            print(i)
```

The class initializer

Assign the max argument to the max field.

Method of the class

Use the internal state when invoking the method.

In this code, __init__ is the initializer. It runs whenever we want to create an instance of a class:

```
num_printer = NumberPrinter(max=10)
```

Note that inside the class, the __init__ method has two arguments: self and max. The first argument of all the methods always has to be self: this way we can use self inside the method to access the state of the object.

However, when we invoke the method later, we don't pass anything to the self argument: it's hidden from us. So, when we invoke the print_number method on the instance of the NumberPrinter object, we simply put empty parentheses with no parameters:

```
num_printer.print_numbers()
```

This code produces the same output as the function from the previous section.

IMPORTING CODE

Now suppose we want to put some code to a separate file. Let's create a file called useful_code.py and place it in the same folder as the notebook.

Open this file with an editor. Inside the file, we can put the function and the class we just created. In this way, we create a module with the name `useful_code`. To access the function and the class inside the module, we import them using the `import` statement:

```
import useful_code
```

Once it's imported, we can use it:

```
num_printer = useful_code.NumberPrinter(max=10)
num_printer.print_numbers()
```

It's also possible to import a module and give it a short name. For example, if instead of writing `useful_code` we want to write `uc`, we can do the following:

```
import useful_code as uc
```

```
num_printer = uc.NumberPrinter(max=10)
num_printer.print_numbers()
```

This is a very common idiom in scientific Python. Packages like NumPy and Pandas are typically imported with shorter aliases:

```
import numpy as np
import pandas as pd
```

Finally, if we don't want to import everything from the module, we can choose what exactly to import using `from ... import` syntax:

```
from useful_code import NumberPrinter
```

```
num_printer = NumberPrinter(max=10)
num_printer.print_numbers()
```

B.1.4   Installing libraries

It's possible to put our code into packages that are available to everyone. For example, NumPy or Pandas are such packages. They are already available in the Anaconda distribution, but typically they don't come pre-installed with Python.

To install such external packages, we can use the built-in package installer called pip. To use it, open your terminal and execute the `pip install` command there:

```
pip install numpy scipy pandas
```

After the install command, we list the packages we want to install. It's also possible to specify the version of each package when installing:

```
pip install numpy==1.16.5 scipy==1.3.1 pandas==0.25.1
```

When we already have a package, but it's outdated and we want to update it, we need to run `pip install` with the -U flag:

```
pip install -U numpy
```

Finally, if we want to remove a package, we use `pip uninstall`:

```
pip uninstall numpy
```

B.1.5   *Python programs*

To execute Python code, we can simply call the Python interpreter and specify the file we want to execute. For example, to run the code inside our useful_code.py script, execute the following command in the command line:

```
python useful_code.py
```

When we execute it, nothing happens: we only declare a function and a class there and don't actually use them. To see some results, we need to add a few lines of code to the file. For example, we can add the following:

```
num_printer = NumberPrinter(max=10)
num_printer.print_numbers()
```

Now when we execute this file, we see the numbers that `NumberPrinter` prints.

However, when we import a module, internally Python executes everything inside the module. It means that the next time we do `import useful_code` in the notebook, we'll see the numbers printed there.

To avoid it, we can tell the Python interpreter that some code needs to run only when executed as a script, and not imported. To achieve that, we put our code inside the following construction:

```
if __name__ == "__main__":
    num_printer = NumberPrinter(max=10)
    num_printer.print_numbers()
```

Finally, we can also pass arguments when running python scripts:

```
import sys

# declarations of print_numbers and NumberPrinter

if __name__ == "__main__":
    max_number = int(sys.argv[1])        ◁──┘  Parse the parameter as an
    num_printer = NumberPrinter(max=max_number)      integer: by default, it's a string.
    num_printer.print_numbers()          ◁──┐  Pass the parsed argument to
                                              the NumberPrinter instance.
```

Now we can run the script with custom parameters:

```
python useful_code.py 5
```

As a result, we'll see numbers from 0 to 5:

```
0
1
2
3
4
5
```

appendix C
Introduction to NumPy

We don't expect any NumPy knowledge from the readers and try to put all the required information in the chapters as we go along. However, because the purpose of the book is to teach machine learning rather than NumPy, we couldn't cover everything in great detail in the chapters. That's the focus of this appendix: to give an overview of the most important concepts from NumPy in one centralized place.

In addition to introducing NumPy, the appendix also covers a bit of linear algebra useful for machine learning, including matrix and vector multiplication, matrix inverse, and the normal equation.

NumPy is a Python library, so if you're not yet familiar with Python, check out appendix B.

C.1 NumPy

NumPy is short for *Numerical Python* — it's a Python library for numerical manipulations. NumPy plays a central role in the Python machine learning ecosystem: nearly all the libraries in Python depend on it. For example, Pandas, Scikit-learn, and TensorFlow all rely on NumPy for numerical operations.

NumPy comes preinstalled in the Anaconda distribution of NumPy, so if you use it, you don't need to do anything extra. But if you don't use Anaconda, installing NumPy is quite simple with `pip`:

```
pip install numpy
```

To experiment with NumPy, let's create a new Jupyter Notebook and name it appendix-c-numpy.

To use NumPy, we need to import it. That's why in the first cell we write

```
import numpy as np
```

In the scientific Python community, it's common to use an alias when importing NumPy. That's why we add as np in the installation code. This allows us to write np in the code instead of numpy.

We'll start exploring NumPy from its core data structure: the NumPy array.

C.1.1   *NumPy arrays*

NumPy arrays are similar to Python lists, but they are better optimized for number-crunching tasks like machine learning.

To create an array of a predefined size filled with zeros, we use the np.zeros function:

```
zeros = np.zeros(10)
```

This creates an array with 10 zero elements (figure C.1).

```
zeros = np.zeros(10)
zeros

array([0., 0., 0., 0., 0., 0., 0., 0., 0., 0.])
```

Figure C.1   Creating a NumPy array of length 10 filled with zeros

Likewise, we can create an array with ones using the np.ones function:

```
ones = np.ones(10)
```

It works exactly the same as zeros, except the elements are ones.

Both functions are a shortcut for a more general function: np.full. It creates an array of a certain size filled with the specified element. For example, to create an array of size 10 filled with zeros, we do the following:

```
array = np.full(10, 0.0)
```

We can achieve the same result using the np.repeat function:

```
array = np.repeat(0.0, 10)
```

This code produces the same result as the earlier code (figure C.2).

```
array = np.full(10, 0.0)
array

array([0., 0., 0., 0., 0., 0., 0., 0., 0., 0.])
```

```
array = np.repeat(0.0, 10)
array

array([0., 0., 0., 0., 0., 0., 0., 0., 0., 0.])
```

Figure C.2   To create an array filled with a particular number, use np.full or np.repeat.

Although in this example both functions produce the same code, np.repeat is actually more powerful. For example, we can use it to create an array where multiple elements are repeated one after another:

```
array = np.repeat([0.0, 1.0], 5)
```

It creates an array of size 10 where the number 0 is repeated five times, and then the number 1 is repeated five times (figure C.3):

```
array([0., 0., 0., 0., 0., 1., 1., 1., 1., 1.])
```

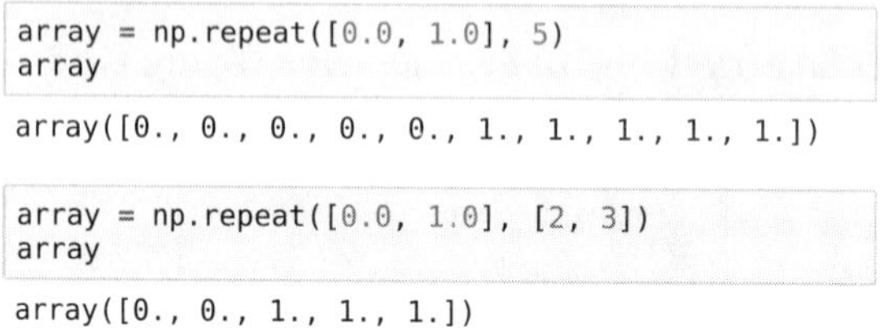

```
array = np.repeat([0.0, 1.0], 5)
array
```

```
array([0., 0., 0., 0., 0., 1., 1., 1., 1., 1.])
```

```
array = np.repeat([0.0, 1.0], [2, 3])
array
```

```
array([0., 0., 1., 1., 1.])
```

Figure C.3 The np.repeat function is more flexible than np.full: it can create arrays by repeating multiple elements.

We can be even more flexible and specify how many times each element should be repeated:

```
array = np.repeat([0.0, 1.0], [2, 3])
```

In this case, 0.0 is repeated two times and 1.0 is repeated three times:

```
array([0., 0., 1., 1., 1.])
```

Like with lists, we can access an element of an array with square brackets:

```
el = array[1]
print(el)
```

This code prints 0.0.

Unlike the usual Python lists, we can access multiple elements of the array at the same time by using a list with indices in the square brackets:

```
print(array[[4, 2, 0]])
```

The result is another array of size 3 consisting of elements of the original array indexed by 4, 2, and 0, respectively:

```
[1., 1., 0.]
```

We can also update the elements of the array using square brackets:

```
array[1] = 1
print(array)
```

Because we changed the element at index 1 from 0 to 1, it prints the following:

```
[0. 1. 1. 1. 1.]
```

If we already have a list with numbers, we can convert it to a NumPy array using np.array:

```
elements = [1, 2, 3, 4]
array = np.array(elements)
```

Now array is a NumPy array of size 4 with the same elements as the original list:

```
array([1, 2, 3, 4])
```

Another useful function for creating NumPy arrays is np.arange. It's the NumPy equivalent of Python's range:

```
np.arange(10)
```

It creates an array of length 10 with numbers from 0 to 9, and like in standard Python's range, 10 is not included in the array:

```
array([0, 1, 2, 3, 4, 5, 6, 7, 8, 9])
```

Often we need to create an array of a certain size filled with numbers between some number x and some number y. For example, imagine that we need to create an array with numbers from 0 to 1:

$$0.0, 0.1, 0.2, ..., 0.9, 1.0$$

We can use np.linspace:

```
thresholds = np.linspace(0, 1, 11)
```

This function takes three parameters:

- The starting number: in our case, we want to start from 0.
- The last number: we want to finish with 1.
- The length of the resulting array: in our case, we want 11 numbers in the array.

This code produces 11 numbers from 0 until 1 (figure C.4).

Python lists can usually contain elements of any type. This is not the case for NumPy arrays: all elements of an array must have the same type. These types are called *dtypes*.

```
thresholds = np.linspace(0, 1, 11)
thresholds
```

```
array([0. , 0.1, 0.2, 0.3, 0.4, 0.5, 0.6, 0.7, 0.8, 0.9, 1. ])
```

Figure C.4   The function `linspace` from NumPy produces a sequence of specified length (11) that starts at 0 and ends at 1.

There are four broad categories of dtypes:

- Unsigned integers (uint): integers that are always positive (or zero)
- Signed integers (int): integers that can be positive and negative
- Floats (float): real numbers
- Booleans (bool): only True and False values

Multiple variations of each dtype exist, depending on the number of bits used for representing the value in memory.

For uint we have four types: uint8, uint16, uint32, and uint64 of size 8, 16, 32, and 64 bits, respectively. Likewise, we have four types of int: int8, int16, int32, and int64. The more bits we use, the larger numbers we can store (table C.1).

Table C.1   Three common NumPy dtypes: uint, int, and float. Each dtype has multiple size variations ranging from 8 to 64 bits.

Size (bits)	uint	int	float
8	$0 .. 2^8 - 1$	$-2^7 .. 2^7 - 1$	–
16	$0 .. 2^{16} - 1$	$-2^{15} .. 2^{15} - 1$	Half precision
32	$0 .. 2^{32} - 1$	$-2^{31} .. 2^{31} - 1$	Single precision
64	$0 .. 2^{64} - 1$	$-2^{63} .. 2^{63} - 1$	Double precision

In the case of floats, we have three types: float16, float32, and float64. The more bits we use, the more precise the float is.

You can check the full list of different dtypes in the official documentation (https://docs.scipy.org/doc/numpy-1.13.0/user/basics.types.html).

NOTE   In NumPy, the default float dtype is float64, which uses 64 bits (8 bytes) for each number. For most machine learning applications, we don't need such precision and can reduce the memory footprint two times by using float32 instead of float64.

When creating an array, we can specify the dtype. For example, when using np.zeros and np.ones, the default dtype is float64. We can specify the dtype when creating an array (figure C.5):

```
zeros = np.zeros(10, dtype=np.uint8)
```

```
zeros = np.zeros(10, dtype=np.uint8)
zeros
```

```
array([0, 0, 0, 0, 0, 0, 0, 0, 0, 0], dtype=uint8)
```

Figure C.5 We can specify the dtype when creating an array.

When we have an array with integers and assign a number outside of the range, the number is cut: only the least significant bits are kept.

For example, suppose we use the `uint8` array `zeros` we just created. Because the dtype is `uint8`, the largest number it can store is 255. Let's try to assign 300 to the first element of the array:

```
zeros[0] = 300
print(zeros[0])
```

Because 300 is greater than 255, only the least significant bits are kept, so this code prints 44.

> **WARNING** Be careful when choosing the dtype for an array. If you acciden-
> tally choose a dtype that's too narrow, NumPy won't warn you when you put
> in a big number. It will simply truncate them.

Iterating over all elements of an array is similar to list. We simply can use a `for` loop:

```
for i in np.arange(5):
    print(i)
```

This code prints numbers from 0 to 4:

```
0
1
2
3
4
```

C.1.2 *Two-dimensional NumPy arrays*

So far we have covered one-dimensional NumPy arrays. We can think of these arrays as vectors. However, for machine learning applications, having only vectors is not enough: we also often need matrices.

In plain Python, we'd use a list of lists for that. In NumPy, the equivalent is a two-dimensional array.

To create a two-dimensional array with zeros, we simply use a tuple instead of a number when invoking `np.zeros`:

```
zeros = np.zeros((5, 2), dtype=np.float32)
```

We use a tuple (5, 2), so it creates an array of zeros with five rows and two columns (figure C.6).

```
zeros = np.zeros((5, 2), dtype=np.float32)
zeros
```
```
array([[0., 0.],
       [0., 0.],
       [0., 0.],
       [0., 0.],
       [0., 0.]], dtype=float32)
```

Figure C.6   To create a two-dimensional array, use a tuple with two elements. The first element specifies the number of rows, and the second, the number of columns.

In the same way, we can use np.ones or np.fill — instead of a single number, we put in a tuple.

The dimensionality of an array is called *shape*. This is the first parameter we pass to the np.zeros function: it specifies how many rows and columns the array will have. To get the shape of an array, use the shape property:

```
print(zeros.shape)
```

When we execute it, we see (5, 2).

It's possible to convert a list of lists to a NumPy array. As with usual lists of numbers, simply use np.array for that:

```
numbers = [            ←──┐  Creates a
    [1, 2, 3],            │  list of lists
    [4, 5, 6],
    [7, 8, 9]
]                              ┐  Converts the list to
                               │  a two-dimensional
numbers = np.array(numbers)  ←─┘  array
```

After executing this code, numbers becomes a NumPy array with shape (3, 3). When we print it, we get

```
array([[1, 2, 3],
       [4, 5, 6],
       [7, 8, 9]])
```

To access an element of a two-dimensional array, we need to use two numbers inside the brackets:

```
print(numbers[0, 1])
```

This code will access the row indexed by 0 and column indexed by 1. So it will print 2.

As with one-dimensional arrays, we use the assignment operator (=) to change an individual value of a two-dimensional array:

```
numbers[0, 1] = 10
```

When we execute it, the content of the array changes:

```
array([[ 1, 10,  3],
       [ 4,  5,  6],
       [ 7,  8,  9]])
```

If instead of two numbers we put only one, we get the entire row, which is a one-dimensional NumPy array:

```
numbers[0]
```

This code returns the entire row indexed by 0:

```
array([1 2 3])
```

To access a column of a two-dimensional array, we use a colon (:) instead of the first element. Like with rows, the result is also a one-dimensional NumPy array:

```
numbers[:, 1]
```

When we execute it, we see the entire column:

```
array([2 5 8])
```

It's also possible to overwrite the content of the entire row or a column using the assignment operator. For example, suppose we want to replace a row in the matrix:

```
numbers[1] = [1, 1, 1]
```

This results in the following change:

```
array([[ 1, 10,  3],
       [ 1,  1,  1],
       [ 7,  8,  9]])
```

Likewise, we can replace the content of an entire column:

```
numbers[:, 2] = [9, 9, 9]
```

As a result, the last column changes:

```
array([[ 1, 10,  9],
       [ 1,  1,  9],
       [ 7,  8,  9]])
```

C.1.3   *Randomly generated arrays*

Often it's useful to generate arrays filled with random numbers. To do this in NumPy, we use the np.random module.

For example, to generate a 5 × 2 array of random numbers uniformly distributed between 0 and 1, use np.random.rand:

```
arr = np.random.rand(5, 2)
```

When we run it, it generates an array that looks like this:

```
array([[0.64814431, 0.51283823],
       [0.40306102, 0.59236807],
       [0.94772704, 0.05777113],
       [0.32034757, 0.15150334],
       [0.10377917, 0.68786012]])
```

Every time we run the code, it generates a different result. Sometimes we need the results to be reproducible, which means that if we want to execute this code later, we will get the same results. To achieve that, we can set the seed of the random-number generator. Once the seed is set, the random-number generator produces the same sequence every time we run the code:

```
np.random.seed(2)
arr = np.random.rand(5, 2)
```

On Ubuntu Linux version 18.04 with NumPy version 1.17.2, it generates the following array:

```
array([[0.4359949 , 0.02592623],
       [0.54966248, 0.43532239],
       [0.4203678 , 0.33033482],
       [0.20464863, 0.61927097],
       [0.29965467, 0.26682728]])
```

No matter how many times we re-execute this cell, the results are the same.

> **WARNING**   Fixing the seed of the random-number generator guarantees that the generator produces the same results when executed on the same OS with the same NumPy version. However, there's no guarantee that updating the NumPy version will not affect reproducibility: a change of version may result in changes in the random-number generator algorithm, and that may lead to different results across versions.

If instead of uniform distribution, we want to sample from the standard normal distribution, we use np.random.randn:

```
arr = np.random.randn(5, 2)
```

> **NOTE** Every time we generate a random array in this appendix, we make sure we fix the seed number before generating it, even if we don't explicitly specify it in the code — we do it to ensure consistency. We use 2 as the seed. There's no particular reason for this number.

To generate uniformly distributed random integers between 0 and 100 (exclusive), we can use `np.random.randint`:

```
randint = np.random.randint(low=0, high=100, size=(5, 2))
```

When executing the code, we get a 5×2 NumPy array of integers:

```
array([[40, 15],
       [72, 22],
       [43, 82],
       [75,  7],
       [34, 49]])
```

Another quite useful feature is shuffling an array — rearranging the elements of an array in random order. For example, let's create an array with a range and then shuffle it:

```
idx = np.arange(5)
print('before shuffle', idx)

np.random.shuffle(idx)
print('after shuffle', idx)
```

When we run the code, we see the following:

```
before shuffle [0 1 2 3 4]
after shuffle  [2 3 0 4 1]
```

C.2 NumPy operations

NumPy comes with a wide range of operations that work with the NumPy arrays. In this section, we cover operations that we'll need throughout the book.

C.2.1 Element-wise operations

NumPy arrays support all the arithmetic operations: addition (+), subtraction (−), multiplication (*), division (/) and others.

To illustrate these operations, let's first create an array using `arange`:

```
rng - np.arange(5)
```

This array contains five elements from 0 to 4:

```
array([0, 1, 2, 3, 4])
```

To multiply every element of the array by two, we simply use the multiplication operator (*):

```
rng * 2
```

As a result, we get a new array where each element from the original array is multiplied by two:

```
array([0, 2, 4, 6, 8])
```

Note that we don't need to explicitly write any loops here to apply the multiplication operation individually to each element: NumPy does it for us. We can say that the multiplication operation is applied *element-wise* — to all elements at once. The addition (+), subtraction (–) and division (/) operations are also element-wise and require no explicit loops.

Such element-wise operations are often called *vectorized*: the for loop happens internally in native code (written C and Fortran), so the operations are very fast!

NOTE   Whenever possible, use vectorized operations from NumPy instead of loops: they are always a magnitude faster.

In the previous code, we used only one operation. It's possible to apply multiple operations at once in one expression:

```
(rng - 1) * 3 / 2 + 1
```

This code creates a new array with the result:

```
array([-0.5, 1. , 2.5, 4. , 5.5])
```

Note that the original array contains integers, but because we used the division operation, the result is an array with float numbers.

Previously, our code involved an array and simple Python numbers. It's also possible to do element-wise operations with two arrays if they have the same shape.

For example, suppose we have two arrays, one containing numbers from 0 to 4, and another containing some random noise:

```
noise = 0.01 * np.random.rand(5)
numbers = np.arange(5)
```

We sometimes need to do that for modeling not-ideal real-life data: in reality there are always imperfections when data is collected, and we can model these imperfections by adding noise.

We build the noise array by first generating numbers between 0 and 1 and then multiplying them by 0.01. This effectively generates random numbers between 0 and 0.01:

```
array([0.00435995, 0.00025926, 0.00549662, 0.00435322, 0.00420368])
```

We can then add these two arrays and get a third one with the sum:

```
result = numbers + noise
```

In this array, each element of the result is the sum of the respective elements of the two other arrays:

```
array([0.00435995, 1.00025926, 2.00549662, 3.00435322, 4.00420368])
```

We can round the numbers to any precision using the round method:

```
result.round(4)
```

It's also an element-wise operation, so it's applied to all the elements at once and the numbers are rounded to the fourth digit:

```
array([0.0044, 1.0003, 2.0055, 3.0044, 4.0042])
```

Sometimes we need to square all the elements of an array. For that, we can simply multiply the array by itself. Let's first generate an array:

```
pred = np.random.rand(3).round(2)
```

This array contains three random numbers:

```
array([0.44, 0.03, 0.55])
```

Now we can multiply it by itself:

```
square = pred * pred
```

As a result, we get a new array where each element of the original array is squared:

```
array([0.1936, 0.0009, 0.3025])
```

Alternatively, we can use the power operator (**):

```
square = pred ** 2
```

Both approaches lead to the same results (figure C.7).

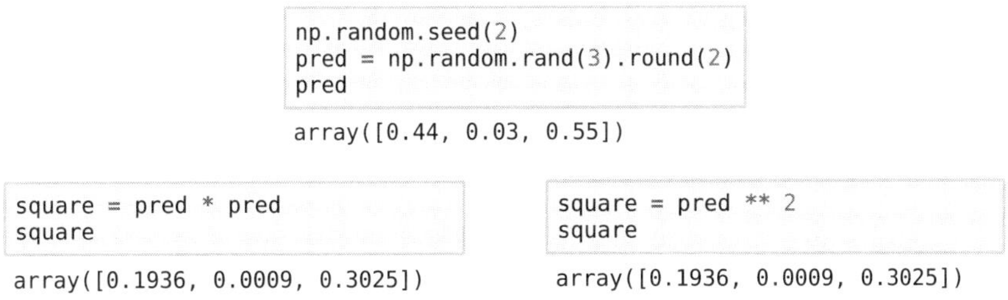

```
np.random.seed(2)
pred = np.random.rand(3).round(2)
pred
```

```
array([0.44, 0.03, 0.55])
```

```
square = pred * pred
square
```

```
square = pred ** 2
square
```

```
array([0.1936, 0.0009, 0.3025])
```

```
array([0.1936, 0.0009, 0.3025])
```

Figure C.7   There are two ways to square the elements of an array: multiply the array with itself or use the power operation (**).

Other useful element-wise operations that we might need for machine learning applications are exponent, logarithm, and square root:

```
pred_exp  = np.exp(pred)          Computes the exponent
pred_log  = np.log(pred)          Computes the logarithm
pred_sqrt = np.sqrt(pred)         Computes the square root
```

Boolean operations can also be applied to NumPy arrays element-wise. To illustrate them, let's again generate an array with some random numbers:

```
pred = np.random.rand(3).round(2)
```

This array contains the following numbers:

```
array([0.44, 0.03, 0.55])
```

We can see the elements that are greater than 0.5:

```
result = pred >= 0.5
```

As a result, we get an array with three Boolean values:

```
array([False, False, True])
```

We know that only the last element of the original array is greater than 0.5, so it's `True` and the rest are `False`.

As with arithmetic operations, we can apply Boolean operations on two NumPy arrays of the same shape. Let's generate two random arrays:

```
pred1 = np.random.rand(3).round(2)
pred2 = np.random.rand(3).round(2)
```

The arrays have the following values:

```
array([0.44, 0.03, 0.55])
array([0.44, 0.42, 0.33])
```

Now we can use the greater-than-or-equal-to operator (>=) to compare the values of these arrays:

```
pred1 >= pred2
```

As a result, we get an array with Booleans (figure C.8):

```
array([ True, False, True])
```

```
pred1 = np.random.rand(3).round(2)
pred1
```

```
array([0.44, 0.03, 0.55])
```

```
pred2 = np.random.rand(3).round(2)
pred2
```

```
array([0.44, 0.42, 0.33])
```

```
pred1 >= pred2
```

```
array([ True, False,  True])
```

Figure C.8   Boolean operations in NumPy are element-wise and can be applied to two arrays of the same shape for comparing values.

Finally, we can apply logical operations — like logical and (&) and or (|) — to Boolean NumPy arrays. Let's again generate two random arrays:

```
pred1 = np.random.rand(5) >= 0.3
pred2 = np.random.rand(5) >= 0.4
```

The generated arrays have the following values:

```
array([ True, False, True])
array([ True, True, False])
```

Like arithmetical operations, logical operators are also element-wise. For example, to compute the element-wise and, we simply use the & operator with arrays (figure C.9):

```
res_and = pred1 & pred2
```

As a result, we get

```
array([ True, False, False])
```

The logical or works in the same way (figure C.9):

```
res_or = pred1 | pred2
```

```
pred1 = np.random.rand(3) >= 0.3
pred1
```

```
array([ True, False,  True])
```

```
pred2 = np.random.rand(3) >= 0.4
pred2
```

```
array([ True,  True, False])
```

```
pred1 & pred2
```

```
array([ True, False, False])
```

```
pred1 | pred2
```

```
array([ True,  True,  True])
```

Figure C.9   Logic operations like logical and logical or can also be applied element-wise.

This creates the following array:

```
array([ True, True, True])
```

C.2.2 *Summarizing operations*

Whereas element-wise operations take in an array and produce an array of the same shape, the summarizing operations take in an array and produce a single number.

For example, we can generate an array and then calculate the sum of all elements:

```
pred = np.random.rand(3).round(2)
pred_sum = pred.sum()
```

In this example, pred is

```
array([0.44, 0.03, 0.55])
```

Then pred_sum is the sum of all three elements, which is 1.02:

$$0.44 + 0.03 + 0.55 = 1.02$$

Other summarizing operations include min, mean, max and std:

```
print('min = %.2f' % pred.min())
print('mean = %.2f' % pred.mean())
print('max = %.2f' % pred.max())
print('std = %.2f' % pred.std())
```

After running this code, it produces

```
min = 0.03
mean = 0.34
max = 0.55
std = 0.22
```

When we have a two-dimensional array, summarizing operations also produce a single number. However, it's also possible to apply these operations to rows or columns separately.

For example, let's generate a 4 × 3 array:

```
matrix = np.random.rand(4, 3).round(2)
```

This generates an array:

```
array([[0.44, 0.03, 0.55],
       [0.44, 0.42, 0.33],
       [0.2 , 0.62, 0.3 ],
       [0.27, 0.62, 0.53]])
```

When we invoke the max method, it returns a single number:

```
matrix.max()
```

The result is 0.62, which is the maximum number across all elements of the matrix.

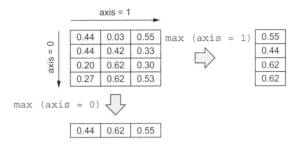

Figure C.10 We can specify the axis along which we apply the operation: `axis=1` means applying it to rows, and `axis=0` means applying it to columns.

If we now want to find the largest number in each row, we can use the `max` method specifying the axis along which we apply this operation. When we want to do it for rows, we use `axis=1` (figure C.10):

```
matrix.max(axis=1)
```

As a result, we get an array with four numbers — the largest number in each row:

```
array([0.55, 0.44, 0.62, 0.62])
```

Likewise, we can find the largest number in each column. For that, we use `axis=0`:

```
matrix.max(axis=0)
```

This time the result is three numbers — the largest numbers in each column:

```
array([0.44, 0.62, 0.55])
```

Other operations — `sum`, `min`, `mean`, `std`, and many others — can also can take `axis` as an argument. For example, we can easily calculate the sum of elements of every row:

```
matrix.sum(axis=1)
```

When executing it, we get four numbers:

```
array([1.02, 1.19, 1.12, 1.42])
```

C.2.3   Sorting

Often we need to sort elements of an array. Let's see how to do it in NumPy. First, let's generate a one-dimensional array with four elements:

```
pred = np.random.rand(4).round(2)
```

The array we generate contains the following elements:

```
array([0.44, 0.03, 0.55, 0.44])
```

To create a sorted copy of the array, use `np.sort`:

```
np.sort(pred)
```

It returns an array with all the elements sorted:

```
array([0.03, 0.44, 0.44, 0.55])
```

Because it creates a copy and sorts it, the original array `pred` remains unchanged.

If we want to sort the elements of the array in place without creating another array, we invoke the method `sort` on the array itself:

```
pred.sort()
```

Now the array `pred` is sorted.

When it comes to sorting, we have another useful thing: `argsort`. Instead of sorting an array, it returns the indices of the array in the sorted order (figure C.11):

```
idx = pred.argsort()
```

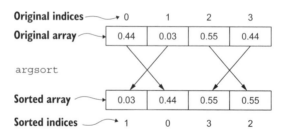

Figure C.11   The function `sort` sorts the array, whereas `argsort` produces an array of indices that sort the array.

Now the array `idx` contains indices in the sorted order:

```
array([1, 0, 3, 2])
```

Now we can use the array `idx` with indexes to get the original array in the sorted order:

```
pred[idx]
```

As we see, it's indeed sorted:

```
array([0.03, 0.44, 0.44, 0.55])
```

C.2.4 *Reshaping and combining*

Each NumPy array has a shape, which specifies its size. For a one-dimensional array, it's the length of the array, and for a two-dimensional array, it's the number of rows and columns. We already know that we can access the shape of an array by using the shape property:

```
rng = np.arange(12)
rng.shape
```

The shape of rng is (12), which means that it's a one-dimensional array of length 12. Because we used np.arange to create the array, it contains the numbers from 0 to 11 (inclusive):

```
array([ 0, 1, 2, 3, 4, 5, 6, 7, 8, 9, 10, 11])
```

It's possible to change the shape of an array from one-dimensional to two-dimensional. We use the reshape method for that:

```
rng.reshape(4, 3)
```

As a result, we get a matrix with four rows and three columns:

```
array([[ 0,  1,  2],
       [ 3,  4,  5],
       [ 6,  7,  8],
       [ 9, 10, 11]])
```

The reshaping worked because it was possible to rearrange 12 original elements into four rows with three columns. In other words, the total number of elements didn't change. However, if we attempt to reshape it to (4, 4), it won't let us:

```
rng.reshape(4, 4)
```

When we do it, NumPy raises a ValueError:

```
---------------------------------------------------------------------------
ValueError                                Traceback (most recent call last)
<ipython-input-176-880fb98fa9c8> in <module>
----> 1 rng.reshape(4, 4)

ValueError: cannot reshape array of size 12 into shape (4,4)
```

Sometimes we need to create a new NumPy array by putting multiple arrays together. Let's see how to do it.

First, we create two arrays, which we'll use for illustration:

```
vec = np.arange(3)
mat = np.arange(6).reshape(3, 2)
```

The first one, vec, is a one-dimensional array with three elements:

```
array([0, 1, 2])
```

The second one, mat, is a two-dimensional one with three rows and two columns:

```
array([[0, 1],
       [2, 3],
       [4, 5]])
```

The simplest way to combine two NumPy arrays is using the np.concatenate function:

```
np.concatenate([vec, vec])
```

It takes in a list of one-dimensional arrays and combines them into one larger one-dimensional array. In our case, we pass vec two times, so as a result, we have an array of length six:

```
array([0, 1, 2, 0, 1, 2])
```

We can achieve the same result using np.hstack, which is short for horizontal stack:

```
np.hstack([vec, vec])
```

It again takes a list of arrays and stacks them horizontally, producing a larger array:

```
array([0, 1, 2, 0, 1, 2])
```

We can also apply np.hstack to two-dimensional arrays:

```
np.hstack([mat, mat])
```

The result is another matrix where the original matrices are stacked horizontally by columns:

```
array([[0, 1, 0, 1],
       [2, 3, 2, 3],
       [4, 5, 4, 5]])
```

However, in case of two-dimensional arrays, np.concatenate works differently from np.hstack:

```
np.concatenate([mat, mat])
```

When we apply np.concatenate to matrices, it stacks them vertically, not horizontally, like one-dimensional arrays, creating a new matrix with six rows:

```
array([[0, 1],
       [2, 3],
       [4, 5],
       [0, 1],
```

```
         [2, 3],
         [4, 5]])
```

Another useful method for combining NumPy arrays is `np.column_stack`: it allows us to stack vectors and matrices together. For example, suppose we want to add an extra column to our matrix. For that we simply pass a list that contains the vector and then the matrix:

```
np.column_stack([vec, mat])
```

As a result, we have a new matrix, where `vec` becomes the first column, and the rest of the `mat` goes after it:

```
array([[0, 0, 1],
       [1, 2, 3],
       [2, 4, 5]])
```

We can apply `np.column_stack` to two vectors:

```
np.column_stack([vec, vec])
```

This produces a two-column matrix as a result:

```
array([[0, 0],
       [1, 1],
       [2, 2]])
```

Like with `np.hstack`, which stacks arrays horizontally, there's `np.vstack` that stacks arrays vertically:

```
np.vstack([vec, vec])
```

When we vertically stack two vectors, we get a matrix with two rows:

```
array([[0, 1, 2],
       [0, 1, 2]])
```

We can also stack two matrices vertically:

```
np.vstack([mat, mat])
```

The result is the same as `np.concatenate([mat, mat])` — we get a new matrix with six rows:

```
array([[0, 1],
       [2, 3],
       [4, 5],
       [0, 1],
       [2, 3],
       [4, 5]])
```

The np.vstack function can also stack together vectors and matrices, in effect creating a matrix with new rows:

```
np.vstack([vec, mat.T])
```

When we do it, vec becomes the first row in the new matrix:

```
array([[0, 1, 2],
       [0, 2, 4],
       [1, 3, 5]])
```

Note that in this code, we used the T property of mat. This is a matrix transposition operation, which changes rows of a matrix to columns:

```
mat.T
```

Originally, mat has the following data:

```
array([[0, 1],
       [2, 3],
       [4, 5]])
```

After transposition, what was a column becomes a row:

```
array([[0, 2, 4],
       [1, 3, 5]])
```

C.2.5   *Slicing and filtering*

Like with Python lists, we can also use slicing for accessing a part of a NumPy array. For example, suppose we have a 5 × 3 matrix:

```
mat = np.arange(15).reshape(5, 3)
```

This matrix has five rows and three columns:

```
array([[ 0,  1,  2],
       [ 3,  4,  5],
       [ 6,  7,  8],
       [ 9, 10, 11],
       [12, 13, 14]])
```

We can access parts of this matrix by using slicing. For example, we can get the first free rows using the range operator (:):

```
mat[:3]
```

It returns rows indexed by 0, 1, and 2 (3 is not included):

```
array([[0, 1, 2],
       [3, 4, 5],
       [6, 7, 8]])
```

If we need only rows 1 and 2, we specify both the beginning and the end of the range:

```
mat[1:3]
```

This gives us the rows we need:

```
array([[3, 4, 5],
       [6, 7, 8]])
```

Like with rows, we can select only some columns; for example, the first two columns:

```
mat[:, :2]
```

Here we have two ranges:

- The first one is simply a colon (:) with no start and end, which means "include all rows."
- The second one is a range that includes columns 0 and 1 (2 not included).

So as a result, we get

```
array([[ 0,  1],
       [ 3,  4],
       [ 6,  7],
       [ 9, 10],
       [12, 13]])
```

Of course, we can combine both and select any matrix part we want:

```
mat[1:3, :2]
```

This gives us rows 1 and 2 and columns 0 and 1:

```
array([[3, 4],
       [6, 7]])
```

If we don't need a range, but rather some specific rows or columns, we can simply provide a list of indices:

```
mat[[3, 0, 1]]
```

This gives us three rows indexed at 3, 0, and 1:

```
array([[ 9, 10, 11],
       [ 0,  1,  2],
       [ 3,  4,  5]])
```

Instead of individual indices, it's possible to use a binary mask to specify which rows to select. For example, suppose we want to choose rows where the first element of a row is an odd number.

To check if the first element is odd, we need to do the following:

1 Select the first column of the matrix.
2 Apply the mod 2 operation (%) to all the elements to compute the remainder of the division by 2.
3 If the remainder is 1, then the number is odd, and if 0, the number is even.

This translates to the following NumPy expression:

```
mat[:, 0] % 2 == 1
```

At the end it produces an array with Booleans:

```
array([False, True, False, True, False])
```

We see that the expression is `True` for rows 1 and 3 and `False` for rows 0, 2, and 5.

Now we can use this expression to select only rows where the expression is `True`:

```
mat[mat[:, 0] % 2 == 1]
```

This gives us a matrix with only two rows: rows 1 and 3:

```
array([[ 3,  4,  5],
       [ 9, 10, 11]])
```

C.3   *Linear algebra*

One of the reasons NumPy is so popular is its support of linear algebra operations. NumPy delegates all the internal computations to BLAS and LAPACK — time-proven libraries for efficient low-level computations — and this is why it's blazingly fast.

In this section, we take a short overview of the linear algebra operations we need throughout the book. We start with the most common ones: matrix and vector multiplications.

C.3.1   *Multiplication*

In linear algebra, we have multiple types of multiplication:

- Vector-vector multiplication: multiplying a vector by another vector
- Matrix-vector multiplication: multiplying a matrix by a vector
- Matrix-matrix multiplication: multiplying a matrix by another matrix

Let's take a closer look at each of them and see how to do them in NumPy.

VECTOR-VECTOR MULTIPLICATION
Vector-vector multiplication involves two vectors. It's typically called *dot product* or *scalar product*; it takes two vectors and produces a *scalar* — a single number.

Suppose we have two vectors, u and v, each of length n; then the dot product between u and v is

$$u^T v = \sum_{i=1}^{n} u_i v_i = u_1 v_1 + u_2 v_2 + \ldots + u_n v_n$$

NOTE In this appendix, the elements of a vector of length n are indexed from 0 to $n-1$: this way it's easier to map the concepts from the mathematical notation to NumPy.

This directly translates to Python. If we have two NumPy arrays u and v, the dot product between them is

```
dot = 0

for i in range(n):
    dot = u[i] * v[i]
```

Of course, we can take advantage of vectorized operations in NumPy and calculate it with a one-line expression:

```
(u * v).sum()
```

However, because it's quite a common operation, it's implemented inside NumPy in the dot method. So, to calculate the dot product, we simply invoke dot:

```
u.dot(v)
```

MATRIX-VECTOR MULTIPLICATION

Another type of multiplication is matrix-vector multiplication.

Suppose we have a matrix X of size m by n and a vector u of size n. If we multiply X by u, we get another vector of size m (figure C.12):

$$Xu = v$$

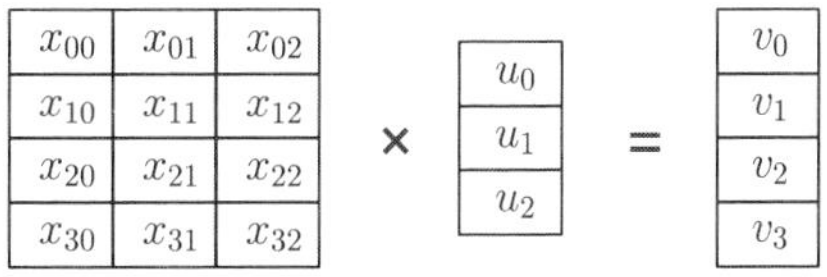

Figure C.12 When we multiply a 4 × 3 matrix by a vector of length 3, we get a vector of length 4.

We can think of the matrix X as a collection of n row-vectors x_i, each of size m (figure C.13).

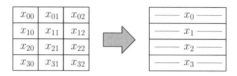

Figure C.13   We can think of the matrix X as of four row-vectors x_i, each of size 3.

Then we can represent matrix-vector multiplication Xu as m vector-vector multiplications between each row x_i and the vector u. The result is another vector — vector v (figure C.14).

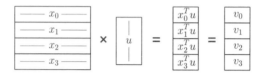

Figure C.14   The matrix-vector multiplication is a set of vector-vector multiplications: we multiply each row x_i of the matrix X by the vector u and as a result get the vector v.

Translating this idea to Python is straightforward:

```
v = np.zeros(m)          ⊲─────┘ Creates an empty vector v

for i in range(m):       ⊲─────┘ For each row x_i of X
    v[i] = X[i].dot(u)   ⊲─────── Computes the ith element of
                                  v as a dot product x_i * u
```

Like with vector-vector multiplication, we can use the dot method of the matrix X (a two-dimensional array) to multiply it by vector u (a one-dimensional array):

```
v = X.dot(u)
```

The result is the vector v — a one-dimensional NumPy array.

MATRIX-MATRIX MULTIPLICATION

Finally, we have a matrix-matrix multiplication. Suppose we have two matrices, X of size m by n and U of size n by k. Then the result is another matrix V of size m by k (figure C.15):

$$XU = V$$

The easiest way to understand matrix-matrix multiplication is to consider U as a set of columns: $u_0, u_1, \ldots, u_{k-1}$ (figure C.16).

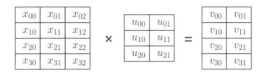

Figure C.15 When we multiply a 4 × 3 matrix *X* by a 3 × 2 matrix *U*, we get a 4 × 2 matrix *V*.

Figure C.16 We can think of *U* as a collection of column vectors. In this case, we have two columns: u_0 and u_1.

Then matrix-matrix multiplication XU is a set of matrix-vector multiplications Xu_i. The result of each multiplication is a vector v_i, which is the ith column of the resulting matrix V (figure C.17):

$$v_i = Xu_i$$

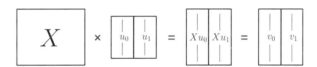

Figure C.17 We can think of matrix-matrix multiplication *XU* as a set of matrix-vector multiplications $v_i = Xu_i$, where u_is are the columns of *U*. The result is a matrix *V* with all the v_i's stacked together.

To implement it in NumPy, we can simply do this:

```
V = np.zeros((m, k))          ◁─────  Creates an empty matrix V

for i in range(k):            ◁─────  For each column uᵢ of U
    vi = X.dot(U[:, i])       ◁───┐
    V[:, i] = vi    ◁───┐          Computes vᵢ as matrix-vector
                        │          multiplication X * uᵢ
        Passing vᵢ as the │
        ith column of V   │
```

Recall that U[:, i] means getting the ith column. Then we multiply X by that column and get vi. With V[:, i], and because we have assignment (=), we overwrite the ith column of V with vi.

Of course, in NumPy there's a shortcut for that — it's again the dot method:

```
V = X.dot(U)
```

C.3.2   *Matrix inverse*

The inverse of a square matrix X is the matrix X^{-1} such that $X^{-1}X = I$, where I is the identity matrix. The identity matrix I doesn't change a vector when we perform matrix-vector multiplication:

$$Iv = v$$

Why do we need it? Suppose we have a system:

$$Ax = b$$

We know the matrix A and the resulting vector b, but don't know the vector x — we want to find it. In other words, we want to *solve* this system.

One of the possible ways of doing it is

- Compute A^{-1}, which is the inverse of A, and then
- Multiply both sides of the equation by the inverse A^{-1}

When doing so, we get

$$A^{-1}Ax = A^{-1}b$$

Because $A^{-1}A = I$, we have

$$Ix = A^{-1}b$$

Or

$$x = A^{-1}b$$

In NumPy, to compute the inverse, we use np.linalg.inv:

```
A = np.array([
    [0, 1, 2],
    [1, 2, 3],
    [2, 3, 3]
])

Ainv = np.linalg.inv(A)
```

For this particular square matrix A, it's possible to compute its inverse, so Ainv has the following values:

```
array([[-3.,   3.,  -1.],
       [ 3.,  -4.,   2.],
       [-1.,   2.,  -1.]])
```

We can verify that if we multiply the matrix with its inverse, we get the identity matrix:

```
A.dot(Ainv)
```

The result is indeed the identity matrix:

```
array([[1., 0., 0.],
       [0., 1., 0.],
       [0., 0., 1.]])
```

> **NOTE** If all you want is to solve the equation $Ax = b$, then you don't really have to compute the inverse. From a computational point of view, calculating the inverse is an expensive operation. Instead, we should use np.linalg .solve, which is a magnitude faster:
>
> ```
> b = np.array([1, 2, 3])
> x = np.linalg.solve(A, b)
> ```

In this book, when computing the weights for linear regression, we use the inverse for simplicity: it makes the code easier to understand.

There are matrices for which there's no inverse. First of all, it's not possible to invert nonsquare matrices. Also, not all square matrices can be inverted: there are *singular* matrices — matrices for which there exists no inverse matrix.

When we try to invert a singular matrix in NumPy, we get an error:

```
B = np.array([
    [0, 1, 1],
    [1, 2, 3],
    [2, 3, 5]
])

np.linalg.inv(B)
```

This code raises LinAlgError:

```
-------------------------------------------------------------------------
LinAlgError                         Traceback (most recent call last)
<ipython-input-286-14528a9f848e> in <module>
      5 ])
      6
----> 7 np.linalg.inv(B)
```

```
<__array_function__ internals> in inv(*args, **kwargs)

<...>

LinAlgError: Singular matrix
```

C.3.3   *Normal equation*

In chapter 2, we used the normal equation to compute the weights vector for linear regression. In this section, we briefly outline how to arrive at the formula but without going into details. For more information, please refer to any linear algebra textbook.

This section may look math-heavy, but feel free to skip it: it will not affect your understanding of the book. If you studied the normal equation and linear regression in college, but already forgot most of it, this section should help you refresh your memory.

Suppose we have a matrix X with observations and a vector y with results. We want to find such vector w that

$$Xw = y$$

However, because X is not a square matrix, we cannot simply invert it, and the exact solution to this system doesn't exist. We can try to find an inexact solution and do the following trick. We multiply both sides by the transpose of X:

$$X^T Xw = X^T y$$

Now $X^T X$ is a square matrix, which should be possible to invert. Let's call this matrix C:

$$C = X^T X$$

The equation becomes

$$Cw = X^T y$$

In this equation, $X^T y$ is also a vector: when we multiply a matrix by a vector, we get a vector. Let's call it z. So now we have

$$Cw = z$$

This system now has an exact solution, which is the best approximation solution to the system we originally wanted to solve. Proving this is out of the scope of the book, so please refer to a textbook for more details.

To solve the system, we can invert C and multiply both sides by it:

$$C^{-1}Cw = C^{-1}z$$

Or

$$w = C^{-1}z$$

Now we have the solution for w. Let's rewrite it in terms of the original X and y:

$$w = (X^TX)^{-1}X^Ty$$

This is the normal equation, which finds the best approximate solution w to the original system $Xw = y$.

It's quite simple to translate to NumPy:

```
C = X.T.dot(X)
Cinv = np.linalg.inv(C)
w = Cinv.dot(X.T).dot(y)
```

Now the array w contains the best approximate solution to the system.

appendix D
Introduction to Pandas

We don't expect any Pandas knowledge from the readers of this book. However, we use it extensively throughout the book. When we do, we try to explain the code, but it's not always possible to cover everything in detail.

In this appendix, we give a more in-depth introduction to Pandas, covering all the features we use in the chapters.

D.1   Pandas

Pandas is a Python library for working with tabular data. It's a popular and convenient tool for data manipulation. It's especially useful when preparing data for training machine learning models.

If you use Anaconda, it already has Pandas preinstalled. If not, install it with `pip`:

```
pip install pandas
```

To experiment with Pandas, let's create a notebook called appendix-d-pandas and use it for running the code from this appendix.

First, we need to import it:

```
import pandas as pd
```

Like with NumPy, we follow a convention and use an alias, `pd`, instead of the full name.

We start by exploring Pandas from its core data structures: DataFrames and Series.

D.1.1 *DataFrame*

In Pandas, a *DataFrame* is simply a table: a data structure with rows and columns (figure D.1).

	Make	Model	Year	Engine HP	Engine Cylinders	Transmission Type	Vehicle_Style	MSRP
0	Nissan	Stanza	1991	138.0	4	MANUAL	sedan	2000
1	Hyundai	Sonata	2017	NaN	4	AUTOMATIC	Sedan	27150
2	Lotus	Elise	2010	218.0	4	MANUAL	convertible	54990
3	GMC	Acadia	2017	194.0	4	AUTOMATIC	4dr SUV	34450
4	Nissan	Frontier	2017	261.0	6	MANUAL	Pickup	32340

Figure D.1   A DataFrame in Pandas: a table with five rows and eight columns

To create a DataFrame, we first need to create some data that we'll put in the table. It can be a list of lists with some values:

```
data = [
    ['Nissan', 'Stanza', 1991, 138, 4, 'MANUAL', 'sedan', 2000],
    ['Hyundai', 'Sonata', 2017, None, 4, 'AUTOMATIC', 'Sedan', 27150],
    ['Lotus', 'Elise', 2010, 218, 4, 'MANUAL', 'convertible', 54990],
    ['GMC', 'Acadia',  2017, 194, 4, 'AUTOMATIC', '4dr SUV', 34450],
    ['Nissan', 'Frontier', 2017, 261, 6, 'MANUAL', 'Pickup', 32340],
]
```

This data is taken from the price-prediction dataset we use in chapter 2: we have some car characteristics like model, make, year of manufacture, and transmission type.

When creating a DataFrame, we need to know what each of the columns contains, so let's create a list with column names:

```
columns = [
    'Make', 'Model', 'Year', 'Engine HP', 'Engine Cylinders',
    'Transmission Type', 'Vehicle_Style', 'MSRP'
]
```

Now we're ready to create a DataFrame from it. For that, we use pd.DataFrame:

```
df = pd.DataFrame(data, columns=columns)
```

It creates a DataFrame with five rows and eight columns (figure D.1).

The first thing we can do with a DataFrame is look at the first few rows in the data to get an idea of what's inside. For that, we use the head method:

```
df.head(n=2)
```

It shows the first two rows of the DataFrame. The number of rows to display is controlled by the n parameter (figure D.2).

```
df.head(n=2)
```

	Make	Model	Year	Engine HP	Engine Cylinders	Transmission Type	Vehicle_Style	MSRP
0	Nissan	Stanza	1991	138.0	4	MANUAL	sedan	2000
1	Hyundai	Sonata	2017	NaN	4	AUTOMATIC	Sedan	27150

Figure D.2   Previewing the content of a DataFrame with `head`

Alternatively, we can use a list of dictionaries to create a DataFrame:

```
data = [
    {
        "Make": "Nissan",
        "Model": "Stanza",
        "Year": 1991,
        "Engine HP": 138.0,
        "Engine Cylinders": 4,
        "Transmission Type": "MANUAL",
        "Vehicle_Style": "sedan",
        "MSRP": 2000
    },
    ... # more rows
]

df = pd.DataFrame(data)
```

In this case, we don't need to specify column names: Pandas automatically takes them from the fields of the dictionaries.

D.1.2   *Series*

Each column in a DataFrame is a *Series* — a special data structure for containing values of one type. In a way, it's quite similar to one-dimensional NumPy arrays.

We can access the values of a column in two ways. First, we can use the dot notation (figure D.3, A):

```
df.Make
```

The other way is to use brackets notation (figure D.3, B):

```
df['Make']
```

The result is exactly the same: a Pandas Series with the values from the Make column.

If a column name contains spaces or other special characters, then we can use only the brackets notation. For example, to access the Engine HP column, we can use only brackets:

```
df['Engine HP']
```

(A) The dot notation   **(B) The brackets notation**

Figure D.3 **Two ways of accessing a column of a DataFrame: (A) the dot notation and (B) the brackets notation**

The bracket notation is also more flexible. We can keep the name of a column in a variable and use it to access its content:

```
col_name = 'Engine HP'
df[col_name]
```

If we need to select a subset of columns, we again use brackets but with a list of names instead of a single string:

```
df[['Make', 'Model', 'MSRP']]
```

This returns a DataFrame with only three columns (figure D.4).

```
df[['Make', 'Model', 'MSRP']]
```

	Make	Model	MSRP
0	Nissan	Stanza	2000
1	Hyundai	Sonata	27150
2	Lotus	Elise	54990
3	GMC	Acadia	34450
4	Nissan	Frontier	32340

Figure D.4 **To select a subset of columns of a DataFrame, use brackets with a list of names.**

To add a column to a DataFrame, we also use the brackets notation:

```
df['id'] = ['nis1', 'hyu1', 'lot2', 'gmc1', 'nis2']
```

We have five rows in the DataFrame, so the list with values should also have five values. As a result, we have another column, id (figure D.5).

```
df['id'] = ['nis1', 'hyu1', 'lot2', 'gmc1', 'nis2']
df
```

	Make	Model	Year	Engine HP	Engine Cylinders	Transmission Type	Vehicle_Style	MSRP	id
0	Nissan	Stanza	1991	138.0	4	MANUAL	sedan	2000	nis1
1	Hyundai	Sonata	2017	NaN	4	AUTOMATIC	Sedan	27150	hyu1
2	Lotus	Elise	2010	218.0	4	MANUAL	convertible	54990	lot2
3	GMC	Acadia	2017	194.0	4	AUTOMATIC	4dr SUV	34450	gmc1
4	Nissan	Frontier	2017	261.0	6	MANUAL	Pickup	32340	nis2

Figure D.5   To add a new column, use the brackets notation.

In this case, id didn't exist, so we appended a new column to the end of the Data-Frame. If id exists, then this code overwrites the existing values:

```
df['id'] = [1, 2, 3, 4, 5]
```

Now the content of the id column changes (figure D.6).

```
df['id'] = [1, 2, 3, 4, 5]
df
```

	Make	Model	Year	Engine HP	Engine Cylinders	Transmission Type	Vehicle_Style	MSRP	id
0	Nissan	Stanza	1991	138.0	4	MANUAL	sedan	2000	1
1	Hyundai	Sonata	2017	NaN	4	AUTOMATIC	Sedan	27150	2
2	Lotus	Elise	2010	218.0	4	MANUAL	convertible	54990	3
3	GMC	Acadia	2017	194.0	4	AUTOMATIC	4dr SUV	34450	4
4	Nissan	Frontier	2017	261.0	6	MANUAL	Pickup	32340	5

Figure D.6   To change the content of a column, use the brackets notation as well.

To delete a column, use the `del` operator:

```
del df['id']
```

After running it, this column disappears from the DataFrame.

D.1.3   Index

Both DataFrame (figure D.7, A) and Series (figure D.7, B) have numbers on the left; these numbers are called an *index*. The index describes how we can access rows from a DataFrame (or a Series).

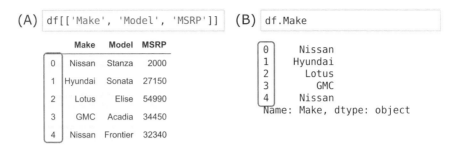

Figure D.7   Both DataFrame and Series have an index — the numbers on the left.

We can get the index of a DataFrame using the `index` property:

```
df.index
```

Because we didn't specify the index when creating a DataFrame, it uses the default one, a series of autoincrementing numbers starting from 0:

```
RangeIndex(start=0, stop=5, step=1)
```

The index behaves in the same way as a Series object, so everything that works for Series also works for the index.

Although a Series has only one index, a DataFrame has two: one for accessing rows, and the other for accessing columns. We already used Index for columns, when selecting individual columns from the DataFrame:

```
df['Make']
```
←——| **Uses the column index
to get the Make column**

To get the column names, we use the `columns` property (figure D.8):

```
df.columns
```

```
df.columns

Index(['Make', 'Model', 'Year', 'Engine HP', 'Engine Cylinders',
       'Transmission Type', 'Vehicle_Style', 'MSRP'],
      dtype='object')
```

Figure D.8   The `columns` property contains the column names.

D.1.4   *Accessing rows*

We can access rows in two ways: using `iloc` and `loc`.

First, let's start with `iloc`. We use it to access the rows of a DataFrame using their positional numbers. For example, to access the first row of the DataFrame, use the index 0:

```
df.iloc[0]
```

This returns the content of the first row:

```
Make               Nissan
Model              Stanza
Year                 1991
Engine HP             138
Engine Cylinders        4
Transmission Type  MANUAL
Vehicle_Style       sedan
MSRP                 2000
Name: 0, dtype: object
```

To get a subset of rows, pass a list with integers — row numbers:

```
df.iloc[[2, 3, 0]]
```

The result is another DataFrame containing only the rows we need (figure D.9).

---

df.iloc[[2, 3, 0]]

	Make	Model	Year	Engine HP	Engine Cylinders	Transmission Type	Vehicle_Style	MSRP
2	Lotus	Elise	2010	218.0	4	MANUAL	convertible	54990
3	GMC	Acadia	2017	194.0	4	AUTOMATIC	4dr SUV	34450
0	Nissan	Stanza	1991	138.0	4	MANUAL	sedan	2000

Figure D.9   Using `iloc` to access rows of a DataFrame

We can use `iloc` for shuffling the content of a DataFrame. In our DataFrame, we have five rows. So, we can create a list of integers from 0 to 4 and shuffle it. Then we can use the shuffled list in `iloc`; this way, we'll get a DataFrame with all the rows shuffled.

Let's implement it. First, we create a range of size 5 using NumPy:

```
import numpy as np

idx = np.arange(5)
```

It creates an array with integers from 0 to 4:

```
array([0, 1, 2, 3, 4])
```

Now we can shuffle this array:

```
np.random.seed(2)
np.random.shuffle(idx)
```

As a result, we get

```
array([2, 4, 1, 3, 0])
```

Finally, we use this array with `iloc` to get the rows in shuffled order:

```
df.iloc[idx]
```

In the result, the rows are reordered according to the numbers in idx (figure D.10).

```
df.iloc[idx]
```

	Make	Model	Year	Engine HP	Engine Cylinders	Transmission Type	Vehicle_Style	MSRP
2	Lotus	Elise	2010	218.0	4	MANUAL	convertible	54990
4	Nissan	Frontier	2017	261.0	6	MANUAL	Pickup	32340
1	Hyundai	Sonata	2017	NaN	4	AUTOMATIC	Sedan	27150
3	GMC	Acadia	2017	194.0	4	AUTOMATIC	4dr SUV	34450
0	Nissan	Stanza	1991	138.0	4	MANUAL	sedan	2000

Figure D.10   Using `iloc` to shuffle the rows of a DataFrame

This doesn't change the DataFrame that we have in `df`. But we can reassign the `df` variable to the new DataFrame:

```
df = df.iloc[idx]
```

As a result, `df` now contains a shuffled DataFrame.

In this shuffled DataFrame, we can still use `iloc` to get rows by using their positional number. For example, if we pass `[0, 1, 2]` to `iloc`, we'll get the first three rows (figure D.11).

```
df.iloc[[0, 1, 2]]
```

	Make	Model	Year	Engine HP	Engine Cylinders	Transmission Type	Vehicle_Style	MSRP
2	Lotus	Elise	2010	218.0	4	MANUAL	convertible	54990
4	Nissan	Frontier	2017	261.0	6	MANUAL	Pickup	32340
1	Hyundai	Sonata	2017	NaN	4	AUTOMATIC	Sedan	27150

Figure D.11   When using `iloc`, we get rows by their position.

However, you have probably noticed that the numbers on the left are not sequential anymore: when shuffling the DataFrame, we shuffled the index as well (figure D.12).

df								
	Make	**Model**	**Year**	**Engine HP**	**Engine Cylinders**	**Transmission Type**	**Vehicle_Style**	**MSRP**
2	Lotus	Elise	2010	218.0	4	MANUAL	convertible	54990
4	Nissan	Frontier	2017	261.0	6	MANUAL	Pickup	32340
1	Hyundai	Sonata	2017	NaN	4	AUTOMATIC	Sedan	27150
3	GMC	Acadia	2017	194.0	4	AUTOMATIC	4dr SUV	34450
0	Nissan	Stanza	1991	138.0	4	MANUAL	sedan	2000

Figure D.12 When shuffling the rows of a DataFrame, we also change the index: it's no longer sequential.

Let's check the index:

```
df.index
```

It's different now:

```
Int64Index([2, 4, 1, 3, 0], dtype='int64')
```

To use this index to access rows, we need `loc` instead of `iloc`. For example:

```
df.loc[[0, 1]]
```

As a result, we get a DataFrame with rows indexed by 0 and 1 — the last row and the row in the middle (Figure D.13).

df.loc[[0, 1]]								
	Make	**Model**	**Year**	**Engine HP**	**Engine Cylinders**	**Transmission Type**	**Vehicle_Style**	**MSRP**
0	Nissan	Stanza	1991	138.0	4	MANUAL	sedan	2000
1	Hyundai	Sonata	2017	NaN	4	AUTOMATIC	Sedan	27150

Figure D.13 When using `loc`, we get rows using the index, not the position.

It's quite different from `iloc`: `iloc` doesn't use the index. Let's compare them:

```
df.iloc[[0, 1]]
```

In this case, we also get a DataFrame with two rows, but these are the first two rows, indexed by 2 and 4 (figure D.14).

```
df.iloc[[0, 1]]
```

	Make	Model	Year	Engine HP	Engine Cylinders	Transmission Type	Vehicle_Style	MSRP
2	Lotus	Elise	2010	218.0	4	MANUAL	convertible	54990
4	Nissan	Frontier	2017	261.0	6	MANUAL	Pickup	32340

Figure D.14 Unlike `loc`, `iloc` gets rows by the position, not index. In this case, we get rows at positions 0 and 1 (indexed by 2 and 4, respectively).

So, `iloc` doesn't look at the index at all; it uses only the actual position.

It's possible to replace the index and set it back to the default one. For that, we can use the `reset_index` method:

```
df.reset_index(drop=True)
```

It creates a new DataFrame with a sequential index (figure D.15).

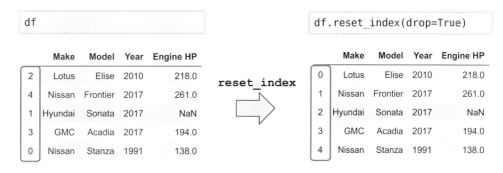

Figure D.15 We can reset the index to sequential numbering by using `reset_index`.

D.1.5 Splitting a DataFrame

We can also use `iloc` to select subsets of a DataFrame. Suppose we want to split a DataFrame into three parts: train, validation, and test. We'll use 60% of data for training (three rows), 20% for validation (one row), and 20% for testing (one row):

```
n_train = 3
n_val = 1
n_test = 1
```

For selecting a range of rows, we use the slicing operator (:). It works for DataFrames in the same way it works for lists.

Thus, for splitting the DataFrame, we do the following:

```
df_train = df.iloc[:n_train]
df_val = df.iloc[n_train:n_train+n_val]
df_test = df.iloc[n_train+n_val:]
```

① Selects rows for train data

② Selects rows for validation data

③ Selects rows for test data

In **①**, we get the train set: `iloc[:n_train]` selects rows from the start of the DataFrame until the row before n_train. For n_train=3, it selects rows 0, 1, and 2. Row 3 is not included.

In **②**, we get the validation set: `iloc[n_train:n_train+n_val]` selects rows from 3 to 3 + 1 = 4. It's not inclusive, so it takes only row 3.

In **③**, we get the test set: `iloc[n_train+n_val:]` selects rows from 3 + 1 = 4 until the end of the DataFrame. In our case, it's only row 4.

As a result, we have three DataFrames (figure D.16).

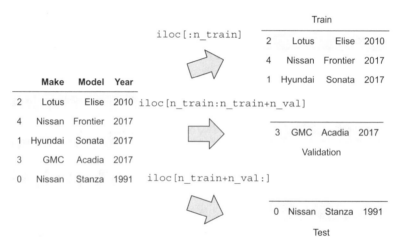

Figure D.16 Using `iloc` with the colon operator to split the DataFrame into train, validation, and test DataFrames

For more information about slicing in Python, refer to appendix B.

We've covered the basic Pandas data structures, so now let's see what we can do with them.

D.2 *Operations*

Pandas is a great tool for data manipulation, and it supports a wide variety of operations. We can group these operations into element-wise operations, summarizing operations, filtering, sorting, grouping, and more. In this section, we cover these operations.

D.2.1 *Element-wise operations*

In Pandas, Series support *element-wise* operations. Just as in NumPy, element-wise operations are applied to each element in a Series, and we get another Series as a result.

All basic arithmetic operations are element-wise: addition (+), subtraction (−), multiplication (*), and division (/). For element-wise operations, we don't need to write any loops: Pandas does it for us.

For example, we can multiply each element of a Series by 2:

```
df['Engine HP'] * 2
```

The result is another Series with each element multiplied by 2 (figure D.17).

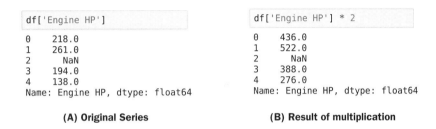

(A) Original Series   **(B) Result of multiplication**

Figure D.17 As with NumPy arrays, all basic arithmetic operations for Series are element-wise.

As with arithmetic, logical operations are also element-wise:

```
df['Year'] > 2000
```

This expression returns a Boolean Series, with `True` for elements higher than 2000 (figure D.18).

(A) Original Series   **(B) Result**

Figure D.18 Logical operations are applied element-wise: in the results, we have `True` for all the elements that satisfy the condition.

We can combine multiple logical operations with logical and (&) or logical or (|):

```
(df['Year'] > 2000) & (df['Make'] == 'Nissan')
```

The result is also a Series. Logical operations are useful for filtering, which we cover next.

D.2.2   *Filtering*

Often, we need to select a subset of rows according to some criteria. For that, we use Boolean operations together with the bracket notation.

For example, to select all Nissan cars, put the condition inside the brackets:

```
df[df['Make'] == 'Nissan']
```

As a result, we have another DataFrame that contains only Nissans (figure D.19).

```
df[df['Make'] == 'Nissan']
```

	Make	Model	Year	Engine HP	Engine Cylinders	Transmission Type	Vehicle_Style	MSRP
1	Nissan	Frontier	2017	261.0	6	MANUAL	Pickup	32340
4	Nissan	Stanza	1991	138.0	4	MANUAL	sedan	2000

Figure D.19   To filter rows, put the condition for filtering inside brackets.

If we need a more complex selection condition, we combine multiple conditions with logical operators like and (&) and or (|).

For example, to select cars made after 2000 with automatic transmission, we use and (figure D.20):

```
df[(df['Year'] > 2010) & (df['Transmission Type'] == 'AUTOMATIC')]
```

```
df[(df['Year'] > 2010) & (df['Transmission Type'] == 'AUTOMATIC')]
```

	Make	Model	Year	Engine HP	Engine Cylinders	Transmission Type	Vehicle_Style	MSRP
2	Hyundai	Sonata	2017	NaN	4	AUTOMATIC	Sedan	27150
3	GMC	Acadia	2017	194.0	4	AUTOMATIC	4dr SUV	34450

Figure D.20   To use multiple selection criteria, combine them with logical and (&).

D.2.3 String operations

Although for NumPy arrays it's possible to do only arithmetic and logical element-wise operations, Pandas supports string operations: lowercasing, replacing substrings, and all the other operations that we can do on string objects.

Let's take a look at Vehicle_Style, which is one of the columns in the DataFrame. We see some inconsistencies in the data: sometimes names start with lowercase letters and sometimes with uppercase ones (figure D.21).

```
df['Vehicle_Style']

0      convertible
1           Pickup
2            Sedan
3          4dr SUV
4            sedan
Name: Vehicle_Style, dtype: object
```

Figure D.21   The Vehicle_Style column with some inconsistencies in the data

To resolve this, we can make everything lowercase. For usual Python strings, we'd use the lower function and apply it to all the elements of the series. In Pandas, instead of writing a loop, we use the special str accessor — it makes string operations element-wise and lets us avoid writing a for loop explicitly:

```
df['Vehicle_Style'].str.lower()
```

The result is a new Series with all the strings styled in lowercase (figure D.22).

```
df['Vehicle_Style'].str.lower()

0      convertible
1           pickup
2            sedan
3          4dr suv
4            sedan
Name: Vehicle_Style, dtype: object
```

Figure D.22   To lowercase all strings of a Series, use lower.

It's also possible to chain several string operations by using the str accessor multiple times (figure D.23):

```
df['Vehicle_Style'].str.lower().str.replace(' ', '_')
```

```
df['Vehicle_Style'].str.lower().str.replace(' ', '_')
0       convertible
1            pickup
2             sedan
3           4dr_suv
4             sedan
Name: Vehicle_Style, dtype: object
```

Figure D.23 To replace characters in all strings of a Series, use the `replace` method. It's possible to chain multiple methods together in one line.

Here, we make everything lowercase and replace spaces with underscores, all at once.

The column names of our DataFrame are also not consistent: sometimes there are spaces, and sometimes there are underscores (figure D.24).

	Make	Model	Year	Engine HP	Engine Cylinders	Transmission Type	Vehicle_Style	MSRP
0	Lotus	Elise	2010	218.0	4	MANUAL	convertible	54990
1	Nissan	Frontier	2017	261.0	6	MANUAL	Pickup	32340
2	Hyundai	Sonata	2017	NaN	4	AUTOMATIC	Sedan	27150
3	GMC	Acadia	2017	194.0	4	AUTOMATIC	4dr SUV	34450
4	Nissan	Stanza	1991	138.0	4	MANUAL	sedan	2000

Figure D.24 The DataFrame: column names are not consistent.

We can also use string operations to normalize the column names:

```
df.columns.str.lower().str.replace(' ', '_')
As a result, we have:
Index(['make', 'model', 'year', 'engine_hp', 'engine_cylinders',
       'transmission_type', 'vehicle_style', 'msrp'],
      dtype='object')
```

This line of code returns new names, but it doesn't change the column names of the DataFrame. To modify them, we need to assign the results back to `df.columns`:

```
df.columns = df.columns.str.lower().str.replace(' ', '_')
```

When we do so, the column names change (figure D.25).

We can solve such inconsistency problems in all the columns of our DataFrame. For that, we need to select all the columns with strings and normalize them.

To select all strings, we can use the `dtype` property of a DataFrame (figure D.26).

	make	model	year	engine_hp	engine_cylinders	transmission_type	vehicle_style	msrp
0	Lotus	Elise	2010	218.0	4	MANUAL	convertible	54990
1	Nissan	Frontier	2017	261.0	6	MANUAL	Pickup	32340
2	Hyundai	Sonata	2017	NaN	4	AUTOMATIC	Sedan	27150
3	GMC	Acadia	2017	194.0	4	AUTOMATIC	4dr SUV	34450
4	Nissan	Stanza	1991	138.0	4	MANUAL	sedan	2000

Figure D.25   The DataFrame after we normalized the column names

```
df.dtypes

make                    object
model                   object
year                     int64
engine_hp              float64
engine_cylinders         int64
transmission_type       object
vehicle_style           object
msrp                     int64
dtype: object
```

Figure D.26   The `dtypes` property returns the types of each column of a DataFrame.

All the strings columns have their dtype set to `object`. So, if we want to select them, we use filtering:

```
df.dtypes[df.dtypes == 'object']
```

That gives us a Series with `object` dtype columns only (figure D.27).

```
df.dtypes[df.dtypes == 'object']

make                 object
model                object
transmission_type    object
vehicle_style        object
dtype: object
```

Figure D.27   To get only columns with strings, select the `object` dtype.

The actual names are stored in the index, so we need to get them:

```
df.dtypes[df.dtypes == 'object'].index
```

This gives us the following column names:

```
Index(['make', 'model', 'transmission_type', 'vehicle_style'], dtype='object')
```

Now we can use this list to iterate over string columns and apply the normalization for each column separately:

```
string_columns = df.dtypes[df.dtypes == 'object'].index

for col in string_columns:
    df[col] = df[col].str.lower().str.replace(' ', '_')
```

This is what we have after running it (figure D.28).

	make	model	year	engine_hp	engine_cylinders	transmission_type	vehicle_style	msrp
0	lotus	elise	2010	218.0	4	manual	convertible	54990
1	nissan	frontier	2017	261.0	6	manual	pickup	32340
2	hyundai	sonata	2017	NaN	4	automatic	sedan	27150
3	gmc	acadia	2017	194.0	4	automatic	4dr_suv	34450
4	nissan	stanza	1991	138.0	4	manual	sedan	2000

Figure D.28 **Both column names and values are normalized: names are lowercase, and spaces are replaced with underscores.**

Next, we cover another type of operation: summarizing operations.

D.2.4 *Summarizing operations*

Just as we do in NumPy, in Pandas we have element-wise operations that produce another Series, as well as summarizing operations that produce a summary — one or multiple numbers.

Summarizing operations are quite useful for doing exploratory data analysis. For numerical fields, the operations are similar to what we have in NumPy. For example, to compute the average of all values in a column, we use the mean method:

```
df.msrp.mean()
```

Other methods that we can use include

- sum: Computes the sum of all values
- min: Gets the smallest number in the Series

- max: Gets the largest number in the Series
- std: Computes the standard deviation

Instead of checking these things separately, we can use describe to get all these values at once:

```
df.msrp.describe()
```

It creates a summary with the number of rows, mean, min, and max, as well as standard deviation and other characteristics:

```
count         5.000000
mean      30186.000000
std       18985.044904
min        2000.000000
25%       27150.000000
50%       32340.000000
75%       34450.000000
max       54990.000000
Name: msrp, dtype: float64
```

When we invoke mean on the entire DataFrame, it computes the mean value for all the numcrical columns:

```
df.mean()
```

In our case, we have four numerical columns, so we get the average for each:

```
year               2010.40
engine_hp           202.75
engine_cylinders      4.40
msrp              30186.00
dtype: float64
```

Likewise, we can use describe on a DataFrame:

```
df.describe()
```

Because describe already returns a Series, when we invoke it on a DataFrame, we get a DataFrame as well (figure D.29).

```
df.describe().round(2)
```

	year	engine_hp	engine_cylinders	msrp
count	5.00	4.00	5.00	5.00
mean	2010.40	202.75	4.40	30186.00
std	11.26	51.30	0.89	18985.04
min	1991.00	138.00	4.00	2000.00
25%	2010.00	180.00	4.00	27150.00
50%	2017.00	206.00	4.00	32340.00
75%	2017.00	228.75	4.00	34450.00
max	2017.00	261.00	6.00	54990.00

Figure D.29   To get the summary statistics of all numerical features, use the
`describe` **method.**

D.2.5   *Missing values*

We didn't focus on it previously, but we have a missing value in our data: we don't
know the value of engine_hp for row 2 (figure D.30).

	make	model	year	engine_hp	engine_cylinders	transmission_type	vehicle_style	msrp
0	lotus	elise	2010	218.0	4	manual	convertible	54990
1	nissan	frontier	2017	261.0	6	manual	pickup	32340
2	hyundai	sonata	2017	NaN	4	automatic	sedan	27150
3	gmc	acadia	2017	194.0	4	automatic	4dr_suv	34450
4	nissan	stanza	1991	138.0	4	manual	sedan	2000

Figure D.30   There's one missing value in our DataFrame.

We can see which values are missing using the `isnull` method:

```
df.isnull()
```

This method returns a new DataFrame where a cell is True if the corresponding value
is missing in the original DataFrame (figure D.31).

However, when we have large DataFrames, looking at all the values is impractical.
We can easily summarize them by running the `sum` method on the results:

```
df.isnull().sum()
```

```
df.isnull()
```

	make	model	year	engine_hp	engine_cylinders	transmission_type	vehicle_style	msrp
0	False	False	False	False	False	False	False	False
1	False	False	False	False	False	False	False	False
2	False	False	False	True	False	False	False	False
3	False	False	False	False	False	False	False	False
4	False	False	False	False	False	False	False	False

Figure D.31   To find missing values, use the `isnull` method.

It returns a Series with the number of missing values per column. In our case, only engine_hp has missing values; others don't (figure D.32).

```
df.isnull().sum()

make                    0
model                   0
year                    0
engine_hp               1
engine_cylinders        0
transmission_type       0
vehicle_style           0
msrp                    0
dtype: int64
```

Figure D.32   To find columns with missing values, use `isnull` followed by `sum`.

To replace the missing values with some actual values, we use the `fillna` method. For example, we can fill the missing values with zero:

```
df.engine_hp.fillna(0)
```

As a result, we get a new Series where NaNs are replaced by 0:

```
0    218.0
1    261.0
2      0.0
3    194.0
4    138.0
Name: engine_hp, dtype: float64
```

Alternatively, we can replace it by getting the mean:

```
df.engine_hp.fillna(df.engine_hp.mean())
```

In this case, the NaNs are replaced by the average:

```
0       218.00
1       261.00
2       202.75
3       194.00
4       138.00
Name: engine_hp, dtype: float64
```

The `fillna` method returns a new Series. Thus, if we need to remove the missing values from our DataFrame, we need to write the results back:

```
df.engine_hp = df.engine_hp.fillna(df.engine_hp.mean())
```

Now we get a DataFrame without missing values (figure D.33).

```
df.engine_hp = df.engine_hp.fillna(df.engine_hp.mean())
df
```

	make	model	year	engine_hp	engine_cylinders	transmission_type	vehicle_style	msrp
0	lotus	elise	2010	218.00	4	manual	convertible	54990
1	nissan	frontier	2017	261.00	6	manual	pickup	32340
2	hyundai	sonata	2017	202.75	4	automatic	sedan	27150
3	gmc	acadia	2017	194.00	4	automatic	4dr_suv	34450
4	nissan	stanza	1991	138.00	4	manual	sedan	2000

Figure D.33   The DataFrame without missing values

D.2.6   *Sorting*

The operations we covered previously were mostly used for Series. We also can perform operations on DataFrames.

Sorting is one of these operations: it rearranges the rows in a DataFrame such that they are sorted by the values of some column (or multiple columns).

For example, let's sort the DataFrame by MSRP. For that, we use the `sort_values` method:

```
df.sort_values(by='msrp')
```

The result is a new DataFrame where rows are sorted from the smallest MSRP (2000) to the largest (54990) (figure D.34).

```
df.sort_values(by='msrp')
```

	make	model	year	engine_hp	engine_cylinders	transmission_type	vehicle_style	msrp
4	nissan	stanza	1991	138.00	4	manual	sedan	2000
2	hyundai	sonata	2017	202.75	4	automatic	sedan	27150
1	nissan	frontier	2017	261.00	6	manual	pickup	32340
3	gmc	acadia	2017	194.00	4	automatic	4dr_suv	34450
0	lotus	elise	2010	218.00	4	manual	convertible	54990

Figure D.34 To sort the rows of a DataFrame, use `sort_values`.

If we want the largest values to appear first, we set the `ascending` parameter to `False`:

```
df.sort_values(by='msrp', ascending=False)
```

Now we have the MSRP of 54990 in the first row and 2000 in the last (figure D.35).

```
df.sort_values(by='msrp', ascending=False)
```

	make	model	year	engine_hp	engine_cylinders	transmission_type	vehicle_style	msrp
0	lotus	elise	2010	218.00	4	manual	convertible	54990
3	gmc	acadia	2017	194.00	4	automatic	4dr_suv	34450
1	nissan	frontier	2017	261.00	6	manual	pickup	32340
2	hyundai	sonata	2017	202.75	4	automatic	sedan	27150
4	nissan	stanza	1991	138.00	4	manual	sedan	2000

Figure D.35 To sort the rows of a DataFrame in descending order, use `ascending=False`.

D.2.7 *Grouping*

Pandas offers quite a few summarizing operations: sum, mean, and many others. We previously have seen how to apply them to calculate a summary over the entire Data-Frame. Sometimes, however, we'd like to do it per group — for example, calculate the average price per transmission type.

In SQL, we'd write something like this:

```
SELECT
    tranmission_type,
    AVG(msrp)
FROM
    cars
```

```
GROUP BY
    transmission_type;
```

In Pandas, we use the `groupby` method:

```
df.groupby('transmission_type').msrp.mean()
```

The result is the average price per transmission type:

```
transmission_type
automatic    30800.000000
manual       29776.666667
Name: msrp, dtype: float64
```

If we'd like to also compute the number of records per each type along with the average price, in SQL, we'd add another statement in the SELECT clause:

```
SELECT
    tranmission_type,
    AVG(msrp),
    COUNT(msrp)
FROM
    cars
GROUP BY
    transmission_type
```

In Pandas, we use `groupby` followed by `agg` (short for "aggregate"):

```
df.groupby('transmission_type').msrp.agg(['mean', 'count'])
```

As a result, we get a DataFrame (figure D.36).

df.groupby('transmission_type').msrp.agg(['mean', 'count'])

	mean	count
transmission_type		
automatic	30800.000000	2
manual	29776.666667	3

Figure D.36   When grouping, we can apply multiple aggregate functions using the `agg` method.

Pandas is quite a powerful tool for data manipulation, and it's often used to prepare data before training a machine learning model. With the information from this appendix, it should be easier for you to understand the code in this book.

appendix E
AWS SageMaker

AWS SageMaker is a set of services from AWS related to machine learning. Sage-Maker makes it easy to create a server on AWS with Jupyter installed on it. The notebooks are already configured: they have most of the libraries we need, including NumPy, Pandas, Scikit-learn, and TensorFlow, so we can just use them for our projects!

E.1 AWS SageMaker Notebooks

SageMaker's notebooks are especially interesting for training neural networks for two reasons:

- We don't need to worry about setting up TensorFlow and all the libraries.
- It's possible to rent a computer with a GPU, which enables us to train neural networks a lot faster.

To use a GPU, we need to adjust the default quotas. In the next section, we tell you how to do this.

E.1.1 Increasing the GPU quota limits

Each account on AWS has quota limits. For example, if our quota limit on the number of instances with GPUs is 10, we cannot request an eleventh instance with a GPU.

By default, the quota limit is zero, which means that it's not possible to rent a GPU machine without changing the quota limits.

To request an increase, open the support center in AWS Console: click Support in the top-right corner and select Support Center (figure E.1).

Next, click the Create Case button (figure E.2).

Now select the Service Limit Increase option. In the Case Details section, select SageMaker from the Limit Type dropdown list (figure E.3).

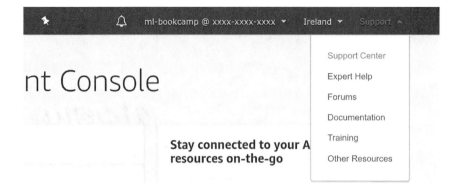

Figure E.1   To open the support center, click Support > Support Center.

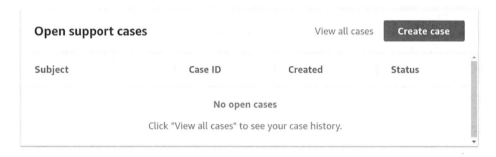

Figure E.2   In the support center, click the Create Case button.

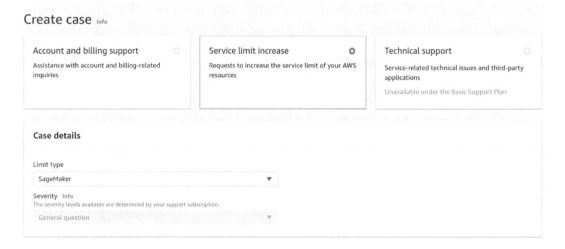

Figure E.3   When creating a new case, select Service Limit Increase > SageMaker.

After that, fill in the quota increase form (figure E.4):

- Region: select the closest to you or the cheapest. You can see the prices here: https://aws.amazon.com/sagemaker/pricing/. Resource type: SageMaker Notebooks.
- Limit: ml.p2.xlarge instances for a machine with one GPU.
- New limit value: 1.

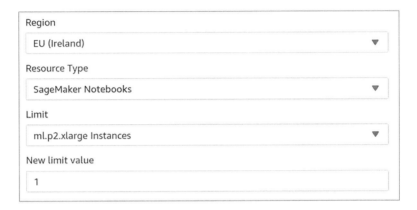

Figure E.4   Increase the limit for ml.p2.xlarge to one instance.

Finally, describe why you need an increase in quota limits. For example, you can type "I'd like to train a neural network using a GPU machine" (figure E.5).

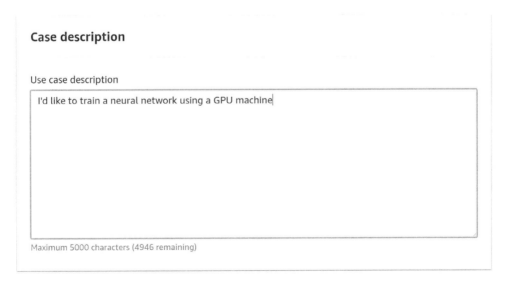

Figure E.5   We need to explain why we want to increase the limit.

We're ready; now click Submit.

After that, we see some details of the request. Back in the Support Center, we see the new case in the list of open cases (figure E.6).

Open support cases   View all cases   **Create case**

Subject	Case ID	Created	Status
Limit Increase: SageMaker	7403143411	29 seconds ago	Unassigned

Figure E.6   The list of open support cases

It typically takes one to two days to process the request and increase the limits.

Once the limit is increased, we can create a Jupyter Notebook instance with a GPU.

E.1.2   Creating a notebook instance

To create a Jupyter Notebook in SageMaker, first find SageMaker in the list of services (figure E.7).

Find Services
You can enter names, keywords or acronyms.

🔍 Sa   ✕

Amazon SageMaker
Build, Train, and Deploy Machine Learning Models

Lightsail
Launch and Manage Virtual Private Servers

AWS Cost Explorer
Visualize and Explore Your AWS Costs and Usage

Figure E.7   To find SageMaker, type SageMaker in the search box.

NOTE   SageMaker notebooks are not covered by the free tier, so it costs money to rent a Jupyter Notebook.

For an instance with one GPU (ml.p2.xlarge), the cost of one hour at the moment of writing is

- Frankfurt: $1.856
- Ireland: $1.361
- Northern Virginia: $1.26

The project from chapter 7 requires one to two hours to complete.

> **NOTE** Make sure you are in the same region where you requested the quota limits increase.

In SageMaker, select Notebook Instances, and then click the Create Notebook Instance button (figure E.8).

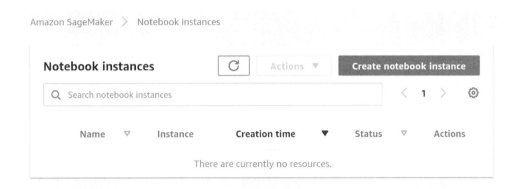

Figure E.8   To create a Jupyter Notebook, click Create Notebook Instance.

Next, we need to configure the instance. First, enter the name of the instance as well as the instance type. Because we're interested in a GPU instance, select ml.p2.xlarge in the Accelerated Computing section (figure E.9).

In Additional Configuration, write 5 GB in the Volume Size field. This way, we should have enough space to store the dataset as well as save our models.

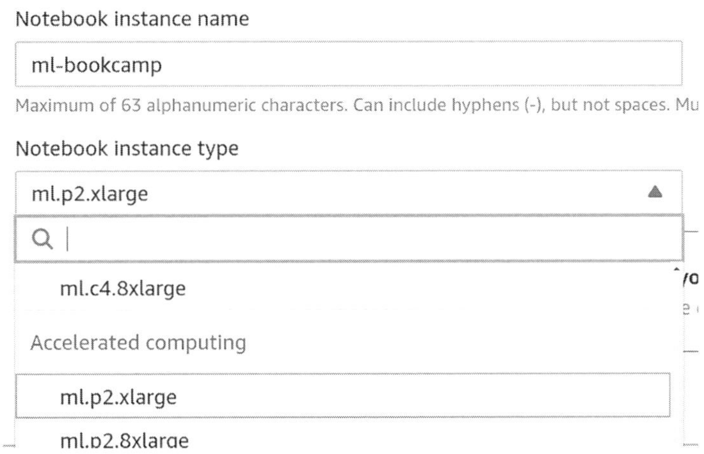

Figure E.9   The Accelerated Computing section contains instances with GPUs.

If you previously used SageMaker and already have an IAM role for it, select it in the IAM Role section.

But if you're doing it for the first time, select Create a New Role (figure E.10).

Permissions and encryption

IAM role
Notebook instances require permissions to call other services including SageMaker and S3.
AmazonSageMakerFullAccess IAM policy attached.

Create a new role ▲
Create a new role
Enter a custom IAM role ARN
Use existing role

Figure E.10   To use a SageMaker notebook, we need to create an IAM role for it.

When creating the role, keep the default values, and click the Create Role button (figure E.11).

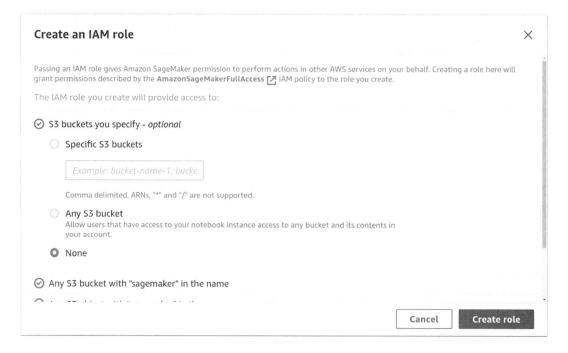

Figure E.11   The default values for the new IAM role are sufficient.

Keep the rest of the options unchanged:

- Root access: Enable
- Encryption key: No custom encryption
- Network: No VPC
- Git repositories: None

Finally, click the Create Notebook Instance to launch it.

If for some reasons you see a ResourceLimitExceeded error message (figure E.12), make sure that

- You have requested an increase in quota limits for the ml.p2.xlarge instance type.
- The request was processed.
- You're trying to create a notebook in the same region where you requested the increase.

 ResourceLimitExceeded
The account-level service limit 'ml.p2.xlarge for notebook instance usage' is 0 Instances, with current utilization of 0 Instances and a request delta of 1 Instances. Please contact AWS support to request an increase for this limit.

Figure E.12 If you see the ResourceLimitExceeded error message, you need to increase the quota limits.

After creating an instance, the notebook appears in the list of notebook instances (figure E.13).

Now we need to wait until the notebook changes status from Pending to InService; this may take one to two minutes.

Once it's in the InService state, it's ready to be used (figure E.14). Click Open Jupyter to access it.

Next, we see how to use it with TensorFlow.

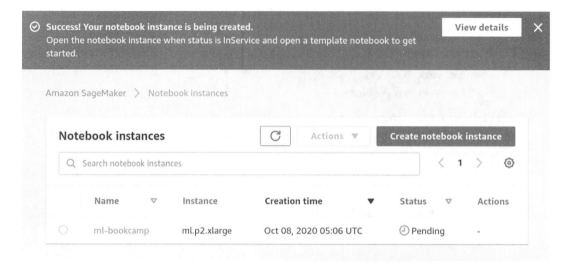

Figure E.13   Success! The notebook instance has been created.

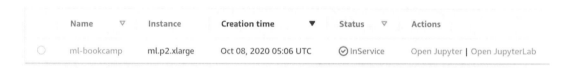

Figure E.14   The new notebook instance is in service and ready to be used.

E.1.3   *Training a model*

After clicking Open Jupyter, we see the familiar interface for Jupyter Notebook.

To create a new notebook, click New, and select conda_tensorflow2_p36 (figure E.15).

This notebook has Python version 3.6 and TensorFlow version 2.1.0. At the time of writing, this is the newest version of TensorFlow available in SageMaker.

Now, import TensorFlow and check its version:

```
import tensorflow as tf
tf.__version__
```

The version should be 2.1.0 or higher (figure E.16).

Now go to chapter 7 and train a neural network! After training is finished, we need to turn off the notebook.

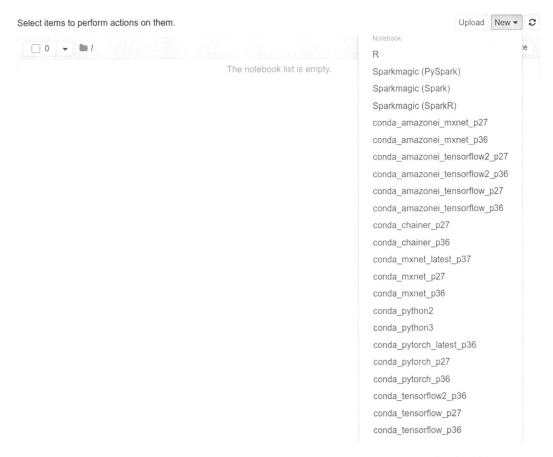

Figure E.15 To create a new notebook with TensorFlow, select conda_tensorflow2_p36.

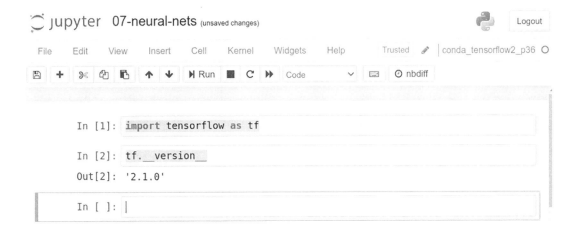

Figure E.16 For our examples, we need at least TensorFlow version 2.1.0.

E.1.4 *Turning off the notebook*

To stop a notebook, first select the instance you want to stop, and then select Stop in the Actions dropdown list (figure E.17).

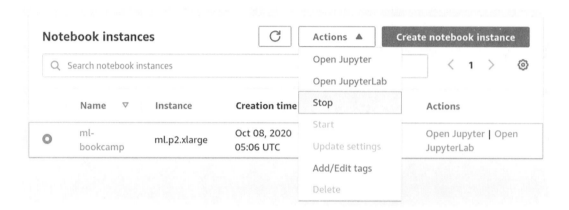

Figure E.17   To turn off a notebook, select the Stop action.

After doing this, the status of the notebook will change from InService to Stopping. It may take a few minutes before it fully stops and changes status from Stopping to Stopped.

> **NOTE**   When we stop a notebook, all our code and data are saved. The next time we start it, we can continue where we left off.

> **IMPORTANT**   The notebook instances are expensive, so make sure you don't accidentally leave it running. SageMaker is not covered by the free tier, so if you forget to stop it, you'll receive a huge bill at the end of a month. There's a way to set a budget in AWS to avoid huge bills. See the documentation about managing costs at AWS: https://docs.aws.amazon.com/awsaccountbilling/ latest/aboutv2/budgets-managing-costs.html. Be careful, and turn off your notebook when you no longer need it.

Once you finish working on a project, you can delete the notebook. Select a notebook, and then choose Delete from the dropdown list (figure E.18). The notebook must be in the Stopped state to delete it.

It will first change status from Stopped to Deleting, and after 30 seconds, it will disappear from the list of notebooks.

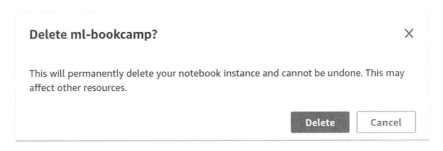

Figure E.18 After you finish chapter 7, you can delete the notebook.

index

Symbols

"%" operator 359
== operator 98
>= operator 99

A

ACCOUNT variable
    308
accuracy 98, 100, 110
activation function 254
activation parameter
    253
actual_churn 123
actual_no_churn 123
add method 366
agg function 82
AMI (Amazon Machine
    Image) 347
Anaconda 334, 355
Anaconda, installing
    326–331
  on Linux 326–328
  on macOS 331
  on Windows 328–331
API Gateway 272, 291
append function 362
apply command 311
apply method 85–86
@app.route 161
area under ROC curve
    (AUC) 144–147, 153,
    181
argmax method 268
argsort 390

arrays
  NumPy arrays 375–379
  randomly generated
    arrays 382–383
  two-dimensional NumPy
    arrays 379–381
ascending parameter 425
assets feature 194
astype(int) function 72
astype(int) method 54
AUC (area under ROC
    curve) 144–147, 181
auc function 145
AVG(churn) 82
AWS (Amazon Web Services)
  creating Kubernetes clusters
    on 305–307
  deleting EKS clusters 324
  Elastic Beanstalk 175–178
  Lambda 271–291
    code for lambda
        functions 277–278
    converting model to TF Lite
        format 274
    creating API Gateway
        285–290
    creating lambda
        functions 281–285
    preparing Docker
        images 279–281
    preparing images 274–276
    pushing image to AWS
        ECR 281
    TensorFlow Lite 273
    using TF Lite model
        276–277

renting servers on 338–356
  accessing billing
    information
    342–344
  configuring CLI
    355–356
  connecting EC2 to
    instances 352–354
  creating EC2
    instances 345–352
  registering 339–342
  shutting down EC2
    instances 354–355
SageMaker notebooks
    427–436
  creating notebook
    instances 430–433
  increasing GPU quota
    limits 427–430
  training model 434
  turning off notebooks
    436
AWS CLI 306, 332, 342,
    355

B

bias term 34, 36, 38–39, 42,
    58
binary classification 8
BinaryCrossentropy 246
break statement 361
BROWSER variable 334
build command 173
business understanding
    step 10–11

C

calculate_mi function 85
car-price prediction project
    19–20
  downloading dataset 19–20
  exploratory data analysis
    20–32
    checking for missing
      values 28–29
    reading and preparing
      data 22–25
    target variable analysis
      25–28
    toolbox for 21–22
    validation framework
      29–32, 51
  linear regression 19, 27,
    32, 34, 38, 40–44, 54,
    58–59
  predicting price 43–62
    baseline solution 43–45
    handling categorical
      variables 53–57
    regularization 57–61
    RMSE 46–49
    simple feature
      engineering 51–52
    using model 61–62
    validating model 50–51
car prices dataset 19
CategoricalCrossentropy 246
categorical variables
  handling 53–57
  one-hot encoding for 88–92
cd command 172
cd notebook 331
checkpointing 251, 263–264
churn 65–66, 69, 72, 76–77
churn array 98
churn-prediction:latest 174
churn prediction project 66–87,
  155–159
  dependency
    management 166–174
    Docker 170–174
    Pipenv 166–170
  exploratory data analysis
    75–77
  feature engineering 88–92
  feature importance
    analysis 78–87
    churn rate 76–84, 87–88,
      92–93, 96, 100, 102–103,
      105–111

correlation coefficient
    86–87
    mutual information 85–86
    risk ratio 80–84
  initial data preparation 67–75
  loading model with
    Pickle 158–159
  logistic regression 92–100
  model interpretation
    100–107
  saving model with Pickle
    156–157
  serving with Flask 163–166
  Telco churn dataset 67
  using model 108–110,
    155–156
churn rate 78–80
churn variable 72
classes 369–370
classification 5, 7–9
  evaluation metrics for
    113–153
    classification accuracy
      114–117
    confusion table 119–129
    dummy baseline 117–118
    parameter tuning 147–151
    ROC curves 129–147
  machine learning for 65–112
    exploratory data
      analysis 75–77
    feature engineering 88–92
    feature importance
      analysis 78–87
    initial data preparation
      67–75
    logistic regression 92–95
    model interpretation
      100–107
    Telco churn dataset 67
    using model 108–110
code reusability 369–371
  classes 370
  functions 369–370
  importing code 370–371
collections 362–369
  dictionaries 367–368
  list comprehension 368–369
  lists 362, 364–366, 368–369,
    371
  sets 366
  slicing 364–365
  Tuples 365–366
colsample_bytree parameter
  222

columns property 409
column_stack function 42
combining operations 391–394
compile method 247
conditions 360
configure command 356
confusion table 114, 118–132,
  152–153
  calculating with NumPy
    122–126
  overview of 119–122
  precision and recall 126–129
container 169–174, 176
context parameter 278
continue statement 361
contract feature 86
contract variable 88
control flow 359–362
  conditions 360
  for loops 360–361
  while loops 361–362
convolutional layers
  (CNN) 234–237, 240–243
convolutional neural networks
  225, 230–234, 240
  getting predictions 233–234
  using pretrained model
    230–233
correlation coefficient 86–87
create_preprocessor
  function 275
credit risk scoring project
  181–190
  data cleaning 182–187
  dataset 181–182
  dataset preparation 187–190
  decision trees 190–203
    decision tree classifier
      191–194
    decision tree learning
      algorithm 194–201
    parameter tuning for
      decision tree
      201–203
  gradient boosting 210–222
    model performance
      monitoring 213–214
    parameter tuning
      214–220
    testing final model
      220–222
    XGBoost 211–213
  random forests 203–210
    parameter tuning 207–210
    training 206–207

CRISP-DM (Cross-Industry Stan-
    dard Process
    for Data Mining) 9–10
  business understanding
    10–11
  data preparation 11
  data understanding 11
  deployment 12
  evaluation 12
  modeling 11

D

data augmentation 259–264
DataFrame (df) 22–24, 30–31,
    50, 53, 73
DataFrames
  overview of 405–406
  splitting 413–414
data preparation step 11
data.shape argument 299
data understanding step 11
data variable 280
debt dataset 198
DecisionTreeClassifier 191
decision trees 180–223
  data cleaning 182–187
  dataset 181–182
  dataset preparation 187–190
  decision tree classifier
    191–194
  decision tree learning
    algorithm 194–201
    impurity 196
    selecting best feature for
      splitting 199
    stopping criteria 199–201
  default 180–181, 183, 189,
    191–196, 198, 212, 214–
    216, 218–219
  gradient boosting 210–222
    model performance
      monitoring 213–214
    parameter tuning 214–220
    testing final model 220–
      222
    XGBoost 211–213
  parameter tuning for
    201–203
  random forests 203–210
    parameter tuning 207–210
    training random
      forest 206–207
decode_prediction
    function 231

deep learning 9
  neural networks 224–270
    convolutional 230–234
    downloading dataset 226–
      227
    GPUs vs. CPUs 225–226
    internals of model 234–240
    loading images 228–230
    TensorFlow and Keras 228
    training model 240–264
    using model 265–268
  serverless 271–291
    code for lambda
      functions 277–278
    converting model to TF Lite
      format 274
    creating API Gateway
      285–290
    creating lambda
      functions 281–285
    preparing Docker
      images 279–281
    preparing images 274–276
    pushing images to AWS
      ECR 281
    TensorFlow Lite 273
    using TensorFlow Lite
      model 276–277
def keyword 369
del operator 189, 408
dense layers 234, 237–241, 243,
    255
dependency management
    166–174
  Docker 170–174
  Pipenv 166–170
deploying machine learning
    models 154–179
  AWS Elastic Beanstalk
    175–178
  dependency
    management 166–174
    Docker 170–174
    Pipenv 166–170
  loading model with
    Pickle 158–159
  model serving 159–166
    Flask 161–166
    web services 160–161
  saving model with Pickle
    156–157
  using model 155–156
deployment 12, 292–293,
    304–305, 310–314,
    317–318

–deploy parameter 172
describe command 315
describe method 186, 421
df (DataFrame) 22, 73
df.columns 418
df.dtypes 70
df_full_train 220
df.head() function 23, 68,
    182
df_num variable 43
df parameter 74
df_test 50, 73, 220
df_train 50, 220
df_train_full 188
df_train_full dataframe 75
df_val 50, 220
df variable 411
dictionaries 367–368
dict_train 189
DictVectorizer 91, 189
display function 83
DMatrix 211
Docker
  dependency
    management 170–174
  installing 337–338
    on Linux 337–338
    on macOs 338
    on Windows 338
  preparing images 279–281,
    307–310
    Gateway image 309–310
    TensorFlow Serving
      image 307–309
Dockerfile 171–173
docker run command 296
dot function 38
dot method 38, 397
dot product 37–40
dropout 254–258
Dropout layer 255
droprate parameter 256
dtype property 418
dtypes 377
dummy baseline 117–118
dump function 156

E

EC2 (Elastic Compute Cloud)
  connecting to instances
    352–354
  creating instances 345–352
  shutting down instances
    354–355

EDA (exploratory data
    analysis) 20–32
    checking for missing
        values 28–29
    churn prediction project
        75–77
    reading and preparing
        data 22–25
    target variable analysis
        25–28
    toolbox for 21–22
    validation framework
        29–32
EKS (Elastic Kubernetes
    Service) 305
EKS cluster 306, 318
eksctl tool 306
element-wise operations
    NumPy 383–387
    Pandas 415–416
ensemble learning 180, 203
    gradient boosting 210–222
        model performance
            monitoring 213–214
        parameter tuning
            214–220
        testing final model
            220–222
        XGBoost 211–213
    random forests 203–210
        parameter tuning for
            207–210
        training 206–207
ensemble package 206
Entering the event loop 297
enumerate function 363
-e parameter 297
epoch 247–252, 256–257, 263
epochs parameter 247
error array 48
errors='coerce' option 71
eta parameter 215
eval_metric parameter 215
evaluate method 266
evaluation metrics, for
    classification 113–153
    classification accuracy
        114–117
    confusion table 119–129
        calculating with
            NumPy 122–126
        overview of 119–122
        precision and recall
            126–129
    dummy baseline 117–118

parameter tuning 147–151
    finding best
        parameters 149–151
    k-fold cross-validation
        147–149
ROC curves 129–147
    area under 144–147
    creating 140–144
    evaluating model at multi-
        ple thresholds 131–134
    ideal model 136–139
    random baseline
        model 134–136
    true positive rateand false
        positive rate 130–131
evaluation step 12
event parameter 278
export_text function 192
extra-index-url parameter 273
ExtraTreesClassifier 222

F

false negatives 121–123, 125,
    127–129, 133, 153
false positive (s) 121–123,
    125–131, 133, 136, 138,
    140–144, 152–153
false positive rate (FPR)
    130–131
fashion classification 225–230
    convolutional neural
        networks 230–234
    getting predictions
        233–234
    using pretrained
        model 230–233
    downloading dataset 226–227
    GPUs vs. CPUs 225–226
    internals of model 234–240
        convolutional layers 234–
            237
        dense layers 237–240
    loading images 228–230
    TensorFlow and Keras 228
    training model 240–264
        adding more layers 252–
            254
        adjusting learning
            rate 249–251
        creating model 242–245
        data augmentation 259–
            264
        loading data 241–242
        regularization 19, 57–61, 64

regularization and
    dropout 254–258
saving model and
    checkpointing 251–252
training larger models 264
training model 245–248
transfer learning 240
using model 265–268
    evaluating model 266
    getting predictions
        267–268
    loading model 265
feature 5, 7, 11
feature engineering 19, 63
    car-price prediction
        project 51–52
    churn prediction project
        88–92
    one-hot encoding for categori-
        cal variables 88–92
feature importance 66, 78,
    105–106, 110
feature importance analysis
    78–87
    churn rate 78–80
    correlation coefficient 86–87
    mutual information 85–86
    risk ratio 80–84
feature maps 235–236
feature matrix 8
feature_names parameter 193
feature vector 5–6, 8
fillna method 44, 423
filtering operations
    NumPy 394–396
    Pandas 416
filters 234–236, 240, 242
fit method 91, 247
fitting 2, 8
Flask 161–166
float16 type 378
float32 type 378
float64 type 378
flow_from_directory
    method 241
FN (false negative) 121
for loops 24, 360–361, 379,
    417
FP (false positive) 121
-f parameter 311
FPR (false positive rate)
    130–131
FROM statement 172
functional component 244
functions 369–370

G

Gateway
  creating API Gateway
      285–290
  creating Gateway service
      301–304
  deployment for 313–314
  preparing Gateway
      image 309–310
  service for 314–316
gender variable 78
get command 319
get_feature_names method 91
get method 367
g function 34
GKE (Google Kubernetes
      Engine) 306
GPUs (graphical processing
      units)
  CPUs vs. 225–226
  increasing quota limits
      427–430
gradient boosting 180–181,
      210–222
  model performance
      monitoring 213–214
  parameter tuning 214–220
  testing final model 220–222
  XGBoost 211–213
GradientBoostingClassifier 211
grouping operations 425–426

H

hard predictions 97
head() method 74, 405
height_shift_range=30
      parameter 262
hello-world container 338
histograms 21, 25, 28, 45
histplot function 27
horizontal autoscaling 304
horizontal_flip=True
      parameter 262
host machine 170

I

identity matrix 58–59
idx array 31, 390
if-else statement 190
ImageDataGenerator 241
Image object 231
imbalanced dataset 77

img variable 231
import statement 115, 371
impurity 196, 198–199, 201
imput_shape parameter 231
include_top parameter 242
indexes 408–409
ingress 304
__init__ method 370
input_shape argument 264
inputs parameter 244
install command 168
int16 type 378
int32 type 378
int64 type 378
int8 type 378
isnull() function 71
isnull method 422
items method 368
-it flag 174

J

JSON (Javascript Object
      Notation) 163
jsonsify 164
Jupyter
  invoking model from
      297–301
  running 331–335
    on Linux 331–334
    on macOS 335
    on Windows 334

K

Kaggle CLI 20
Kaggle CLI, installing 335–336
Keras 224–225, 228, 230,
      241–242, 246–247, 251,
      253–255, 261, 266, 269
keras_image_helper library 275
keras.losses package 246
KERAS_MODEL_NAME
      parameter 323
key field 336
keys method 368
KFold class 148
k-fold cross-validation 147–149
KFServing 293, 317–319
  deploying TensorFlow models
      with 318–319
  transformers 321–323
kubectl get inferenceservice
      323
kubectl tool 306

Kubeflow 292–293, 306, 325
  model deployment with
      317–324
    accessing model 319–321
    deleting EKS clusters 324
    deploying TensorFlow
        models with KFServing
        318–319
    KFServing
        transformers 321–324
    testing transformers
        323–324
    uploading model to
        S3 317–318
  overview of 293
Kubernetes 292–294, 324–325
  model deployment with
      304–317
    creating clusters on
        AWS 305–307
    deployment for
        Gateway 313–314
    deployment for TF
        Serving 310–312
    overview of 304–305
    preparing Docker
        images 307–310
    service for Gateway
        314–316
    service for TF Serving
        312–313
    testing service 316–317
  overview of 293

L

lambda environment 280
lambda functions
  code for 277–278
  creating 281–285
lambda_handler function 278
learning rate 215–217, 246,
      248–251, 253, 263
len function 22, 67, 188, 363
LinAlgError 57, 401
linear algebra 396–403
  matrix inverse 400–401
  multiplication 396–400
    matrix-matrix
        multiplication 398–400
    matrix-vector
        multiplication 397–398
    vector-vector
        multiplication 396–397
  normal equation 402–403

linear models 93
LinearRegression 110
linear regression 32, 35, 37, 41–42, 58
linear_regresson function 45
linspace function 115
Linux
  connecting to EC2 instances on 352–353
  installing Anaconda on 326–328
  installing Docker on 337–338
  installing Python on 326–328
  running Jupyter on 331–334
Linux subsystems for windows 328, 334
list comprehension 368–369
lists 362–364
LoadBalancer Ingress 316
load function 158
load_img function 228
load_model function 265
local run command 176
logistic regression 66, 88, 92–100, 102, 108, 110–112
LogisticRegression class 96
logits 246–247
log transformation 26–27, 32
long tail 25–28, 32
lower function 417

M

machine learning 1–17
  for classification 65–112
    exploratory data analysis 20–32, 75–77
    feature engineering 88–92
    feature importance analysis 78–87
    initial data preparation 67–75
    logistic regression 92–100
    model interpretation 100–107
    Telco churn dataset 67
    using model 108–110
  for regression 18–64
    downloading dataset 19–20
    exploratory data analysis 20–32
    linear regression 32–41
    predicting price 43–62
    training linear regression model 41–42

modeling and validation 12–16
  process 9–12
    business understanding 10–11
    data preparation 11
    data understanding 11
    deployment 12
    evaluation 12
    iteration 12
    modeling 11
  rule-based systems vs. 4–7
  supervised 7–9
  when not to use 7
macOS
  connecting to EC2 instances on 354
  installing Anaconda on 331
  installing Docker on 338
  installing Python on 331
  running Jupyter on 335
make_model function 256
make_request function 302
map method 184
matrix inverse 374, 400–401
matrix-matrix multiplication 396, 398–400
matrix-vector multiplication 396–400
max argument 370
max_depth parameter 192
max_features parameter 222
max method 389, 421
max operation 388
mean() method 49, 76
mean method 124, 420
mean operation 388
MeanSquaredError 246
mean squared error (MSE) 47–48
metric 114, 119, 129, 144–145, 147, 152
metrics package 85, 141
microservice 160
min_child_weight parameter 218
min_leaf_size parameter 201
min method 420
min operation 388
missing values 21, 43–44
  checking for 28–29
  Pandas 422–424
ModelCheckpoint class 251
Model class 244

model deployment 154, 179
modeling step 11–16
MODEL_INPUT_SIZE parameter 323
model interpretation 100–107
MODEL_LABELS parameter 323
MODEL_NAME parameter 299
MODEL_NAME variable 297
model selection 16–17
model_selection module 73
model_selection package 148
model serving 159–166
  Flask 161–166
  web services 160–161
models package 265
monthlycharges variable 87
MSE (mean squared error) 47
multiclass classification 8
multiplication 396–400
  matrix-matrix multiplication 398–400
  matrix-vector multiplication 397–398
  vector-vector multiplication 396–397
mutual information 85–86
mutual_info_score function 85

N

name argument 275
NaN (not a number) 71
negative examples 93
n_estimators parameter 206
neural networks 224–270
  convolutional neural networks 230–234
    getting predictions 233–234
    using pretrained model 230–233
  downloading dataset 226–227
  GPUs vs. CPUs 225–226
  internals of model 234–240
    convolutional layers 234–237
    dense layers 237–240
  loading images 228–230
  TensorFlow and Keras 228
  training model 240–264
    adding more layers 252–254
    adjusting learning rate 249–251

neural networks *(continued)*
    creating model 242–245
    data augmentation
        259–264
    loading data 241–242
    regularization and
        dropout 254–258
    saving model and
        checkpointing 251–252
    training larger model
        264
    training model 245–248
    transfer learning 240
    using model 265–268
        evaluating model 266
        getting predictions
            267–268
        loading model 265
–no-browser parameter 332
–no-cache-dir setting 172
nodes 304–305
noise array 384
normal distribution 27–28
normal equation 41–42, 57,
    374, 402–403
not a number (NaN) 71
n parameter 405
np.arange function 377
np.array function 377
np.column_stack 393
np.concatenate function
    392
np.eye function 58
np.fill function 380
np.full function 375
np.hstack function 392
np.linalg.inv function 41,
    400
np.linalg.solve 401
np.linspace function 137, 377
np.ones function 375
np.random module 382
np.random.rand 382
np.random.randint 383
np.random.randn 382
np.random.seed function 31
np.repeat function 137, 376
np_to_protobuf function 299
np.vstack function 393
np.zeros function 375
nthread parameter 215
NumberPrinter class 370
NumberPrinter object 370
numerical instability 19, 57–58,
    61, 63–64

NumPy 374–403
    arrays
        NumPy arrays 375–379
        randomly generated
            arrays 382–383
        two-dimensional NumPy
            arrays 379–381
    calculating confusion table
        with 122–126
    linear algebra 396–403
        matrix inverse 400–401
        multiplication 396–400
        normal equation
            402–403
    operations 383–396
        element-wise
            operations 383–387
        reshaping and
            combining 391–394
        slicing and filtering
            394–396
        sorting 389–390
        summarizing
            operations 388–389

O

objective parameter 212
one-hot encoding 53, 83, 89,
    91–92, 96, 101, 103–104,
    109
onlinesecurity feature 86
open function 157
operations
    NumPy 383–396
        combining 391–394
        element-wise
            operations 383–387
        filtering 394–396
        reshaping 391–394
        slicing 394–396
        sorting 389–390
        summarizing 388–389
    Pandas 414–426
        element-wise
            operations 415–416
        filtering 416
        grouping 425–426
        missing values 422–424
        sorting 424–425
        string operations 417–420
        summarizing 420–421
optimizers 245–246
overfitting 191–192, 199–200,
    214, 222

P

Pandas 404–426
    accessing rows 409–413
    DataFrames
        overview of 405–406
        splitting 413–414
    indexes 408–409, 411–413,
        419
    operations 414–426
        element-wise
            operations 415–416
        filtering 416
        grouping 425–426
        missing values 422–424
        sorting 424–425
        string operations 417–420
        summarizing
            operations 420–421
    Series 406–408
parameter tuning 147–151
    finding best parameters
        149–151
    for decision trees 201–203
    for random forests 207–210
    for XGBoost 214–220
    k-fold cross-validation
        147–149
partner variable 79
PATH variable 327
pb_result variable 300
pd.DataFrame 405
-p docker command 176
Pickle 155–158, 173
    loading models with 158–159
    saving models with 156–157
ping function 161
Pipenv 166–170
pipenv install 172
pip install 165–166, 273, 372,
    374, 404
pip uninstall 372
positive examples 93
-p parameter 174, 297
precision 114, 126–129,
    151–152
pred array 390
predict_churn array 123
predict function 148, 155, 303
predict method 212, 233
predict_no_churn array 123
predict_proba method 96, 191
predict_single function 156
pred variable 300
prepare_X function 50

preprocessing_function 261
preprocess_input function 231,
    274
print function 357
print_number method 370
probability 95
process_response function
    302
Python 357–373
    installing 326–331
        on Linux 326–328
        on macOS 331
        on Windows 328–331
    variables 357–373
        code reusability 369–371
        collections 362–369
        control flow 359–362
        installing libraries 371–372
        Python programs 372–373
PYTHONUNBUFFERED
    variable 172

R

random forest 180–181,
    203–210, 213, 215, 220,
    222
    parameter tuning for
        207–210
    training 206–207
RandomForestClassifier 206
random_state parameter 74,
    206
ranking 8
read_csv function 22, 67
recall 114, 126–131, 151–153
REGION variable 308
regression 8–9
regression, machine learning
    for 18–64
    downloading dataset 19–20
    exploratory data analysis
        20–32
        checking for missing
            values 28–29
        reading and preparing
            data 22–25
        target variable analysis
            25–28
        toolbox for 21–22
        validation framework
            29–32
    linear regression 32–41
    predicting price 43–62
        baseline solution 43–45

handling categorical
    variables 53–57
regularization 57–61
RMSE 46–49
simple feature
    engineering 51–52
using model 61–62
validating model 50–51
training linear regression
    model 41–42
regularization 57–61, 254–258
ReLU (Rectified Linear
    Unit) 254
repeat function 118
replace method 186
request 164
reset_index method 413
reshape method 391
reshaping operations 391–394
results variable 165, 277
return statement 369
ridge regression 58
risk 80–84, 111
risk ratio 80–84, 105
RMSE (root mean squared
    error) 46–49
rmse function 48
ROC (receiver operating
    characteristic) curves 114,
    129–147, 152–153
    area under 144–147
    creating 140–144
    evaluating model at multiple
        thresholds 131–134
    ideal model 136–139
    random baseline model
        134–136
    true positive rate and false
        positive
        rate 130–131
roc_auc_score function 145
roc_curve function 141
rom_logits=True parameter 246
root mean squared error 46, 48
rotation_range=30
    parameter 262
round method 186, 385
rule-based systems 4–7
run command 169

S

S3, uploading model to 317–318
sagemaker 226, 228
save_best_only 252

saved_model_cli 296
saved_model format 295–296,
    317
save_weights method 251
scalars 396
score 95
SE (squared error) 46
seed parameter 215
SELECT clause 426
self argument 370
Series 404, 406–409, 415–421,
    423–424
series parameter 85
serverless deep learning
    271–291
    code for lambda
        functions 277–278
    converting model to TF Lite
        format 274
    creating API Gateway
        285–290
    creating lambda
        functions 281–285
    preparing Docker
        images 279–281
    preparing images 274–276
    pushing images to AWS
        ECR 281
    TensorFlow Lite 273
    using TensorFlow Lite
        model 276–277
service 293–294
sets 362, 366
shape property 380
shear_range=10 parameter 262
shell command 168
show command 296
side effect 52
sigmoid 93–95, 102, 107
silent parameter 215
singular matrices 57, 401
sklearn.linear_model
    package 110
slicing operations
    NumPy 394–396
    Python 364–365
soft predictions 97
solver parameter 96
sorting operations
    NumPy 389–390
    Pandas 424–425
sort method 390
sort_values method 424
source code, accessing
    336–337

sparse=False parameter 91
ssh command 328
status variable 187
std method 421
std operation 388
stopping criteria 199–201
str accessor 417
str attribute 24
string.format method 359
string operations 417–420
subsample parameter 222
summarizing operations 414, 425
 NumPy 388–389
 Pandas 420–421
sum method 124, 420
supervised machine learning 7–9
–system parameter 172

T

target_size 229, 275
target variable 6–8
target variable analysis 25–28
techsupport feature 86
Telco churn dataset 67
TensorFlow 224–226, 228
TensorFlow Lite 272–273, 276
 converting model to TF Lite format 274
 using TF Lite model 276–277
TensorFlow Serving 297, 309
 deployment for 310–312
 preparing images 307–309
 service for 312–313
 serving models with 293–304
 creating Gateway service 301–304
 invoking model from Jupyter 297–301
 running locally 296–297
 saved_model format 295–296
 serving architecture 294–295
tenure variable 87
test_size parameter 74
-t flag 173
tf.make_tensor_proto function 299

TF_SERVING_HOST variable 302
T function 68
TN (true negative) 120
to_dict method 90
to_numeric function 71
total_charges 71
totalcharges variable 87
TP (true positive) 120
TPR (true positive rate) 130–131
T property 394
trainable parameter 242
train_ds parameter 247
train function 148, 212
training 2
training=False parameter 244
training set 17
train_test_split 188
train_test_split function 73
transfer learning 240, 248
transform method 91
tree package 191
true negatives 120, 125–126, 128–129, 133, 153
true positives 120, 124, 126–127, 129–130, 133–134, 136, 153
tuple assignment 358
tuples 358–359, 362, 365–366
type: LoadBalancer 315

U

-U flag 372
uint16 type 378
uint32 type 378
uint64 type 378
uint8 type 378
underfits 249
username field 336

V

validation
 modeling and 12–16
 validating models 50–51
 validation frameworks 29–32
validation_data parameter 247
validation set 13, 16–17
value_counts 187

value_counts() method 76
ValueError 391
values property 44
variables 357–373
 code reusability 369–371
 classes 370
 functions 369–370
 importing code 370–371
 collections 362–369
 dictionaries 367–368
 list comprehension 368–369
 lists 362–364
 sets 366
 slicing 364–365
 Tuples 365–366
 control flow 359–362
 conditions 360
 for loops 360–361
 while loops 361–362
 installing libraries 371–372
 Python programs 372–373
vector 244
vectorization 48
vectorized operations 384, 397
vector-vector multiplication 396–398
vertical_flip=False parameter 262
virtual environments 167–170, 172, 175
-v parameter 297

W

web service 154, 159–163, 165–166, 175, 179
weights of a model 35–36, 42
weights parameter 231
wget 295
which command 328
while loops 361–362
width_shift_range=30 parameter 262
Windows
 connecting to EC2 instances on 354
 installing Anaconda on 328–331
 installing Docker on 338
 installing Python on 328–331
 running Jupyter on 334

X

Xception 231
XGBoost
    gradient boosting 211–213
    parameter tuning for
        214–220
xi variable 34

X_train 50
X_val 50
X variable 319

Y

YMLLoadWarning 211
y_pred array 50, 98

y_train 50
y_val 50

Z

zoom_range=0.2 parameter
    262